CONSTRUCTING
THE SPANISH EMPIRE
IN HAVANA

CONSTRUCTING THE SPANISH EMPIRE IN HAVANA

State Slavery in Defense and Development, 1762–1835

EVELYN P. JENNINGS

Louisiana State University Press
Baton Rouge

Published by Louisiana State University Press
www.lsupress.org

Designer: Barbara Neely Bourgoyne
Typeface: Quadraat

Jacket illustration: *Habana*, Smith Hermanos & Co., 1851

Library of Congress Cataloging-in-Publication Data
Names: Jennings, Evelyn P., author.
Title: Constructing the Spanish Empire in Havana : state slavery in defense and development,
    1762–1835 / Evelyn P. Jennings.
Description: Baton Rouge : Louisiana State University Press, [2020] | Includes bibliographical
    references and index.
Identifiers: LCCN 2020014682 (print) | LCCN 2020014683 (ebook) | ISBN 978-0-8071-7394-7
    (cloth) | ISBN 978-0-8071-7464-7 (pdf) | ISBN 978-0-8071-7465-4 (epub)
Subjects: LCSH: Slavery—Cuba—Havana—History. | Forced labor—Cuba—Havana—History. |
    Plantations—Cuba—Havana—History. | Public works—Cuba—Havana—History. | Slave
    trade—Spain—History. | Havana (Cuba)—Economic conditions. | Spain—Colonies—
    America—Administration.
Classification: LCC HT1079.H38 J36 2020 (print) | LCC HT1079.H38 (ebook) | DDC
    306.3/6309729124—dc23
LC record available at https://lccn.loc.gov/2020014682
LC ebook record available at https://lccn.loc.gov/2020014683

For Bill, who lived with this story for so long

CONTENTS

ACKNOWLEDGMENTS

I have incurred many debts, both personal and professional, over the many years and iterations of this project. My first expression of gratitude must go to my first graduate adviser, Clara E. Lida, from many years ago at SUNY at Stony Brook, who always insisted on meticulous preparation and intellectual rigor, and who suggested, as I cast about for a research topic, Why not Cuba? Another of my graduate advisors at Stony Brook, Eugene Lebovics, was especially helpful and encouraging on my return to graduate school after a long hiatus.

I owe many debts to the Frederick Douglass Institute for African and African-American Studies and the History Department at the University of Rochester, where I first began working on state enslavement in Cuba. Two fellowships from the Douglass Institute allowed me to complete my graduate work and finish writing an early version of this study. I must thank, particularly, Joseph E. Inikori and Larry E. Hudson, the directors of the Douglass Institute during my time as a graduate student at the University of Rochester, and fellow Institute fellow Jim Bryant. The History Department at the University of Rochester also supported my graduate work with the Egon Berlin Prize for research in European history, the Sanford Elwitt Memorial Prize for travel and research, and a dissertation writing fellowship that helped support trips to Spain, Cuba, and New York City.

I would especially like to acknowledge my many debts, both personal and professional, to my University of Rochester graduate advisor, Stanley L. Engerman. I have benefited in numerous ways from his encyclopedic knowledge of the fields of comparative slavery, labor history, and Atlantic economic history. He read countless drafts of papers, grant applications, and a nearly final version of this book manuscript and has guided all with his careful attention to the details of evidence and interpretation. I hope I have internalized many of those small queries in the margins in colored pencil that have saved me from flights of fanciful interpretation or abuse of evidence: *Timing? Links?* Any remaining errors of fact or interpretation are my own.

I also have benefited from Stan's great generosity, good humor, and patience and from the warmth and encouragement of his late wife, Judy. As Joan Rubin noted at a UR conference in Stan's honor in the early 2000s, everyone loves Stan Engerman; I feel particularly privileged to have had the opportunity to learn why. Other advisors in the UR History Department read some or all of my early versions of the chapter on fort building and offered good guidance, usually on how to pare things down and sharpen an argument, in particular Dorinda Outram, Joseph Inikori, Alice Conklin, and Larry Hudson.

At a very early stage of this project, I traveled to Cuba and benefited from the vast knowledge and generosity of the late Francisco Pérez Guzmán, who was willing to spend time talking with me, even though I had no idea what I was doing. He was also kind enough to give me a copy of his indispensable book, *La Habana: clave de un imperio*. I am also grateful for the help and kindness of the staff members in the reading room at the Archivo Nacional in Havana on a later, brief trip to that repository.

My first research adventure at the Archive of the Indies in Seville was aided immensely by Pablo Tornero Tinajero, who encouraged me to explore the intendants' papers, which ultimately formed the basis for much of chapter 3 on the fortification projects. Other colleagues in Seville who provided support and conversation include Igor Pérez Tostado at the Universidad Pablo de Olavide, who invited me to speak to colleagues and graduate students in the Department of Geography, History, and Philosophy in 2007. In Madrid, many thanks especially to Consuelo Naranjo Orovio and María Dolores González-Ripoll from the Consejo Superior de Investigaciones Científicas for their hospitality and for sharing their important works on Cuba. Other colleagues in Spain who have been generous with their time and work are José Antonio Piqueras Arenas and Joan Casanovas Codino, the latter of whom was a fellow graduate student at Stony Brook long ago. Thanks also to Vicky Hayward for food and fellowship while I was in Madrid, and congratulations on the publication of her book, *The New Art of Cookery*, which we discussed many years ago. In New York City, my thanks to Collette Stallone for her hospitality at a time when I had so little money to pursue this research.

I am grateful to librarians and archivists at repositories in the United States, including the Library of Congress, the New York Public Library, and the interlibrary loan staff at St. Lawrence University. I am particularly grateful to Mary Haegert, Emily Walhout, and Susan Halpert at the Houghton Library at Harvard University for help with materials in the José Augusto Escoto Cuban History and Literature Collection, and particularly for helping me find the papers on Havana's enslaved artillerymen and their families after those papers were moved and recataloged.

Since this project has taken so long to complete, I have shared parts of it at many conferences over the years and have benefited from comments from fellow scholars of Cuba and the Atlantic world, and of labor history and slavery studies. I cannot enumerate all who have helped over time, but they include Manuel Barcia, Pepijn Brandon, Matt Childs, Sir John Elliott, Ada Ferrer, Alejandro de la Fuente, Niklas Frykman, David Geggus, Jane Landers, Alex Lichtenstein, William Phillips, Joel Quirk, Marcus Rediker, Pernille Røge, Elena Schneider, Marcel van der Linden, and Molly Warsh. A special thanks to Sherry Johnson for answering questions over the years, sharing her work, and encouraging me to apply for the Lydia Cabrera Award for Cuban Historical Studies in 2004, which funded a sabbatical return trip to the Spanish archives. Another special thanks to John Donoghue, who has been a good friend, interlocutor on all these topics, and coauthor and coeditor of our essay collection, *Building the Atlantic Empires*.

In my almost twenty years at St. Lawrence University, I am grateful for the financial support of a William G. Bradbury Award for junior faculty research and seven grants from the History Department's Vilas funds for research and travel, without which my archive and library travel would have been impossible. All of my colleagues in the SLU History Department have been supportive over the years I have worked on this project: Donna Alvah, Matt Carotenuto, Anne Csete, Judith DeGroat, Howard Eissenstat, Elun Gabriel, Liz Regosin, Melissane Schrems, and Mary Jane Smith. Ilia Casanova-Marengo has been a good friend and colleague over the years, as well. I'm sorry someone beat us to publishing an English translation of *Cecilia Valdés*. I also would like to thank my fellow associate deans, Sarah Barber, Kimberly Flint-Hamilton, Elun Gabriel, and Marina Llorente, whose encouragement through our weekly writing group meetings kept me on course for the final push to finish the manuscript.

I am grateful to Brill Publishers for permission to include some portions of my essay "The Sinews of Spain's American Empire" in this book. I also thank the *International Review of Social History* for permission to include some of my essay "Paths to Sweet Success" in chapter 5.

My last debts, but certainly not my least, are to my family and friends. To my good friend of many years, Hector Cobb, thanks are due for his enthusiasm for my work and for sharing my passion for studying history. I thank my sister, Nancy, and my parents, Bill and Betty Powell, for their love and support and for a timely infusion of funds that made possible my first research trip to Spain. I am sad that my parents did not live to see this book in print. My sons, Ryan and Raurri, have cheered on this work for more than half of their lives and for that I am grateful. Finally, my love and gratitude to my husband, Bill, who has endured the most as I worked on "the book"—long absences while I traveled to archives, years that I sat at the dining room table typing away. His love and support made this effort possible and fruitful. I dedicate this book to him.

CONSTRUCTING
THE SPANISH EMPIRE
IN HAVANA

PROLOGUE

On each of my trips to Cuba, I have gone on an evening excursion to La Cabaña, the massive fortress across the bay of Havana, built in the late eighteenth century. The fort was almost its own city, with barracks for hundreds of soldiers. On my first visit, in 1999, the excursion included a reenactment of the fort's Spanish garrison firing the cannon blast that had announced the nightly closing of the doors to Havana's city wall, until the wall was torn down in the mid-nineteenth century. There were a few groups of tourists out that night, but most of the people there for the *cañonazo* were Cubans—young people hanging out in groups, couples on dates, families out with their children.

The reenactors, dressed as Spanish soldiers, marched up to the cannon platform and fired off a loud blast that had spectators covering their ears and laughing. Then our party toured the museums that are now housed in the fort to learn that, in addition to the fort's role as a bulwark against invasion, various groups had faced a firing squad there over the years—from Cuban anticolonial fighters in the nineteenth century to opponents of twentieth-century strongmen Gerardo Machado and Fulgencio Batista. After the triumph of the 1959 revolution, Che Guevara set up his headquarters in the fort and executed some of Batista's officers there.

When I visited La Cabaña most recently, in 2016, with a group of college students from upstate New York, the *cañonazo* ceremony had become an epic spectacle, but not because the reenactment itself had changed much; it hadn't. Rather, it was a spectacle of Cuba's transformation into a tourist mecca. There were busloads of tourist groups, young and old, particularly groups of American college students, much like our own, who were eager to see Cuba "before it changes." The crowd was so large that I couldn't see the reenactment itself, so I joined hundreds of others who tried to watch it using a cell phone, with my arm in the air. After the blast, people streamed back to their buses and taxis. A few milled through the museum exhibits, which still show some of the fort's bloody history, but most were more intent on having a drink or checking out the many booths with souvenirs that are now available at every tourist stop on the island.

Havana's colonial architecture in the old city—the area within the boundaries of the now demolished city wall, which includes the four fortresses guarding the city's harbor—was designated a UNESCO World Heritage site in 1982, and the preservation and restoration of Old Havana continues to be a state priority. The attention and resources devoted to Havana's colonial heritage seemed odd to me, given the revolution's anti-imperial character, though as a historian I am grateful. One can see that the colonial plazas and forts are an obligatory stop for tourists visiting the city and generate much-needed revenue for the state. Some ordinary Cubans have benefited as well—vendors, bartenders, guides, musicians, and artists all around Old Havana urge tourists to spend some money. It is clear that these historical remnants will be a fundamental part of Cuba's economy going forward.

One historical detail that was not reenacted or noted on plaques in Havana's impressive forts, however, was the human dimension of how they came to be. Who built these massive structures on limestone cliffs? Who dug the foundations and trenches? Who cut and hauled the stone? How did these Herculean projects affect the people who built them and the city's economy and development? This book is an effort to provide some answers to those questions.

INTRODUCTION

When German scientist Alexander von Humboldt wrote about his impressions of Havana as he sailed into its port in December 1800, he noted that the political importance of Cuba derived not only from its size as the largest island in the Caribbean, its fertile soil, and the characteristics of its people. Its importance also was due to "the advantages offered by the geographic position of Havana" in the Gulf of Mexico, "precisely where . . . a multitude of paths cross that serve the commerce of the peoples [of the region], . . . where the lovely port of Havana is situated, fortified by nature and even more by art." For Humboldt, the natural components of the landscape were secondary to the "art" of "cultivated nature" and the colonial city's built environment.[1]

Humboldt described the view on entering the port of Havana as one of the most "cheerful and picturesque" in the Americas. The mouth of the port was defended by two forts, La Punta and El Morro, both begun in 1589 as Havana became the gathering point for the imperial silver fleets on their return to Spain. The narrow channel leading to the bay of Havana was guarded by two additional forts: La Fuerza, the city's oldest fort, to the west, and the massive La Cabaña, built after the 1762–1763 British occupation of Havana, which "crown[ed] the rocks to the east of the port." Three additional forts guarded the western approaches to the city. The channel opened into a "clover-shaped," deepwater bay, prompting Humboldt to note that the majestic royal palms were overshadowed in a "city half covered by a forest of masts and sails of vessels," highlighting the naval and commercial importance of Cuba's capital.[2]

Havana's commercial vitality in 1800, which Humboldt described, was the result of the striking transformations Cuba underwent in the second half of the eighteenth century. The broad contours of these transformations, enumerated by

Humboldt and well examined by later historians, resulted from the shift from an economy based on imperial service in the Havana region to a plantation economy based on sugar.[3] For Humboldt, a key factor in this transformation was external, as Havana benefited significantly from the collapse of the sugar economy of Saint-Domingue during the Haitian Revolution to become one of the premier commercial cities of the world.[4]

One effect of Cuba's development as a plantation economy was the rapid expansion of African enslavement. From the mid-eighteenth century onward, Spanish officials began advocating for increased importation of enslaved Africans to Cuba to better develop the island's economy and to defend the territory from imperial rivals.[5] By the early 1800s, many among Cuba's elite remained enthusiastic about the continued necessity of enslaved Africans' labor to the island's prosperity, though, in the lengthening shadow of the Haitian Revolution, they worried more about slave rebellion and cultural degeneration.[6] Though Humboldt visited Cuba as a guest of the Spanish state and of wealthy Cuban slave owners, his observations of the lot of the enslaved moved him to say that slavery was the "worst of evils" and was not ameliorated by the supposedly "gentle" norms of Spanish law.[7]

Some of Humboldt's other observations resonated more with his Cuban contemporaries and with later historians of slavery on the island. In particular, he commented on striking differences between the lives of the enslaved in Havana and those working on sugar plantations in the countryside. "What a distance between a slave who serves in the house of a rich man in Havana and in Kingston, or who works on his own account only giving to his owner a daily payment, and the slave subjected to a sugar mill!" Humboldt reflected the perceptions of both owners and slaves at the time, who saw differences in the relative severity of work regimes and material circumstances between urban and rural sites of enslavement. As he observed, "The carriage driver is threatened with the coffee plantation, the coffee worker with the sugar mill."[8]

Humboldt emphasized the geopolitical and economic role that Havana played in the Spanish Empire and noted the physical manifestations of the city's importance—the massive fortifications guarding its shores and the multitude of trading ships in its port. He was also a keen observer of the demographic and social changes wrought by sugar production, but he did not comment on the close connections between the fortification of Havana and the expansion of the plantation economy and enslavement. Similarly, later historiography has tended to focus more on the role of sugar in Cuban development, more rarely on the Spanish state's role in effecting the transformation of Cuba from an economy dominated by imperial service into a plantation colony.[9]

This book joins these two histories to show the key role played by the Spanish state's defense policies and projects in the transformation of Cuba into a plantation society based on slavery. As such, it examines the institutions and officials of imperial governance in Spain and Cuba as they devised and adapted labor policies to carry out public works, foregrounding how state ownership and employment of enslaved workers shaped the lives of those doing the work and Cuba's development into a plantation economy.

This study also complicates Humboldt's broad dichotomy between the lives of those enslaved in Havana and those enslaved on plantations. In fact, there were varied sites of state enslavement in Havana itself, some with clear parallels to the punishing labor regimes on sugar plantations, others with opportunities for some autonomy for the enslaved in both work and social life. Additionally, though this study focuses especially on the forced labor of the enslaved in state projects, the enslaved were only one group of coerced workers among a range of others, which always included convicts and, by the 1830s, also included indentured immigrants. Thus, the experiences of people enslaved by the Spanish state in Havana are examined to understand the political economy of labor coercion in this imperial space—when, how, and why the state marshaled enslaved workers for defense and development in Havana over the eighteenth and early nineteenth centuries.

State Slavery in Havana and the Political Economy of Empire

Havana is a particularly fruitful site for examining the Spanish state's use of enslaved labor. The city was founded around 1515 on a promontory of land that, as Humboldt affirmed, formed the western point of the mouth to one of the best harbors in the world.[10] Two points of land almost enclose Havana's bay, a body of water close to four kilometers in width and in length and deep enough to accommodate easily hundreds of sailing vessels. The prevailing winds, which blow perpendicularly across the opening of the bay, facilitated both entrance and exit. The flow of the sea's currents through the Caribbean and into the Atlantic toward Spain made Cuba a natural site for gathering ships making the circuit from Europe through the Caribbean and then returning.

To the south of the bay's opening, other natural features combined to make the site of Havana almost peninsular in character. Its eastern limit was the enclosed bay, while to the west lay swamps and a difficult coastline. Beyond the swamps and to the south stretched thick woods.

The ease of entry to the bay, however, made the city vulnerable to attack from the sea. When Havana was a colonial backwater, this was a threat to its residents but not an urgent defense consideration for the Spanish crown. Once the convoy system was instituted, in 1543, to escort the fleets back to Spain, Havana's defense brought greater imperial resources to Cuba and launched the first period of sustained growth on the island.

One of the crucial components of this growth was the state's use of enslaved laborers to construct fortifications and service the fleets. Since the indigenous population of the island was drastically reduced within the first fifty years of European conquest and settlement and Spanish immigration was low, the labor of enslaved Africans became central to economic development on the island.[11] From the mid-sixteenth century onward, Havana was the key to and the safeguard of Spanish Atlantic and Caribbean trade routes, vital to the entire imperial economy and its defense. To defend and develop Havana to protect the treasure fleets, the Spanish crown invested in the city, using huge sums of money generated from other, wealthier areas of the empire.[12] Up through the first half of the eighteenth century, it was not the extraction of minerals or the production of agricultural commodities for export that drove economic development in Cuba; instead, it was the exigencies of imperial trade and defense centered in the city of Havana.

Always struggling with a labor shortage on the island, the crown had to import forced laborers to do the work of building fortifications, constructing and repairing the ships of the fleet, and the myriad other services required by a busy imperial port. Thus, through the process of building and defending its American colonies, the Spanish state helped to create Havana's thriving urban economy based on enslaved labor, such that, by the late 1760s, the city had the largest contingent of state slaves in the American empire.

Enslavement by the state for its own projects was not new when Spaniards ventured to the Caribbean in the fifteenth century. Spanish monarchs had owned and employed enslaved people on the peninsula for centuries, and enslaved workers' status, treatment, and access to manumission were codified and negotiated in practice, long before the era covered in this study began. Through the eighteenth century, many of those enslaved in state service were king's slaves, esclavos del rey, purchased by the Spanish crown and employed at many sites of imperial power in Cuba—for shipbuilding and fort construction projects, at the docks, in the tobacco warehouses, in military garrisons, and in the offices and residences of officials.

The importance of state-owned enslaved workers engaged in public tasks surged in the mid-eighteenth century, then diminished by the mid-nineteenth century, but the policies, practices, and precedents established by the state to carry out its projects in the 1760s formed a bridge between colonial or "first" slavery, as it had developed in Cuba from the sixteenth century, and the modern or "second" slavery system of the nineteenth century.[13] The first priority of the Spanish efforts to reconstruct the infrastructure of the empire in Havana was to preserve the island as a colony, not to produce a commodity. Yet Spain's projects in Havana from the 1760s to 1820 often were at the leading edge of waves of transformation toward a modern, slave-based economy that did produce tropical commodities in Cuba, shaping and being shaped by capitalist imperatives, especially in labor and commodity markets, the slave trade being a commerce that joined the two.

The execution of public works projects in Havana was important to plantation development, in part due to the parallels between the types of work regimes required in both settings. Before the middle of the nineteenth century, fort, ship, road, and building construction were the only enterprises in Cuba that could employ hundreds, and occasionally thousands, of unfree workers at a given moment. The work required for public projects was largely difficult, dangerous, draining, and often deadly for those forced to dig, mine, and haul wood, earth, and stone in the tropical heat and damp. The unskilled work on public construction projects rarely attracted free wageworkers in sufficient numbers or at sufficiently low wages to ensure completion on a budget. Therefore, analogous to plantation labor recruitment before emancipation, many public projects could only be undertaken if a majority of workers were under some kind of coercion. Forced labor in public works was also a tool of the Spanish state to discipline unruly subjects and enemies and to benefit from their labor.

Thus, state enslavement and its relation to other forms of forced labor was at the heart of the political economy of the Spanish Empire. The state determined laws and regulations for the slave trade up to the last decade of the eighteenth century, affecting markets both local and international. The state set regulations for the behavior of and treatment of its enslaved subjects, though these regulations were not always followed in practice. Finally, because state projects often were the largest employers of both enslaved and other forced workers, they were sites where work regimes and mixes of types of laborers were worked out in practice so that, in some cases, they could later be applied elsewhere.

War Work, Constructive Labor, and Development

Warfare is central to the story of state slavery in Cuba, as well. As the first European power to claim a global empire in the sixteenth century, Spain spent much of the seventeenth and eighteenth centuries trying to defend that claim and the flows of imperial trade against the predations and growing power of its European rivals, on land and at sea. Building, maintaining, and defending the infrastructure of an empire was hard work. Thus, this study contends that it was not only commodity production and manufacturing that produced value and drove economic transformations in a given site.[14] Rather, warfare and defense prompted Spanish officials to devise a series of evolving policies and practices toward its own enslaved workers and those it employed in constructive labor, which increased slave imports to Cuba, shaped the opportunities available to planters interested in producing tropical exports, and modeled labor organization on large-scale projects, both public and private. The escalating state demand for and employment of labor in the second half of the eighteenth century drove deep changes in markets, work regimes, and, ultimately, in the relationships between the state and its subjects in Cuba, both enslaved and free.[15]

For example, the urgency of defense concerns after 1763 pushed the Spanish crown to make changes in Cuba's level of integration into Atlantic markets, unraveling centuries of mercantilist constraints on trade. With crown approval, state actors in Cuba gradually loosened restrictions on slave trading to mobilize thousands of enslaved workers for fort building in the 1760s and in the process allowed greater numbers of enslaved Africans to be purchased by private planters. State demand expanded markets not only for labor but also for foodstuffs, wood, bricks, stone, and ironwork as officials sought to marshal the necessary tools and materials for building and repairing ships, forts, and roads over decades. To fund these massive enterprises, officials diverted capital to Havana from the imperial flows of Mexican silver and through donations from wealthy Cubans. Securing local resources in the service of imperial defense also required considerable interaction between state actors and Cuban elites. Accommodating many of the demands of those elites further opened the island to Atlantic markets for enslaved workers and the sugar they produced.

New sources and sites of power developed as a result of officials' willingness to facilitate plantation expansion, allowing Cuban-born planters to gain considerable influence in Madrid and in colonial administration in Havana. By the first third of the nineteenth century, these wealthy creoles established quasi-governmental organizations that undertook public works in their own interests, with a particular focus on the transportation infrastructure of Cuba, as sugar cultivation expanded out from Havana. The impulse behind these transportation infrastructure projects was less directly tied to imperial service and more clearly connected to expanding sugar production.

In the period under study here, the 1760s up to 1835, there was significant interpenetration of interests among colonial officials and Cuban elites. Some of the highest Spanish officials on the island, such as the captains general and intendants, were also plantation owners. By the 1820s, two wealthy Cuban-born slave owners became intendants. Additionally, the Spanish crown's need to retain Cuba, first as a crucial way station for the silver fleets returning to the metropole and later as the wealthiest of its colonies in a shrinking empire, necessitated working closely with Cuban elites, not only to increase the slave trade to the island but also to collaborate on controlling the enslaved as their numbers grew.

As the foregoing suggests, the state is defined broadly in this study as an institution that included both metropolitan and colonial branches, staffed by shifting groups of officials, representing a variety of interests and perspectives. There often was an interpenetration of public and private actors and interests at play. One common element that united virtually all state actors and their collaborators, at least during the years from the 1760s through the early 1830s, was the importance of defending and developing Cuba and maintaining slavery and the colonial bond with Spain, even though disagreement developed about the best policies to meet those goals.

The laws, decrees, and practices of the Spanish state also shaped ideological and social norms in Cuba, defining hierarchies of status and access for all its subjects. The crown and its representatives expressed their power through both force and grace, within the norms of a paternalism that could be bloody and cruel as well as merciful. In this study of state slavery in Cuba, we see that Spanish law defined slavery as unnatural and allowed multiple paths to freedom. The enslaved were children of God, potential or practicing Christians, with some rights to religious practice and family life. In addition, the enslaved availed themselves of these openings in the Spanish legal system to seek redress and to pursue freedom for themselves and their loved ones. Spanish officials and codes also valued military service and sacrifice and rewarded even the enslaved for fighting for the king.[16]

The often collaborative relationship between metropolitan officials and creoles finally broke down by the 1830s, after Spain's loss of its mainland colonies, shifting the political economy of labor yet again. Spanish officials extended the state's power through the criminal justice system to control potentially disruptive populations, such as recaptured fugitive slaves, political prisoners, and people defined as vagrant, and to put them to work on public projects. As the employment of slaves in the private plantation sector soared, their enslavement by the state shrank and ceased to be an important component of state officials' labor recruitment strategy. However, both the state and private employers still demanded laborers over whom they could exert some control, especially with regard to their mobility and work discipline, even as plantation production of sugar expanded.

Thus, this examination of enslavement on the part of the Spanish state shows that the constructive labor of empire was a vital component of the evolving political economy of forced labor in Cuba, and by implication in the empire. The Spanish state's policies and practices as a slave owner and employer in public works in the eighteenth and early nineteenth centuries shaped and sometimes led the expansion of enslavement and plantation development in Cuba.

Historical Processes and Perspectives

Work on this project has spanned many years and therefore has been informed by and seeks to inform several lines of historical inquiry. It was conceived within the vibrant field of slavery studies and is framed by the protean scholarship on European imperialisms, both of which were often animated by comparative questions. The intervening years of research and writing in those fields and in my own thinking have widened the lenses through which I examine state slavery in Havana. The unit of analysis has remained the city of Havana, and the main actors continue to be people enslaved by the colonial state and the many officials who recruited, deployed, and disciplined them and debated their fates. However, Havana's state slaves are now situated in multiple and interconnected contexts, extending beyond the city, the island of Cuba, or the Spanish Empire. In seeking to fully understand and interpret their working lives, the setting is local but the flows of goods, people, ideas, and historical processes are often Atlantic and sometimes global in scope. Hence, at least for this project, a long period of gestation has enriched the story.

The classic melding of studies of slavery and European imperialisms was Frank Tannebaum's *Slave and Citizen*, which found the experiences of and prospects for freedom and social mobility available to enslaved Africans and their descendants in the Iberian empires to be significantly different from those available to people living in the British Empire. Through his historical comparison, Tannenbaum hoped to explain significant differences in race relations in the United States and Latin America by the mid-twentieth century.[17]

Citing Humboldt and others, Tannenbaum's work also suggested the relative openness of enslavement in Cuba, especially for skilled slaves in cities, compared to slaves on the plantations of the Anglophone Caribbean and North America.[18] Such a characterization of urban enslavement has validity and continues to frame studies of slaves' experiences in the cities of the Americas.[19] However, many of the examples of urban work done by thousands of Havana's state slaves discussed in this book break down sharp distinctions between the experiences of urban and rural enslavement upon which Humboldt, Tannenbaum, and others have remarked. More recent scholarship contends that it is more analytically valuable to identify "spaces of slavery" within cities and to see how the enslaved worked and lived there.[20] Even in state employment in Havana, the terms of work, living conditions, levels of autonomy, and possibilities of achieving freedom varied considerably among the enslaved who were laboring in digging the foundations of forts, building imperial ships, transporting lime and earth, or serving in the city's artillery company. Colonial officials' expectations and rationales for employing enslaved versus other types of coerced workers also varied across the many sites of state work in the city.

Interestingly, state slavery in Europe's American empires is little studied, in spite of the fact that all the major colonizing powers owned or employed slaves for much of the colonial era. State slavery in Cuba has received more attention than state slavery in other parts of Spain's American empire, particularly in the work of Francisco Pérez Guzmán on Havana and María Elena Díaz on state slaves in Santiago de Cuba.[21] Díaz studied the *cobreros*, the king's slaves of El Cobre, in eastern Cuba, who stand in sharp contrast to most of the royal slaves discussed in this book.[22] The *cobreros*' experience was also uncommon in the wider history of enslavement in the Americas.[23] However, interesting parallels do emerge when we examine the enslaved and formerly enslaved who fought for the Spanish crown to defend the empire in Havana, as we shall see in chapter 4.

The relative lack of scholarly attention to both urban and state enslavement more broadly in the Atlantic world is due in part to the fact that the majority of enslaved Africans brought to the Americas were destined for plantation labor.[24] Additionally, the implicit (or sometimes explicit) biases and binaries that have framed the questions posed by scholars about the differences between urban or rural plantation slavery, or enslavement in British or Spanish colonies, or the relative modernity of British economic and political development versus Spanish development have directed scholarly attention away from studies of slaves working outside areas of export commodity production and of the interactions among various sites of slavery.[25] One of the goals of this book is to bridge these divides to tell a more cohesive story of slavery's development in Cuba through the example of state enslavement in Havana.

In Cuban historiography on slavery, Marxist and nationalist categories and narratives have had the strongest influence. Cuban historians often combined deep research in Cuban archives with debates about the nature of the Cuban plantation economy and its relationship to capitalism, especially in the nineteenth century. Some Cuban scholars argued that enslavement was a precapitalist mode of labor and that Cuba's continuation as a colony of Spain until 1898 prohibited the development of capitalist social relations in the island's dependent plantation economy.[26] Other Cuban historians have argued that the island's plantation economy remained "traditional" or "colonial and dependent" into the latter half of the 1800s. Even when some measure of capitalist development was acknowledged, slavery was seen as the obstacle to a fully modern economy.[27]

Other avenues of scholarship chose to focus more on the details of social relations on the island's plantations and less on whether those relations conformed to a priori categories defining capitalism. Evidence of slaves' agency in seeking greater autonomy, and even freedom, contrasted with the more mechanistic Marxian story of the inexorable march of capitalist social relations toward free wage labor.[28] Here, the slave system appears to be flexible and adaptable as the political economy of the Spanish and other Atlantic empires shifted away from slavery in the later nineteenth century. Cuban planters' efforts to diversify their labor forces are evidence of the resilience of the slave system rather than of its internal contradictions and crisis. Still, rather than embracing wage labor exclusively, Cuban planters remained attached to the control over work discipline that slavery afforded them, and as full emancipation neared, in 1886, they tried to recreate as many elements of that control as possible with contract laborers, convicts, and free workers.[29]

Historians of Cuban slavery have been attentive to the many connections between Cuba's plantation economy and the commercial networks of other European powers for slave trading, for importing goods from wheat to locomotive engines, and for sugar markets as evidence of the island's colonial dependence.[30] However, more recently, scholars have begun to situate the development of slavery in Cuba in a more holistic Atlantic or global framework.[31] One example, from the late 1980s, is the work of historical sociologist Dale Tomich, who introduced the notion of "second slavery" to create a framework that would allow the examination of the interrelations of slavery and capitalism beyond analyses that had isolated the one from the other or that failed to attend to "the specificity and complexity of local histories" and their interactions "with processes of the world economy."[32] Tomich and those who have followed his lead in using this framework to understand slavery in the Americas have identified sugar production in Cuba, along with the production of cotton in the southern United States and coffee in southeastern Brazil, as prime examples of the dramatic reformulation of slavery after the abolition of the transatlantic slave trade and the revolutionary upheavals of the later eighteenth and early nineteenth centuries.[33] Most relevant for this book is that fact that Cuba was the only one of the three cases in which state slavery for the construction of imperial infrastructure played a prominent, though unacknowledged, role in effecting the transition.

To best understand state slavery in Havana, factors of influence and interaction must be considered at multiple levels of analysis. Therefore, works on Atlantic, imperial, and global labor history have been helpful in framing the analysis in this book. Numerous scholars of labor history, especially since the early 2000s, have called for abandoning stark juxtapositions of freedom and unfreedom among workers and of narratives of transition from one form of labor to another.[34] The flowering of Atlantic history also helped shift focus from oppositional comparative questions to examine the flows of people and goods around the Atlantic and/or the entanglements in the region across the many boundaries, real and imagined, of ethnicity, territory, empire, gender, race, status, and class.[35]

Peter Linebaugh and Marcus Rediker's work on the motley crews of transatlantic piracy, naval service, and slave trading has been deeply influential in shaping the fields of Atlantic and global labor history and for helping me situate state slavery in Cuba within larger narratives. As they note in The Many-Headed Hydra, "The emphasis in modern labor history on the white, male, skilled, waged, nationalist, propertied artisan/citizen or industrial worker has hidden the history of the Atlantic proletariat of the seventeenth, eighteenth, and early nineteenth centuries."[36] Their Atlantic proletariat included people who worked under various degrees of coercion (the sailors and slaves of their subtitle). Many of these people were "the hewers of wood and drawers of water" who "transformed the face of the Earth by building the infrastructure of 'civilization.'"[37] Such a capacious definition of proletarians, and by implication of capitalism, allows historians to examine existing social relations of work, rather than trying to explain why those relations did or did not conform to a priori categories or viewing long periods of history as "transitional" on the way to an ideal form of capitalism. Similarly, in a narrative of capitalist development, such a definition allows a place for the workers who built, maintained, and defended the infrastructure of empires, along with those producing commodities.

Like Linebaugh and Rediker's tale of the English motley crew, much of the writing on slavery and capitalism has focused on the Anglo-Atlantic, and an implicit bias in favor of the Anglo-Atlantic as normative has persisted in the field.[38] Building on the arguments of Eric Williams and others, several twenty-first-century analyses have put slavery at the center of examinations of industrialization and the development of modern Western societies, with their main focus on Britain and its American colonies.[39] For instance, rather than seeing the increasing role of slavery in the United States in the eighteenth and nineteenth centuries as somehow backward, transitional, or anomalous, scholars of the new history of capitalism in the United States have argued that enslavement was the "beating heart" of capitalist development for centuries and that "the constant shifting recombination of various systems of labor" are constituent elements of the process.[40] A crucial phase of this development was what Sven Beckert has called "war capitalism," a period from the sixteenth to the eighteenth centuries when warfare and imperial expansion, based mostly on forced labor, was an engine of transformation.[41]

The story in this book examines what could be called a second phase of war capitalism in the Spanish Empire, which drove capitalist development and transformed the political economy of labor in Cuba in the late 1700s and 1800s. War capitalism as manifested in Cuba did not lead to industrialization in Spain and creation of a parallel empire of sugar, though capital accumulated in slave trading and sugar production in Cuba helped to propel other types of industrial development in Spain.[42] The analysis here shows that Spain's confrontations with the aggressive violence and acquisitiveness of the British state in the eighteenth and early nineteenth centuries did compel Spanish officials to invent new ways to mobilize capital and labor, to initiate a reinvention of slavery, and to open the way to the expansion and ultimate industrialization of sugar production on the island.

Even within the later era of second slavery in the Atlantic world, networks of trade, production processes, labor recruitment, and work regimes were again transformed, by abolitionism, new technologies, and political reconfigurations of nations and empires. The story told here ends in 1835, just as the Cuban elite took definitive steps toward building the first railroad line on the island, using new configurations of forced labor that for the first time included contract laborers. Thereafter, an ascendant and confident class of creole planters continued to pursue innovations in sugar processing technologies, in railroad building, and in the warehousing of sugar. They also forged new trade relationships outside the Spanish Empire, as Cuban sugar production industrialized.[43]

This case study of Havana in the late eighteenth and early nineteenth centuries shows the ubiquity of coercion and the simultaneity of varied labor forms, first employed effectively by the Spanish colonial state in its defense and infrastructure projects, and later adapted, at least in part, to plantations.[44] The precise mix of type of worker and degree of coercion at any state work site in Havana shifted over time, but this is not a story of a transition from unfree to free labor. Rather, as Cuba was more tightly integrated into global capitalist networks of trade and labor, violence and coercion remained fundamental characteristics of workers' relationships to their employers. But enslavement as the dominant form of coercion became more entrenched in plantation production and less so in imperial labor for the state.

Additionally, the relationship of state slaves to the crown, their enslaver, varied according to their levels of skill and their roles in defending the island, and these roles were transformed by the expansion of the plantation economy. Military service, even by the enslaved, could bring higher status and rewards. A complex blend of economic imperatives, cultural norms and traditions, and internal and external political considerations framed state actors' decisions about resorting to enslavement as a mode of labor recruitment, deployment, and control and produced significant variation in experiences over time, even among those enslaved to do the king's work in a local setting such as Havana.

The new histories of capitalism and global labor history I have discussed here have put more emphasis on the role of states in creating and protecting the physical, legal, and ideological context for the accumulation of capital through territorial expansion and forced labor.[45] A return to scholarly interest in the political economies of empire also has refocused attention on state actors and their roles in shaping economic development, both in theory and in practice. However, studies of political economy, from its early articulations in the eighteenth century to twenty-first-century histories, focus mostly on states' approaches to commerce and less on their roles in shaping policy and labor practice, which I focus on here.[46]

The Spanish crown framed the political economy of imperial commerce through laws and decrees, seeking to set the terms of trade within and beyond the empire, regulating shipping, tariffs, duties, and protocols. Metropolitan officials thereby defined and sought to punish smugglers and pirates and made war to enforce the empire's exclusive vision of commerce, though successful enforcement was impossible. The extensive needs of this protectionist state were the engine of growth and development in Cuba for at least two and a half centuries.[47] In the case of Spanish Cuba, it was the engine of capital accumulation and redistribution as the inpouring of silver from Mexico was invested in land and labor in Cuba (and elsewhere) and in the construction of imperial defense works and state-owned enterprises such as mines.

The imperial state had the power to mobilize resources in extremis in ways that private individuals could not, such that by the eighteenth century the state organized most war-making and infrastructure building projects. To carry out these massive efforts, state officials partnered with private individuals and institutions to recruit laborers in local, imperial, and even global labor markets. Hence, in this study, I strive to attend to the many interrelations of people and processes, at multiple levels of analysis, to understand a particular form of slavery (enslavement by the Spanish state) in a particular space and time (Havana from the 1760s into the 1830s).

Ultimately, this book is a story of the tremendous labor required to construct, maintain, and defend the Spanish Empire in Havana. That labor did not produce commodities for a market, but it was intimately and transformatively related to such production. Instead, those workers, many of them enslaved, built and reproduced the Spanish Empire in this key Caribbean port. By attending to spaces of slavery within a larger context of capitalist relations, not only of production but also of construction and reproduction, we come to a fuller understanding of the deep embedment of force and violence in the development of capitalism. Because the actors in this story (the state's officials and its enslaved workers) were not primarily producers for a market, the most interesting questions are about how their lives and work affected development and the reformulation of social relations in varying spatial contexts over time—in Havana or Cuba, in the Spanish Empire or the Atlantic, and even occasionally on a global scale. The physical construction of the Spanish Empire in Cuba was a key component of Atlantic capitalism, and state enslavement for that construction was crucial to the development of plantation slavery in Cuba in the nineteenth century.

Sources

Because this book focuses on the political economy of state enslavement in Havana, the bulk of the sources consulted were generated by the Spanish governmental bureaucracy. The voices telling the stories here are largely those of Spanish officials struggling over resources to carry out complex projects. Some aspects of the daily lives of the people enslaved by the king are revealed through monthly registers of their numbers and tasks, through lists of people confined to the hospital or missing from work, or through officials' letters describing their housing, sustenance, and punishments. The expressed thoughts and feelings of Havana's royal slaves are often obscured in these sources, yet I have tried to capture the experiences of enslaved individuals where possible.

Due to the British siege and occupation in 1762, Cuba was Spain's first American colony to experience administrative and military restructuring under the Spanish Bourbon monarchy. The bulk of the primary sources for the discussion of the eighteenth century in this book are documents generated by Spanish colonial bureaucrats in their efforts to both reform and defend Havana after 1763. The urgency created by the occupation prompted the crown to reform the existing bureaucratic structure on the island by importing to Cuba a variant of the French intendancy system, under the direction of a newly appointed captain general with more extensive powers than those granted to any other colonial official, except a viceroy. The intendant also had broad powers, being charged with overseeing economic development, public works, finance, war, and justice.

The papers of the intendants were particularly useful for this study. Since many of the colonial officials assigned to Cuba in the eighteenth century were also military men, some of this documentation is housed in the military archive of Simancas, Spain. In keeping with the Bourbons' impulse to centralize administration, Charles III initiated the collection of documents on the Indies into one archive in 1785. The process of remitting documents on the Indies to this Archivo

General de Indias in Seville continued well into the twentieth century. In 1975, numerous documents generated from 1760 onward that had been housed in Simancas were sent to the Archivo General in Seville, though the Archivo General de Simancas remains a critical repository for the period.[48]

The papers generated by the colonial officials directly responsible for the planning and execution of the massive defense program—the captain general, the intendants, the engineers, and military supervisors at the construction sites—form the core of this study's discussion of the period from 1763 to the 1790s. These collections also contain the reports these officials sent to Spain to keep the secretary of state apprised of the progress (or lack thereof) on the fortification projects. Other scholars have used these documents to examine the military and commercial reforms undertaken during this period, but scholarly attention to their rich detail on state enslavement has been slight.[49] As documents generated within the colonial bureaucracy, they provide insights into the institutions and actors involved in the process of decision-making at this critical juncture in Spanish colonial history. They also contain detailed quantitative data on the recruitment, deployment, and distribution of the enslaved and other laborers, forced and free, in the extensive fortification projects begun after 1763. As a metropolitan archive, these documents are strongest at representing the voices of Spanish bureaucrats trying to carry out the daunting array of public works in their charge, with limited resources. These sources also have information on the lives and experiences of individual slaves.

The primary materials for the discussion of workers enslaved by the state in public works in the nineteenth century are of more diverse provenance. By the 1830s, Spanish colonial officials on the island no longer had exclusive control of infrastructure projects such as road and bridge building or the recruitment of the enslaved for state service. Most helpful in piecing together information on public works in this period has been the documents housed in the Archivo Histórico Nacional in Madrid under the headings "Estado" (State) and "Ultramar" (Overseas). These collections were supplemented with documents from the Seville archive.

I was able to consult a just few documents in the Archivo Nacional de la República de Cuba in Havana on a brief trip to the island in 2012. As with the sources for the eighteenth century, this documentation tends to give a top-down view of the lives of enslaved workers engaged in public works, but it is a particularly relevant view for answering the questions posed in this book—questions about the changing geopolitical and economic circumstances influencing the deployment of enslaved labor by the Spanish state, and their impact on Cuban economic development.

Structure and Argument

This exploration of state enslavement in Havana from 1762 to 1834 is divided into five chapters framed by an introduction and brief conclusion. Because the evolution of the Spanish state's use of enslavement for its own projects throughout the empire has not been studied in detail, chapter 1 summarizes the historical relationship between the Spanish state and forced labor on the peninsula, in its Mediterranean and Atlantic colonies, and in the New World from the fifteenth through the seventeenth centuries.

The extent of state enslavement in each of the colonial settings was shaped in part by colony type. Settlement colonies required more work. Colonists needed food, water, and shelter, and the new site had to be defended from pirates, colonial rivals, and hostile natives. In the initial stages of conquest and settlement, the funds and the labor for all of these activities were often provided by private individuals, fortified with various types of incentives by the state. However, most colonies were eventually brought under closer supervision by the Spanish crown, putting the responsibility for infrastructure and defense back on the state.

Hence, chapter 1 focuses on the three areas in which the majority of state workers were deployed: in military, naval, and defense works; in the development of infrastructure; and in production in state enterprises. This discussion highlights a number of patterns of political and economic imperatives emerging in Spain's Old World possessions, which later shaped the use of state enslaved workers in Cuba. Several factors influenced decisions about the use of crown slaves versus other types of forced or free laborers in state projects, including the type of work to be performed, the possible hazards to workers, and the cost effectiveness of enslaved versus other forced or free labor. The chapter ends with a typology of forms of state enslavement, which is thereafter used to analyze state slavery in the subsequent chapters.

Chapter 2 discusses cycles of Atlantic warfare and their impact on defense and development priorities in Cuba, especially the Bourbons' renewed attention to strengthening the royal navy in the early eighteenth century. Traditional patterns of state enslavement—small groups of strategically employed royal slaves supplemented with hired enslaved people, and other workers forced and free—sufficed to expand the navy and to better commercialize tobacco production.

Sugar production also was encouraged by changes in tax and tariff policies and with modest encouragement of slave importation through a chartered joint-stock company, the Royal Company of Havana (RCH). Traditional patterns of labor employment did not suffice for increasing the land fortifications of the city, and these defense works ultimately failed in the face of a massive land and sea attack by British forces in 1762. Policies to foment sugar production did produce growth, but the demand for enslaved labor on plantations was not fully satisfied.

Both the state and the RCH relied on the strategic employment of the enslaved in their respective endeavors: the Havana shipyard, the tobacco *factoría*, warehouses, and transport. All of these endeavors prospered by using long-standing labor practices. The labor requirements of the Bourbons' plans for building land fortifications in Havana by 1760 are contrasted with naval regeneration and the tobacco monopoly. Little progress was made in land defenses before 1762, due to problems in recruiting sufficient labor to begin them. The chapter ends with the British siege and occupation of Havana from 1762 to 1763, with attention to both sides' use of the enslaved in battle and as auxiliaries.

Chapter 3 is a detailed analysis of state enslavement for defense and ship construction in Cuba after the Seven Years' War. The Spanish crown initiated government and commercial reforms to generate the necessary funds and labor to protect Havana from renewed war with Britain. In particular, the crown loosened restrictions on slave trading to help recruit thousands of enslaved Africans to repair and expand Havana's defense works. In the process, many thousands more of the enslaved were sold to the private sector. To increase revenue, the state renegotiated its relationship with the native Cuban elite, creating conditions that favored increased private investment in sugar expansion and slavery from the 1760s onward.

The process of refortifying Havana also reconfigured the state's relationship with a large portion of its own slaves, particularly those employed in fort building. Because of the size and urgency of these projects, the Spanish state enforced work regimes not common to Cuban slavery previously, particularly in the city: gang labor, a highly skewed gender ratio in favor of men, punishing regimens that produced high mortality, and limited access to manumission.

The unusually extensive use of royal slaves in fort construction is then contrasted with the return to strategic use of those enslaved by the king in the reopened shipyard, to analyze the factors influencing these differences, such as shifting defense priorities, the structure of the labor market and the labor alternatives available at a given moment, the types of work to be performed, possible hazards to workers, and the state's fiscal resources. In fact, the intense initial resort to the labor of royal slaves for fort building obtained only from 1764 to 1769. Thereafter, until the completion of the forts in the 1790s, the state divested itself of its least skilled enslaved workers in favor of convict labor. However, the commercial reforms enacted to recruit enslaved labor for public works were retained and expanded, as the Bourbons' defense needs aided plantation development. The brief moment of urgent resort to the labor of thousands of state slaves for defense in the 1760s had long-term consequences for the social relations between the enslaved and their employers, both state and private, and between metropolitan officials and the Cuban elite.

Chapter 4 discusses Spain's varied military use of the enslaved from the second half of the eighteenth century into the early nineteenth. In one case, the working and living arrangements of royal slaves in Havana's reformed artillery units were starkly different from those of the fort workers. Here, the state recruited equal numbers of enslaved men and women with the intention of forming a skilled cadre of artillery workers who could enjoy private living quarters, special uniforms, and family life. In the offensive campaigns against British colonies in the circum-Caribbean during the American War of Independence (1779–1783), Spain made some use of free militiamen of color, but it employed few of its enslaved workers in battle. The enslaved people it did use tended to be auxiliaries, who did the difficult work of digging trenches and hauling armaments and supplies. Finally, warfare against revolutionary France (1793–1795) in Saint-Domingue, in the context of a massive slave rebellion, forced Spain to ally with black military leaders who had freed themselves through force of arms, thereafter complicating issues of their reward and resettlement in a Spanish Caribbean empire ever more committed to slavery.

This analysis concludes with a comparison of state enslavement in the military and in defense construction as the Atlantic context of all these activities shifted over the eighteenth century. The extensive resort to royal slaves in both defense construction and the military during specific moments in the 1700s ultimately created both fiscal and political problems for the state and discouraged a return to such practices in the nineteenth century. The chapter ends with a discussion of the momentous changes wrought by war and revolution in the Atlantic world from 1790 to 1825 and how these changes affected Havana's role in imperial trade and defense. With the loss of the mainland empire, especially of Mexico, Cuba became Spain's main source of colonial revenue, due to the explosive growth of the plantation economy based on enslaved labor. The island also was the empire's main base of operations to counter US, British, and French interests in North America and the Caribbean. The demographic transformation of Cuban society from 1792 onward, from a white majority to a majority of people of African descent, also heightened Spanish officials' attention to internal defense against slave rebellion, to potential alliances between free people of African descent and the enslaved, and to the wisdom of relying so heavily on white creoles, free people of African descent, and royal slaves for the island's defense and development.

Chapter 5 focuses on infrastructure projects in Havana, particularly road building and urban renewal, organized by the colonial state or by quasi-state institutions such as the Havana Consulado from the 1770s until 1835. It revisits several important currents of change discussed in chapters 3 and 4 that affected the deployment of state slaves in defense construction and military organization—the growing prosperity and political power of the Cuban creole elite, massive importations of enslaved Africans, waves of revolution and warfare in Europe and the Americas—and examines their effects on the state's patterns of labor organization for public projects. Spain was alternately at war with France and England or with its own colonists for many of these years, with periods of respite in the 1770s and between 1783 and 1793. A return to the costly and extensive employment of royal slaves of the 1760s was impossible, and large public works projects still had trouble recruiting sufficient laborers without some kind of coercion.[50]

Chapter 5 also shows how Spanish officials in Cuba recruited new groups of laborers, such as the burgeoning population of fugitive slaves, and harnessed their labor for the state while they awaited reclamation by their enslavers. Colonial officials in Cuba also turned setbacks such as the British–Spanish treaties abolishing the transatlantic slave trade in the empire into a source of forced laborers, through the captain general's control over the enslaved Africans freed by the terms of those treaties—the *emancipados.* "Enlightened" policing under the Bourbons also generated growing numbers of prisoners who were sentenced to labor in public works. In this era, royal slavery was a minor supplement to the state's expanding powers of labor coercion in other sectors and over a subset of the enslaved who had fled their captivity. This chapter also shows that greater integration into capitalist markets for commodities such as sugar did not cause a shift to greater resort to free laborers in public works. Rather, the growth of slavery in the private sector and British abolitionism reduced the state's ability to employ the enslaved, but not the officials' insistence on the need for coercion to do public work.

Thus, this book demonstrates the importance of imperial states in shaping the interplay between enslavement and the development of capitalism—both their better-studied importance in stimulating development in the private sector and their less-studied importance as recruiters and employers of labor in public works as a part of that process. It expands the discussion of the state's influence on the experience of enslavement beyond considerations of law and policy directives to examine the Spanish state as an owner and employer of the enslaved.

This project also situates the case of state enslavement in Cuba within the history of the complex processes that formed the modern Atlantic world—the construction of empires in the Americas and the workers who carried it out; the varied processes of expansion and the experiences of African enslavement (and its ultimate demise), from the point of view of those who endured it; and the restructuring of European colonialism in the Americas over the eighteenth and nineteenth centuries. If the "sinews" of imperial power and war were embedded in a state's access to money,[51] they also were embedded in that state's access to muscle—in this case, the coerced labor of the enslaved.

My hope in writing this book has been to reveal the tremendous labor of thousands of enslaved people that is embedded in the massive structures of Havana's defensive colonial infrastructure but is today largely invisible. By unearthing the story of how the policies and practices of the Spanish state to recruit and employ enslaved labor remade Cuba, we see more clearly a darker side of the colonial heritage that now attracts tourists to the forts guarding Havana's port. And we understand more fully how the work of constructing empires helped to construct capitalism as well.

1

SLAVERY AND THE STATE

Precedents in Spain and Cuba to 1700

The kingdoms of Spain had a long and continuous history with the institution of slavery, from ancient times into the modern era.[1] Though few slaves remained in Spain by the nineteenth century, slavery was not officially abolished on the peninsula until 1836. Full abolition did not come to its colony in Cuba until 1886. Over this extensive period, the Spanish crown also had a long and continuous history as an owner and employer of slaves, especially in military occupations and public works.

By the end of the fifteenth century the enslaved in Spain were a diverse mix of peoples, mostly employed in urban settings or as domestic servants.[2] As Spain embarked on imperial expansion after 1492, peninsular models of enslavement were brought to the Americas and adapted to both local circumstances and the empire's widening military and defensive needs. A mix of historical precedent in law, of practice, and of expediency shaped an evolving political economy of forced labor in the Spanish Empire over the sixteenth and seventeenth centuries as officials increasingly resorted to enslaved labor for state work, both on the peninsula and in Cuba. By approximately 1700, the main characteristics of state slavery in the Spanish Empire were well established and their application by colonial officials in Cuba profoundly reshaped slavery and the development of Havana over the eighteenth century.

Historical Precedents

The clearest historical antecedents of the Spanish Empire's approach to enslavement are found in the Roman era of conquest and colonization of the peninsula, though both law and practice were modified many times over the two millennia before final abolition. Hundreds of thousands of people were enslaved by the Romans as they slowly extended their rule across the Iberian peninsula from 218 BCE to the end of the first century BCE. Romans employed slaves in large-scale enterprises in agriculture as well as in urban service, artisanal jobs, and domestic service. Publicly owned slaves also were important to Rome's Iberian colonization, as they would later be to Spain's imperial expansion, in such jobs as building and maintaining roads and aqueducts.[3]

Another important practice brought by the Romans was the state's appropriation and control of mineral deposits. Public slaves composed most of the workforce in Iberian silver mines under the Roman Republic. Under the Roman Empire, the state began renting out the mines and the workforce became more varied, mixing public and rented slaves with free workers.[4] Spanish monarchs in the modern era also experimented with various administrative models and diverse groups of forced and free laborers in its mines at home and in the Americas, while jealously guarding their royal portion of the empire's mineral wealth.

The collapse of the Roman Empire brought successive waves of conquerors to Spain, who maintained and modified the practice of slavery. The use of large numbers of slaves in agriculture and public works declined, but the institution endured and became even more diverse after the Muslim conquest in the eighth century. Important for the story of enslavement in the Spanish Caribbean were the extensive Muslim slave trading networks, especially with sub-Saharan Africa, which brought significant numbers of black slaves to Spain for the first time.[5] In the 1400s, expeditions by Portuguese traders further expanded Europe's access to African slaves. By 1525, black slaves in Seville numbered more than 3,200 and free and enslaved Africans had participated in many Spanish expeditions of conquest.[6] The Muslim practice of extensive employment of slaves as soldiers was rare in the Spanish American empire, though in times of crisis slaves were armed for colonial defense. More common was the employment of slaves to build and maintain Spain's extensive system of fortifications, especially in the Caribbean.[7]

The Christian kingdoms of medieval Spain most often employed slaves in small numbers, as auxiliaries to other servile or free workers, in contrast to the more typical Roman and Muslim practice of extensive employment of slaves in agriculture, urban employments, and the military.[8] More influential over the long term were Roman legal norms governing slavery that were rediscovered and included in the codification of Castilian law known as *Las Siete Partidas del*

Rey Don Alfonso el Sabio, in the 1260s. Even after new slave codes were produced in 1789 and 1845 in response to the growth of plantation economies in the Spanish Caribbean, the *Siete Partidas* legal framework continued to shape thinking and interactions among slaves, their owners, and the state in Spain and its colonies.[9]

The *Siete Partidas*'s most explicit antecedents were imperial Roman legal norms, later tempered by those of the Christian Bible and the Catholic Church.[10] Slavery was characterized as an institution with deep historical roots, but also one that was evil and against natural reason.[11] The code tried to bridge the contradiction between the ancients' view of enslavement as an appropriate state for inferior beings and aspects of Christian thought that viewed the slave as a human being with a soul, capable of attaining salvation and deserving of mercy.[12]

The authority of masters was upheld throughout the code, but the *Siete Partidas* also allowed the enslaved certain rights along with their obligations to obey and serve their owners. Slaves were to have some personal security, with provisions against murder without judicial authorization or against extreme mutilations such as castration.[13] If a slave was Christian, she or he was entitled to similar access to the sacrament of marriage and the support for parenthood enjoyed by a free person. For the Church, it was the consent of the marriage partners, not their civil status, that was crucial to the legitimacy of the union.[14] All the provisions on marriage favored allowing enslaved spouses to enjoy conjugal life. Free persons also could marry slaves, as long as the free partner understood that the other was enslaved and both were Christians. As in Roman law, a child followed the status of the mother, whether enslaved or free.[15]

The *Siete Partidas* provisions on slaves attaining their freedom have generated much scholarly debate about the nature of enslavement in the Spanish colonies.[16] Recalling the value placed on liberty by the ancients, the code declared that "all the laws in the world constantly favor freedom."[17] The power to free rested largely with slave owners, who could completely free their slaves or apply conditions to the manumission. Enslavers could grant freedom through a testament or could will their direct descendants to do so.[18]

On the other hand, the code also provided several clear paths to freedom through which the enslaved could and did exercise considerable agency.[19] The *Siete Partidas* recognized that some slaves deserved freedom for their own good works, often the performance of an act of extraordinary service to the state; the king would then grant their freedom and compensate their owners. Such acts of service included denouncing a virgin's rapist or army deserters and reporting counterfeit money. For a slave who discovered treason against the king or his realm, no compensation had to be paid.[20] In the Americas there is ample evidence of the state rewarding slaves who fought bravely and loyally for the monarch, though not all who fought gained their freedom.[21]

Another important Roman precedent, the *peculium*, allowed slaves to acquire and retain some control of modest amounts of money or property, though legally their enslavers owned it.[22] An enslaved person could pursue freedom through self-purchase by saving earnings over time and entrusting the money toward his or her price to a third party. When the full price had been set aside, this party was to buy the enslaved person from the enslaver to set him or her free. It was stipulated that the enslaved could take the third party to court if the agreement was not carried out.[23] The code hedged the leveling possibilities of such policies by emphasizing the origin of the power to free. Enslaved people who were freed had to continue to love and honor their former enslavers, never being disrespectful to them, defaming them, or attempting to litigate against them for past wrongs. Masters were permitted to rescind freedom if the freed tried to dishonor them, but the enslaved could take their masters to court in protest.[24]

These various provisions of the *Siete Partidas* framed the institution of slavery in Spain with a basic humanitarian and Christian regard for the enslaved's temporal and spiritual lives and a relative openness to the achievement of freedom. The code was developed at a time when enslaved people were not a large portion of the overall peninsular population and tended to work closely with their owners as domestic servants or artisans. By the late fifteenth century, the enslaved population in Spain was growing in size and diversity, including Muslims captured in war on the peninsula and in North Africa, sub-Saharan Africans purchased from Portuguese traders, and enslaved people of many ethnicities purchased through the Mediterranean slave trade. As Castilian conquerors moved into the Canary Islands and the Caribbean, natives of those areas also appeared among the enslaved in Spain. The Spanish crown's practice with regard to its enslaved subjects maintained the commitment to paternalism and Christian principles expressed in the *Siete Partidas*, but these ideals were tempered by local circumstances and the defense and development imperatives of the empire.

State Slavery in Spain: Defense and Development

The Spanish crown's territorial and military commitments expanded over the sixteenth and seventeenth centuries, and it increasingly resorted to slavery and other forms of forced labor to meet those needs. A brief look at two sites of significant employment of royal slaves on the peninsula highlights several points that are important in our subsequent analysis of state slavery in Cuba. First, assigning king's slaves to state projects was a practice of long standing, but was only one choice among a range of coerced laborers in state employ. Crown interest in recruiting and employing enslaved workers peaked when slaves were abundant and their cost to the royal treasury was lowest, as in the last quarter of the sixteenth century.

Several other factors also could compel the state to increase its use of royal slaves, such as when a project was particularly urgent or stalled, or when both free and other forced laborers were in short supply. Such factors later shaped the state's practice in 1760s Cuba. In addition, the Spanish state's many imperial commitments, which by the mid-1500s had extended around the globe, were expensive. Thus, when they were compelled to commit royal slaves to a given task, state officials had to balance defense or development imperatives against the need to protect the state's investment in their bodies and labor.

Warfare was a key factor in determining both the demand for and the supply of enslaved people in state employ as the Spanish Empire expanded. War between Christian and Muslim kingdoms in Spain and the Western Mediterranean produced hundreds of thousands of captives from the late 1400s to the 1760s, and both sides claimed the right to enslave those captured.[25] In Spain, the siege of Malaga in 1487 generated between 11,000 and 15,000 slaves. Expeditions against the Moriscos (Moors) of Alpujarras, north of Granada, consigned some 25,000 to 30,000 defeated rebels to enslavement from 1568 to 1571. Even two centuries later, raiding along the North African coast by Spanish corsairs, from 1710 to 1789, produced close to 6,000 captives for state projects.[26] The supply of the enslaved through capture was therefore uneven over time, and enslaved workers had to be supplemented by others as the labor needs of the state grew with the size and complexity of the empire.

The most voracious demand for forced labor in military employ was in Spain's Mediterranean galleys. One historian estimates that as many as 150,000 slaves toiled there from the sixteenth century to the galleys' abolition in 1748.[27] Even these staggering numbers were insufficient, and late fifteenth-century monarchs Ferdinand and Isabella supplemented their contingents of galley slaves with convicts sentenced to hard labor at the oars. As wages for free oarsmen rose over the sixteenth century, the crown came to rely almost exclusively on forced laborers by the late 1500s.[28]

State records list several kinds of slaves in the galleys, reflecting their method of acquisition and the state of hostilities with Spain's Mediterranean rivals. The largest number of the enslaved were Muslims, who became *esclavos del rey*, captured or purchased by the crown as prisoners of war. The king took charge of another category of the enslaved deemed too dangerous to be entrusted to private owners—*arraeces*, the captains of Muslim corsair vessels.[29] There were also renegades, Christians who had gone over to serve Muslim rulers, and rebellious Moriscos. By the eighteenth century, the largest group among royal slaves in Spain was Muslims from North Africa, or *moros*. Galley records also show natives of Argel, or *turcos*, small numbers of Jewish slaves, and *negros*, or sub-Saharan Africans, some of who had been enslaved by the captured Muslims.[30]

In addition, the king acquired enslaved people through donations from private owners. Enslavers could ingratiate themselves to the crown and punish particularly incorrigible slaves by donating them to service in the king's galleys. These voluntary donations by enslavers were at their height at the end of the sixteenth century, when the supply of slaves in Spain was at its peak and the cost for donors was lower. By 1578, 50 percent of the rowers in Spain's Genoa squadron were enslaved. When the supply of slaves was tighter, in 1639 and 1647, the king was compelled to exact forced donations of enslaved rowers for "temporary service" and to sentence more criminals to work in the galleys.[31] When urgency outweighed frugality, the crown also would purchase Muslim slaves for the galleys, if the above methods of acquisition proved inadequate.[32]

Though their provenance differed, on board the ships, the legal differences between slaves and convicts were blurred. Their food and clothing allotments were equivalent and the principal occupation of both groups was rowing. As the galleys became outmoded in naval warfare over the seventeenth century and the ships spent more time in port, both slaves and convicts were sent ashore to do heavy work on the docks, in arsenals, and in the transport of water, wood, and other supplies.[33]

State interests did recognize differences among forced laborers in several circumstances. The enslaved generally served in perpetuity and were too valuable to be given the death penalty for serious crimes, except in extreme circumstances. They were more likely to incur such exemplary punishments as the cutting off of an ear or nose. Into the eighteenth century, many Muslim *esclavos del rey* were exchanged for Christian slaves held in North Africa, a practice that could moderate treatment, as Spanish officials sought to avoid retaliation against their compatriots held captive in Muslim lands.[34]

Conditions of life for most king's slaves in the galleys were, in any case, hard, characterized by draining work, corporal punishment, disease, and monotonous and sometimes inadequate rations and clothing allotments. Yet this dismal existence was tempered by the crown's desire to promote Christianity and even occasional, if grudging, tolerance for Muslim religious practice. Slaves who remained Muslims were only freed through ransoms and exchanges, while conversion to Christianity offered at least the possibility of attaining freedom through manumission.[35] Though not all who converted were freed, converts could be assigned to less onerous tasks such as personal service or work in hospitals and convents, which allowed them to attend mass and removed them from the potential ridicule of their former coreligionists. Evidence from the eighteenth century shows that Muslim *esclavos del rey* were allowed to prepare and bury their dead, according to their custom, in a Cartagena mosque that the enslaved purchased and maintained with their own contributions.[36]

In an early modern parallel to Roman practice, the Spanish crown also employed royal slaves at the mercury mines in Almadén, where state intervention was based on empire-wide development interests less directly tied to military needs. More *esclavos del rey* worked in the galleys than at Almadén, but the state's policies in the mines illuminate two points important to understanding state slavery more generally. First, the crown was too overextended to direct and staff all of the many projects needed to defend and develop the empire, but it would selectively take charge of sites and workers it deemed imperative. Second, the state was also unable to afford the incarceration of the many groups of people it deemed dangerous, and it used state work as both punishment for transgressors and compensation for affronts to public order.

As tremendous reserves of silver were discovered in Mexico and Peru in the 1530s and 1540s, the processing of silver became a state imperative, because mercury was an essential ingredient in the process of refining silver ore. In 1566, the crown released convicts to the Almadén mine's concessionaires to help them meet mercury quotas. As crown finances became more desperate in 1645, the state took direct control of the mining operations and its labor force in an attempt to ensure an adequate supply of mercury. Similarly, the king confiscated Cuba's copper mines and the slaves employed there in 1670.[37]

In recruiting labor, the physical demands of mining at Almadén were considered less onerous than galley service, but officials recognized that constant exposure to mercury, especially in the furnaces, posed grave health risks for laborers assigned there. The crown sought a limited but expendable supply of workers who could be exploited without consideration of the hazards of mercury poisoning. Free workers could rarely be recruited to do this work, and most royal slaves were too valuable for such hazardous duty. Instead, the state purchased rebellious or troublesome slaves at reduced prices from private owners, specifically for the mines, simultaneously minimizing state expenditures and disciplining a dangerous social group. The enslaved contingent of mine workers continued to grow until the abolition of the galleys in 1748, when Spanish courts began sending more convicts to the mines.[38]

Harnessing the labor of potentially disruptive subjects, both enslaved and free, evolved as a common characteristic of state labor policies on both sides of the Atlantic over the colonial period. The types of work carried out by state workers also were quite similar in Spain and its American colonies. Military service and defense projects predominated, followed by mining and the many tasks essential to a maritime empire—aboard ships, in arsenals, in dockyards and warehouses, in transport, and in personal service.

The considerations driving state decisions about recruitment and employment of slaves and other forced laborers show important parallels as well. The crown operated within the legal framework expressed in the *Siete Partidas*, with the king as the patriarch who attended to the welfare and spiritual development of his charges, along with their discipline and punishment. This sometimes benevolent, but abstract, role was tempered by the crown's need to balance its many military commitments and expenses and by local authorities' regulation of their specific communities.

Several important differences between state slavery in Spain and in its American empire developed over time, and the Cuban case illustrates these changes well. The main difference was in the provenance and acquisition of royal slaves. Warfare continued to drive the demand for workers enslaved by the state in the New World, but it was much less often the method of acquiring those enslaved people in Cuba, especially after the first flush of conquest and settlement in the mid-1500s.

State Slavery in Sixteenth-Century Cuba: Defense and Development
Columbus arrived in the Caribbean in 1492 as a member of a Mediterranean culture in which the practice of enslavement was deeply embedded. He offered his patron, Queen Isabella of Spain, enslaved American natives as potential com-

modities when he failed to find the riches of Asia.[39] Isabella refused to endorse an Atlantic trade in Amerindians, banning their enslavement, in 1500, with the exception of those who practiced cannibalism or rebelled against Spanish political or religious authority. In 1530, the crown tried to ban all future enslavement of natives, only to rescind the prohibition in 1534, in the face of protests from settlers. The crown finally returned to a ban on native enslavement in the New Laws, promulgated in 1542, though Spanish capture and enslavement of Amerindians was never eliminated.[40]

In lieu of outright enslavement, the crown and Spanish settlers adapted the peninsular practice of granting lands and people to Christian conquerors of Muslim areas, known as *encomienda*, to ensure a labor supply and the conversion of the Amerindians. In the New World, the natives retained their lands, but Spanish *encomenderos* were granted control of the labor of groups of Indians in return for undertaking their instruction in European habits and Christianity.

The *encomienda* system did not preserve the indigenous populations as the crown had hoped, and it was soon clear that others would be needed to carry out the many tasks required to sustain the colonies, particularly in the Caribbean. Disease, warfare, and overwork reduced the native population of Cuba to a few thousand souls within fifty years of conquest, prompting settlers' requests for the importation of enslaved Africans as laborers. Since Iberians had imported enslaved blacks to the peninsula since the 1440s, Spaniards had access to the channels of that slave trade and were favorably disposed toward sub-Saharan Africans as workers.[41] Even the passionate advocate for American native rights, Bartolomé de Las Casas, saw African enslavement as an acceptable substitute for the abuses visited on the Indians, until he recanted near the end of his life.[42]

Chattel slaves were among those who were sent to the Americas, but the enslaved population of Spain's colonies came to differ markedly from that of the peninsula. In spite of its long experience with enslaved Muslims at home, the Spanish crown sought to contain the problem of religious conformity throughout its overseas realm by prohibiting the emigration of Muslims, whether slave or free, to the New World. Ferdinand and Isabella cautioned the first governor of Santo Domingo not to "give permission to come there Moors, nor Jews, nor heretics, nor [ir]reconcilables, nor persons newly converted to our faith, except if they are negro slaves or other slaves born in the power of Christians, our subjects and natives."[43] There is scattered evidence that, in spite of royal restrictions, some Muslim slaves did make it to the Americas.[44] Overall, however, in Cuba and throughout Spain's expanding American empire in the first twenty-five years of conquest and settlement, the enslaved were either American natives or Christianized, black Africans acquired through the Portuguese slave trade in West Africa.[45]

Africans, enslaved and free, were involved in all of the major expeditions of the conquest era, as servants and as auxiliaries in battle.[46] Official authorization for African enslavement in the New World came in 1501, when the crown allowed the first royal governor of Hispaniola, Nícolás de Ovando, to bring Christianized enslaved people from the peninsula to his new post when he shipped out the following year.[47] In these first years of settlement, the crown also transplanted state enslavement to the Americas; in 1505, it assigned seventeen royal slaves to help mine gold in the Caribbean colonies.[48]

The earliest importations of enslaved people were largely free of duties, but the crown soon moved to extract some revenue from the practice and to control the types of enslaved workers as their numbers in the new colonies began to rise.[49] In 1510, King Ferdinand gave permission to ship a maximum of two hundred slaves for sale to settlers or for work on royal properties. By 1513, it was necessary to pay for a license to export slaves to the Indies, though the numbers of the enslaved were initially small.[50] The crown also moved quickly to keep close control over travel to the Indies by requiring the authorization of all immigrants, both forced and free. Legal importations of enslaved people from the peninsula soon proved inadequate, and in 1518 the first license was granted to import enslaved workers directly from Africa to the New World colonies.[51]

The Spanish claimed Cuba in 1511, during this early wave of settlement, and soon faced a similarly catastrophic loss of life among the natives. By 1551, the king had granted a license to import three hundred enslaved Africans to the island.[52] Thus, within the first decades of conquest and settlement, many of the features of Spanish slavery had been adapted to its Caribbean colonies, including state licensing and taxing of slave procurement, a shift from capture in warfare to purchase as the primary mode of recruitment, a varied provenance of slaves (though the mix of peoples was distinct on either side of the Atlantic), and a blend of slaves owned by the crown and by private enslavers in state employments such as mining.

Economic development in Cuba enjoyed a brief postconquest boom, based on some modest deposits of gold and the provisioning of the expeditions of conquest to mainland Central and South America. Enslaved Africans worked with Amerindian laborers in farming and livestock rearing and in placer mining. By the 1540s, however, some of the major deposits of precious metals in Mexico and Peru were producing silver and mercury, and the promise of greater wealth elsewhere led to an exodus of population from Cuba. By the mid-sixteenth century, the Spanish population on the island had fallen to some forty householders and their families, who struggled to eke out a sustenance; the native population had been reduced to several small villages.[53] Cuba had become a colonial backwater, far from the centers of American wealth that were rich in mineral and human resources.

Piracy and Defense in Havana

The rich veins of silver in Mexico and Tierra Firme, and the interests of Spain and its European rivals in tapping them, ultimately benefited Cuba, particularly Havana. Pirate attacks moved from the eastern Atlantic into the Caribbean, forcing the Spanish crown to experiment with defense initiatives supported by growing investments of state money, manpower, and supervision.[54] Still, given Spain's many military commitments, defense policy was largely reactive, following the rhythms of war and peace in Europe and threats or attacks in the Caribbean.

War with France brought repeated French pirate attacks on towns and shipping in the middle decades of the sixteenth century, prompting Spanish efforts to protect the treasure galleons and secure port towns around the Caribbean. After a French fleet occupied Havana in 1537, the king authorized Cuba's new governor, Hernando de Soto, to build the island's first forts—one in Santiago de Cuba (the capital until 1553) and one in Havana.[55] Construction of the Fortaleza del Adelantado at the mouth of the channel entering the bay of Havana got under way in June of 1539. These early fortifications were very modest, however, and much of the actual construction and the later manning of the fort fell to the colony's residents, a difficult task for Havana's few hundred people in the mid-1500s.[56]

Early attempts at land defenses were mirrored by developments at sea to protect Spanish shipping. The crown had been reluctant to invest its own funds to protect shipments by individual merchants, but private defense efforts had proved unreliable. One glaring example was corsair Jean Fleury's capture of two of the three treasure ships sent by Hernán Cortés from Mexico to Charles I. The crown began requiring larger fleets of ships, with armed escorts, for the transatlantic voyage, and by the 1550s Havana had become a gathering point for vessels returning to Spain with the empire's growing gold and silver remittances.[57]

The promise of more people coming to Havana with the fleets inspired the initial steps in constructing the city's first important public project outside the military defense complex. Proposals to build the Zanja Real, a trench or conduit to bring freshwater from the Chorrera River to Havana, appeared in 1544, funded by a local tax (*sisa*) on wine, meat, and soap. A host of problems similar to those that plagued all public works—insufficient funding and manpower, and conflicts over jurisdiction—would hamper its completion for almost fifty years.[58]

Even with its growing strategic importance, Havana remained vulnerable and something of a frontier settlement into the 1550s. Most of its buildings were wood and palm leaf huts like the indigenous *bohíos*. All of the earliest fortifications in Cuba had been built with local funds and labor, but fears of renewed attacks by the French induced Charles I to begin subsidizing the island's defenses with monies and manpower from New Spain. In 1552, he ordered a *situado*, or subsidy, of 3,000 pesos sent from Veracruz, along with twenty black slaves to carry out needed work on Havana's Fortaleza. The governor in Havana informed the king the following year that funds had not yet arrived, a harbinger of future problems. Spanish officials in Cuba continued to suffer the irregular or tardy arrival of the Mexican *situados* into the 1700s.[59]

In July 1555, French corsair Jacques de Sores attacked and burned Havana, destroying the fort and leaving intact only the two stone houses and part of the Zanja Real.[60] Once word reached Spain of the Sores attack, the royal bureaucracy moved with uncharacteristic speed to secure the city. Since the convoy system had languished during the 1550s, the crown experimented with small squads of naval vessels to patrol the Caribbean, but these were inadequate to halt pirate attacks.[61]

A more sustained effort was mounted to plan and approve funds for substantial land fortifications to guard Havana's harbor. The process of building the city's first major fort highlights several issues that characterized state defense works throughout the period from the sixteenth century to the end of the eighteenth century. Virtually all public projects in Cuba suffered from problems in organizing and maintaining sufficient monies and manpower to see them to completion. Even in cases in which the crown took the initiative, the state's many-layered system of institutions and people, from the king to local authorities like the town councils, or *cabildos*, all competed for resources to advance their particular interests. These interests were sometimes in concert, sometimes in conflict within the state's bureaucracy and with private individuals and groups, who often became the state's creditors and contractors in public works. Also, once Cuba's defenses required resources from outside the island, delays regularly disrupted projects. Thus, the implementation of defense plans through the various layers of state and private interests and institutions across the Atlantic could be frustratingly slow. Ultimately, however, royal money and attention brought development as the local economy expanded to provide workers, materials, and services to state projects.

Technical expertise and skilled labor to build the fort known as La Real Fuerza were recruited in Spain, though it took two years to hire an engineer, stonecutters, and masons and to gather the necessary tools; their dispatch to Cuba took eight months. The foundation trenches were begun only in December 1558, and the pace of work was slow. Exasperated with the lack of progress, between 1560 and 1562 the crown replaced the engineer and dispatched a group of crown slaves to ease the shortage of laborers.[62]

The new engineer found a host of problems. Money was still tight, even with the New Spain subsidy for Cuban defense. Various interest groups, from the colonial governor to local contractors, had diverted resources and workers to their own uses while the king was appointing the second engineer.[63] Though the crown had reserves of its own enslaved workers to commit to the project, these royal slaves were only a supplement to wage laborers and enslaved workers furnished by city residents. In 1572, 191 royal slaves arrived in the slave ship *San Pedro*, destined to work on Havana's fortifications. Though not all of these slaves survived or remained in the city, by 1575 almost two hundred slaves were working to complete La Fuerza.[64] Fort construction was also a site of forced labor for various troublesome elements of the local population—vagrants "of various colors," a few indigenous people, and even fourteen French pirates captured off the coast of Matanzas.[65]

Havana's La Fuerza became a liability to the royal treasury, without much chance of a timely remedy, as the fort absorbed almost 75 percent of the total empire-wide expenditure for fortifications from 1548 to 1563. The project proceeded in fits and starts for the next twelve years (perhaps prolonged by the outright bankruptcy of the Spanish crown in 1575), finally to be certified for occupancy in 1577.[66] Hence, the first serious attempt to fortify the city and harbor of Havana took a frustrating twenty-two years to complete.[67]

The attempt by French Protestants to colonize Florida from 1562 to 1565 inspired a new round of measures to improve Caribbean defenses. The Spanish crown realized that a more comprehensive system of defense was needed, now that larger-scale invasion forces had been added to the threat represented by corsair raiding. The convoy or fleet system had been reinstituted in the 1561 as a more cost-effective measure than a permanent patrol squadron. Havana's port was thus confirmed as the meeting site for the fleets from New Spain and the South American mainland (Tierra Firme) before they returned to Spain.[68]

On land, the building of stone fortresses in Caribbean ports was reinforced by the establishment of permanent garrisons in key areas along the fleet's convoy route (Florida, Havana, San Juan de Ulúa, and San Juan de Puerto Rico). The first steps toward a permanent garrison in Havana were taken in January 1567 with the arrival of two hundred men.[69] The soldiers proved a disruptive element, due in part to their own behavior and in part to conflicts between civil and military authorities over jurisdiction. Cuba's governor accused soldiers of killing *vecinos*, or local householders, and committing outrages with local women without punishment. Soldiers' grievances included serious backlogs in pay and miserable rations that forced them to run up debts with local vendors to sustain themselves.

After putting down several minor revolts among the soldiers, the governor tried to assign them to help local workers dig trenches for La Fuerza, while free stoneworkers and slaves raised the fort's stone walls.[70] The garrison was reduced to fifty men in 1570, and funds for their pay were now taken from the Mexican *situado*. By the late 1500s, however, the cohort returned to around 450 men, a testament to the importance that the crown attached to the city in the system of imperial commerce and defense.[71]

"El Draque" and Havana's Defense
In the last three decades of the sixteenth century, Spain confronted militant Protestantism in Northern Europe, and the rhythms of that conflict were reflected in Dutch and English piracy and Spanish defensive measures in the Caribbean. Francis Drake's career was a particularly painful reminder of Spanish vulnerability. On an expedition to the Panamanian isthmus in early 1573, he conspired with both runaway slaves and the French to attack a Spanish mule train bringing gold and silver to Nombre de Dios.[72] His circumnavigation of the globe between 1578 and 1580 brought foreign ships into the Spanish Pacific for the first time as he raided and plundered at will along the coast of South America and in the Philippines.

In response, in the late 1570s, the Spanish crown made another attempt to protect the vulnerable coasts of its Caribbean colonies by sending galleys to the region as coastal patrols, something that had been avoided for most of the sixteenth century because of the galleys' poor navigation in the high seas of the

Atlantic crossing. Labor recruitment for galley service soon became a problem. In a 1576 proposal to the king, a well-respected resident of Havana (*habanero*) estimated that each galley would require a crew of fifty, with 250 black slaves at the oars. Instead, two galleys arrived in Havana in 1586 with a mixed crew of four hundred forced laborers, or *galeotes*. In spite of royal prohibitions, some members of the crew were *moros* and *turcos*.

Even after applying strategies used to staff the Mediterranean galleys to re-supply the Cuban squad—adding convicts from Mexico and some captured pirates and smugglers—such a large number of forced laborers was difficult and expensive to maintain in the New World. By 1596, most of the *galeotes* had died or completed their sentences, leaving only 104 men, forty-five of whom were serving life sentences. Some were so old as to be useless at the oars. Though they had proved quite effective at deterring corsair predations, the colonial galleys fell into disrepair by the 1590s.[73]

In 1585, Drake returned to the Caribbean to sack and plunder Cartagena, in present-day Colombia, and Santo Domingo, in Hispaniola. In Havana, news of Drake's expedition ignited a desperate scramble to protect the city by importing one hundred soldiers from Mexico, forming militia companies that included both whites and free people of color, with *vecinos* and their servants digging trenches for batteries. *Habaneros'* efforts saved their city from a direct attack by "El Draque," who instead preyed on the less well-defended Saint Augustine in Florida. Returning to the Eastern Atlantic in 1587, Drake stormed the peninsular port of Cadiz, destroying tons of shipping and supplies and delaying Phillip II's ill-fated attack on England until 1588.[74]

This low ebb in military strength, while demoralizing for Spain, ultimately proved to be a boon for Cuba.[75] Although Havana had been spared a direct attack, Drake's many raids convinced the crown that the convoys and a few fortifications scattered around the Caribbean were insufficient to guard the Indies fleets and their ports of call. A real system of fortifications was needed, along with the rebuilding of the Spanish navy.

Naval Defense

In contrast to the galleys, the building and manning of military ships for the Atlantic fleets were based largely in the northern regions of Spain, where the use of enslaved labor was less extensive. With a rapidly growing peninsular population in the first half of the sixteenth century, the merchant and military fleets were able to recruit some 40,000 men, mostly among the native born. Though both Spanish population growth and trade with the Indies declined by the early seventeenth century, military demand for sailors increased as Spain got involved in the Thirty Years' War. From 1639 to 1646, an urgent need for crews in warships against the French and the Dutch compelled the crown to hire foreign ships and sailors, especially in the Mediterranean ports of Ragusa, Naples, and Genoa.[76]

Wages for sailors tended to be better than those for rural day laborers but lagged behind wages in the merchant marine, meaning that military recruitment could suffer in the competition for sailors. Price inflation over the late sixteenth and early seventeenth centuries was not matched by wages, leaving most seamen struggling to sustain themselves and their families, though the crown offered several months' advance on wages as an inducement to enlistment. The constant warfare that engaged Spain's armies for most of the century also reduced the numbers available to be recruited as sailors. The fact that soldiers were valued more highly than sailors in Castile's martial culture probably undermined popular enthusiasm for naval service as well.[77]

As Spain became embroiled on many fronts during the Thirty Years' War (beginning in 1618), it had to raise naval expeditions to fight in both American and European waters and fleets to carry out the Indies trade and its protection. By 1625, the Spanish state imposed a mandatory registration plan known as the matrícula to generate a listing of all men in Spain with any seafaring experience, with tax exemptions for voluntary registrants and penalties for those who tried to escape it. When thousands of men needed to be recruited for a fleet, royal officials or their contractors would use these lists for naval levies in various regions of Spain. In times of crisis, the crown resorted to forced service, though such coercion was not unique to the Spanish navy; all early modern powers resorted to such tactics to maintain a navy.[78]

Labor recruitment in peninsular shipbuilding also faced shortages from the end of the sixteenth century onward, for a number of reasons. One was the general demographic decline on the peninsula. Another was the crown's unreliability as an employer. As the insolvency of the Spanish treasury became more acute, the navy was undermined at numerous points throughout the process of building and outfitting a fleet. The craftsmen necessary for shipbuilding, especially carpenters and caulkers, were increasingly in short supply and often suffered long periods without pay. The state tried to compel free workers to report for ship construction with threats of fines, imprisonment, or confiscation of property, though compulsion had its limits. When money ran out, workers would desert the shipyards and return home, leaving officials to decide whether pursuit was worth the expense.[79]

With no permanent navy in the sixteenth century, Spain relied on the rental of private vessels for royal service. In the early decades of the seventeenth century, after the humiliating English defeat of the Spanish Armada in 1588, the crown increasingly moved to state contracts with private shipbuilders to construct vessels for naval service. Greater state control allowed the crown to regulate the size and characteristics of ships needed for both trade and warfare.

The first half of the seventeenth century severely challenged state resources as Spain mounted large fleets to combat interlopers and pirates in the Caribbean, to attempt to dislodge the Dutch from the coast of Brazil, and to retake its colonies in the Netherlands through warfare on land and at sea. By 1639, with the naval defeat at the Battle of the Downs, the Spanish royal fleet lay in ruins and its cadre of experienced naval officers had been lost. Though the annual fleets to the Indies continued to sail, they were forced to operate under a cloud of short funds and crisis. The necessary rebuilding was hobbled because the numbers of willing royal servants who volunteered to construct ships for the king had dwindled by the 1650s, a consequence of successive crown bankruptcies.[80]

The consequences of Spain's naval catastrophes from the late 1580s onward were more salutary for Cuba, as the 60 percent reduction in the tonnage of the navy forced royal officials to find the resources to rebuild its armada and protect the empire.[81] Havana received new rounds of situado funding for fort construction, mining, and shipbuilding. Among the orders Phillip II gave to the new governor, Juan de Tejeda, in 1589, was a directive for the construction of two new forts—the Castillo de los Tres Reyes del Morro, on the eastern point of Havana's harbor, and the fort of San Salvador de la Punta, on the western point. He also was to establish a shipyard in Havana to help rebuild the Spanish navy and to finish the Zanja Real in order to guarantee the city's water supply.[82]

The organization of the new fort projects reflects several precedents, set during the building of Havana's Fortaleza in the 1530s, which continued into the eighteenth century. In terms of labor recruitment, many of the most skilled among the workers had to be brought from Europe. The Italian engineer Bautista Antonelli returned to Cuba in 1589 to begin the forts, employing masons, carpenters, and ironworking experts brought from Spain with the promise of attractive wages. The skilled workers numbered between fifty and seventy people, supported by more than one hundred *peones*, or unskilled people, working for a daily wage, or *jornal*. The blend of less skilled workers was similar to the mix employed in the early years of the sixteenth century, comprising vagrants, hired slaves, and crown slaves from elsewhere in the empire. Antonelli also tried to reduce his labor costs by recruiting *galeotes* who had completed their sentences, to hew stone for the forts, replacing free stoneworkers with much higher wages.[83]

By 1603, only sixty *esclavos del rey* remained working at El Morro and had to be supplemented with 137 more to advance the project. In 1608, the crown wanted to help fortify Cartagena de Indias and ordered the engineer to shift Havana's most skilled and healthy king's slaves there. In 1647, seven years after El Morro was officially completed, only twenty-six king's slaves were still assigned there. Four were assigned to the launch that served to transport people and goods from Havana to El Morro, eleven were still fit to work, and another eleven were considered "useless," due to their advanced age. Balancing paternalism and the bottom line, the crown continued to maintain its elderly slaves "while they lived," but over the next few years it sought to sell the able-bodied, in part to save the salaries of the supervisors assigned to them.[84]

Between 1589 and 1640, the crown invested substantial amounts to build El Morro and La Punta. Another stream of *situado* funds was assigned to develop copper mines in eastern Cuba and a foundry in Havana to provide artillery for the new forts. The Havana foundry was a short-lived experiment (1598–1607), but the copper reserves of Santiago de Cuba developed into the most sustained and extensive mining project in the Spanish Caribbean. As with the mercury mines of Almadén, the initial exploitation of Cuban copper from 1530 to the 1590s had been left to concessionaires, though none was very successful. In the 1570s, the king allowed one concessionaire to bring in foreign mining experts and to purchase slaves to improve production.[85]

In response to a mounting English threat in 1597, Phillip II took a more direct interest in the Santiago mines, though their administration was still contracted out to an *asentista*, or contractor. The crown assigned *situado* funds to the mining operation and promised the first administrator two hundred slaves, but these workers were slow to arrive. Contractor Sánchez de Moya began to piece together a workforce by commandeering fifty-nine slaves from a slave ship arriving in Santiago, which included men, women, and children. He also brought thirteen more slaves from Havana, and rented or purchased eight slaves from local owners, to begin mining in 1599 with a total of eighty enslaved workers.

In 1603, eighty-two of the promised two hundred slaves arrived from Spain. Even as the enslaved population grew, Sánchez de Moya had to assign some of the workforce to food production to sustain the settlement, reducing the numbers of people devoted to mining. More purchases of slaves, and natural reproduction, increased the size of the enslaved population at the mines to 339 people by 1620. Production had increased into the 1610s, but fell off thereafter under a new *asentista*, though the community of the enslaved remained.[86]

From at least the 1550s, small ships for Caribbean commerce were built in Havana, Bayamo, Mariel, and other island ports, though enslaved labor played a lesser role in shipbuilding than in mining. To carry out his charge to establish a shipyard to construct frigates and galleons for the imperial navy, Havana's Governor Tejeda found abundant quantities of high-quality wood for shipbuilding, but he worried about recruiting labor and finding the necessary hardware and supplies. As with the fort projects, the governor had to import skilled labor. Writing in 1591, as he sent four Cuban-constructed ships to Spain, Tejeda reported his need to take forty carpenters and some caulkers from the Indies fleets' crews to complete the next six ships ordered by the king. "In this land," he lamented, "there are only one master [shipbuilder] and five or six carpenters."[87] Later in the same year, he was able to hold forty-two carpenters from the fleet, at royal expense, for ship construction, though he said he would have to let them go in December if supplies were slow in arriving.

In contrast to the forts and copper mines, the shipyard's labor force seems to have been composed largely of free workers supplemented with sailors on salaries and rations and slaves hired out from local owners. Though the governor fretted over the numbers of workers available, the fleets provided waves of skilled workers and others for months at a time. Therefore, the shipyard did not require such substantial purchases of royal slaves to carry out its work as were required at the copper mines. Wages were also high in the shipyard, even for hired slaves, whose *jornales* were the same as or close to those of free caulkers and carpenters.[88] The work was probably less onerous than fort construction, as well, encouraging enslavers to reap the most benefit with less risk by hiring their slaves out to shipbuilding.[89]

In spite of Tejeda's sometimes gloomy assessments of resources in Cuba, he also managed to finish the long-stalled project of the Zanja Real. Work on the water conduit had been stymied by engineering problems, disasters such as hurricanes and cave-ins, and inconsistent application of monies and labor. The

Havana *cabildo* received royal approval for the local consumption tax to fund the project in the late 1540s, and it contracted out oversight of the work many times over the next fifty years without much progress being made. Havana *vecinos* contributed the labor of some of their enslaved workers, or small groups of ten to thirty slaves were diverted from the Fuerza fort, but as one dispirited governor in the 1570s put it, "What they do one day falls in the next."[90]

The combined engineering knowledge of Antonelli and the vigilance of Tejeda finally brought the *zanja* into Havana in 1592. In addition to his duties on the El Morro and La Punta forts, Antonelli rebuilt a dam for the *zanja* and supervised its completion. Tejeda attended to the project "day and night," and though it went over budget, he told the king that its benefits to the city, its garrison, and the fleets were worth the cost.[91]

Defense and Development in the Late 1500s
The wave of defense and naval construction in the late 1500s was an important element in the first real spurt of growth in the city after a century of decline relative to the mainland centers of the empire. Havana became one of the fastest growing urban centers in the Americas from the late 1500s into the first decades of the 1600s.[92] Besides permanent island residents, the population could swell by several thousand when the Indies fleet was in port. The necessity of provisioning the fleet encouraged the growth of ranching and truck farming in the hinterland of the town. By the late 1500s, Havana also had seven shipyards, and the specialized tasks needed to repair and outfit ships brought skilled laborers from around the empire. The ships' crews had to be fed, clothed, housed, and entertained, spawning fifty taverns in the city in the 1570s. Fort and ship construction also increased demand for locally produced building materials such as wood and lime. Increased capital from royal subsidies and growing trade fostered the establishment of the first sugar mills in the Havana region after 1595, though the scale of their operations was small.[93]

In addition, residents could make money by renting their enslaved workers to the state or by hiring people enslaved by the crown for their private businesses. One historian estimates that royal slaves hired out to Havana residents provided the equivalent of 33,707 workdays to private employers between 1578 and 1580 alone, half of them carried out by female enslaved workers. By being lax in collecting payment for those workdays, the state effectively "subsidiz[ed] the local economy with His Majesty's labor force."[94] As Havana's residents accumulated capital, they purchased increasing numbers of enslaved workers themselves. Over the last decade of the sixteenth century, 1,069 enslaved Africans entered legally through Havana. By the early seventeenth century, Africans and their descendants represented almost half of Havana's total population, though the share of royal slaves in the city's population had declined.[95]

New Challenges in the Seventeenth Century

For virtually the entire seventeenth century, Spain was at war with one or more of its European rivals, bringing even more direct challenges to its monopoly of trade and settlement in the Americas.[96] With the formation of the Dutch West India Company in 1621, the Dutch embarked on outright invasion and colonization in areas of Spain's empire (the crowns of Spain and Portugal being united from 1580 to 1640), occupying parts of northeast Brazil in the 1620s and 1630s and capturing the Caribbean island of Curaçao. The Spanish suffered the further humiliation of having the silver fleet of 1628 captured by Piet Heyn off the coast of Cuba.

The English, too, had encroached on Spanish territory by taking the Caribbean islands of Barbados, Saint Kitts, and Nevis. Although Oliver Cromwell's Western Design failed in its attack on Santo Domingo in 1654, the English were successful in taking the relatively undefended island of Jamaica. This conquest gave them an ideal base from which to harass the Spanish and carry out smuggling and piracy around the Caribbean. As further proof of the threat the English represented, they captured the silver fleet off the coast of Cádiz in 1656. Compounding these predations, Spain's resources were stretched to the limit fighting land wars on the European continent.[97]

For Cuban officials, concerns about the proximity of rival colonies prompted a new round of defense constructions in the 1630s and 1640s, especially along the northern coast to the east and west of Havana. Between 1634 and 1649, small forts were built with mostly local funds and labor at the mouths of the Chorrera River to the west and the Cojímar River to the east, to prevent enemy landings and access to the interior.[98]

The fortifications of the late 1500s had made the sea approaches to the Havana bay reasonably secure. But with the English now in Jamaica, the earlier proposals for a city wall were revived to shore up the western land approaches to Havana. Estimates of the costs of building a land wall for the city in 1601 included the purchase by the king of "100 slaves from Guinea" to work with a dozen or so wage-earning stonecutters and masons; this was similar to the workforce used to build El Morro and La Punta. However, the project languished for decades as earmarked *situado* funds from New Spain repeatedly failed to arrive.

After the English sack and brief occupation of Santiago de Cuba in 1662, the Havana governor, Francisco Dávila Orejón, finally began the work of digging a protected trench along the proposed line of the wall, west of the city, by exhorting *habaneros* to donate their own labor or the labor of their slaves. Actual construction finally commenced in the winter of 1674.[99] *Situado* funds ultimately covered 56.4 percent of the construction costs, while the local consumption taxes provided 41.8 percent. The workforce consisted of a mix of people similar to those used in earlier state defense projects—some king's slaves, black and white day laborers, and convicts from New Spain. The wall project also seems to have attracted significant amounts of labor donated by city residents.[100] A wall that encircled the landward side of the city was completed by 1683, but work continued into the 1740s to construct a section along the bay side of the city and to keep the completed segments in repair.[101]

The English presence in Jamaica also brought greater royal attention to the copper mines of Santiago de Cuba. In 1670, with production at a standstill and defense a greater concern, the crown confiscated the El Cobre mines and the workers enslaved by the former owners became king's slaves. In this isolated, rural area far from the thriving port of Havana, a unique example of state slavery evolved that was quite different from that experienced by the state's slaves in the capital. Labor in the mines, and for other public works, like building Santiago's fortifications, was organized on a rotating basis, more like the corvée labor familiar in Europe or the labor exactions made on indigenous communities in other areas of the Spanish Empire. In El Cobre, with a small population and less access to the imports and trade that passed through Havana, the crown allowed the enslaved miners their own plots of land for their subsistence and that of their families. Because a settled population could better provide defense in an emergency, the crown was willing to grant privileges to the miners of El Cobre that were not usually granted to state slaves in other places. They had families, served in the militia, sat on the town council, and considered the land they worked their own, by grant of the king.[102]

The enslaved *cobreros* struggled to be recognized as a legitimate community, a pueblo, within the Spanish colonial system. They protested labor exactions they found burdensome or unjust, particularly a royal order to send some of their number to Havana to help build the city wall in 1674.[103] They used both legal tactics (petitions and litigation) and extralegal tactics (*marronage*, or flight) to resist the state's efforts to either sell them or reassign them to Havana's public works. They litigated against Spanish officials they felt abused their special status as slaves of the king. Over the next century, El Cobre's slaves were able to negotiate a unique arrangement among the royal slaves employed in Cuba, one which gave them considerably more autonomy and status than most of the king's slaves living in Havana.

~~~

The foregoing discussion highlights the characteristics of the Spanish state's relationships to forced labor in state projects as they evolved on the peninsula and in Cuba over the first two centuries of conquest and colonization. The legal framework elaborated to deal with enslavement in medieval Spain continued to inform the state's approach to the enslaved people it later employed in Spain and in the Americas. The crown upheld the authority and right to property of enslavers but tempered them with Christian values and the state's needs in times of crisis. In practice, Muslim slaves, as infidels and prisoners of war, warranted limited crown concern for their welfare, unless they could be ransomed or traded for Christian captives in Muslim lands. The indigenous peoples of the Americas, as subjects of the monarch and potential converts to Christianity, evoked an outpouring of debate about their nature, treatment, and fate, which led to the official abolition of their enslavement by 1542. As royal charges, Africans elicited much less concern and discussion; their enslavement was often seen as an alternative to the enslavement of Amerindians.[104] Ultimately, the state encouraged a basic humanitarian concern for adequate subsistence and treatment for all enslaved people, within the confines of a paternalism that mandated the obligations of both masters and those they enslaved.

This ideal was constrained by a number of variables that affected the ways in which the state employed the different types of forced laborers at its disposal. For royal officials charged with the execution of state projects, slavery was but one form of forced labor among several that were usually employed in concert. The king's own enslaved workers were viewed as valuable resources to be employed strategically, the value of their skills and persons conserved. Penal laborers were seen as distinct from the enslaved for a variety of reasons that will be discussed at length in subsequent chapters, but the deployment of each group for a given task was often organized in tandem. The preponderance of one group over an-other was determined by two main factors: the empire-wide network of institu-tions, practices, and pools of available laborers; and the shifting circumstances of a particular time and place in which a task or project was carried out. Most of Cuba's enslaved people came from Africa, often passing through the slave trading depots of neighboring Caribbean islands such as Jamaica. Cuba's most important channels for recruiting convict laborers flowed through New Spain.

There was considerable similarity in the types of work performed by *esclavos del rey* in Spain and its American possessions throughout the colonial period, as military and defense needs predominated. State slaves constructed and repaired fortifications and ships, worked in arsenals and mines, and built roads and ca-nals. They also worked at ancillary tasks in ports, dockyards, and warehouses; in transport occupations; and in personal service. Royal slaves were well integrated into the economic life of Havana. Though they usually lived in separate quarters, their lives were quite similar to those of other enslaved people in urban areas in Spain and its American colonies.[105] The crown's methods of acquiring slaves also were similar on both sides of the Atlantic—through purchases from private individuals or slave traders, donations, judicial sentences, or capture in warfare.

Though methods of acquisition were similar, the provenance of enslaved people on either side of the Atlantic differed considerably. Access to a mobile pool of its own laborers was one important part of Spanish defense strategy, well established on the peninsula before 1492 and adapted to local conditions in the Americas. From all of the complexities of precedent and practice discussed here, five general models of state enslavement can be identified as they evolved in Cuba over the colonial period. Listing them separately is valuable for analysis and clarification, but the historical examples were rarely so clear cut, as the examples included here and discussed later in the book will attest.

1. *Itinerant squads of royal enslaved workers sent from one site to another, often as a quick fix for stalled projects.* Their numbers were usually small, ten to twenty enslaved workers, and more rarely fifty to one hundred. Even the preceding brief out-line of state slavery before 1700 is replete with examples: seventeen royal enslaved workers sent from Spain to aid gold mining in Hispaniola, fifty-two sent to Cuba's eastern copper mines, enslaved workers from La Fuerza diverted to constructing the *zanja*, enslaved workers from Havana's El Morro sent to build forts in Cartagena, attempts to send enslaved people from El

Cobre to build Havana's city wall. State officials used such tactics with other forced workers, as well as with *forzados*, or convict laborers, from the galleys or with garrison soldiers who were assigned to the forts. Shifting workers to various sites was also fundamental to the crown's overall defense strategy in the Caribbean—Mexico provided enslaved people and convicts to Havana forts for centuries, and Havana sent laborers to projects in other colonies such as Puerto Rico or Florida.[106]

2. *Enslaved people as militia fighters, soldiers, auxiliaries, and allies in battle.* Such employment of the enslaved was fundamental to Spain's ability to conquer and defend vast areas of the Americas, though the Spanish Empire never purchased large numbers of the enslaved to form army units, on the English Caribbean model of the West India Regiments.[107] In addition to the enslaved joining Havana's other residents to defend against Francis Drake in the 1580s and the *cobreros'* militia in eastern Cuba, already mentioned, subsequent chapters will provide numerous examples from the eighteenth century: enslaved men manning the cannons of El Morro during the British siege, serving in Havana's artillery companies, accompanying Spanish troops on expeditions to Pensacola and Mobile, and freeing themselves by fighting in the name of the Spanish king against revolutionary France in Saint-Domingue.

3. *Small groups of royal enslaved workers trained and retained in strategic roles.* As the defense complex of Havana expanded, especially in the eighteenth century, the state began to keep permanent contingents of royal slaves to ensure the availability of trained laborers in strategically important tasks. The *cobreros* again provide an example, and chapter 4 discusses other skilled groups of the enslaved in Havana's shipyard and artillery corps.

4. *A community of enslaved families in the king's service.* When the crown needed a group of enslaved workers at a particular site over an extended period, it sometimes explicitly endorsed and promoted the formation of family groups as a way to reduce the cost of maintaining the community, benefit from the labor of enslaved men's wives, and enhance the loyalty and permanence of the group. The work the state sought to guarantee was often important to defense and therefore was often gendered specifically for men (such as in fort construction, mining, or manning artillery). Their wives' labor, both repro-

ductive and productive, was to support the community and relieve the royal treasury. Their progeny would enrich the crown and provide a new generation of apprentices to the skilled work of their parents. Officials proposed such communities more often than they were employed, but the copper miners of El Cobre and the enslaved artillerymen of Havana were successful ones in the eighteenth century.

5. *Large-scale deployment of the enslaved for construction*. This model of state slavery was likely the most arduous for the enslaved workers forced to endure it. Large building projects like forts required substantial numbers of unskilled laborers to dig and haul earth, stone, and other materials. As such, the forts of Havana were sites of punitive labor for centuries—punishing unruly enslaved people or runaways, smugglers, army deserters, and convicts from around the empire. In Cuba, where wages remained high for most of the colonial period, free workers rarely could be recruited in sufficient numbers over the many years needed to complete these projects. Reminiscent of Roman models of public enslavement in building infrastructure, and of the galleys and arsenals of the Iberian peninsula, fort building in Havana required progressively larger commitments of the enslaved as the threats to the Spanish Empire increased. In the late sixteenth and seventeenth centuries, enslaved fort workers numbered up to about two hundred people. By the 1760s, the state employed thousands of the enslaved to refortify the city against the British.

The Spanish state's employment of enslaved people in its many projects in Havana over the colonial period brought development that enriched its free residents and helped to create conditions of life and work for the enslaved that often were distinct from those on other Caribbean islands with early plantation-based economies. The urban locus of much state work in Cuba and its demand for skilled labor opened some opportunities for the enslaved to hire out and earn money within a juridical framework that supported and facilitated the pursuit of freedom. The importance of manumission to the historical development of Cuban slavery is clear in numerous instances over the colonial period, and in the growth of the largest free population of color in the Caribbean by the eighteenth century.[108]

In Cuba manumission also evolved to include customary features such as self-purchase by installments, or *coartación*, which created a group of enslaved people who had an intermediate status between enslavement and freedom.[109] Once a slave had made the initial payment on his or her freedom, the price could not be changed. His or her new status as a *coartado/a* (one whose enslaved status had been "cut" by a payment toward freedom) allowed the slave to look for a new owner with or without cause. When a *coartado/a* was sold, the new owner was only entitled to the portion of the *coartado/a*'s labor that had not yet been paid for by the slave.[110]

Many authors point to this practice as crucial to the special character of urban enslavement in Cuba, with some claiming that it was unique to the island, but subsequent work has shown it was more widely practiced.[111] The size of Cuba's free population of color suggests, however, that the extent of manumission may have been unique, at least up to the late 1700s. Since the Spanish state was the island's single largest employer of the enslaved, at least into the eighteenth century, its norms and practices helped create this slave system, one relatively open to the pursuit of freedom by the enslaved.

Up through the seventeenth century, Spain was able to defend and maintain its empire using a relatively ad hoc and reactive policy with a moderate number of state enslaved workers as a key resource. Labor was recruited in an often haphazard and expedient way. The crown bought and sold small groups of its own enslaved workers, rented out others from private owners, cajoled "donations," and assigned convicts to sites around the Caribbean as the strategic urgency of the moment demanded. Revenue was similarly patched and pieced together from public and private sources. Luckily for Spain, its rivals faced similar constraints in the sixteenth and seventeenth centuries, and its defensive efforts proved sufficient to retain all of the most important parts of the American empire. Pirate attacks, even from the likes of Francis Drake, could not dislodge the Spanish.

The eighteenth century presented Spain with a challenge to its New World hegemony that was different in both kind and degree. The military power of England, especially at sea, forced the Spanish state to reform itself to generate the necessary funds and labor to protect the key to the empire, in Havana. Spain also had to expand the recruitment and deployment of its own enslaved workers to meet that challenge.

2

WAR, REGENERATION, AND
THE LIMITS OF REFORM UNDER
THE EARLY BOURBONS,
1700–1762

At the dawn of the eighteenth century, Spain's new Bourbon monarchs identified as their central goals better defense of the empire against the military and territorial incursions of their Western European rivals, especially England, and an increase in the Indies revenue received by the crown. The paths to the realization of these goals were mutually dependent and intertwined. Higher crown revenues necessitated development initiatives such as increasing the production of silver in the American mainland's mines and of tropical commodities in places like Cuba, but ultimately success depended on the arrival in Spain of those products and the taxes and duties paid on them. Their safe arrival required good Caribbean defenses and a strong navy, both of which depended on marshaling resources to rebuild and maintain them. A key factor in the success or failure of the crown's imperial political economy of defense and development was labor. Under Spain's early Bourbon monarchs, Philip V and Ferdinand VI, and during the first years under Charles III, the crown's policies toward slave trading shifted, and resort to forced labor more generally increased, but long-standing patterns of state enslavement were largely maintained.

Early Bourbon Efforts in Defense and Development, 1701–1740
Due to the crown's focus on the retention of its European empire during the late sixteenth and early seventeenth centuries, Spain was unable to prevent a growing

number of American territorial acquisitions by England and France. After 1650, the Spanish crown was forced to recognize these acquisitions in treaties that gave each nation a foothold in the Caribbean, from which they were able to penetrate Spanish imperial commerce and occasionally intercept the flow of silver to the metropole.[1]

When the last Hapsburg monarch, Charles II, died without issue in November 1700, his will named as his successor Philip of Anjou, grandson of Louis XIV of France. This decision touched off more than a decade of fighting, on the peninsula and beyond, as the Western European imperial powers contested Philip's accession to the Spanish throne. In 1701, Philip claimed the throne of an empire of vast wealth, but the crown had steadily lost control of that wealth over the preceding century. Bullion had flowed through Spain to pay for expensive military campaigns in the Netherlands, Italy, and the Mediterranean, but little stayed on the peninsula to stimulate development. In trade and manufacturing, the Spanish Empire had become largely a dependency of its Western European rivals for goods, capital, and shipping.[2]

The empire's problems and their solutions were intimately related. To defend the empire, the new administration in Madrid would have to generate more revenue from the Americas through trade and development. To develop the colonies and reap the benefits of increased trade, the empire would have to better defend its territories on land and its commercial traffic at sea. All of these enterprises would require the labor of many thousands of people, both forced and free.

The strengthening of Spain's military forces was a clear priority for Philip V when he arrived in Madrid, as both the army and navy were in ruins. Havana was a key site in his plan for military regeneration.[3] The city continued to be a strategic hub as the collection point for the silver fleets, and it was the target of escalating aggression, especially from England. In response, the crown devoted increasing attention and resources, both human and material, to the city's defense and development.

Havana's military role expanded in the 1700s as it became the base of operations to disrupt the most threatening incursions of England and France into North America—Carolina, Campeche, and Jamaica in the case of England, and Saint-Domingue, New Orleans, and Mobile for France. Defense policy also needed to address the losses to the Spanish treasury from smuggling and contraband originating from the bases established in the non-Spanish colonies of the Western Caribbean.[4] To the minds of Philip V's ministers, all of these military functions required a resurgent navy, a project that consumed much of their energy and resources up to 1760.

Beyond assuring the flow of silver from the Americas to Spain, the Bourbons looked to colonies like Cuba to produce goods for colonial trade that would generate revenue for the state. As in the sixteenth and seventeenth centuries, defense needs and development were still closely intertwined in imperial policy generally, and for Cuba in particular, but the foci of development efforts for areas outside the main American mining sectors shifted under the early Bourbons. By the early 1700s, English and French colonies in the Caribbean had begun to show the profit potential of plantation production of tropical commodities. For Cuba, this translated into official study of and experimentation with institutions and policies to better regulate the production and trade in tobacco and to encourage the production of sugar for export.

All plans for defense projects and for the expansion of tobacco and sugar production relied in some measure on slavery for their success. During the first half of the eighteenth century, the labor requirements of fortification repairs, extension of the city wall of Havana, and ship construction in its shipyards remained similar to what they had been in the preceding centuries. The crown continued to use state-owned slaves strategically, along with hired enslaved workers, in defense projects in Cuba, but rarely in groups larger than several hundred. Convicts and free workers also were part of the mix of laborers in virtually every state project. To expand production of tobacco and sugar, however, Cuba needed a larger and more reliable source of slaves, though the crown proved ambivalent about the wisdom of significantly increasing the size of the island's enslaved population.

Rebuilding the Navy

Warfare in Europe over the seventeenth century had diverted a greater proportion of Spanish resources to the needs of the army. By 1700, the Spanish navy suffered from the lack of centralized administration and from its reliance on foreign shipbuilders to restock its fleets. Spain's reliance on galleys also was eclipsed under the early Bourbons, as the galleys were abolished in 1748. The forced laborers, both enslaved and prisoners, who had once been employed at the oars were now sent to work in peninsular arsenals in towns such as Cartagena, to help rebuild the navy.[5]

Efforts to strengthen the navy under Philip V and Ferdinand VI sought to consolidate and centralize the administration of the navy and to increase its size and power. A crucial component of the Bourbons' naval revival was access to shipyards capable of building and repairing the large vessels necessary for Atlantic transport and defense. With its vast forests of hardwoods and its position as a key imperial port, Havana had been a center for shipbuilding and repair since the second half of the sixteenth century. This role was revitalized at the beginning of the eighteenth century as Havana's harbor became a haven for French warships during the War of the Spanish Succession.[6]

One of the crown's first steps toward naval renewal was an order for two large ships to be constructed in Havana in 1701. A proposed budget for this construction, by master carpenter José Ruiz de Campos, offers a window into the labor practices in the shipyard that remained constant for most of the eighteenth century. One of the most important tasks in the building process was obtaining and preparing the wood necessary for the ships' construction. Teams of workers had to be sent to the forested outskirts of the city; in some cases, these workers had to cut their own roads to areas with the needed wood. After the timber was cut, teams of oxen and mules would drag it back to the shipyard or to a nearby river for transport by boat.

Such an arduous process required axmen and animal drivers as well as sawyers. Ruiz de Campos estimated that their salaries represented about 24 percent of the labor cost of constructing one ship. Salaries for thirty seamen also were included, at just under 12 percent, perhaps to be recruited from among those who were often in port waiting for the sailing of the royal fleets. For shipyard construction, Ruiz de Campos's cost estimates assumed a free, skilled workforce of carpenters, caulkers, sawyers, and ironworkers whose wages represented almost 40 percent of the total labor costs, showing the shipyard's historic preponderance of free, skilled labor.[7]

Since more than one ship had been ordered by the crown, Ruiz de Campos offered a plan to save money on future construction by employing thirty enslaved workers and training them for all the tasks needed to find, cut, and transport wood to the shipyard. In this way, the master carpenter contended, "With the first ship they will be trained and on the rest the salaries will be saved."[8] Later patterns suggest that the crown found this advice useful, as the shipyard continued to function effectively over the century with a majority of free workers augmented by naval seamen and a strategic but limited use of slaves, most often employed as cohorts of trained workers (especially sawyers) in the cutting and transport of wood.

Even with a well-functioning labor regime at a primary shipyard, the royal navy still needed major restructuring. Near the end of the war of succession, in 1712, Philip established a commission to study the navy and recommend changes. One legacy of the Hapsburg era was that Spain had "almost as many navies as realms" in 1700.[9] A year after peace was negotiated, in 1714, Philip V moved to consolidate these various navies under a single entity, the royal armada. He also appointed José Patiño as the general intendant of the navy in 1717, bringing a man of considerable talent to the project of naval reform. As Patiño moved to rationalize naval administration, he initiated the codification of the many disparate orders issued over previous decades into a series of ordinances, standardizing policies on wages, equipment, and measures. Additionally, the transatlantic fleets' general sailing orders and timetables were published.[10]

Patiño also made plans for Spain to resume large-scale shipbuilding to increase the size of its fleets, as only two ships had been built between 1700 and 1709. Renewed royal attention brought heartening results. From 1700 to 1716, nine ships of the line were built in royal shipyards, three of them in Havana. During Patiño's twenty-year tenure as marine intendant, and later as minister of the navy and Indies (1726–1736), Havana's shipyard produced twenty-two of the fifty-eight ships of the line and two of the six frigates that were built in royal yards.[11]

Increasing the number of ships in the royal navy necessitated recruiting crewmen to sail them. Since the seventeenth century, the crown had relied on voluntary naval service and had experimented several times with establishing a maritime registry of all seamen in Spain, all with limited success. Under Patiño's leadership, the state tried to entice more men to naval service, in 1726, by offering exemptions from army levies to all seamen who registered with their local authorities. The navy's labor shortage continued in the next decade, prompting more focused efforts to identify and recruit sailors. A royal decree in 1737 ordered local officials to register all sailors and shipwrights in their districts. Registration was still officially voluntary, but the decree mandated that virtually all occupations at sea would now be open only to those who registered. Foreign seamen who were Catholics, if they were married to Spanish women or were willing to settle in Spain, were also encouraged to register.[12]

All registrants were rewarded with some privileges, including the aforementioned relief from army levies and the right to have any civil or criminal charges made against them heard in Admiralty courts. If they were actually called to royal service, the king offered typically paternalist benefits to registrants, such as an enlistment bonus to sustain their families while they were at sea, a pension if they were disabled, and a guarantee that superiors were to treat them "with sweetness and good form." Seamen who deserted His Majesty's navy, however, could expect punishments ranging from fines or service without pay to forced labor in North African presidios or the galleys, depending on the severity of the offense.[13]

Both shipbuilding and naval service continued to rely on some form of voluntary labor over the first half of the eighteenth century, even as Spain's military commitments increased with renewed warfare in 1739. The shipbuilding program also may have benefited from the improved registry of sailors. By the late 1730s, more than 39,000 men and boys had been entered in the naval registry, and in some localities, such as Cadiz, up to 10 percent of registrants were also shipwrights.[14] While these skilled sailors (from merchant or naval vessels) awaited orders to sail, quartered in ports such as Havana, they were a potential source of skilled labor for hire in the shipyard.

Though the early Bourbon efforts at naval renewal and other defense improvements did not require major changes in labor recruitment and deployment, they did necessitate funding on a new scale. Spain had been able to defend Havana and the Caribbean's sea-lanes in the sixteenth and much of the seventeenth centuries, funded by relatively modest infusions of silver from Mexico.[15] Remittances for Caribbean defense had oscillated between approximately 30,000 to 45,000 pesos per year, on average, from the 1590s to the 1620s. In the mid-1600s, remittances for defense rose to an average of some 150,000 to 175,000 pesos per year. By the 1720s, however, annual defense remittances averaged more than 1 million pesos per year for the first time, and Havana received the lion's share of the funds for Caribbean defense over the rest of the eighteenth century.

Two factors played into the city's need for such large infusions of funds. As the data on shipbuilding indicates, Havana was a crucial site for the Bourbons' plans for naval regeneration, yet the island's relative underdevelopment meant that it had never generated sufficient revenue to cover even its own defense needs.[16] Even as Cuba's tax revenues rose by more than a factor of six from 1700 to 1760, Mexican *situado* funds assigned to Havana rose more than tenfold.[17] Fortunately for the Spanish crown, Mexican silver production also surged over the eighteenth century, to approximately 100 million pesos annually at midcentury and more than 200 million pesos per year by 1810.[18]

Up to 1740, the crown relied on both Mexican silver and the capital of private individuals to fund individual ship construction. Private capital was solicited and all the major steps in the building process were contracted out, while the crown retained ownership of the shipyard, its materials, and the technical direction of construction. Recruiting the laborers necessary for construction was the responsibility of the contractor. In essence, the crown sought a financier who would loan the state the funds necessary to construct a ship, often in return for some kind of royal favor—a trade concession, an exemption, or a monopoly.

A petition by Havana merchant Diego de Salazar in the early 1730s provides an example of such an arrangement. His initial petition outlined the assets he commanded, as proof of his wealth and his ability to fund ship construction: three hundred black slaves, three sugar mills, three tobacco mills, three farms, five houses, more than 150,000 pesos in merchandise, and various people who owed him money. Salazar's assets and interests combined all the main engines of economic development in colonial Cuba—slaveholding, tobacco and sugar production, and state defense projects—challenging older historiography that saw these pursuits as divergent and even contradictory.[19]

Salazar ultimately agreed to build four ships for the crown, and his contract reveals how little control he had over the actual building process. The crown chose the master shipwright Juan de Acosta to supervise the construction.[20] Salazar was obliged to have the ships built according to official specifications, following all the "stated measurements," while the state was supposed to facilitate the importation of the necessary iron hardware from Spain, at a discount. Salazar also agreed to mortgage property, including some of his own slaves, to a total of 50,000 pesos, as insurance. If any slaves died during the contract period, Salazar would have to replace them at his own expense.[21]

The papers included in the file with Salazar's contract give only a glimpse of a few of the laborers involved in these ships' construction—in this case, criminals. One report detailed problems with private individuals cutting wood in areas reserved for the royal shipyard. Even though such private lumbering was prohibited in 1719, it remained a perennial enforcement concern into the first half of the nineteenth century. To address this problem, the Cuban captain general ordered a military official to end the illegal lumbering and to punish the poachers with a fine of twenty-five pesos. Several days' labor in the shipyard was the penalty for repeat offenders.[22]

The merchant Salazar's contract also contained the price the crown agreed to pay for the ships at their completion: two for 77,000 pesos and two for 67,000.[23] Salazar was an exceptionally wealthy volunteer, willing to finance royal shipbuilding. However, on the whole, the crown had a poor record as a partner in shipbuilding and financiers like Diego de Salazar rarely presented themselves in sufficient numbers to advance the Bourbons' ambitious agenda for naval regeneration.[24]

Another problem for the shipbuilding program in Havana was the lack of space in its shipyard. In 1713, the crown had ordered the building of a royal shipyard in one of the oldest parts of the city, constrained between the La Fuerza fort and the treasury building, with only one major slipway and no space for all the warehouses and other buildings necessary for the yard and its arsenal (the manufacturing complex). To increase royal oversight in the shipyard, in 1734 the crown appointed a naval commissioner, Lorenzo de Montalvo Ruiz de Alarcón. One of his first tasks was to move the shipyard to a larger site on the southwestern rim of town, outside the city walls, to accommodate the quickened pace of shipbuilding. By the late 1730s, the new shipyard was operating, and over the next decade Montalvo added a sawmill and a masting sheer, used to install masts on large ships, to Havana's shipbuilding complex.[25]

By the mid-eighteenth century, the Spanish Bourbons had made progress in rebuilding the royal navy without making radical changes in long-standing patterns of labor recruitment. The marine registry for naval service identified many thousands of sailors and shipwrights who could also repair and help build ships in places like Havana. The state's access to navy seamen as a pool of laborers for tasks in port blurred the line between voluntary and forced labor, since it is not clear how freely sailors chose to work in the shipyard. But the seamen's labor may have obviated the need for greater resort to both royal and privately owned slaves in Havana's shipyard as the king's orders for new ships mounted. Accomplishing the Bourbons' goals in tobacco and sugar production, on the other hand, required greater reliance on the slave trade to recruit workers.

Tobacco, Sugar, and Slaves

The interrelations of war and defense with trade and development in early eighteenth-century Cuba are illustrated by the crown's efforts to regulate and derive greater revenue from the trafficking of the enslaved and the production and trade of tobacco and sugar on the island. With respect to the slave trade, Spain found itself at a continual disadvantage to other powers over the entire eighteenth century. Spanish merchants had rarely been involved in the importation of enslaved people directly from Africa to the Americas, and Spain's debilitated state at the opening of the century meant negotiating the rights of foreigners to said trade from a position of weakness.

The War of the Spanish Succession forced Spain to open the slave trade to its American colonies to both of its European rivals. In 1702, in return for French support in the war, Philip V granted the French Guinea Company the exclusive slave trade *asiento*, or monopoly contract.[26] Along with the right to introduce 48,000 *piezas de Indias* over the next ten years, the French company was granted favors not enjoyed by earlier *asentistas*: permission to trade in previously closed ports of the empire, such as Buenos Aires and Callao, and to transport materials necessary for ship repair and the provisioning of enslaved people and naval crews to its own warehouses in a number of American ports, as well as relief from the obligation to register its ships with the Casa de Contratación. In spite of these privileges, the French Guinea Company was unable to fulfill its contract and went bankrupt in 1710.[27]

At the conclusion of the war of succession, in return for recognition of Philip V's claim to the Spanish throne, the English extracted even more extensive commercial concessions. One of the treaties negotiated to end the war mandated the transfer of the Spanish slave trade *asiento* to the English queen, who then awarded it to the recently chartered South Sea Company (SSC). The company agreed to bring 144,000 *piezas de Indias* (or 4,800 annually) to Spanish America over the thirty-year contract period, and the company enjoyed commercial privileges similar to those granted in the preceding French *asiento*. For instance, the SSC's slave merchants could accept gold or silver or "*frutos del país*," often tobacco or sugar, as payment for slaves. They could import provisions for their ships, crews, and slave cohorts and sell any excess goods in the local market. In addition, the SSC gained unprecedented legal access to Spanish American markets through an annual "permission ship," a 500-ton English vessel allowed to import goods for sale at the Portobello trade fair, in present-day Panama.[28]

English traders could now exploit both legal and illegal channels of trade in Spanish America, and some groups in the Spanish Empire realized benefits from these agreements as well. The Spanish crown extracted from the English a payment of 200,000 *escudos* for the royal treasury and imposed high duties on slaves imported by the South Sea Company. In Cuba, producers of tobacco and sugar had a new outlet for their harvests through payment for enslaved workers and other goods purchased from company merchants. For the crown, the benefits ultimately were mitigated by the new opportunities for fraud and smuggling.[29]

The SSC had uneven success during its exclusive slave trading contract. It introduced its first cargo of fifty enslaved Africans to Cuba in 1715. Though slave imports waxed and waned thereafter, in part due to interruptions when Spain and England were at war (from 1719 to 1721 and 1727 to 1729), the SSC introduced 6,062 slaves (measured as 5,116 *piezas de Indias*) through Havana, and another 503 (or 486 *piezas*) through Santiago de Cuba, from 1715 to 1734.[30]

In spite of its legal monopoly on slave trading to the Spanish Empire, the company failed to meet its annual quota of 4,800 *piezas* and suffered losses during its first two decades of operation. Some losses were due to the inherent risks and costs of slave trading, not the least of which were diseases and deaths suffered by the enslaved during the grueling Atlantic crossing or while awaiting sale in Caribbean ports. Also, Cuban entrepreneurs often were short of capital, so they would make a down payment to slave merchants and then pay the rest of the price at a future date, in *frutos* such as snuff or sugar.[31] Such payments in kind were subject to physical deterioration and price fluctuations, increasing potential risks and losses for the SSC. Finally, goods lost or confiscated during wartime embargos were not always compensated. Thus, the greatest benefits of the *asiento* for the SSC most likely lay elsewhere. As royal officials in Havana investigating smuggling operations by the company concluded, "Slave trading covered an enormous interloping commerce that produced even greater profits than the one in slaves."[32]

One such commerce was the trade in tobacco, and here the Spanish state established its own monopoly to create another source of revenue for the royal treasury. Though other American colonies (Virginia and Brazil, for example) produced tobacco, Cuba's leaf was particularly prized in European markets. Tobacco processing in Seville had been a state monopoly since the early seventeenth century, as part of an effort to reduce fraud and increase state tobacco revenues. In the late 1600s, the crown sought to extend its monopoly and to control the colonial production of the leaf in Cuba. By 1702, tobacco contributed more than 14 percent of the crown of Castile's net revenues; eleven years later the percentage had risen to almost 25 percent.[33] Recognizing the profitability of tobacco to the treasury, in 1717, Philip V established a royal tobacco monopoly in Cuba (the first in its American colonies), which would purchase all of the island's production at set prices and thereby regulate both the quantity and quality of the tobacco sent to Seville's cigar and snuff factories.[34]

The Bourbons had several goals in implementing the tobacco monopoly. At the top of the list was restricting the processing of tobacco to designated manufacturing centers, especially those in Seville, and ensuring sufficient leaf for peninsular demand, something the open market in tobacco was unable to provide.[35] A second goal was the reduction of the contraband trade in tobacco, especially to English traders and smugglers, which was virtually impossible in an open market. A third, related goal was to ensure that the bulk of the revenue generated by the tobacco trade went to the crown.[36]

To achieve these goals, the crown experimented with several different commercial organizations of the tobacco monopoly. Under foreign *asientos*, tobacco and slave trading intersected from 1701 to 1739 as both the French Guinea Company and the South Sea Company sold slaves to tobacco producers in return for leaf tobacco or snuff. Within the state tobacco monopoly, there was an initial period of direct state purchases; then the crown allowed more participation by local merchants in the 1720s. By 1734, officials in Madrid had decided that a private contractor might run the monopoly more efficiently and awarded *asientos* to three different individuals over the next six years.[37]

As with ship construction, monies from the Mexican *situado* were designated to cover the state's tobacco purchases. The amounts dedicated to buying tobacco rose from 200,000 pesos in 1723 to 500,000 pesos in 1744, a clear sign of the importance that the crown attached to tobacco.[38] The tobacco monopoly also suffered from irregular arrivals of the *situado* funds, which produced a host of problems: disgruntled growers, when payments were in arrears; and rising indebtedness among the growers and the *factoría* itself, as both relied more heavily on borrowing in local capital markets to sustain their operations.[39] One historian has concluded that the tobacco trade in Cuba was less an exclusive monopoly and more a shared business of the state and the wealthy local elite.[40] This insight can be extended to most of the enterprises in which the state was a major player in awarding contracts, regulating production and distribution, or deploying labor— shipbuilding, slave trading, and tobacco.

The state's hand was less visible in the island's sugar sector, in part because, unlike tobacco, the metropole did not process the sugar harvested in its colonies. Instead, the crown mostly wanted to extract revenue from the trade in sugar. Its main roles in encouraging sugar production were in organizing the recruitment of forced laborers through the slave trade *asiento*, defending against resistance by the enslaved, and setting taxes and duties.

In practice, the state's management of the *asiento*, taxes, and duties initially worked against sugar expansion in Cuba. The French and English slave trade monopolies, in the early 1700s, tended to keep slave prices as high as 350 to 450 pesos per person, and, as noted, planters often were forced to secure credit for their slave purchases.[41] To ensure adequate lumber for shipbuilding, in 1719 the crown forbade woodcutting for sugar mills. Cuban planters also found it difficult to compete with sugars imported into Cadiz from the French Caribbean, beginning in 1727. Royal tax policy on sugar charged import duties, sales tax, and a high freight rate when sugar was transported in royal ships.[42]

These unfavorable conditions encouraged Cuban planters to organize and press their case in Madrid. They argued that they needed tax relief, since the difficult prospects in the sugar sector were driving planters out of sugar production entirely or into ranching or tobacco growing. The latter would have been particularly unwelcome to Madrid officials, since they were trying to limit tobacco production to the amounts needed for the royal factories, to reduce smuggling. Cuban planters ultimately gained concessions in 1730, when the king lowered both import duties and the sales tax and reduced freight rates in royal vessels.[43]

Planters also looked to colonial troops and authorities to protect them against rebellion, as the African-born population among the enslaved began to increase. The first major slave revolt on the island erupted in 1727, to the south of Havana, on the Quiebra Hacha plantation belonging to the first Count of Casa Bayona. In an ill-conceived act of contrition several days before Easter, the count reenacted with his slaves Jesus's washing of the feet of his disciples at the Last Supper. The enslaved participants may have construed the act as a sign of the count's weakness, and shortly thereafter, enslaved people on his and a number of surrounding plantation rebelled, causing "grave insults, deaths, and sacrileges, stealing the sacred garments and chalices [from the church] and placing this city [Havana] in great danger."[44] An infantry company from the capital and local residents ultimately crushed the rebellion, but fears of concerted revolt by the enslaved continued to animate Cuban planters, at least until the specter of revolution by the enslaved in Saint-Domingue in the 1790s provided an even more frightful example.

Commercial Warfare

The new Bourbon administration's efforts to improve defenses and spur development in Cuba had met with some success in Havana and in the empire by the late 1730s. By 1739, a total of eighteen ships had been constructed in Havana's shipyard, fourteen of them ships of the line. Royal attention and resources to naval regeneration had produced what one historian has described as "a professional navy of considerable strength with its own independent systems of construction, supply, and maintenance."[45] In land-based defenses, much of the work needed on the city's wall was finished, virtually enclosing the urban core by midcentury.[46] Some attempts had been made to derive greater benefit for the state from the tobacco trade and to encourage sugar production; Indies revenues had risen appreciably.[47]

The success of these early efforts encouraged Spain to contest more vigorously the commercial inroads granted to England by treaty after the War of the Spanish Succession and extended through fraud and smuggling. With renewed Anglo–Spanish warfare in 1739, Spain effectively abrogated those treaties and sought to reassert greater control over its colonial trade and to realize greater advantage for the metropole. For Cuba, resurgent Spanish mercantilism took the relatively innovative form of a chartered joint-stock company. The company's contract with the crown brought together defense projects in shipbuilding and strengthened Spain's presence in the northern rim of the Caribbean with development initiatives in slave trading, tobacco, and sugar production.[48] The necessity of such a concerted effort on both fronts was demonstrated by the dire threat posed by the English military response to Spain's attempts to reassert its power in the Caribbean.

English traders' efforts to smuggle goods into Spanish American markets, and Spain's attempts to interdict this illicit commerce, were a continual source of tension from the signing of the treaties ending the War of Spanish Succession onward. Spanish officials resented what they saw as undue advantage forced upon them by defeat, and they railed against the South Sea Company and private traders who went beyond the concessions allowed by the slave trade *asiento*, and by the provisioning and permission ships. Spanish *guardacostas* (coast guard vessels) stepped up their interdiction and searches of ships, sometimes confiscating merchandise as contraband. Privateers from Cuban ports harassed English traders and seized ships and goods.[49] Spanish officials in colonial ports such as Havana also tried to extract additional taxes, duties, fees, and bribes both from legal agents of the SSC and from smugglers. These tensions ultimately erupted in war between England and Spain in 1739.[50]

The Caribbean theater of this warfare put defenses in the region to the test as England mounted serious attempts to capture strategic Spanish ports in Cuba and elsewhere. To cut Spain's trade routes to its mainland colonies, English forces attacked and destroyed the port of Portobello on the Isthmus of Panama, menaced Havana, and blockaded Santiago de Cuba for two months in 1740. The next year, the English returned to Santiago, landing 3,000 men reinforced by 1,000 enslaved auxiliaries from Jamaica, but disease and fierce resistance repelled the attack. A subsequent attack on Santiago, in 1748, also was repulsed, by the town's shore batteries.[51] Among the defenders of Santiago de Cuba were the enslaved royal militiamen of El Cobre. Havana's militia companies, on the other hand, were all free men, both whites and men of color. Ultimately, the fortifications and defenders of both cities foiled the English assaults.[52]

The English also mounted a massive amphibious attack against Cartagena de Indias, in 1741, and laid siege to that port for six weeks. Here the attackers numbered some 12,000 fighting men supported by 180 ships. Cartagena's defenders barely topped 3,200 men in both the army and naval units, supplemented with six hundred indigenous archers, used mostly as workers. English troops landed successfully but were never able to breach the fort of San Felipe de Barajas, which protected the land approaches to the city. After facing fierce resistance and suffering thousands of casualties due to injuries and disease, Admiral Vernon and his forces retreated. Spain's long-standing Caribbean defense strategy of fortified ports, small permanent garrisons, and local volunteers prevailed, if only by a hairbreadth.[53]

Though Madrid policy makers were justifiably proud of the Spanish victory at Cartagena, the military assault on Spain's Caribbean trade routes brought even more opportunity for the English to trade illegally with Spanish America. During the war years from 1739 through 1748, both English and North American interlopers traded actively in ports all around the Caribbean, providing foodstuffs, naval stores, manufactured goods, and slaves, often in exchange for silver. Spanish officials could do little to control smuggling and sometimes had to rely on illegal traders themselves to procure much-needed provisions.[54]

Even after the war, the Spanish eschewed a wholesale return to earlier patterns of restricted trade. For instance, though Admiral Vernon had held Portobello for only two months, thereafter Spain ceased using the convoy system of galleons to trade with its South American colonies.[55] The flotas ultimately were revived for the Cadiz–Veracruz shipping route, in 1757, but for the rest of the American empire such a closed system of trade was no longer possible. The wartime expedient of issuing individual licenses to unescorted merchant ships was extended into the 1750s, and smuggling remained an open wound in the imperial body.[56] With the success of its Caribbean defense system against the English assault, Spain had won the battle, but it nonetheless lost the war to control imperial trade.

Combining Defense and Development: The Royal Company of Havana

For Cuba, war had brought the de facto end of the South Sea Company's privileged access to Spanish American trade, and Spanish officials reverted briefly to granting licenses or contracts to individuals to carry out the trade in tobacco and in enslaved Africans. A contract with one Martín Ulibarri y Gamboa for 1,000 *piezas de Indias* was never fulfilled, so Cuban slaveholders had to rely on the illegal slave trade until a new source could be organized.[57]

By the late 1730s, both state officials and private entrepreneurs in Cuba saw benefit in combining trade and defense activities under the auspices of a single institution. The third *asentista* of the tobacco monopoly in Cuba, Martín de Aróstegui, parlayed his individual privilege into a much larger contract for a royally chartered trading company that addressed many of the crown's goals for defense and development. The Royal Company of Havana, chartered in 1740, illustrates well the interplay of public and private interests in all state business, including the recruitment and deployment of the enslaved for defense and development projects. The limits of the company's success in the fulfillment of its many charges by the 1760s later pushed the state to take more direct control of both defense and development initiatives when faced with a new English assault on Havana in 1762.[58]

The chartered company, financed through offerings of joint stock, was a relatively recent innovation in the eighteenth-century Spanish Empire, but it had been a successful tool for state and private collaboration in the development and imperial expansion of Spain's mercantilist rivals in Holland, England, and France since the mid-seventeenth century. Several such companies had been chartered in Spain by the 1720s and 1730s, but a new feature of the Royal Company of Havana was its base in the colonial capital and the extensive participation by Cubans.

The list of investors who purchased shares shows a wide range of social and economic levels of participation in the RCH. Of the 139 people who bought shares (at five hundred pesos each) from March 1740 to January 1744, almost 70 percent (ninety-seven) invested in fewer than ten shares. A modest investment did not always correspond to lower social status, however, as eight of the small investors were members of the titled nobility. The largest investors were the king and queen, with one hundred shares, followed by the eighty shares purchased by Martín Aróstegui, the prime mover in the negotiations to establish the RCH. The 1740 company charter facilitated investment by capital-poor Cuban tobacco growers by permitting them the exclusive right to buy portions of a share. Tobacco growers and sugar mill owners were also the only investors allowed to buy up to four shares with "good quality fruits" rather than with gold or silver currency.[59]

Over the first five years of its operation, the RCH sold 1,460 shares for a total of 730,000 pesos of capital, well short of the 1 million pesos anticipated at its founding. Not all shareholders paid cash for their shares, either. The Spanish monarchs stipulated that their one hundred shares be financed with the duties collected on goods traded by the RCH. Thus, its plight was similar to that of the tobacco monopoly of the early 1700s; the company began its operations considerably undercapitalized and had to resort to early borrowing at high interest to cover its expenses.[60]

The charter of the Royal Company of Havana shows the interpenetration of crown and colonials' interests in defense and trade in tobacco, sugar, and slaves. The company was given a monopoly on a range of exports from and imports to Cuba in exchange for specific services to the monarch. Both the crown and Cuban entrepreneurs sought to profit by controlling the tobacco trade. The sharp dealing and low prices paid by earlier *asentistas* had encouraged smuggling and discouraged many Cuban tobacco growers from selling to the state. Therefore, the RCH was to pay "advantageous prices to stimulate an improvement in cultivation" and to remit to the royal treasury 15 percent of the funds generated annually by the tobacco trade. The company also was to pay good prices for sugar and oversee its transport to Cadiz, and to help provide more enslaved workers to sugar planters.[61]

Among its other services to the crown, the RCH was to provision the garrisons or presidios of Havana, Saint Augustine, and Apalache as Spain sought to strengthen its frontier against English and French expansion in North America. The company also was expected to outfit and transport to Florida from the Canary Islands a cohort of five hundred families as settlers. The company was to provide twenty pesos in start-up funds per family, along with farm implements, defensive weapons, and church bells and altar implements for ten churches, though as of 1748 the directors had not fulfilled these charges. Beyond providing goods and settlers to the empire's outposts in southeastern North America, the crown asked the company to use its trade through the presidio in Apalache to win over the native peoples by building a "store or warehouse of goods for the purpose of attracting the Indians and dissuading them from friendship with Foreigners."[62]

In return for these services, the RCH was allowed to import textiles, ironware, wines, brandies, and oil from Spain, along with foodstuffs such as flour. To aid in carrying out its general charge of increasing commerce on the island, the company was granted certain exemptions from import restrictions and duties. Another privilege the king granted specifically to Aróstegui for his services as the Royal Company director was the enjoyment of the *fuero militar* (military privileges) while the contract was in force.[63]

After negotiating the founding charter of the RCH, Martín Aróstegui signed a second contract, in 1741, obligating the company to even more extensive royal service—the building of three to four ships per year for the royal navy, over the next decade. The crown had found a way around the shortage of individual financiers for shipbuilding through the RCH contract. Everything necessary for each ship was the financial responsibility of the company, including the cutting and preparation of wood and the manufacture of cannons and other ironwork in Havana's arsenal.[64] The crown would pay for each ship in three installments, using funds from the Mexican *situado*, to a fixed total of 75,000 pesos for large warships and 19,000 pesos for the smallest boats. According to the contract, the company was not obligated to continue construction if payments were seriously in arrears. The company also agreed to send the new ships to Spain and to give passage to returning officials and troops at its own expense.[65]

These many services to the crown and imperial defense soon became a burden. Over the first three years of its contract, the RCH was able to finish only two seventy-gun ships of the line. Accounts from November 1744 on the expenses incurred in constructing the two ships, named the *Invencible* and the *Reina*, showed a total cost of 253,968 pesos 3 reales, while the crown paid only the fixed price of 150,000 pesos for both vessels, leaving the RCH to cover a loss of almost 104,000 pesos. In 1745, the company reported losses of 114,958 pesos 5 reales on the construction of two sixty-gun ships, the *Conquistador* and the *Dragón*. From the first, ship construction for the royal navy was a losing proposition for the RCH, much as it had been for earlier contractors.[66]

Over the next two years, the company struggled to accommodate changing orders from Madrid and the irregular delivery of supplies from Spain, due in part to the disruptions of war. By 1745, the king was writing to the directors of the RCH through Patiño's successor in the ministry of the navy, the Marquis de Ensenada, to express his displeasure with the slow pace of naval construction in the Havana shipyard. The directors replied that several problems retarded completion of vessels, one being that the crown had changed the number and size of the vessels it requested, from four ships of sixty cannons to three ships of seventy cannons and two of eighty. When the new order arrived in Havana, the wood for the four smaller ships had already been cut and was on its way to the shipyard. The directors maintained that the change to larger ships necessitated sending larger groups of workers farther from the city to find the required timbers. The company also had to instruct the ironworks in Vizcaya to suspend manufacture of parts for the old order and change to those for the larger vessels, all of which delayed construction and increased expenses. The directors contended that they were working with "a knife at the throat from all the enormous losses on each ship" and were therefore doing everything "that human possibility permits" to fulfill their obligations to the crown. They even intimated that the crown's failure to pay for all of its shares in the company had made it difficult for them to fund the importation of materials for shipbuilding.[67]

Expenses continued to mount, as the RCH had to maintain the shipyard and raise new structures as needed. In particular, the addition of a masting sheer, called "La Machina," was completed, largely at company expense, along with added slipways for the new arsenal complex outside the city walls and administrative and storage buildings. To provide some of the supplies that were slow in arriving from Spain, factories were established to make rope from local resources and to sew sails. Another of the company's duties to the crown, beyond building new ships, was the careening and repair of royal vessels already in service, a total of thirty ships from 1740 to 1746.[68]

The RCH had to conduct all its business under the watchful eyes of the king's naval commissioner, Lorenzo de Montalvo, appointed to the Havana shipyard in 1734, and of the former contractor-shipwright Juan de Acosta.[69] In 1746, Montalvo and Acosta advised the RCH directors on how to best organize the cutting and transport of wood and reported to Minister Ensenada on the company's activities. They noted that in addition to purchasing more teams of oxen and hiring more woodcutters, the company had devoted a schooner and five smaller boats to the transport of wood by water to the shipyard.[70]

All of these many endeavors required hundreds of workers to successfully fulfill the RCH's obligation to build royal ships. The shipyard, its arsenal, and the docks teemed with people carrying out the king's business, some of whom were employed by the RCH, some by other contractors, and others directly by the state. Although the RCH imported roughly 10,000 enslaved Africans from 1740 to 1760, it did not retain a large portion of those enslaved workers for its own projects; most were likely sold to private owners.[71]

The company's strategic employment of its own enslaved people, combined with other kinds of laborers, paralleled the state's labor practices in its own projects. The RCH maintained a small contingent of approximately thirty-five to forty enslaved workers in its tobacco warehouse and as carters to transport tobacco back and forth from the docks, but the largest cohort of its enslaved worked in naval construction.[72] By 1748, there were thirteen woodcutting sites around Havana, with a mix of 350 to 400 enslaved and free workers.[73] The RCH had some slaves and other workers of its own harvesting timbers from Havana's hinterland, but it also bought substantial quantities of wood from private individuals, then paid to have it delivered to the *astillero*.[74] At the shipyard itself, the company employed 236 of its own slaves in the sawmill, who were valued at 70,800 pesos, or three hundred pesos each, a price that suggests they had acquired some skill at their work.[75]

Still, nearly two-thirds of the approximately eight hundred workers in the Havana shipyard were free people employed as carpenters, caulkers, masons, ironworkers, and the like.[76] Free workers, especially those with skills, generally commanded high salaries, which may explain the company's choice to train a group of its own enslaved sawyers. Cuban historian Levi Marrero's work on prices and salaries in mid-eighteenth-century Cuba suggests that the island was indeed *tierra cara* (an expensive land), with high salaries even for *peones*, at four to six reales per day. Skilled craftsmen working in the shipyard received as much as thirteen to fifteen reales per day. These salaries were in addition to the workers' daily ration, at a cost of one to one and a half reales per day, customarily provided by the employer.[77]

There also are scattered references to enslaved workers employed in the capital directly by the state in the early 1700s. Clearing Havana's bay of sediment and debris was an ongoing task that fell under the state's purview. For this work, the state maintained a pontoon boat manned by a boatswain, sailors, royal slaves, and prisoners, mostly from New Spain. Royal slaves also manned the launch that ferried people and provisions to the El Morro fort, across the bay from the city of Havana.[78] For the proposed building of the shipyard's masting sheer in 1747, the budget included crown purchases of enslaved workers with expertise in carpentry and bricklaying.[79] Skilled royal slaves from other parts of the island, such as El Cobre in the east, were sometimes sent to Havana for work in the forts and the naval yard.[80]

In the first half of the 1700s, the Bourbons' plans to rebuild the royal navy in Havana were advanced through the well-tested labor practices of sending small contingents of royal slaves from one part of the island to the capital, purchasing small groups of enslaved people to be trained in particular skills, and retaining some of those groups of the enslaved for strategic work over time, as in the sawing and preparation of timber for the *astillero*. When the RCH took over the task of constructing ships for the royal navy, it, too, continued the prevailing labor patterns, which included a preponderance of free workers supplemented with contingents of the enslaved in strategic work. Only in the cutting and processing of timber did the RCH, like previous contractors, make significant use of the enslaved and other coerced workers, such as convicts. Yet, even with a well-established labor regime, the costs of both enslaved and free labor remained high, and the RCH failed to cover its expenses in building ships for the crown.

Given the history of problems in generating a profit in shipbuilding, it is doubtful that the directors of the Royal Company of Havana hoped to do more than break even on that aspect of their contract with the crown. Losses accumulated from the king's first order, and by 1748 the company's directors were petitioning him for a release from their obligation to produce ships for the navy, due to the tremendous losses they had suffered in that endeavor. They went so far as to claim that the company itself was a "slave" to various interests on the island and requested liberation from its rightful "owner," the king. The directors also complained that the company benefited from few of the concessions and exemptions granted in the initial contract with the crown, and that even the two permits to import slaves "had turned out not at all favorably."[81]

As with the South Sea Company's *asiento*, the RCH procured slaves through English traders in Jamaica and enjoyed freedom from duties for provisions imported for their maintenance. The slave trade to Cuba continued to be one of the few avenues for legal trade with foreigners, and it masked considerable contraband trading in slaves and provision goods.[82] Despite having a source of enslaved labor relatively close at hand, the directors said that they had lost much time and money trading enslaved people, partly through trying to comply with royal wishes. The enslaved sold in Cuba had been priced "with great equity in favor of the public by order of Your Majesty." "Not a few" had also been lost to illness and death, and a hospital had to be maintained for their care. At the end of the day, the company claimed a loss of 103,588 pesos that had not been recouped through slave sales by the end of 1748.[83]

To be able to continue benefiting the realm through its many services, such as "improving and trading fruits, employing vassals, [and] increasing navigation," the company included in the petition a list of sixty actions necessary to "rectify" its difficult position. Not surprisingly, the main change the directors pleaded for was relief from building ships for the royal navy. They also asked for relief from all responsibility for transporting and establishing in Florida families from the Canary Islands, though they would continue to supply the presidios in the region and the storehouse in Apalache. In spite of the directors' gloomy catalog of problems, they suggested that another grant of a contract to import slaves might help them offset some of their other losses.[84] Most likely they had come to see future potential in the provision of slaves as both tobacco and sugar production expanded on the island and wanted to continue enjoying the freedom to import other goods as a lucrative ancillary to slave trading.

The clearest statement of the importance of expanding slavery in Cuba, for both the imperial project and economic growth, came from the RCH's lawyer, Bernardo de Urrutia y Matos, in his study of Cuban development, published in 1743. Much of the text reads as an apologia for the RCH and a legitimation of its continued privileges, but Urrutia also took pains to link the crown's interests in the island's defense and economic development to the expansion of slavery. He wondered how the island had defended itself before the establishment of the RCH in 1740, and he answered his own query with some hyperbole: "The king had no *negros* nor did he build fortifications beyond a part of a wall." He also noted that Havana seemed unable to subsist on more money than most towns of equal size in Spain because "in Spain they work more and spend less."[85] For the author, the remedy lay in the RCH's continued direction of commerce and development, and in a better workforce.

Urrutia enumerated the many ways that the RCH had improved commerce on the island, but he opined that Cuba would be unable to compete with other smaller and less fertile Caribbean islands that produced more until it, too, enjoyed "abundant and cheap slaves." For Urrutia, the timely provision of "comfortably priced" slaves to Cuba was one of the most important policy issues facing the crown, because slaves were the key to all development and thereby to the improvement of royal revenues.[86] He articulated a seamless vision of meeting the goals of the early Bourbons' plan of renewal in Cuba by continuing the RCH's role as its major trader:

> The ends are advanced mutually because with fruits slaves are purchased, with slaves more fruits will be made, and with more fruits and more slaves reales and

pesos will be made, there is business on the Island, and the King has much that will serve him on her with the residence of squadrons, factories and careenage of ships, remission of timbers, purchase of tobacco, maintenance of presidios, outfitting of mines, wealth of vassals, improvement of populations and commercial traffic, that all conspire to increase the Public Treasury and put the Island in an impregnable state, and [be the] strongest bulwark against enemies in America.[87]

The crown saw enough benefit to Cuba in the company's activities to allow it to end the obligation to build royal ships in 1749, but the directors had to complete the ships already under construction—two eighty-gun ships and three of seventy guns.[88] Within a year, the company directors were desperately short of funds and proposed cutting the wages of arsenal workers in half, at least until *situado* funds arrived from Mexico. Without such a wage reduction, they foresaw having to suspend work altogether. A group of the arsenal's shipwrights sent a written protest to the royal commissioner of the navy, Montalvo, contending that the workers would be unable to sustain their families at half pay. Unpersuaded, Montalvo approved the shift to half pay as the best way to address royal interests and finish the ships without delay. The shipwrights whose skills and pay scales were specific to shipbuilding had little choice but to accept the wages offered, hoping to be compensated when Mexican funds arrived.[89]

Though both the workers and the company directors were discouraged by the difficulties of completing royal ships on the crown's terms, the state clearly had benefited. The period from 1700 to 1760 saw 63 percent of the largest ships of the line produced in Havana's shipyard over the entire century, 16.2 percent in the 1741–1749 period under the RCH contract. The building of large ships in Havana slumped in the 1750s, but overall the crown had been successful at organizing the expansion of its navy by modifying the contract system to include the Royal Company of Havana and shifting much of the risk and cost to private entrepreneurs.[90]

The Royal Company's frustrating experience as a crown shipbuilder was somewhat offset by gains realized in the trading of tropical commodities, especially of tobacco. However, just prior to the English attack in 1762, the crown rescinded the company's most lucrative privileges with two significant changes to development policy (in 1760): a reimposition of a full state monopoly on tobacco purchases and a new tax on sugar production. Both changes reflected in some measure the Royal Company of Havana's success in harnessing the revenue potential of tobacco and stimulating the production of sugar. Shortly after the crown relieved the company of the obligation to build ships, in 1752, the king suspended the directors and ordered a review of the RCH books and business practices. During the long investigation, the RCH lost its exclusive right to the tobacco *asiento*.[91]

Though there clearly were irregularities in the RCH's operations—too many family members on the payroll, lavish gifts and expenses—the directors' profits from tobacco trading convinced the crown that it would do well to rethink its modest 15 percent share of that revenue. In 1760, the state reverted to running its own monopoly, establishing the tobacco *factoría* or administrative district in Havana and ending the company's most profitable privilege in trade.[92] Given the considerable growth in sugar production in Cuba over the previous two decades, in 1760 the crown moved to end the RCH's preferential treatment and to realize more revenue from the trade in sugar, establishing a new tax, the *ramo de azucares*, a 5 percent levy on sugar harvests that was collected in kind in December.[93]

Neither policy shift necessitated any major changes in labor policy, however. Once the Havana tobacco *factoría* was established, the crown allotted a small amount of money to purchase twelve *esclavos del rey* at three hundred pesos each, plus their daily ration and clothing allowance. In keeping with labor policies in other state enterprises such as the shipyard, a small but permanent squad of royal enslaved laborers was recruited to work in the state warehouse and to transport its tobacco to the docks.[94]

Land Defenses

The early Bourbons accomplished naval regeneration by outsourcing many aspects of ship construction while centralizing the administration of the navy. In contrast, land defenses traditionally were more tightly controlled by the crown in imperial hubs such as Havana, through state-constructed fortifications supported by light companies of Spanish troops. After an uprising of Cuban tobacco growers occupied Havana's Plaza de San Francisco and drove out the governor in 1717, the crown combined the light companies in the plaza with some 1,000 reinforcements to form the first fixed battalion in Spanish America.[95]

For land defenses, the king assigned royal engineers, who were often military officers, to supervise fort building. Financing came directly from Mexican *situado* funds, not private financiers or the trading companies. In the early 1750s, Madrid increased the Havana garrison's troop strength from 1,200 to 2,080 men and reorganized the command structure. The artillery company added men, for a total of 172. The crown also centered defense planning and resources for the northwestern rim of the Caribbean in Havana, but no major conceptual changes were made to the strategy of relying on local forts, locally based troops, and climate to deter attackers.[96]

Madrid's emphasis on naval rearmament and the apparent success of Havana's existing fortifications in deterring English threats through the 1750s focused plans for land defenses on maintenance rather than new building. Royal engineer Carlos Desnaux reported to Cuban Captain General Francisco Güemes y Horcacitas in 1744 that the port was well guarded with its constellation of forts and batteries. What was most needed, he thought, were repairs and extensions to the city's wall. The portion facing the sea could not resist "half a day's attack" in its current condition.

In keeping with long-standing state policy that relied on strategic use of the enslaved to advance urgent projects, Desnaux thought royal slaves were underutilized because they were scattered around the city doing minor repairs. Instead, the king's slaves, "with whom all the works are done," should be quickly assigned to the wall to put the project in motion. The engineer also suggested specific repairs to the Punta fort and constant vigilance in keeping the fascines and forts' foundations well maintained against heavy rains. He contended that once the defense of the various land approaches to Havana had been "sharpened," enemy forces would be slowed sufficiently to allow the climate, so "contrary to the temperament of the English," to do its work. Nothing but a formal siege, he said, could take the city, a prescient conclusion.[97]

The new captain general appointed in 1747, Francisco Cagigal de la Vega, was less sanguine about the city's defenses. In November 1749, he informed the minister of the Indies that "there is no human force that could restrain enemies from possessing this precious prisoner," and he continued to recommend a major investment in fortification works for the next decade.[98]

The forts built at the end of the sixteenth century had made the mouth of the bay of Havana reasonably secure. The El Morro castle guarded the point of land facing the city across the bay, and the smaller La Punta fort guarded the point of land on the western side of bay's opening. The La Fuerza fort guarded the port area of the city proper. A serious problem was the high ground surrounding the capital. Three hills to the west provided potential sites for enemy artillery to dominate that approach to the city. Across the bay to the east, the largely undefended hill of La Cabaña overlooked Havana's strongest fort, El Morro.

Renewed war between France and England in 1753 gave greater urgency to plans for new fort construction to better secure the land approaches to Havana. Charles III's formal alliance with France through the Third Family Pact in August 1761 ensured Spain's entry into the global conflict that was the Seven Years' War. With open war imminent, Cagigal's replacement as captain general, Juan de Prado y Portocarrero, arrived in Cuba in 1760. He had wide-ranging instructions to deal with the insecurity posed by the undefended heights around the city, but ministerial disagreement had left to Prado the choice of beginning with the western hills or with La Cabaña. Two French engineers accompanied him to survey the city's fortifications and make proposals. One engineer, Francisco Ricaud, echoed Cagigal's dismal judgment: "Tears will be shed much too late if this tragedy is not remedied . . . If Havana is not secured, the American colonies will fall of their own weight, without New Spain being able to subsist." Ricaud identified the construction of a major fort on La Cabaña as most urgent, and Prado agreed.[99] Such a fort would stall land forces of an enemy and reduce them to harrying tactics, allowing time for climate and disease to defeat the attackers.[100]

The island's perennial shortage of labor proved to be an obstacle to advancing the fortification of La Cabaña. When Prado reviewed the existing cohort of royal slaves and *forzados*, he found about three hundred people, too few to undertake the construction of a large fort. The crown promised to send troops, munitions, and tools to facilitate the project, but an outbreak of yellow fever in the summer of 1761 derailed labor recruitment. It felled the chief engineer, many of the Spanish troops and laborers, and the small contingent of slaves.[101] Prado requested that the viceroy of New Spain send him as many prisoners as could be spared and authorized two Havana residents to purchase slaves in Jamaica. Neither effort recruited many workers, though a group of prisoners from Veracruz brought some relief.

Britain declared war against Spain in January 1762, but even six months later little had been accomplished on the fort project—some trees had been cleared from La Cabaña hill, and part of a ramp to facilitate the movement of materials had been started. Prado had greater success fulfilling his charge to restore and mount all the artillery of the plaza, which had fallen into serious disrepair. After a thorough inventory, Havana workshops built gun carriages and cannon supports and repaired artillery for the El Morro and La Punta forts and the city's batteries.[102]

This modest accomplishment, however, would not save the city. When a British invasion force of more than two hundred ships and a combined total of more than 28,000 men, including 2,400 enslaved Africans, appeared off Havana in June 1762, the city and its defenders were woefully unprepared.[103] Contemporaries and later historians have given many reasons for the city's vulnerability: poor judgment and leadership by officials in Havana, poor training of the local militia, lack of ammunition for troops and artillery, and a lack of fortifications on the hills surrounding the city. All of these problems played a role, but the decisive failure to secure the high ground in Havana's outskirts, especially at La Cabaña, was a direct result of failure to marshal the necessary labor to build fortifications there—a strategic error that the crown had to remedy speedily after losing Havana to a British siege and occupation.

The British Attack

On June 6, 1762, a combined force of the British army and navy arrived off Cojímar, about six miles to the east of Havana. By the next afternoon, the British had landed their troops. Overcoming the slight resistance of Cuban defenders stationed in an old tower in Cojímar, the British army began its westward advance on El Morro, the largest of the Cuban fortresses guarding the city's harbor. With covering fire from British ships positioned offshore, the army continued to advance over the next several days, crossing the Cojímar River and taking the town of Guanabacoa, about three miles to the east of Havana.[104]

On June 7, Cuban Captain General Prado belatedly called together a Junta de Guerra (war council) to direct the defense operations. Over the next four days, close to 2,000 people evacuated the city, the beginning of a flood of evacuees that may have totaled 30,000 in all.[105] A contingent of cavalry and troops was sent to halt the British advance in the east, but they were easily scattered by fire from the British ships offshore. Prado ordered parapets and batteries to be erected and trenches dug on the hill of La Cabaña. He also ordered the extramural area west of the city to be burned to deprive the enemy of wooded cover in the western land approaches to the city.

A particularly ill-fated measure was the sinking of several large men-of-war in the mouth of the harbor to prevent a British entry into the port. A similar measure had been used successfully to defend Cartagena de Indias in 1741, but the geography of Havana's port should have dissuaded Prado from applying it there. It is unlikely that the British would have risked their ships in such a narrow channel guarded by the three forts, El Morro and La Punta at the bay's mouth, and the Fuerza in the channel. Instead, the sinkings trapped eighteen warships of Havana's squadron within the harbor and gave the British free rein offshore to import and transfer supplies and reinforcements and to open a new offensive front west of the city.[106]

By June 9, British troops were camped all along the shore area between Cojímar and El Morro. A British officer in the invasion party wrote in his journal that the fort could be successfully attacked if "the ships were not exposed to the fire of the *puntal-fort* and *batteries* on the western side, and that such a diversion from the ships would facilitate our approaches."[107] Although the officer's optimism was ultimately borne out, the British were to pay a high price for taking El Morro.

By June 11, a British force had attacked and taken possession of the heights of La Cabaña, to the south of El Morro. Another naval expedition had sailed west of Havana, made a landing, and subdued the small fortress at the mouth of the Chorrera River, ensuring a water supply for the invading forces and undermining that of the city. In spite of the fact that the Spanish were well aware of the importance of the heights of La Cabaña to the defense of the city, the invaders had established themselves there with little resistance.[108]

On June 29, Spanish Captain General Prado belatedly sent a contingent of six hundred men across the bay to try to burn out the British batteries, but they were repulsed, with heavy Spanish losses. Within three days of landing, the British effectively dominated an arc to the seaward sides of the city, anchored in the hills to the east and west. With their construction of a battery on the heights of La Cabaña, British artillery bombarded the city, its harbor, and defenses from land and sea for forty-eight days.[109]

From mid-June onward, Havana's remaining hope was the strength of El Morro and the invading forces' susceptibility to tropical diseases. As the British had planned, they caught the Spanish in Havana largely unprepared and quickly controlled all but the southern approaches to the city. However, it soon became obvious to British commanders that the laws of European warfare in the Caribbean might undermine this engagement as well. The attacking forces began to succumb to yellow fever, in combination with other "fluxes and fevers" to which Europeans in the tropics were prone.[110]

By the beginning of July, early British optimism had been substantially muted by the difficulties of the siege. As an officer remarked in his journal, "The *Morro* was now found to be *tuffer work* and the *Spaniards more resolute than was at first imagined. Our people grew fatigued by the heat and hard labour, and want of water near them was a sensible distress.*"[111] The Spaniards in El Morro continued to fight with considerable vigor, repelling enemy advances at close range with rifle fire and hand grenades.[112] The fort's large guns also maintained a withering barrage, in part due to the fierce fighting of men of color. As the same British officer noted, "The fire of the enemy was rather superior to ours, as they were very brisk in remounting their canon [sic], and had many slaves at work."[113]

In fact, both sides employed enslaved people of African descent in this conflict. The British expedition commanders had had orders to purchase slaves in Martinique and some of the smaller islands, along with forming a group of slaves commandeered in Jamaica for the Havana campaign.[114] Once in Cuba, "five mulattoes, eighty-four negroes, and one Indian" deserted the Spanish to join the British attackers in exchange for their freedom.[115]

On the Spanish side, in addition to the enslaved helping work the artillery in El Morro, on June 26 a group of thirteen privately owned slaves who were in the fort carried out a raid on a British advance party, with "machetes in hand," killing one, taking seven prisoner, and putting the rest to flight. The crown ultimately rewarded their brave service with a grant of freedom. The group's leader, the African-born enslaved man Andres Gutierrez, was manumitted and later commanded a company of Havana's black militia.[116] Also in late June, Captain General Prado recruited a squad of one hundred privately owned slaves. One historian credits them with capturing some pieces of British artillery and killing at least two hundred of the invaders.[117]

Havana also was defended by companies of local militia, among them several companies of free militiamen of color. British officers commented on the high numbers of militiamen of color in the several engagements with Spanish defenders. The officer quoted earlier described the force of about six hundred men that came across the bay to try to burn out the British batteries as consisting of "mostly Mulatos and Negros, with some seamen."[118] On July 18, Havana militia forces and the enslaved attached to their units overcame the British batteries at Taganana, put the British troops to flight, and took eighteen British prisoners, who were sent to the city as prizes of the engagement. Again the bravery of 104 of the enslaved participating in this raid was rewarded with a grant of liberty.[119] The militiamen fighting to the east of Havana against the bulk of British forces fared worse, however. During their ill-fated attack to try and retake La Cabaña on July 22, they suffered heavy losses. A British officer described the group: "These poor wretches, . . . left above 400 dead upon the spot, many wounded and about seventy prisoners."[120]

Even with the disarray of Spanish troops and Cuban militiamen, by late July nearly 5,000 British army troops and 3,000 of the naval contingent were unfit for duty, the vast majority lost to sickness rather than injuries.[121] The British siege was revived by 1,400 reinforcements from the British North American colonies, who began arriving on July 27, and a new strategy of mining the foundations of El Morro.[122]

Finally, at two o'clock on the afternoon of July 30, a mine in the northeast bastion of El Morro exploded, sending the sentries flying. The British took advantage of the initial panic provoked by the explosion to scale the walls with ladders and storm the fort. The invading British put to death hundreds of the fort's defenders, many of whom were men of color.[123] With El Morro in British hands, the Spanish had little recourse but to evacuate and then shell the fort from the western banks of the bay, reducing much of it to rubble. As the British now completely controlled the eastern banks of the harbor, they proceeded to finish the battery on the Cabaña heights. After Captain General Prado refused to surrender on August 10, the British shelled the city. By three o'clock on the afternoon on August 11, flags of truce appeared all over Havana and Prado asked for a cease-fire.[124]

The siege claimed a heavy toll on both sides. The Spanish garrison ended the fight with only 631 veteran soldiers; the naval squadron with 735 men.[125] Victory came not a moment too soon for the British. By August 11, one officer's battalion was so weakened that "we have not above 150 men fit for duty."[126] Of the 5,366 men from the British army who died, 4,708 of them succumbed to disease. Of 4,668 naval casualties, only sixty-eight died in battle. Though yellow fever had saved numerous Spanish American cities attacked by the British in the eighteenth century (among them, Cartagena de Indias and Santiago de Cuba), it failed to rescue Havana in time.[127] Great Britain's willingness and ability to send such a large invading force and to continue to reinforce it over the course of the two-month siege helped the British to prevail. But for Spain, the British victory threw into sharp relief the misuse and overextension of Spanish resources in the face of Britain's growing military and naval strength.

The British Occupation
The terms of defeat and occupation were not draconian, but the additional losses must have rubbed salt in the wounds of the embattled Spanish Empire. The articles of capitulation, signed on August 11, gave the British possession of the town and the port of Havana but maintained the Catholic religion and preserved the

Catholic Church's goods and property. Most *habaneros* were allowed to remain in their homes, to continue to exercise their various occupations, and to enjoy the free use of their goods.[128]

The losses to the crown, however, were substantial and particularly painful, given the defense and development objectives of the early Bourbons over the first half of the eighteenth century. The resurgent Spanish navy lost thousands of men, twelve warships, three frigates, and several small boats. Then the British burned the ships under construction in the shipyard.[129] Any silver or tobacco belonging to the Spanish crown now belonged to the British. All the *esclavos del rey* were to be turned over to people designated by the British commander of the city.[130] The bitterest pill may have been the confiscation of more than 1.8 million pesos in silver and trade goods belonging to the Spanish royal treasury, the Royal Company of Havana, and merchants in Spain.[131]

Many historians of Cuba have viewed the occupation as the moment when the Spanish mercantilist monopoly was effectively broken by the British declaration of free trade in Havana's port. According to this view, free trade stimulated sugar expansion, particularly by providing free access to the Atlantic slave trade. Later work by historians suggests that the occupation merely made visible expansion and trade that had been proceeding illegally under the Spanish. In fact, as early as 1740, the crown had begun to allow Cuban sugar tax-free access to the Spanish market, which encouraged expansion and provided protection from international fluctuations in price. There also had been many decades of interaction among the peoples of the British and Spanish empires, with Havana as a hub.[132]

With regard to the effect of the British occupation on the importation of enslaved Africans to Havana, the number of the enslaved in the city in the 1760s, and of royal slaves, is difficult to determine exactly. In the mid-1750s, the population of the entire island was probably around 160,000, with perhaps one-quarter of those people being enslaved. The population of Havana was around 35,000 people, with a somewhat larger portion of slaves. Estimates of the number of enslaved Africans imported through Havana during the British occupation, from 1762 to 1763, are 3,000 to 4,000 persons, though not all of these enslaved people stayed in Havana after being sold.[133] As we will see in the next chapter, the Spanish state moved quickly to increase the city's enslaved population for fort building by more than 4,000 people when the occupation ended in the summer of 1763, suggesting that slave imports under the British were not uniquely large or transformative.[134]

The early Bourbon monarchs made some progress toward their goals of better defense and greater economic development in Cuba up to 1760. Shipbuilding was booming and tobacco and sugar production were both generating more revenue for the state. All of these initiatives had been accomplished with only modest innovations in state policy with regard to slave trading, through the Royal Company of Havana, and with little change in patterns of state enslavement in the shipyard. Where innovation was needed but not enacted was in marshaling the resources to rapidly construct fortifications in the hills surrounding the city. This shortsightedness ultimately opened the way for the British victory in 1762.

If the British occupation was not the transformative event on all fronts that some have claimed, it did reinforce existing trends toward the expansion of slavery and sugar production in Cuba. Additionally, the occupation did have a transformative effect on Bourbon defensive strategy and its implementation, especially in terms of labor recruitment. The poor leadership and misfortune of Captain General Prado and others was punished by the crown, but the investigation into the causes of the defeat also brought to light convincing evidence of the necessity for a new, comprehensive plan of defense for Cuba, the completion of which required a large-scale resort to state slavery.

3

FORTIFYING HAVANA, 1763–1790

Before the British occupation in 1762, Spain's strategy for defending Havana by land relied on its garrison soldiers and local militia, along with a system of three forts at the entrance to the port, a fortified wall surrounding the city proper, and a protective line of minor batteries and guard towers along the coast to the east and west of the city.[1] The funding and the labor required to build, maintain, and man these defenses had been cobbled together by the crown and colonial administrators in Cuba over two hundred years, using a circuit of monies and people that flowed around the circum-Caribbean and across the Atlantic from Spain as availability, costs, and urgency allowed. The capitulation of Havana to the British was humiliating proof of the inadequacies of this system by the mid-eighteenth century.

Defense concerns had informed the Bourbons' program of colonial reform since the early 1700s, along with efforts to centralize and rationalize the administration of the Indies. The Bourbons also were keen to foment the economic development of the American colonies and increase revenue, in part to sustain needed improvements in colonial defenses. The extremity of Havana's vulnerability, and the likelihood of renewed hostilities, finally spurred officials in Spain to reform Cuba's permanent garrison and militias; some changes also were made at the navy yard. Still, preparations of Havana's arsenal and military units for renewed war did not require an extensive employment of royal slaves. Instead, the state relied on more common patterns of employing squads of specialized slaves for specific tasks in ship and fort construction, at the docks, in the tobacco factory, and in state warehouses and offices.

After the British occupation, the navy yard returned to using the largely free labor force that had carried out shipbuilding in Havana since the sixteenth century, with small squads of royal slaves assigned to tasks such as cutting and preparing wood and carpentry. For the new land defenses planned for Havana, however, the crown sought to avoid the lengthy delays and shortages of workers and supplies that had hindered earlier projects by assuming direct oversight of the repairs and fort construction around the city, beginning in 1763.[2] The returning Spanish captain general, the Count of Ricla, was charged with quickly organizing the necessary resources for this work, including thousands of workers, most of whom, in the initial stages, were to be king's slaves.

This extensive resort to state enslavement in the 1760s was unique in Cuba's experience with the state as a slave owner. Though brief, this extraordinary moment in the history of state enslavement in Cuba had far-reaching effects on slave trading and ownership in the private sector and on the island's economic development more generally. The state's massive fort building projects after the British occupation also necessitated particularly harsh work regimes for crown slaves in Cuba, which muted earlier patterns of royal paternalism and the opportunities to pursue freedom. By the 1770s, the state returned to the more strategic and limited use of workers enslaved by the king that had characterized fort building since the sixteenth century, supplementing the fort's workforce with convicts and levies of free workers—a pattern of labor organization that would characterize public works in Havana into the nineteenth century. But the reforms of defense and development strategies and practices initiated the rapid increase of importations of enslaved Africans into Cuba, expanded plantation production, and transformed the state's relationships with its subjects, both free and enslaved.

First Steps, 1763–1765

The Spanish crown initiated a multifaceted program of review and reform in Madrid even before the peace to end the Seven Years' War was concluded in 1763. Charles III consolidated and centralized ministerial control by establishing the Junta de Ministros, uniting the ministers of state, war, finance, the navy, and the Indies in weekly sessions to evaluate and reform colonial policy.[3] Another part of the crown's review included a court of inquiry into the capitulation of Havana, as the defeated Captain General Prado and the rest of the Junta de Guerra on the island were ordered back to Spain. Prado's inept leadership was clearly an important factor in the loss of Havana, and some of his military decisions seem questionable in hindsight. His inability to keep La Cabaña's heights out of British hands ultimately allowed them to take El Morro. Yet the building of a major fort on La Cabaña required a huge infusion of funds, labor, and materials, all of which Prado was unable to secure during his short tenure on the island.[4] The fort of El Morro had taken twenty years to build; Prado had been given barely one year. While the captain general was ultimately convicted of negligence, the investigation also brought to light convincing evidence of the need for a new, comprehensive plan of defense for Cuba.[5]

The general outlines of this defense plan were in place by the time the Treaty of Paris was signed, in February 1763. In contrast to Spain's former administrative policies, which encouraged overlapping jurisdictions and lengthy consultation, the king appointed the Count of Ricla as captain general of Cuba, with wide-ranging powers to reorganize and improve the island's defenses, both its fortifications and its armed forces.[6] The new plan included Ricla's bold proposal for the better arming and training of the colonists as disciplined militias to create a large, effective reserve force at a lower cost. This proposal risked a significant shift in political and military power to the colonials, but Spain's vast commitments and limited resources allowed few other options.[7]

Repairing and expanding the land fortifications of Havana were, in some ways, the most difficult operations, especially in terms of recruiting the necessary manpower. In the island's labor market of chronic shortage, wages for all kinds of work remained high. Forcing free colonists to do the backbreaking work of fort building, or commandeering privately owned slaves over many years, could have sown the seeds of rebellion, an outcome that the crown was keen to avoid after coming so close to losing the island. The plan to build three new forts, with La Cabaña slated to be one of the largest in the empire, plus repairs to El Morro and the city's wall, would require thousands of workers just to get started. Pools of coerced laborers in those numbers could only be procured quickly through the Atlantic slave trade.

Charles III and his ministers were, therefore, acutely aware of the high costs involved in their desire to militarize and better fortify Cuba. The crown's plans for Cuba included a careful review of its population, economy, trade, and development potential. Returning Spanish administrators also sought to conciliate and co-opt Cuban colonists into greater responsibility for their own defense, offering rewards and incentives to join the new militia companies and asking them to pay higher taxes in return for commercial concessions.

The first of Ricla's instructions was to oversee the evacuations of the British from Cuba and of the Spanish from Florida. Once in possession of the island, he was to begin immediate repair of the city's fortifications and to undertake the reorganization of the military forces on the island. The king and his administrators knew that sufficient manpower would be crucial to both these efforts, so while Ricla's instructions were similar to those given his predecessors, he had far more authority to enact policies that would speed recruitment.[8]

The count arrived in Havana in late June 1763 and moved quickly to discharge his duties. From July 7 to July 10, English forces were evacuated from Havana. By late July, Ricla was writing to the minister of the Indies, Julián de Arriaga, about his initial efforts to organize the fortification projects. The king had promised the new captain general at least twelve engineers, plus funds and *forzados* from New Spain. To offset the extreme shortage of skilled workers on the island, Ricla requested that 120 masons and forty stonecutters be sent from Spain as quickly as possible.[9] Rather than granting the *asiento* for slave importation to a single person or company, the king also authorized the captain general to purchase slaves on royal account through whatever channels necessary, "in foreign colonies or transported from the coast of Guinea in shipments under my flag, or foreign ones, on commission, or contract with some of my subjects or their companies, extending [these shipments] even to the precise provision of private residents of the Island, whose estates must lack so much of this help due to the late war."[10] The extremity of Havana's defense needs in 1763 gave Ricla the crown's permission to act directly as a slave buyer for the state and to facilitate the sale of enslaved workers to private individuals as well.

Ricla did have access to some enslaved laborers on his arrival in Cuba, but their numbers were small, given the massive fortification projects on his agenda. Eight *esclavos del rey* were evacuated to Havana from Saint Augustine, Florida, in late 1763 as part of the transfer of power to the British.[11] The crown also owned small groups of enslaved people in various state enterprises around Havana—the tobacco factory, the shipyard, and the existing forts. In 1761, before the British invasion, the crown had approved a proposal by Spanish trader José Villanueva Pico to import up to 1,000 slaves per year to Cuba, but the war had interrupted fulfillment of the contract. Over objections by the Royal Company of Havana, Villanueva's agent, José Uque de Osorio, was ultimately able to import some 697 enslaved people, from 1763 to 1765, who were purchased on royal account.[12]

Some *habaneros* were also eager to support the new defense efforts by offering funds and workers. Ricla was able to begin the clearing of trees from the hill of La Cabaña with seven hundred workers, many of them slaves donated by neighboring sugar plantation owners for a period of two months.[13] Still, the captain general had access to only five hundred or six hundred enslaved workers specifically for fortification work in the first month following his arrival in Cuba, a number wholly inadequate for the state's defense needs.

On August 1, 1763, Ricla issued a proclamation soliciting proposals to increase the numbers of enslaved Africans brought to the island.[14] One response was a contract offered in that same month by one Nicolas Colonado, who proposed bringing four hundred to five hundred slaves over four months. He would sell to the crown at 180 pesos each, while the public would pay 270 pesos for *piezas* (adults), 240 for *mulecones* (youths), and 200 for *muleques* (children).[15] In another contract proposal, Colonado agreed to deliver to the king 3,000 enslaved people, adults and youths, at 145 pesos over two years, and 2,000 to the public over four years at 265 pesos for adults, 235 pesos for youths, and 200 pesos for children. In addition, he would be allowed to export molasses, paying only a 5 percent tax, and would have exclusive rights to import flour at two barrels per enslaved person imported, for the duration of the contract.[16]

The main terms of this proposal appeared in most of the others put forth at this time—slave sales to the crown at close to half the price proposed for public sales, and concessions to traders to import commodities such as flour and to export tropical products such as molasses free of duties or only lightly taxed. Another striking feature of these proposals was the preponderance of English and Irish traders involved in some part of the process of delivering enslaved people to Havana. Since Spain did not have factories on the coast of West Africa before the end of the eighteenth century, its colonists had to rely on foreign traders to supply them with slaves.[17] Trade had to pass through the hands of Spanish and Cuban merchants to comply with Spanish commercial regulations, which raised retail prices of most commodities, including slaves.[18]

Although British troops had left Cuba by mid-July 1763, a number of British merchants were allowed by treaty to remain as they wound up their business affairs on the island. Some offered their services to the Royal Company of Havana as importers of slaves, a boon for the company, since it had lost the state tobacco monopoly and faced greater competition from private traders.[19] Among their most ambitious proposals was a contract by the Irish slave trader Cornelius Coppinger for the introduction of 7,000 enslaved workers through the RCH over a period of fifteen months.[20] There were to be 3,000 of the enslaved for the fortification works (1,000 *piezas* and 2,000 *mulecones*) at 150 pesos each, and 4,000 more for sale to the public. To speed the fortification projects, the company proposed importing five hundred enslaved workers immediately, then two shipments of 1,500 slaves each over six months, and 3,000 over the final six months.[21] The crown resisted allowing Coppinger to import such large numbers of slaves "in order that English commerce not become rooted in these places,"[22] but the king's desire for long-term exclusion of English merchants from Cuban trade rested on the fiction that British merchants were not already firmly entrenched and even indispensable. The fortification projects would have been impossible without English traders' contracts for slaves and for supplies such as flour and bricks.[23]

The RCH, via its British contractors, did introduce more than 5,000 slaves through Havana between December 1763 and the end of 1764. Other, smaller contracts brought another 2,300 slaves to the city through 1765. Therefore, legal imports to the city were close to 8,000 slaves, while contraband trading probably introduced more.[24] Of this total, more than half (4,359) were purchased by the crown for work in the fortifications and came from the following sources:

Royal Company of Havana (through various contractors)	2,716 slaves
Cornelius Coppinger	938
Salillès	8
Joseph Uque	697
Total	4,359 slaves

The vast majority of these new royal slaves (3,959) were men, compared to four hundred women, indicating that the work to be required of them was exceptionally heavy physical labor.[25]

If only about 3,200 enslaved people were imported during the eleven-month British occupation, largely due to Albemarle's profiteering and restrictions on slave sales, earlier historiography's emphasis on the transformative nature of the occupation is incorrect. The figures here for the state's demand for enslaved labor for imperial defense works from 1763 to 1765 was a greater stimulus to imports of enslaved workers in both policy and practice than British free trade and sugar expansion under the occupation had been.[26]

Even though Ricla had been able to purchase enslaved workers at reduced prices for the crown (at an average price of 150 pesos each, a 25 to 50 percent reduction from contemporaneous slave prices), slave purchases still averaged more than 50 percent of the total expenses at the fortification projects during his tenure (table 3.1).[27]

Table 3.1. State Purchases of Slaves for Fort Works, 1763–1765

Year	Slaves purchased	Average price (pesos)	Total (pesos)	Total (reales)	Total annual expenses	Percentage of reales
1763	795	150	119,250	954,000	1,560,875.12	61
1764	1,967	150	295,050	2,362,420	4,445,192.12	53
1765	1,436	140.8	202,235	1,617,864	3,800,320.21	43
Totals	4,198		616,684	4,934,304	9,806,387.45	50

Source: Estado of the expenses and costs of the fortification works of Havana from July 7, 1763, to December 31, 1772, Archive General de Indias, Santo Domingo, 2129. For monetary equivalencies, see John Robert McNeill, *Atlantic Empires of France and Spain: Louisbourg and Havana, 1700–1763* (Chapel Hill: University of North Carolina Press, 1985), 212.

Note: The figures for the number of slaves purchased and their total value in reales are taken from this estado. A footnote to the estado states that the slaves were purchased at prices of 130, 150, and 156 pesos, but since there is no way to determine how many slaves were purchased at the different prices, an average is provided here. The estado's final total in reales has been preserved in the table, though it differs slightly from the total obtained by using the average prices. One peso = eight reales de vellón.

Given this large influx of the enslaved to the city, Ricla also had to organize and fund their maintenance. He wrote numerous letters seeking imports of fabric from Spain for slaves' clothing and contracts with private individuals to provide food for the state's workforce. He made arrangements to set up a new hospital to care for the growing numbers of ill and injured royal slaves and convicts, who were not being adequately cared for in existing facilities. The hospital was staffed with a doctor, two surgeons, three bloodletters, an aide, and a chaplain. The state also assigned an interpreter to help recently arrived enslaved Africans communicate with their doctors. At times, the crown replaced some of the medical personnel with prisoner attendants as a cost reduction measure, though in 1764 the cost of the new hospital alone reached 203,129 reales, or 6 percent of total expenses.[28]

As the crown's defense plan increased the number of soldiers assigned to Havana's garrison, a small group of men enslaved by the king were assigned to the Royal Hospital of San Ambrosio, which cared for sick and injured troops. Records of these employees and servants include the names of the royal slaves assigned there in the late 1760s, a rarity in officials' accounting. The list offers a glimpse of possible backgrounds of some of the enslaved Africans in royal service in this period. In the year 1768, the group consisted of seven to nine men, four or five of whom bore Christian first names and African ethnonyms as surnames: Gerónimo, Martin, and Francisco Caravalí; Antonio Congo; and Joseph María Gangá. Martín Caravalí also was identified as a royal slave imprisoned in the quarters of the enslaved artillerymen of Havana, who will be discussed in chapter 4.[29]

Such ethnonyms often represented broad geographic areas in West Africa and the western part of Central Africa, where enslaved Africans were forcibly embarked to the Americas. The Slave Voyages database estimates that 4,100 enslaved people called Caravalí embarked from ports in the Bight of Biafra, bound for Cuba, over the 1751–1775 period. An estimated 3,300 enslaved people called Lucumí embarked from the area that is now southwestern Nigeria, bound for Cuba, over the same period. Smaller numbers of enslaved people, roughly 1,200, called Gangá, embarked from the area of present-day Sierra Leone, Liberia, and the Windward Coast areas, headed to Cuba, over the twenty-five-year period.[30]

The Count of Ricla's first six months in office also included reviews to assess the service and loyalty of Havana residents during the British siege and occupation.[31] Under Ricla, four titles of Castile were awarded to leading white creoles for their service to the Spanish cause during the British siege and occupation. Another was granted in 1766.[32] The captain general was also keen to reward enslaved people who had extended extraordinary service to the crown during the fighting. Since the defeated Captain General Prado had not been able to fully reward all deserving slaves and their owners, he asked Ricla to complete this task. The king gave Ricla the authority to extend liberty to others among the enslaved who could verify their equally distinguished bravery and service.[33]

The captain general issued a proclamation ordering the 118 enslaved people freed by Prado and their owners to present themselves at the city's government office to certify their grants of freedom. He also called for any slaves who had been badly injured in the siege to appear, along with their owners. So many slaves appeared that Ricla appointed his close aide, Field Marshal Alejandro O'Reilly, to continue the review and to judge the merits of the enslaved people who came forward.[34] Ricla clearly attached importance to both the review process and to public recognition of extraordinary service and sacrifice to the state by slaves, though he ultimately denied the requests of many of the enslaved.

In this initial round, 128 slaves were declared free and were given individual letters of freedom, 118 by Prado and ten more by Ricla, in a first round of review. Three of the freed were so badly maimed as to be "incapable of seeking their sustenance" and were awarded a state maintenance allowance of one real per day.[35] A list with all the names of the manumitted, confirming their free status, was posted in the market square in the Plaza Nueva. This public recognition induced even more slaves to come forward, and Ricla investigated their claims carefully. From this newest group, he identified thirteen more, four of whom were granted full liberty for having been injured during the siege. Three of these four freed men were so severely wounded, "missing legs and arms and one full of wounds," that in addition to their freedom, the state granted them one real per day payment because they were permanently disabled.[36]

For the remaining nine, Ricla adapted the Cuban custom of *coartación*, which recognized a state of partial freedom, to reward six deserving slaves who were "not entirely disabled by different wounds and blows." He granted them partial freedom, "assign[ing them] . . . half of their value so that in this part they would be free, thus providing that their owners, conforming to the custom of this Country, would enjoy from them only half of their service." To the other three slaves who were already *coartados*, Ricla awarded thirty pesos each.[37] Ultimately, the Spanish state rewarded as many as 175 slaves who had fought during the siege.[38]

Ricla's respect for an enslaved person's right to partial freedom upon payment of a portion of their price shows that this aspect of the practice of *coartación* was well established in Cuba by the mid-eighteenth century. Enslaved people continued to claim this right until the end of slavery on the island, in 1886, though private slave owners sometimes contested it vigorously. The state, on the other hand, saw the value to Cuba's defense of rewarding with their freedom, wholly or in part, the enslaved who fought against the British invasion.[39]

Ricla's public awards to slaves who fought during the siege were part of the overall defense plan for the city, as he hoped they would "be a greater stimulus to others" to serve the king as renewed warfare loomed. Since all of the enslaved people freed after the occupation were privately owned slaves, the captain general was also careful to compensate owners whose slaves were killed during the fighting or were thereafter freed by the state. Owners were paid 200 pesos 4 reales per freed person. Some owners demonstrated their loyalty by ceding their slaves' value to the king; others accepted compensation in the form of new slaves or cash.[40]

Commercial Reform

Besides a swift demonstration of the returning Spanish administration's willingness to reward loyal slave owners, Ricla also moved quickly to begin consultations with the Havana elite on commercial reform. Charles III's new minister of finance and war, the Marquis of Esquilache, was determined to effect a thoroughgoing reform of the tax system to fund military reform and expansion. In the fall of 1763, Ricla drafted Father Ignacio Tomás Butler, a well-known Jesuit, to initiate conversations with thirty of Havana's leading families on the subject of economic development on the island and the possibility of raising more revenue through higher taxes. Ricla first sent Butler to convey these objectives to prominent habaneros individually, as a way to gauge their response. With clear signs that changes would be accepted, Butler arranged a collective meeting to discuss more concrete ways to fund Cuban defense. Ultimately, this group voted not to advance any particular plan of reform, "preferring to put themselves in the King's hands" and have him initiate a proposal to which they could then respond. They also agreed to reconvene to examine whatever proposal came forth.[41]

Ricla was heartened by the Havana elite's response and reported to Esquilache that he saw no reason to call a second consultation session. People were "already convinced that one way or another" they would have to fund their own defense, and it was now up to the king to elect the means. The captain general then appointed Joseph Gelabert, a royal treasury official in Havana, to prepare a report on possible ways to raise the necessary funds.[42]

As another part of the effort to understand Cuba's economic potential, Field Marshal O'Reilly left Havana in January 1764 to reorganize militia companies throughout the island, with the additional charge to carry out a visita, or inspection of the island and its resources. His review acquainted him with "how much this precious Island could contribute to the power of the Monarchy and the happiness of Spain" and with the "principal causes of its backwardness." According to O'Reilly, most of Cuba's problems related to trade and the restrictions imperial policy had imposed upon it. In particular, he cited "the dearness, and scarcity of

Negroes, due to the duties that the King exacts, and much more for the contracts, and formalities, that are observed for their introduction."[43]

O'Reilly thought that economic advancement in Cuba would be impossible without the increased importation of enslaved Africans, "since they are the only ones who work in sugar mills, clearing forests, and in the care of livestock." He was particularly harsh in his condemnation of policies that required the slave trade to pass through Spanish hands, since Spain had no factories on the coast of Africa. Most of the slaves imported to the island came in foreign ships anyway, and the Royal Company of Havana, or the Spanish contractor, did little more than add to the market price of slaves by charging "fourteen or more pesos per slave . . . for [simply] lending his name." Therefore, O'Reilly recommended emulating the French, English, and Dutch, whose colonies also relied heavily on enslaved labor, and ending restrictions and duties on the slave trade. The king, he felt, would extract far more revenue from taxes on local products than on the laborers so necessary to produce those goods.[44]

Changes to Slave Trading

O'Reilly's recommendations for increasing the slave trade to the island were already being at least partially implemented in 1764, under Ricla, to rapidly re-cruit a labor force for the fortification projects, yet the crown proved reluctant to open the trade completely to foreigners over the next twenty years. Instead, with the departure of Ricla in 1765, the king sought to engage more Spanish subjects directly in slave trading by granting an exclusive *asiento* to the Company of the Royal Asiento of Black Slaves (also known as the Gaditana Company, since many of its founding members lived in the port of Cádiz).

The many provisions of the company's *asiento* suggest that the crown had sev-eral objectives in granting the monopoly. One was the further development of the languishing colony of Puerto Rico. The company was required to set up its main slave repository and distribution center there until 1772 (thereafter it moved to Havana) and to offer slaves to Puerto Rican buyers at reduced prices. This aspect of the company's charge had little success, as the repository's facilities were often inadequate to house and care for hundreds of enslaved people at one time, leading to high mortality rates. The company also found itself short of the necessary ships to distribute to other Spanish ports the slaves and the goods taken in payment.[45]

With the Gaditana Company's *asiento*, the crown also hoped to reduce the inroads foreign, especially English, slave traders had made in the provisioning of the Spanish colonies. The company tried outfitting expeditions directly to the coast of Africa in 1767 but found few factors there willing to trade, and prices were high when slaves were offered for sale. Company officials quickly realized that they would have to return to the more traditional position as intermediaries or distributors for foreign slave traders in Spanish colonial markets. Though the goal of cutting out foreign traders was never realized, the company was able to import somewhere between 23,000 and 24,000 enslaved Africans to Cuba during its years under royal contract, 1765 to 1779. The crown's more traditional policy on slave trading was less popular with the Havana elite than other aspects of commercial reform. They vigorously protested the new company's monopoly, complaining of high prices, uneven delivery of badly needed enslaved workers, and royal concessions granted to the company to import commodities such as flour.[46]

Other Changes in Commercial Policy

Changes in colonial trade and taxation policy were ultimately more to *habaneros'* liking, though it would require considerable negotiation. The expenses of the state's initial slave purchases between 1763 and 1765, along with the high costs of organizing defense works and maintaining the Havana garrison, prompted Madrid officials to move quickly to implement changes in tax policy. In response to a royal order in late April 1764, Ricla published a preliminary order establishing an increase in the *alcabala*, or sales tax, from 2 percent to 4 percent, along with some other changes in duties on specific goods such as the local liquors *aguardiente* and *sambumbía*.[47]

Wealthy *habaneros* were initially surprised at the quick pace of change and concerned that taxes had been raised without corresponding commercial concessions to help them pay those higher taxes. In the fall of 1764, they met often to draft a petition that detailed the changes they deemed indispensable, changes which echoed those proposed by OReilly's *visita* report. Ricla forwarded their proposal to Spain with his approval.[48]

By October 1765, deliberations on commercial reform in Madrid were concluded with two royal decrees that represented some significant concessions to Cuban interests.[49] There now could be free trade between Spain and its Caribbean colonies (although intracolonial trade was still banned). The Spanish ports of Alicante, Málaga, Cartagena, Barcelona, Santander, Gijón, La Coruña, Seville, and Cádiz all were allowed to trade with Havana. This commerce could be carried in either Spanish or Cuban ships. The partial reform of trade duties of 1764, which had converted older ones based on weight and volume to ad valorem duties, was extended as the *alcabala* rose again, from 4 percent to 6 percent.[50]

The new regulations were particularly advantageous to Cuban sugar interests. Old duties on sugar were abolished and replaced by the 6 percent *alcabala*, to be charged only once, at the time of sale or export. Cuban sugar now also had greater access to the Spanish market and, despite pressure from the French Bourbons, sugar from the French islands was refused privileged access to Spain.

Efforts to simplify taxes on slave imports were less successful. In the royal order of October 16, 1765, the king abolished the earlier *derecho de marca* tax on slave purchases, which he said had often raised prices by close to 15 percent. Fearful of a severe impact on the treasury if all duties were abolished, the king imposed an annual capitation, or head tax, to be collected every six months, on a sliding scale based on age and gender. The head tax proved so cumbersome and complicated that the crown and planters agreed to return to previous *derecho de marca* in 1767.[51]

After 1765, the new *alcabala* generated 40 to 50 percent of the island's revenues, and Cuba contributed a growing percentage of the revenue for its own defense. Yet the island continued to rely on subsidies to finance the bulk of its imperial obligations. Luckily for the empire's finances, royal revenues experienced considerable growth in New Spain during this period, with Mexican *situado* payments to Cuba running between 1 million and 2 million pesos per year into the early 1770s.[52]

Havana's Shipyard

Although the Spanish army garrison and local militia regiments bore most of the burden of the Spanish defeat at Havana, the siege and occupation were also a serious setback for the Spanish navy and its Havana shipyard. During the siege, Captain General Prado had ordered the sinking of several large men-of-war in the narrow channel at the entrance to Havana's port, trapping eighteen serviceable warships within the harbor.[53] The naval commissioner stationed in Havana, Lorenzo de Montalvo, had destroyed or dispersed much of the shipyard's stock of naval stores to deny the British access to them. During the occupation, the British then dismantled and sold virtually anything else of value.

This destruction ultimately opened the way for improvements in both the design and the function of the shipyard and its administration, once the city was returned to Spain in 1763. Montalvo redesigned the shipyard and rerouted the city's freshwater canal to pass through it, to power an enormous sawmill. With new docks and slipways, a new arsenal building, and a sawmill, Montalvo was able to salvage two hulls that had been under construction before the siege and to begin the work on a new ninety-four-gun ship.[54]

Naval account records for the period immediately following the British occupation also show administrative reforms designed to ensure greater crown control over the shipyard, rather than leaving naval construction to the interest and goodwill of private investors. Monies from New Spain's coffers were now assigned directly to a newly established naval treasury, opened in Havana in July 1763, rather than relying on private contractors for financing. By December of that year, Charles III had created a naval intendancy in Havana and appointed Lorenzo de Montalvo to the post. Montalvo now had the authority to oversee both the shipyard and the naval squadron stationed in Havana's harbor, and the crown ended the practice of contracting out the building of ships.[55]

For the rebuilding of the shipyard and the resumption of ship construction, the naval intendant recruited labor, much as the state had been recruiting labor for state projects for centuries. Some enslaved workers were purchased outright by the crown, and the prices paid for these slaves suggest that the crown was looking for skilled workers. One enslaved man, recorded as a sawyer, was purchased for 350 pesos. Two enslaved men were purchased for a wood contractor for 770 pesos each, indicating considerable value to the crown, although their specific occupations were not noted. Still, the numbers of the enslaved purchased directly by the crown for the navy seem to have been small, mostly purchased singly or in pairs.[56]

A handful of king's slaves taken by the British during the occupation were also bought back with crown funds after Havana was returned to Spain in June 1763. Two king's slaves were redeemed for 220 pesos each. Two others, listed as sawyers of the "Casta Caravalí," commanded the higher price of 407 pesos each.[57]

Besides direct purchases, the crown also hired enslaved workers from private owners as needed. For instance, in March 1764, Don Luis de Noriega was paid 541 reales for the labor of his enslaved man, Joseph Noriega, who had worked for almost seven months helping to clear the Rio de la Palma to ease the transport of logs to the shipyard. In April, the crown paid out 2,440 reales for privately owned slaves (although their exact number is not stated) who worked careening royal ships. For December 1764, there are payouts listed to a group of sawyers enslaved to private owners for their work on two gunships, the San Carlos and the San Fernando.[58]

The state also resorted to the criminal justice system to recruit forced laborers for Havana's shipyard. The naval accounts from 1763 to 1765 show periodic payouts of about fourteen pesos per person for the maintenance and transport of convicts sent from New Spain, sometimes in groups of as many as 120 men, to advance the projects.[59] Naval officials also tried to return the shipyard to a full labor contingent by hunting down military and naval deserters and enslaved and convict fugitives. The payments for the return of all types of fugitives were around forty reales, in most cases.[60] Clearly, recruiting convicts and catching fugitives cost the crown considerably less than the outright purchase of enslaved workers. All of these recruitment efforts, however, do not seem to have generated more than approximately 150 forced workers over about three years. The majority of the workers in the shipyard continued to be free laborers working for wages and their daily ration.

One of the most pressing tasks immediately after the return of Havana to Spain in June 1763 was the clearing of the bay. A mixed group of workers, about forty free navy seamen and about forty convicts and king's slaves, were assigned to remove the ships scuttled in the opening of the harbor during the siege.[61]

By the beginning of 1764, the naval accounts begin to show payouts to government contractors for the food and clothing rations of crown slaves and convicts employed in the shipyard and by the naval squadron. Through the figures given for these rations, it is possible to estimate roughly the numbers of enslaved workers and convicts employed in various types of work around the shipyard.[62] The largest group of royal slaves and convicts seems to have been employed in 1764, with a combined total of some 223 persons getting rations from the contractor. Small mixed groups were used in all aspects of the shipyard's operation—clearing channels, construction and repair of ships, sawing timbers, and carpentry and stonemasonry for new buildings. The largest payouts in the shipyard accounts went for the wages of carpenters, caulkers, and other skilled workmen involved in shipbuilding and in repairing or rebuilding the shipyard. While each of these groups most likely had enslaved people working with them in some capacity, most of the laborers in these professions were free.[63] The same pattern appears in the accounts of the naval squadron.[64]

Not only free workers and hired slaves received wages, however. The crown also rewarded its own enslaved laborers, in cash or in kind, for particularly valuable or extraordinary effort. In 1764, Joseph Columbra, a man enslaved by the king, was rewarded with a pair of shoes for his work in the care and cleaning of the accounting office of the arsenal.[65] In September of that year, Ignacio Congo and several companions, all king's slaves, received 485 reales for apprehending another king's slave, Raphael Congo, who had fled when the British took Havana in 1762. Later in the month, nine sawyers who were enslaved by the king received seven reales each for "extraordinary" night work while preparing timber for the ships the *San Carlos* and the *San Fernando*, reflecting the importance of woodworking to the rebuilding of the royal navy.[66] The most striking reward went to Francisco Xavier Cohimbra, a *carpintero de lo blanco* (joiner) enslaved by the king. For his exemplary service, he received "three shirts, three pairs of breeches, a jacket, a pair of shoes, and a pair of stockings" for his "continuous attendance, devotion, and application" to the work of building the water-powered sawmill in Havana's port.[67] Exemplary state service outside of battle could bring rewards of luxury items such as shoes and stockings or even cash, but not grants of freedom.

By the time the accounts for the shipyard and the naval squadron were combined under the supervision of a new treasurer general, in 1765, the number of people enslaved by the king and of convicts employed in both branches had fallen to around one hundred, rising slowly over the months of 1766 and reaching a high of 180 in December.[68] Clearly, the navy and the shipyard made wide use of royal slaves, but even after the devastation of the British siege and occupation, the shipyard was able to return to full production without a major reform of its time-honored practices of labor recruitment and deployment.

～

As Ricla's tenure drew to a close he had faithfully carried out the main tasks of his charge, but some problems remained. The plaza of Havana had been reclaimed and the English army evacuated, though excising their mercantile influence proved impossible.[69] Laborers and materials had been amassed and work had begun on implementing the refortification of the city. And in spite of some tense moments, the Havana elite had cooperated by donating funds and the labor of enslaved workers and by accepting higher taxes in return for greater commercial freedom.

Yet the rising costs of the defense projects quickly raised concerns among colonial officials. As early as 1764, Ricla and his superiors in Madrid were trying to find ways to reduce the costs of assigning royal slaves to various tasks. In response to crown instructions to better guard state warehouses and the custom-house, Ricla created a crew of twelve men enslaved by the king to staff a launch in the bay and monitor the loading and unloading of goods at the docks. To avoid incurring the cost their maintenance, the state planned to give these enslaved workers carts to move goods for private individuals, who would pay the royal treasury directly, creating a fund to support the launch and its crew.[70]

Another proposal suggested establishing a "colony" in the suburbs of Havana, populated by seven hundred male *esclavos del rey* and seven hundred females to marry them. These slaves would be available for labor in the fort works but would also "earn their livelihood with carts working in the city."[71] This plan does not seem to have been implemented, but it may have grown out of the crown's experience with the settled community of king's slaves in El Cobre, in eastern Cuba, which had relieved the crown of much of the cost of their maintenance and had provided a pool of people to fortify and defend the area as needed.[72] In any event, these special groups of royal slaves were small compared to the many assigned to the fort works in their initial stages.

The Fortification Projects, 1765–1769

By early spring of 1765, more than 2,000 workers were employed at the three main sites of fortification work around Havana. Even before such large and complex projects were fully under way, concerns were raised about oversight. Alejandro O'Reilly had been shocked by the disorder of the Cuban military's finances revealed during his *visita*. In December 1763, he had urged Esquilache to appoint an official who would rationalize and monitor military expenditures. By fall of 1764, the king had approved a plan to appoint an intendant, a new royal official, subordinate to the captain general but charged with the vital duties of managing the royal treasury on the island and the fortification projects. Cuba's first intendant, Miguel de Altarriba, took up his post in February 1765.[73]

As table 3.2 shows, when Altarriba arrived in Havana, the largest group of workers in the fort projects over 1765 was recently arrived, enslaved Africans (*bozales*). There was a much smaller group of Hispanized crown slaves (*ladinos*), so that royal slaves constituted between 55 percent and 68.3 percent of the total fortification workforce. Two other groups of enslaved workers were employed on the fortification projects in that year: a group of slaves who had fled the English, most probably during the occupation, and a smaller group of enslaved workers hired out by private owners. Free workers of color also constituted a very small group of the total workforce in 1765. Native Cubans or Spaniards who were designated by Spanish authorities as white (*paysanos*, as opposed to the free people of color designated as *mulatos* or *negros libres*) were a larger portion of the free workers at the forts. The only group whose numbers approached those of the recently arrived, enslaved Africans during 1765 was convict laborers.

Table 3.2. Workers on Fort Projects, March 1765–February 1766

Type of workers	March 1765	April 1765	May 1765	June 1765	July 1765	August 1765	Oct. 1765	Feb. 1766
Native Cubans	55	36	44	43	50	52	50	36
Prisoners	513	446	510	430	616	624	629	632
Free mulattos	23	18	20	22	19	20	16	17
Free blacks	20	16	21	23	30	31	30	29
Ladino royal slaves	13	12	13	13	11	13	13	15
Royal bozales slaves	1,429	1,217	1,352	1,303	1,511	1,473	1,399	1,334
Fugitive slaves	41	46	46	42	49	48	43	55
Slaves of private owners	16	18	18	18	18	20	12	13
Workers in hospital	NA	424	331	378	[375]	[375]	[443]	[237]
Total workers	2,110	2,233	2,355	2,272	2,304	2,281	2,192	2,163
Royal slaves as % of total	68.3%	55.0%	57.9%	57.9%	66.0%	65.1%	64.4%	62.3%
Prisoners as % of total	24.3%	19.9%	21.6%	18.9%	26.7%	27.3%	28.6%	29.2%
Free workers as % of total	4.6%	3.1%	3.6%	3.8%	4.2%	4.5%	4.3%	3.7%

Source: Review extracts of the king's slaves and others in the defense works of Havana, dated March 31, 1765; April 24, 1765; May 28, 1765; June 30, 1765; July 31, 1765; August 24, 1765; October 27, 1765, Archive General de Indias, Santo Domingo, 1647. Review extract for February 23, 1766, Archivo General de Simancas, Secretaría y Superintendencia de Hacienda, 2344.

Note: The numbers of workers in the hospital from July 1765 through October 1765 and for February 1766 are bracketed here because they were not separated out of the other categories by the compilers of the summary tables in those months. Their numbers were reported in the written summaries.

Clearly, enslaved Africans, recently purchased through the Atlantic slave trade, had been crucial to Ricla's plan to quickly reinforce the battered defenses of Havana. Free workers, black and white, were never more than 5 percent of the total workforce. They were usually skilled workers hired to do the careful work of stonecutting and masonry. Because the bulk of the work, especially at the beginning of the projects, involved heavy, unskilled labor, the state resorted to using a mix of coerced laborers. Since convicts (particularly from Spain but also from New Spain and Cuba) were not numerous in 1763, the urgency of the projects and the difficulty of the labor necessitated the state buying and maintaining a large contingent of enslaved workers in its own name to advance its defense program.[74]

Monthly summaries of the workforce at the forts also reflect the state's defense priorities. The work sites for repairs of El Morro and the building of the fortresses of La Cabaña and Atarés accounted for just over 76 percent of the labor force for 1765 (table 3.3). By the last month of 1767 and for most of 1768, there was significant concentration of workers at the fortress of La Cabaña, because the major repairs at El Morro had been finished and work at Atarés had slowed.[75]

Table 3.3. Workers in Three Main Fort Projects as Percent of Total Workforce, 1765

Month	Morro workers	Morro as % of total	Cabaña workers	Cabaña as % of total	Atarés workers	Atarés as % of total	Total workforce
March	557	26.4%	1,152	54.5%	401	19.0%	2,110
April	572	25.6%	611	27.3%	369	16.5%	2,233
May	529	22.4%	615	26.1%	458	19.0%	2,355
June	531	23.3%	570	25.0%	439	19.0%	2,272
July	669	29.0%	559	24.2%	531	23.0%	2,304
August	688	30.1%	528	23/1%	536	23.4%	2,281
October	689	31.4%	497	22.6%	539	24.5%	2,192

Source: Review extracts of the king's slaves and others in the defense works of Havana, dated March 31, 1765; April 24, 1765; May 28, 1765; June 30, 1765; July 31, 1765; August 24, 1765; October 27, 1765, Archive General de Indias, Santo Domingo, 1647. Review extract for February 23, 1766, Archivo General de Simancas, Secretaría y Superintendencia de Hacienda, 2344.

The summaries list some of the many tasks at which those employed on the fortifications worked. Besides those assigned to the fort sites for digging, hauling, and construction, others quarried and cut stone; some made fascines to fill trenches and build batteries. Some worked the ovens and hauled lime and charcoal.[76]

Some specialization among the coerced workers assigned to state defense works is also revealed in the summaries. Though the Count of Ricla had established a squad of royal slave carters on the docks in 1764, the carting of materials around the fort sites was too large an enterprise to staff exclusively with crown slaves. The summaries showed only a small group of twenty-one to twenty-five African-born men enslaved by the king (*bozales del rey*) employed as carters, and their numbers remained constant throughout the period from 1765 through 1768. Although it was only listed separately for two months of 1765, the making of fascines was done exclusively by ninety of the king's slaves.[77]

Other tasks drew mixed groups of workers. The stone quarries were manned by a handful of *paysanos*, some convicts, and groups of several hundred king's slaves. The lime and charcoal ovens employed both convicts and king's slaves, but the proportion of convicts to enslaved workers grew over the period from March 1765 to October 1768. Work in the warehouses (which held foodstuffs, salt, water, and so on for the fort workers) showed a similar progression toward greater reliance on convicts over enslaved workers from 1765 to 1768.

Besides the heavy work of digging trenches and foundations necessary for fort building, some of the those enslaved by the state were assigned to work with the free skilled workers to learn their trade, particularly in carpentry and fascine making. The state preferred to use its own enslaved workers for this for several reasons. In particular, convict laborers were rarely sentenced to fort works in perpetuity. Some had sentences as short as several months; others could reduce their sentences through good behavior. When using crown slaves, however, the fortification projects could count on benefiting from their training for as long as the project demanded, and enslaved workers trained in carpentry could be moved to other construction projects or to the shipyard. Moreover, should the state need to sell them, it would benefit from the higher price that a specifically trained enslaved worker would bring in the tight market for skilled labor on the island.[78]

In addition to the large number of the enslaved working on the forts themselves, smaller groups of king's slaves were employed at a number of sites in Havana. The reports of the Hospital of San Ambrosio (one from 1765 and ten from 1768) listed a total workforce of thirty to thirty-six employees. The hospital, established to care for ailing Spanish troops, employed an average of nineteen free civilians (servants, medical personnel, and administrators), twelve prisoners (some of whom were listed as "Guachinango Indians"), and between seven and nine king's slaves. These lists listed the king's slaves by name, their consistency indicating that a core of seven of these enslaved men worked at the hospital over a number of years.[79]

King's slaves also worked at the other major sites of state enterprises in Havana—the shipyard and the royal tobacco factory—and were employed in myriad other tasks around the city, including work in the homes and offices of the colonial officials stationed in the city. Still, the vast majority of people enslaved by the king, and prisoners, were employed at the fort sites themselves. Table 3.4 summarizes some of this data. In spite of some inconsistencies in the data, due to some groups of workers being listed under fort sites in several months and separately by task in others, general trends in the patterns of state employment are visible. For instance, there was a gradual increase in the numbers of free workers employed, especially at the fort works, over the years from 1765 to 1768. The state also increased its use of convict labor, both at the forts and at other tasks. But this growing use of free workers and convicts did not offset an overall decline in the total number of workers on all the state's defense works by October 1768. It was the decline of the use of enslaved workers of all provenances, particularly of those enslaved by the king, that accounted for the overall decline in the total workforce.

The reasons for the state's diminishing use of those it enslaved were varied, but most seem to be related in some measure to the expense of purchasing and maintaining its own force of enslaved laborers. Though the records of state officials do not make it explicit, it is entirely possible that the state never intended to keep a large contingent of royal slaves at work on the forts over a long period.[80] Instead, in keeping with historical patterns of state slavery in Cuba, once the

Table 3.4. Workers Employed at Fort Sites and at Other Tasks, March 1765–October 1768

	FORT SITES					OTHER TASKS				
Date	Free workers (black and white)	Prisoners	King's slaves	Other slaves	Total on fort sites	Free workers (black and white)	Prisoners	King's slaves	Other slaves	Total other tasks
March 1765	98	513	1,442	57	2,110	NA	NA	NA	NA	NA
April 1765	64	361	771	56	1,220	6	117	458	8	589
May 1765	80	317	966	52	1,415	5	193	479	8	685
June 1765	84	355	840	52	1,331	4	159	476	8	647
July 1765	95	446	1,160	58	1,759	4	170	362	9	545
August 1765	101	466	1,127	58	1,752	2	120	337	10	469
October 1765	94	490	1,087	54	1,725	2	139	325	1	467
January 1766	73	460	1,031	55	1,619	9	139	309	11	468

Table 3.4 (continued)

| | FORT SITES | | | | OTHER TASKS | | | | |
Date	Free workers (black and white)	Prisoners	King's slaves	Other slaves	Total on fort sites	Free workers (black and white)	Prisoners	King's slaves	Other slaves	Total other tasks
December 1767	135	398	1,033	38	1,604	8	166	125	2	301
January 1768	121	470	1,042	19	1,543	8	166	111	2	287
February 1768	123	454	1,033	20	1,630	8	189	126	2	325
March 1768	128	467	1,031	17	1,643	8	186	126	2	322
April 1768	142	455	1,029	17	1,643	8	191	125	2	326
May 1768	139	539	1,020	16	1,714	5	192	122	2	321
June 1768	138	685	959	12	1,794	8	202	112	2	324
July 1768	144	640	860	15	1,659	9	216	105	2	332
September 1768	137	760	842	13	1,752	9	225	102	2	338
October 1768	127	690	803	8	1,628	11	241	100	1	353

Source: Archivo General de Indias, Santo Domingo, 1647, 2122. Data for 1766 is from Archivo General de Simancas, Secretaría y Superintendencia de Hacienda, 2344.

Note: The data for March 1765 does not differentiate fort sites from other tasks, as all workers are listed under the three major fort projects of El Morro, La Cabaña, and Atarés. The sixty prisoners employed in carting were subsumed under the fort sites' listings after 1765. Quarrying and fascine making, which employed some 450 to 475 king's slaves and approximately 105 prisoners, were listed under the fort works at Atarés after August 1765.

initial crisis had passed—once the fort works were begun and other networks for forced and free laborers were tapped—the state could begin to sell some of its own slaves to recoup funds. Labor costs from May 1763 to the end of 1765, which included the purchase of enslaved workers, rations and medical care for the enslaved and for prisoners, the cost of a squad of guards to apprehend deserters, and the salaries of other employees (not including the engineers), constituted 65 percent of the total expenses recorded for fort works between May 1763 and the end of 1765. To try to meet these costs, the Mexican *situado*, or subsidy payment, more than tripled, to an average of nearly 1.5 million pesos per year from 1763 to 1769.[81]

When the new intendant, Miguel de Altarriba, arrived in February 1765, he assumed direct administration of the defense projects and their workers. He negotiated with contractors to purchase more slaves for the crown (1,436 for 1765), and with private owners in Havana and elsewhere, which had been complicated by the departure of many of the British merchants the previous fall.[82]

The significant investment by the state in the purchase and maintenance of a large contingent of crown slaves was compounded by losses of these enslaved workers through disease, desertion, and death. Table 3.5 summarizes the numbers of king's slaves and prisoners in the hospital and shows that a significant portion of the workforce on the fort projects was incapacitated over the first five and one-half years. Also, prisoners were consistently more likely than crown slaves to fall ill, although the figure for October 1768 is something of an anomaly. One reason for this may be that the population of prisoners was constantly being supplemented with new arrivals, particularly from New Spain, while no new king's slaves were purchased after 1765. In the unfamiliar disease environment of Havana, new forced recruits had a greater chance of becoming ill. For instance, the spike in the percentages of prisoners in the hospital from May to July 1768 may be due to the arrival of 294 Guachinango Indians from Mexico in May and June of that year.

Table 3.5. Numbers and Percentages of King's Slaves and Prisoners Ill, July 1765–October 1768

Date	KING'S SLAVES			PRISONERS		
	Ill slaves	Total slaves	% of total slaves	Ill prisoners	Total prisoners	% of total prisoners
July 1765	199	1,522	13.0	175	616	28.4
August 1765	236	1,486	15.9	139	624	22.2
October 1765	222	1,412	15.7	221	629	35.1
December 1767	115	1,158	9.9	109	564	19.3
January 1768	92	1,147	8.0	96	636	15.0
February 1768	78	1,159	6.7	114	643	17.7
March 1768	97	1,157	8.3	84	653	12.8
April 1768	85	1,154	7.3	88	646	13.6
May 1768	114	1,142	9.9	123	721	17.0
June 1768	103	1,077	9.5	213	887	24.0

Table 3.5 (continued)

| | KING'S SLAVES | | | PRISONERS | | |
Date	Ill slaves	Total slaves	% of total slaves	Ill prisoners	Total prisoners	% of total prisoners
July 1768	102	965	10.5	210	856	24.5
September 1768	99	944	10.4	157	985	15.9
October 1768	170	903	18.8	150	931	16.1

Source: Review extracts of the king's slaves and others in the defense works of Havana, dated March 31, 1765; April 24, 1765; May 28, 1765; June 30, 1765; July 31, 1765; August 24, 1765; October 27, 1765, Archive General de Indias, Santo Domingo, 1647. Review extract for February 23, 1766, Archivo General de Simancas, Secretaría y Superintendencia de Hacienda, 2344.

Note: By July 1765, the monthly summaries included a breakdown of the forced laborers in the hospital.

These New Spain natives also seemed to be particularly prone to desertion, as the monthly summaries for the three months list sixty-one Guanchingos as having deserted, out of a total of 110 desertions among all groups of workers (both forced and free) and of soldiers. Desertions among the enslaved are more difficult to gauge precisely. For all the monthly summaries of 1768 that give breakdowns of deserters, the total number of the enslaved reported to have deserted was only sixteen individuals.[83]

In the early years of the fort projects, desertions by the enslaved may have posed a greater problem. The summary of project expenses showed no outlays to stem desertions in the latter half of 1763, but in 1764 and 1765, when 3,403 enslaved people were purchased by the crown, the cost of the desertion guard squad totaled 37,884 pesos. The state continued to fund the desertion squad at lesser levels through 1772.[84] Faced with the flight of esclavos del rey and convict workers to Havana from their posts in El Morro and La Cabaña, in 1764 Ricla imposed a hefty fine of twenty-five ducados on anyone caught ferrying fort workers to the city.[85] Problems with desertion may also help to explain the concentration of prisoners in fort site transport tasks such as carting, which allowed workers considerable mobility, since the desertion of prisoners, while troublesome, would not have represented as much of a loss of crown investment as the desertion of king's slaves.

The numbers of the enslaved who died while working in the fortification projects is more difficult to determine. Cuban historian Francisco Pérez Guzmán estimated a death rate for both people enslaved by the state and convict laborers at about 15 to 20 percent per year. The actual numbers are obscured by the fact that there seems to have been an active trade in state slaves by falsifying deaths and selling the state's enslaved workers to the private sector.[86] Still, fragments of evidence suggest that deaths among the newly arrived enslaved Africans were a serious problem. In a letter to Esquilache detailing problems that increased costs, the main supervisor at the La Cabaña site stressed the need for a prisoner overseer for every fifty enslaved workers because the enslaved "kill each other . . . [or] hang themselves." He also bemoaned corrupt contractors and overseers who skimmed from provisions for the fort laborers, leaving the enslaved to "eat a very short ration from which they deteriorate, sick, and unable to work."[87]

A report from the Hospital de Nuestra Señora del Pilar, established under the Count of Ricla to treat slaves and prisoners, listed the deaths of a total of 534 African-born king's slaves, or 19.3 percent of the newly purchased slaves, between April and October of 1764 alone.[88] While death from disease and injury was difficult for colonial officials to stem, during the same month officials tried to control fraud and desertion by ordering that royal slaves be marked with the cruel practice of branding, scarring them with the symbol of the crown and the letters of the garrison brigade to which they were assigned.[89]

The work regimes endured by both the state's slaves and prisoners also contributed to the high rates of disease, death, and desertion in the labor force. At the fort sites with more than 1,000 workers, the enslaved and convict contingents were generally mustered out separately in brigades of about one hundred men. Each work squad was assigned to and supervised by a specific brigade of soldiers from the Spanish garrison.[90] How workers would have been organized for tasks in settings with smaller, mixed groups of workers is less clear. At the lime kilns, the ratio of prisoners to the enslaved was fairly even until the end of 1765, when prisoners began to predominate. The extant records indicate only one soldier assigned to the kilns through 1765, and then two or three appear in records for 1767 and 1768 as the numbers of workers rose to more than ninety. In the warehouses, as well, the workers were a mixed group, with only one or two soldiers assigned to them over the entire period from 1765 to 1768, even though the numbers of workers increased to more than two hundred by 1768.[91]

The workday at the fort sites began and ended with a roll call and an accounting of any tools issued. The workday in the summer months generally extended to twelve and one-half hours, taking advantage of more hours of daylight. The winter months averaged nine to ten hours per day. Work discipline was maintained by the armed guards assigned to each brigade. There was usually a brief break in the morning for breakfast, a longer break of some three to four hours with the main meal at midday, and dinner after the end of the workday in the evening.

The diet of the enslaved and prisoners assigned to the fort projects consisted of salted meats (usually beef, ham, or sometimes fish), rice, root vegetables, legumes, and some kind of bread, either cassava or wheat. Pérez Guzmán has calculated the range of caloric intake for fort workers between 3,400 and 4,400 calories per day, probably sufficient to sustain the laborers, if all of the rations actually reached them, although it was not an especially varied diet.[92] The enslaved and convicts also were issued three rations of tobacco per day, and those working in particularly draining work were given sambumbía, a drink of sugarcane juice, water, and chilies, as refreshment.[93]

However, when Intendant Altarriba arrived, in early 1765, he reviewed the assigned rations and found them "a gift and copious." In mid-July, he reduced both the size of the rations and their overall cost. He contended that locally produced cassava and salted meats were often more expensive than wheat flour sent from Veracruz, so he relied more heavily on imported flour. Determining that peppers were too expensive, he eliminated them completely from his revised selection of vegetables for workers' rations.[94]

For clothing, those enslaved by the king were issued two suits of garments per year, consisting of pants and shirts of ordinary linen and an overshirt of blue or green for the cold season.[95] For a bit of sun protection, two straw hats were also included. Shoes do not seem to have been a regular part of the clothing allotment.[96]

In terms of housing, the lot of the state's enslaved workers was particularly hard. Because large numbers of the enslaved were acquired by the state quickly, their housing was somewhat makeshift and cramped, even by plantation standards. The typical housing was a barracks constructed at about 137.5 feet in length but only 13.75 feet in width to house 200 to 220 of the enslaved or convicts. There was no division of the space inside the barracks to allow for any privacy, and the beds were generally made of wooden slats. There was little relief, since fort regulations required all workers, enslaved and free, to remain on site during the workweek. These cramped conditions were eased somewhat only as the number of workers confined to the hospital mounted into the hundreds.[97]

The chaplains were supposed to offer religious instruction during meal breaks and to say mass on Sundays and holidays. The aim of this instruction was to ensure that "the spiritual well-being of those souls [of the enslaved], disposed by the grace of baptism, be reconciled with service to the king."[98] Religious instruction by clergy only became the norm in 1764, with official regulation and payment of chaplains assigned to the fort works. Before 1764, these duties were carried out voluntarily by engineers, supervisors, and clergy at various work sites. Only after the state became responsible for some 2,000 newly arrived enslaved Africans did it directly commit itself to funding and regulating the conversion and instruction of its own enslaved workers.

Since the defense projects of the late eighteenth century in Havana were such massive undertakings, the crown could not always conduct all aspects of each project itself. As it had for centuries, state officials contracted out parts of the projects to private *asentistas*. One of the major tasks was the movement of materials around the construction sites. Therefore, in addition to reducing costs by cutting rations, by August 1765, officials proposed reducing the expenses of the projects by contracting out to a private individual the hauling of materials. It was recommended that the state should sell the contractor forty unskilled enslaved men chosen from the fort works, at a price of three hundred pesos each (approximately double the price the state had paid for them).[99] By October, savings to the crown from the contracting out of some of the hauling to Manuel Sánchez were estimated to be more than 50,000 pesos.[100] On the other hand, difficulties in acquiring the necessary building materials in a timely fashion could increase labor costs. In the summer of 1765, the lack of bricks forced the crown to send home with pay several master stonecutters and masons recruited from Spain.[101]

Since the king's enslaved workers were the largest contingent on the fortification projects during its most intense and urgent phase, from 1763 to 1765, officials focused considerable attention on this group to reduce expenses. The highest yearly total, of 1,967 enslaved workers employed by the state, had been reached in 1764.[102] In the following year, the king ordered the intendant to begin selling off enslaved unskilled workers to raise money for the fort works.[103] After 1765, the proportion of the king's enslaved workers to convict laborers began to decline, until by the mid-1770s, prisoners outnumbered the enslaved. The report on fort expenses for 1772 listed 423 slaves still owned by the crown, after the state had recouped some 390,456 pesos by selling many of its enslaved workers. At slave prices current in Cuba at the time, as noted in the intendants' reports of the 1760s (250 to 300 pesos), this would have involved the sale to the private sector of approximately 1,300 to 1,500 enslaved people.[104]

Finishing the Forts

The new captain general, Antonio María de Bucareli, retained some of the extraordinary powers granted to his predecessor, Ricla, and the principal goal of his administration continued to be the realization of the various defense projects.[105] This charge was complicated by natural setbacks and a chronic scarcity of resources. A hurricane in October of 1766 had created a subsistence crisis among the enslaved workers in the king's service, forcing Havana officials to petition the crown for donations of foodstuffs from the governors in Veracruz, Campeche, and Cumaná.[106] Procuring the necessary funding and recruiting sufficient laborers continued to be a major problem in carrying out the fort works. The Mexican *situado* allocation for fortifications had been reduced from 500,000 to 300,000 pesos, a sum Bucareli deemed inadequate for the work necessary on La Cabaña alone. Even this reduced sum could not be counted upon, since the viceroy of New Spain rarely sent the full amount.[107]

At the insistence of the intendant, in May 1768, Bucareli called for the formation of a junta to try to coordinate the fort works and to regulate their expenses. The members included Bucareli; the intendant, Miguel de Altarriba; and the two directing engineers, Silvestre Abarca and Agustín Crame. After consultation and discussion, the junta decided that the only place they could cut expenses was in the excavation of trenches on the forts. Some of this work had been contracted out since 1764. Bucareli tartly remarked that the contractors had left the most difficult parts of the excavation until the last and now would not complete the work without raising the price.[108]

In marked contrast to the strategy used at the start of the fort works in 1763, colonial officials in Havana were not looking to enslaved laborers to carry out this difficult work five years later. Instead, the junta decided that, as prisoners arrived from New Spain, they would be assigned directly to the trenches, dismissing the day laborers presently working there in equal numbers as they were replaced with prisoners. Data for the Havana forts suggest that these prisoners numbered more than 1,000.

New Spain suffered a period of hunger, deprivation, and rising crime during this era of increasing fortification and militarization in Cuba. The colonial state in Mexico also sought to increase the size of the army through levies, which exacerbated popular discontent and the numbers of people who ran afoul of the law. The army's policy of separating men from their poor families for military service was a disruptive practice that caused many new recruits to desert. The streams of prisoners who began to take the place of royal slaves in Havana's fortifications from the 1760s to the 1790s were largely made up of convicts and state prisoners from around Mexico. Some were sent directly to Veracruz's forts; others were transported to Havana to serve their sentences at hard labor. Smaller numbers of prisoners came from Spain. Once in Havana, the majority remained in Cuba, though some were sent on to other Caribbean presidios, such as San Juan in Puerto Rico or Pensacola, Florida.[109]

The junta for the fort projects estimated the costs of completing the trench work at the Atarés fort at 8,000 pesos. Another 4,000 pesos were needed for a gunpowder warehouse, and an additional 9,000 pesos for urgent repairs to the army barracks. To offset these costs, the junta decided that the intendant should take charge of the sale of "some of the slaves less useful for such work, those most likely to lose their value." The junta saw no other way to cut expenses. As Bucareli explained to the minister of the Indies, "With respect to the fact that the number of prisoners and blacks that we have today reaches 1.527 it is necessary to feed them and to cover the rest of the costs that they occasion, nothing can be cut from the train of the works, in masons, stone cutters, carts, lime, bricks, and other necessities, that are needed in order not to make useless the cost of the maintenance of the prisoners and blacks."[110] Even with the sale of those enslaved by the king, Cuban officials hoped that the large works on La Cabaña would be finished within the next three years and that the resulting savings could be applied to beginning work on a smaller fort on the hill of Aróstegui, to the west of the city.

Other sites in Cuba also needed workers to begin strengthening their fortifications. The royal engineer assigned to Santiago de Cuba in 1765, for instance, wrote to Captain General Ricla to complain about the lack of virtually all the resources necessary for fort building in the eastern region. He claimed that there were barely two skilled workers of any value in stone- or ironworking. The trenches and moats had to be dug out of pure rock, necessitating at least twenty-four miners. Though Santiago's fort projects did get under way, the engineer despaired of finding the required skilled and unskilled laborers in a place where "there is not even a cat."[111]

Though the king had a community of royal slaves in the region, the enslaved copper miners of El Cobre had proven difficult to mobilize for fort work, and their numbers were small. By 1768, proposals were floated to send five hundred king's slaves to Santiago to advance stalled work there. One hundred would be sent early, to set up a settlement, cut wood, build housing, and open ovens for charcoal and lime. Such a plan was not carried out, but the proposal is a testament to the relative success of the enslaved copper miners of El Cobre in resisting the kinds of mobilizations and work regimes that obtained at Havana's fort sites.[112]

As royal officials began to reduce the numbers of royal slaves in Havana's defense works, the composition of the workforce at the fort sites began to change, as table 3.6 illustrates. In spite of the junta's intention to reduce the contingent of day laborers in equal measure with the arrival of new prisoners from New Spain, the number of free workers on the fort projects varied only slightly over the five months. The number of those enslaved by the king, on the other hand, was reduced by 317 people, at least 160 of whom were sold to private owners, according to the monthly workforce summaries from June and July 1768. The table indicates that, by the fall of 1768, king's slaves were rapidly declining as the main labor support for the fortification projects in Havana. With a steadier supply of prisoners from New Spain, the state felt able to divest itself of some of its less skilled enslaved workers, to recoup their value and offset the tremendous expenses of the fort works.

It seems that, by 1768, in the changing circumstances of the empire's labor market, the skills acquired by king's slaves in the Havana fort projects, rather than the projects' urgency for imperial defense, determined the retention and deployment of enslaved laborers at the forts. Yet even these changes in the organization and composition of the labor force were insufficient to put the fortifications' financing on a sure footing. Bucareli continued to press the issue of the desperate state of Havana's funding on the minister of the Indies.

Table 3.6. Free Workers, Prisoners, and King's Slaves at Fort Sites, May 1768–September 1768

Month	Free workers	Forzados	Negros del rey	Total
May	140	529	1,020	1,689
June	139	685	959	1,783
July	144	640	860	1,644
September	137	760	842	1,739
October	126	690	703	1,519

Source: "Estado de Revista . . . de los Negros, esclavos del Rey y demas Individuos en las citadadas obras . . . ," May 15, June 19, July 24, and September 18, 1768, Archivo General de Indias, Santo Domingo, 2122.

Note: The heading "Free workers" here includes people listed as paysanos, and mulatos and negros libres.

By the summer of 1768, Bucareli had sent at least a dozen reports to the crown, requesting help and detailing the fort works' many expenses. In June, he complained that, in his twenty-six months of service as captain general, he had counted only one *situado* shipment from New Spain that had arrived in full.[113] The insecurity of *situado* funds forced the captain general to resort to considerable borrowing to keep the projects afloat—some 295,676 pesos in loans for the first four months of 1768.[114] When possible, he solicited donations from wealthy Cubans. Bucareli also tried to cajole other concessions from private merchants. On being notified that 150 slaves were being sent from Puerto Rico to be sold by the company of the royal *asiento*, he immediately apprised the company of the service it could render the king if it were to pass along the value of the slaves' sales to cover funds pending from Veracruz. Feeling confident that the request would be granted, Bucareli found himself "with one less care from the many I suffer due to scarcity."[115]

Bucareli and the fort works junta met again in the summer of 1768 to discuss the projects' funding. They had hoped that the sales of 200 to 250 king's slaves would cover the forts' expenses for two to three months. But the *situado* payment had been reduced by almost half in 1768, forcing Havana residents to absorb more of the costs and to hold debts for the projects. The intendant expressed his sense that the government could no longer expect large amounts of help from local residents, either in loans or in donations, although state debts to private citizens continued to average more than 500,000 pesos per year into the 1770s.[116]

To avoid sending only negative reports to Madrid, in July of 1768, Bucareli sent a letter praising engineer Silvestre Abarca for having been able to carry out increased work at the fort sites in the first six months of 1768, in spite of shortages, such as the artillery that had been mounted on one of the bulwarks of La Cabaña. Characteristically, Bucareli ended his letter by expressing his doubts that this level of accomplishment could be sustained, due to the shortages of funds. By September, Bucareli was warning the metropolitan government that the sale of king's slaves had not been sufficient to cover the fort works' expenses and that the works might have to be shut down completely for lack of funds.[117] A bit of relief arrived from Veracruz at the end of 1769, with 100,000 pesos for Havana and the navy and one hundred convicts.[118]

Early the following year, the engineer in charge of the fort works made some adjustments to the workforce. To reduce costs, Abarca dismissed a group of masons and stone cutters in January and asked the crown for approval to help in returning them and their families to Cádiz. To keep important aspects of the fort projects moving, Abarca moved a brigade of king's slaves from repair works in various places to the Atarés fort site, to help restore the glacis that had fallen there.[119]

In the search for funds, colonial officials resorted to several creative measures to further the fort projects. Operating in a long tradition among officials of the Spanish Empire, Intendant Altarriba appropriated funds designated for other projects and then notified Madrid, "hopeful" that the crown would approve. To continue the important work of removing earth from the Cabaña site and extending the glacis, Altarriba diverted some 116,000 pesos that had passed through his office from Guatemala, destined for Puerto Rico. He assured the king that all this was to the end of carrying out the work on the fortifications with the greatest brevity and without suspending the sale of the king's enslaved workers.[120]

Bucareli's perseverance ultimately was rewarded, as a number of the fortification works around the plaza of Havana were completed during his tenure. When his successor, Felipe de Fondesviela, the Marqués de la Torre, arrived in 1771, only the small castle on the hill of Aróstegui and the major project of La Cabaña remained unfinished. The total sum expended on the fortification projects from the retaking of Havana in June 1763 to the end of 1772 amounted to more than 30 million reales, or about 3.8 million pesos. Table 3.7 shows the yearly totals.

Table 3.7. Total Yearly Expenses on Havana Fort Works, 1763–1772, in Pesos

Year	Total expenses (pesos)
1763 (July–December)	195,109
1764	555,649
1765	475,040
1766	378,390
1767	467,611
1768	405,224
1769	270,363
1770	252,412
1771	363,255
1772	435,579
Total	3,798,632

Source: "Estado que manifiesta los gastos . . . ," July 7, 1763 through December 31, 1772, Archivo General de Indias, Santo Domingo, 2129.

A number of the major fortification projects had been completed or were near completion by the mid-1770s. As shown in table 3.8, the number of people working at the fort sites had fallen from several thousand to an average of roughly 590 people in 1774 and 1775. La Cabaña fort was finally finished in 1776. Hence, the number of workers employed at various tasks around the sites, in warehouses, at carting and woodcutting, at the lime kilns, at skilled trades, and in the hospitals, was now roughly equal to the number employed in actual fort work. Segregation of king's slaves and prisoners by task was more pronounced in the workforce of the 1770s. Warehouse work was carried out almost exclusively by king's slaves, at a ratio of ten to one. The transportation of supplies by both land and water was the exclusive domain of hundreds of prisoners and a mere handful of free workers. As desertion continued to be a serious problem for fort worker administrators throughout the period, the crown sought to reduce losses of its own enslaved workers by employing them in more easily monitored areas.

Table 3.8. Workers at La Cabaña and the Loma de Aróstegui, October 1774–March 1775

Date	Paysanos	Prisoners	Free people of color	King's slaves	Other slaves	Total
October 1774	61	366	16	168	4	615
November 1774	61	387	19	168	4	639
January 1775	80	291	26	161	8	566
February 1775	83	288	24	159	7	561
March 1775	78	287	28	160	7	560

Source: "Estado que comprehende el numero de forzados existentes . . . en la Cavaña, y Loma de Arostegui . . . ," October 30 and November 27, 1774; January 29, February 27, and March 26, 1775, Archivo General de Indias, Santo Domingo, 1211.

The acquisition of a skill by the enslaved remained an important factor in their retention as slaves of the crown. The workers listed by specific skills in the summaries, such as coopers, armorers, masons, and smiths, were all king's slaves. Other occupations had smaller but more mixed groups of workers. The hospitals, for instance, employed only some forty-four workers, including a group of eleven soldiers.

The numbers and breakdown of patients in the hospital (table 3.9) continued to show the greater susceptibility to disease of new immigrants to the island, such as prisoners and soldiers. Among those enslaved by the king who were assigned to the fort works, an average of seventeen to eighteen men were sick in the hospital between fall 1774 and early spring 1775. Among prisoners, the number of sick in the hospital was around ninety, except in January 1775, when their number soared to 171. Soldiers assigned to the fort works also suffered much higher rates of disease; an average of 36.4 percent of them was confined to the hospital over the same period.

Table 3.9. Workers Sick in the Hospital del Pilar, October 1774–March 1775

Date	Paysanos	Prisoners	Free people of color	King's slaves	Other slaves	Soldiers	Yearly totals
October 1774	64	92	30	12	5	64	267
November 1774	58	91	30	12	5	59	255
January 1775	8	171	8	21	2	41	251
February 1775	3	93	9	22	2	47	176
March 1775	16	89	6	21	1	50	183

Source: "Estado que comprehende el numero de forzados existentes . . . en la Cavaña, y Loma de Arostegui . . . ," October 30 and November 27, 1774; January 29, February 27, and March 26, 1775, Archivo General de Indias, Santo Domingo, 1211.

Even though the total workforce employed on the fort projects had decreased by the mid-1770s, the state continued to employ more than 1,000 workers at these sites a full decade after their inception. The most significant change in the state's deployment of labor on defense projects is visible in its divestiture of its contingent of king's slaves in favor of prisoners (see table 3.10).

Table 3.10. Yearly Averages of King's Slaves and Prisoners Employed in Havana Fort Works, 1763–1775

Year	King's slaves	Prisoners	Total number of workers
1763	795	NA	NA
1764	1967	NA	NA
1765	1,396	538	2,249
1766	NA	NA	NA
1767	1,158	964	2,309
1768	1,072	773	2,004
1772	447*	1,130*	1,949*

Table 3.10 (continued)

Year	King's slaves	Prisoners	Total number of workers
1773	400*	1,071*	1,838*
1774	321	980	1,517
1775	319	837	1,318

Source: Review extracts of the king's slaves and others in the defense works of Havana, dated March 31, 1765; April 24, 1765; May 28, 1765; June 30, 1765; July 31, 1765; August 24, 1765; October 27, 1765, Archive General de Indias, Santo Domingo, 1647; review extract for February 23, 1766, Archivo General de Simancas, Secretaría y Superintendencia de Hacienda, 2344; "Estado que comprehende el numero de forzados existentes . . . en la Cavaña, y Loma de Arostegui . . . ," October 30 and November 27, 1774; January 29, February 27, and March 26, 1775, Archivo General de Indias, Santo Domingo, 1211. Averages marked with an asterisk are derived from data in Christian De Vito, "Connected Singularities: Convict Labour in Late Colonial Spanish America (1760s–1800), in Micro-Spatial Histories of Global Labour, edited by Christian G. De Vito and Anne Gerritsen (London: Palgrave, 2018), table 7.1, 175.

Note: The total number of workers includes soldiers, civilians (paysanos), and free people of color.

The state was able to recoup about 63 percent of its initial expenditure for enslaved Africans by selling them to private owners in Cuba as the urgency of the projects diminished and more prisoners became available. Between 1763 and 1765, the crown spent 616,788 pesos on purchases of the enslaved. Sales of king's slaves between 1765 and 1772 netted 390,455 pesos for the royal treasury. The summary of 1772 also listed 423 of the enslaved as still owned by the crown, at a value of 126,900 pesos, an average value of three hundred pesos per enslaved person, or close to double the original price paid by the crown. The summary noted the increasing number of deaths and desertions among those enslaved by the king as a reason for the loss of some 99,432 pesos. Yet the state's power to dictate the price at which it would buy enslaved workers from the asentistas between 1763 and 1765 allowed it to offset some of the immense labor costs of the fortifications projects.[121]

Fort Work in Wartime

As the British colonies in North America moved toward a break with the metropole, concern rose among Spanish officials about the possibility of renewed war with Great Britain. In August 1776, shortly after the American colonies' Declaration of Independence, Charles III sent a royal order to the captain general of Cuba asking him to respond to charges that the fortification works on the island were not being carried out in a timely fashion. The first concern was that, even with four hundred men assigned to it, the final repairs at La Cabaña had not been finished, nor had adequate account been given as to why.

As had been the case for at least a decade, the captain general cited labor shortages as the major constraint on the speedy completion of the fort projects. He informed the king that in none of the six months from January to June had the full four hundred men been employed at La Cabaña. The Cabaña fort site was the base from which workers were deployed, as needed, to all the defense sites of Havana. For instance, workers had been assigned to repair the army barracks and the floor of El Morro. There still was work to be done at the Atarés site, and both the factoría of tobacco and the gunpowder warehouse needed to be finished. Thus, according to Captain General De la Torre, only the following numbers of workers were available for work at La Cabaña between January and June 1776:[122]

January	285
February	284
March	281
April	220
May	112
June	106

Much of the workforce was still involved in the excavation of parts of the fort sites—digging and removing sand and rocks or cutting wood—leaving a reduced number of workers for actual construction. De la Torre reported that, since January 1775, he had communicated to Madrid the necessity of increasing the number of day laborers and prisoners assigned to the projects. Even though the official number of workers on the projects was listed as 1,074, only 758 were employed in and around the fort sites; more than three hundred were sick in the hospital. Without increasing the actual workforce to at least 1,000 able-bodied men, De la Torre predicted that things would not proceed more quickly.[123]

Three monthly summaries for 1775 provide an interesting glimpse of the workers employed in secondary tasks around the defense sites. For instance, the summary of January 1775 lists 655 people at the fort sites, but only 521 actually worked on the forts of La Cabaña and El Príncipe.[124] The distribution of the 134 remaining workers was as follows:

eight worked in the salumería, salting meat;

two were sick in the Hospital of San Lázaro (these may have been soldiers);

fourteen worked on the ferries, bringing supplies across the bay to La Cabaña;

two worked on the boat of the commander of El Morro;

one swept the castle;

twenty-nine of the most invalid were assigned to basket weaving;

two were listed as "crazy";

two were blind;

seven worked in the foodstuffs warehouse of La Cabaña;

ten were woodcutters;

nineteen were in the hospital;

sixteen had deserted; and

twenty-two had been sent to do repairs on the fort of Matanzas, east of Havana.

Unfortunately, the summary does not indicate the status of these 134 workers, but the fact that the state would continue to maintain a group of workers who were unfit for labor suggests that they were enslaved by the king or were prisoners of the state.

By the time Spain entered the American War of Independence against the British, in 1779, some of the major works of fortification in Havana were near completion. But the state still maintained a workforce of some 670 workers into the 1780s to keep the defense works in good repair. The fort sites now employed only about 250 workers, ninety-nine of whom were enslaved by the king. Even with the reduced number of workers in its charge, the state maintained considerable segregation by task, as it had over the previous twenty years. Warehouse work and skilled occupations, such as ironworking and carpentry, were still dominated by king's slaves. Prisoners were the only state workers used on the ferries in the bay, at the slaughterhouse, and in cutting wood. The hospitals still employed a mixed group of workers, although here, too, prisoners predominated.

By the 1780s, the supply of prisoners from New Spain must have been insufficient or interrupted by warfare in the Caribbean, because Havana officials now devoted much of their attention to trying to recruit and control free day laborers.[125] In the fall of 1782, with Spain still at war with Britain and Spanish troops engaged in Florida and the Gulf of Mexico, Captain General Juan Manuel de Cagigal expressed fears that Havana might again be invaded. He discussed the defense works, which were on the point of completion, if only the necessary workers could be recruited and retained. He blamed the "well-known retreat of day laborers, that are more and more scarce daily."[126] The chief engineer, Luis Huet, notified the captain general that 1,800 workers would be necessary to shore up defenses quickly, probably an unrealistic number, given the constraints imposed by militia recruitment during wartime. Cagigal tried to alleviate the shortage by publishing a proclamation in the city, calling for workers at the fort sites. Huet reported that the proclamation netted 398 day laborers who initially presented themselves for work, but shortly thereafter, 193 were missing or had deserted.[127]

Even with free workers, the state found it necessary to use coercion to carry out its public works, and this coercion may have fallen most heavily on free workers of color. In the fall of 1782, Huet wrote to Cagigal, proposing an exemplary punishment of some of the missing free black workers to reduce desertion. Huet claimed to know where a number of them were hiding, and he suggested that they be punished with the wearing of a shackle and chain. The captain general agreed to the chaining of these deserters for several days, "to serve as an example." Even so, by December 1782, Huet declared himself on the point of firing half the workers, so disgusted was he with the state of affairs.[128]

Another method of recruitment, largely restricted to moments of crisis in wartime, was the fortification levy, which targeted both free whites and people of color or enslaved people, who were hired out between the ages of fifteen and fifty years old. The circular sent to local officials stipulated the exclusion of the ill and disabled of both statuses and specifically rejected those deemed unruly, or fugitives among the enslaved. The numbers recruited for fort projects by this method are not clear from the records, but officials also felt the need to directly solicit sugar mill owners for donations of their enslaved workers to the forts. The state did offer to pay the current day laborers' wage of four and one-half reales per day, which suggests real desperation, considering the additional compensation that would have to be paid in the event of serious disease, injury, or the death of privately owned slaves at the forts.[129]

Even with the return of peace between Britain and Spain in 1783, the Spanish crown continued to maintain a workforce of some six hundred people on the fort sites (table 3.11). In marked contrast to the workforce twenty years earlier, prisoners, rather than king's slaves, now dominated as the major source of labor for state projects. A full two decades after the most intense phase of fortification construction in Havana, in which the labor of those enslaved by the king had been crucial, their numbers employed on the fort sites fell to below two hundred people. They continued to be employed in jobs in which royal slaves had predominated since the late 1760s—in warehouses and hospital work, and especially in skilled jobs such as metalworking and carpentry. As we shall see in chapter 4, by the mid-1780s the largest contingent of people enslaved by the king in Havana's defense sector was employed in the Havana artillery company, not in the fortifications. By 1790, only three hundred *forzados* and sixty people enslaved by the king worked regularly in the city's forts.[130]

Table 3.11. Workers on Fortifications, November 1784–January 1785

Date	Paysanos	Prisoners	Free people of color	King's slaves	Other slaves	Total
November 1784	51	338	22	190	3	604
December 1784	47	336	25	187	3	598
January 1785	48	336	25	185	3	597

Source: "Estado que comprehende el Numero de Forzados . . . en la Cavaña y Loma de Arostegui," November 28, 1784, December 31, 1784, January 30, 1785, Archivo General de Indias, Cuba, 1371.

The Spanish state in Cuba had briefly resorted to the extensive recruitment and employment of its own enslaved labor force to begin the largest fortification effort ever mounted in the empire, after the British occupation of Havana. To facilitate and fund its purchase and maintenance of thousands of the enslaved for fort work, the state also transformed Cuba's commercial relationships within the empire and the wider circuits of Atlantic trade. Still, as early as 1765, just as the last contingents of enslaved Africans destined for the fort projects were arriving in Havana, Charles III and royal officials began looking for ways to reduce the expense of this effort.

Officials' recruitment and employment of enslaved workers for the repair and building of Havana's fortifications show the Spanish colonial state using all of the various models of state enslavement outlined in chapter 1 to secure the city after the British occupation. They ultimately returned to the less extensive and more strategic patterns of royal enslavement and employment that had served the empire's defense needs for centuries. But the transformations that accompanied this brief surge in state enslavement were profound.

One of the most significant changes was the opening of the slave trade in the Spanish Empire to facilitate the recruitment of enslaved Africans for defense work in Havana. Officials in Cuba resorted to trading with merchants of their recent British enemy and began to experiment with charging Spanish subjects with carrying out the slave trade to the island, with mixed results. By 1789, the Spanish crown was compelled to declare free trade in enslaved Africans to its colonies. The bulk of the major defense works in Havana had been completed, and the state was no longer a major purchaser of enslaved workers in the city's market. However, major changes to commercial policy and taxation, and the increasing numbers of the enslaved available to planters, ensured that sugar production was poised to dominate the economy of the island.

A number of questions regarding previous interpretations of the nature of enslavement in Cuba also arise from this story. In the historiography of Cuban slavery, 1790 is the date after which most authors begin to talk of the "hardening" of the regime of enslavement, with large importations of slaves, skewed gender ratios in favor of men, gang labor, high mortality, and diminished access to manumission. The evidence here suggests that many of those same conditions obtained in the urban context of state defense projects before the advent of the sugar boom on the island. The labor of constructing the infrastructure of the empire often was as grueling and deadly as sugar production for the enslaved. Punishing work regimes, like those on sugar plantations, were not unique to plantations, or even to rural areas, and the experience of enslavement within a single society, and even within a single city, could vary considerably.[131]

This case of people of African descent enslaved by the king in eighteenth-century Havana highlights the importance of factors such as the geopolitics of imperial defense and the work regimes necessitated by massive projects of public works, more than the factors structuring commodity production, as central to shaping the experiences of the enslaved in state service in Havana. Within the great variety of working and living conditions, the key factors for both the state and its enslaved workers were the nature of the work to be performed, the level of coercion necessary to carry it out, potential resistance, and the structure of the labor market in which decisions about labor deployment were made.

The evidence about the fort projects of the 1763–1790 period also shows that warfare was a crucial catalyst to development, and it highlights the importance of state policy to Cuban economic development. The historical narrative of the development of a slave society in Cuba by the nineteenth century must include the state's defense priorities and actions as an owner and employer of the enslaved, along with private entrepreneurship and the evolving Atlantic markets for provisions and tropical commodities.

The defense projects forged deep linkages throughout the Cuban economy. The state's extraordinary investment in state enslavement in the 1760s was indeed temporary, but the many changes the state enacted to successfully complete the defense projects profoundly altered the allocation and orientation of all major factors of production on the island. The state's demand for land changed previous, more casual attitudes toward land titles and usage by confiscating the land necessary for new forts, warehouses, barracks, and parade grounds. This demand, coupled with population growth, increased land values in and around Havana. After 1779, when the royal treasury began compensating property owners for lands claimed by the state for defense purposes, many small and larger landholders benefited.[132] The crown also was forced to allow the Cuban elite more commercial freedom in return for assuming a greater burden of taxation and militia responsibilities.

Havana's fort projects also affected the structure of the city's labor market for both free and forced workers. The state's demand for labor kept wages high, especially for skilled work, so some free workers benefited. The need for coerced labor on the fort projects was at least as great a stimulant to the slave trade to Cuba in the 1760s as commercial policy under the British occupation had been. State projects alone may have increased the city's enslaved population by 50 percent, while similar numbers of the enslaved were sold into the private sector from 1763 to 1765 as a result of royal contracts with both the Royal Company of Havana and private slave traders. Thus, the Spanish state helped create the economic framework for plantation expansion and modeled the successful deployment of enslaved labor in both skilled trades and in gang labor.

Income within the empire also was redistributed, as much of the great quantities of silver extracted from Mexico over the eighteenth century were funneled into Havana. The local economy was enriched, as the state contracted out many of the necessities of the fort projects—slave procurement, transport, brick manufacture, and lime and charcoal production. The state purchased provisions and supplies for its troops, workers, and projects. It confiscated, purchased, and rented land and buildings in and around the city. The tremendous expenses associated with the fortification projects also made colonial subjects the state's creditors, as *situado* payments fell in arrears. As Allan J. Kuethe has noted, "This inflow of treasure established a level of financial liquidity that was unique in the empire."[133] Although it would be difficult to document, many scholars believe this capital was an important factor in the expansion of sugar production after the Seven Years' War.[134]

Thus, Cuba emerged by 1790 more heavily taxed but more prosperous, more tightly controlled by the metropole government but more open to the emerging Atlantic economy. As the state became less committed to the use of enslaved labor, the private sector became more so. Creole elites were more closely allied with peninsular bureaucrats and the military but were poised to take advantage of economic opportunities, both within and beyond the empire, that the Spanish state would be unable to control.

In the geopolitics of the Atlantic world, Spain was stronger than it had been for some years, and Havana was better defended than almost any city in the Americas. Yet the waves of warfare that engulfed the Atlantic world in the last decades of the eighteenth century left Spain, by the 1820s, virtually bankrupt and stripped of most of its American empire. Enslaved people of African descent were involved in all of Spain's Caribbean military campaigns, but mostly as a minor supplement to free white soldiers and to militiamen, both white and of color. An extraordinary resort to state slavery had allowed Spain to successfully fortify Havana and encourage economic development in Cuba after 1763, but it was the subsequent explosive growth of African enslavement and sugar production in the private sector that would sustain the empire into the nineteenth century.

4

SLAVES IN THE MILITARY,
1763–1800

The Treaty of Paris ended the Seven Years' War in 1763, but it brought an uneasy peace. Britain had expelled the French and expanded its own territory in North America. It had humiliated Spain by capturing Havana and Manila, and it gained the Florida colonies in exchange for ending Havana's occupation. The war had been costly for all the antagonists, and all three states embarked on military and administrative reforms to improve defenses and military readiness, since all the signatories expected that a return to war was likely.[1] Few foresaw, however, that a return to war would come from the outbreak of rebellion in Britain's North American colonies in 1776, or on the plantations of French Saint-Domingue in 1791.

To make war in the eighteenth-century Caribbean, Spain, France, and Britain all resorted to the labor and fighting skills of enslaved people of African descent. Spain had employed hundreds of slaves in various capacities in a desperate though failed attempt to save Havana during the British attack in 1762. Even in defeat, the crown rewarded dozens of those slaves for their service and sacrifice.

Over the next two decades, however, the employment of enslaved men as soldiers in military campaigns outside of Cuba was minor. Instead, during Spain's intervention in the American War of Independence from 1779 to 1783, its military employment of the enslaved followed more traditional patterns based on the strategic use of small groups of slaves. Only when Spain was back on the defensive, during the chaotic warfare following the outbreak of slave rebellion in nearby Saint-Domingue in the 1790s, did the crown resort to recruiting thousands of current and formerly enslaved men to fight in the king's name, later rewarding them for their service, even in defeat.

Both the Atlantic and the Cuban contexts of the late 1790s, in which the policy of alliance and reward of the enslaved for military service was carried out, differed markedly from earlier examples, even one as close in time as the 1762 attack on Havana. By the late 1790s, the balance of power and alliances in Europe and the Caribbean had shifted dramatically. When Spanish officials in Santo Domingo and Cuba began negotiations with the crown's black allies, in 1795, France was no longer the Spanish Bourbons' dynastic ally against Protestant England. Instead, France was now a republican enemy that had abolished slavery, and the black armies who fought for France in Saint-Domingue had forced Spain to withdraw and sue for peace. England had become an ally, though a short-lived one, in the fight to defend slavery.

In Cuba, liberalization of trade after 1778 and the opening of the slave trade after 1789 had stimulated a steady growth of sugar production, and the island's enslaved population increased rapidly as more than 200,000 enslaved Africans were forcibly imported from 1790 to 1820.[2] When the Spanish crown freed more than one hundred enslaved men who had resisted the British attack of the 1760s, they were publicly honored, in the hope that this would encourage others among the enslaved to faithfully defend crown and colony. Even those who were freed remained on the island. In 1793, Spain had been desperate enough to recruit rebels among the enslaved and the free population of African descent in Hispaniola, to try to save its colony in Santo Domingo, but when those allies arrived in Havana's port after the war, the captain general of Cuba refused to even allow them off the ship, insisting that they were a pernicious example of savagery and might incite rebellion in Cuba as well.

By the early nineteenth century, after the enslaved insurgents of Saint-Domingue had freed themselves from slavery and French colonial rule, Cuba had become a plantation colony, with enslaved and free people of color making up a majority of its population. Spanish officials assigned to the island now resisted the employment of slaves in the military, and they even questioned the loyalty of free militiamen of color who had fought so effectively to defend Spanish interests in the Caribbean during the previous generation.[3]

One particularly interesting case of the Spanish state's employment of slaves in military units was the community of one hundred enslaved artillerymen in Havana, who were trained in the use of cannons, to supplement the forces in the reformed artillery corps. The state allowed them many privileges, in contrast to the experience of royal slaves in fort building. When Spain took the offensive in war with England from 1779 to 1783, some of these artillerymen and other auxiliaries served in successful Spanish campaigns against British strongholds in the Gulf of Mexico, such as Manchac and Pensacola. When Spain fought unsuccessfully against the French Republic (1793–1795) in Hispaniola, during the chaotic bloodletting of the Haitian Revolution, it had to join its allies and opponents in trying to recruit the enslaved as soldiers.

Havana's Company of Enslaved Artillerymen

As was detailed in chapter 3, the defense needs of Havana in the 1760s were substantial, and there was a particular need for unskilled laborers in fort building. However, the Bourbons' military reorganization and reform also identified deficiencies in available military personnel that needed rectification to secure Havana. Although armed corps of the enslaved in actual combat were rare in the Spanish Empire, the militarization of Havana after the British occupation ended in 1763 included the creation of an elite corps of people enslaved by the king, who were assigned to the city's artillery companies. From among the more than 4,000 enslaved Africans purchased for state work during Captain General Ricla's tenure, from 1762 to 1763, one hundred men were set apart to serve in the artillery companies and one hundred women were purchased as wives for them.[4]

Here, the crown and its officials assigned a small group of trained slaves to a strategic task: manning and maintaining the cannonry for Havana's defenses. To assure their loyalty and to retain these enslaved men permanently, the state established a community for them, with provisions for family life, material benefits, and special status. The state's organization and regulation of this enslaved company provide a good illustration of the guiding principles that supported state enslavement in Cuba for much of the colonial period—the strategic use of state slaves for colonial defense, close attention to costs and benefits, and a Catholic, deeply gendered paternalism. In other words, the officials saw Havana's enslaved artillerymen and their families both as valuable state resources and as human subjects of the king.[5]

Though it is unclear exactly when Ricla purchased the two hundred male and female enslaved Africans destined for artillery service, payouts to a contractor, for materials and wages to build houses for the enslaved artillerymen and their families, appear in the captain general's accounts as early as February 1764. Leftover wood was used later to construct beds.[6] This special corps was officially formed in February 1765, with a white second lieutenant and two sergeants from the veteran troops of the Havana artillery company as commanders and with four free blacks serving as first corporals to the one hundred enslaved men, who were listed as "servants" in the artillery records.[7]

By February 1766, Intendant Miguel de Altarriba wrote to the Marquis of Esquilache with an update on the status of the enslaved artillerymen and the women purchased to be their wives. Since all two hundred people were classified as *bozales*, having been born in Africa, the crown felt they would need considerable instruction before they could be married and take up their duties. When the intendant tried to arrange the marriages, he found the men "little instructed" and "most unbaptized," and so he assigned some "young men of their own kind, their corporals, and the chaplain of the Hospital of San Ambrosio" to immediately undertake their training in Christian teachings and practice. The women were divided among the "best residents of this City" for similar instruction. By the winter of 1766, Altarriba thought twenty were ready for their marriage vows and that most could marry by Easter. The intendant also requested Esquilache's approval for a special gift of eight reales to each couple to celebrate their wedding.[8]

Within a year of the corps' formation, Altarriba was making a case to Spanish officials for the benefits of a permanent enslaved artillery squad. With four new forts under construction in the city, the skills of these men would be crucial in manning the cannons, since the island suffered from a "lack of soldiers trained in artillery in moments of need." Their families also served the crown well, since "the precious production of their offspring is so useful to the state" and there were "already good signs" that the couples would soon begin having children. To support reproduction, the intendant proposed rewarding each family that had a child within one year with four pesos for diapers, "given their poverty," and giving two pesos to those who had a child by the second year. Those who did not have children would "not receive any help and [would] have to work in their off hours for their maintenance."[9]

The intendant also made a case for granting these enslaved artillerymen and their families privileges, especially compared to those enslaved by the king who were employed in fort construction. In addition to the artillerymen's specially constructed houses and the monetary gifts for marriage and parenthood, the Count of Ricla ordered special uniforms with pants, a waistcoat, shoes, and a cap with an insignia of two crossed cannons on the front. The artillerymen's wives would sew their husbands' uniforms and then be employed in making the more modest clothing designated for the state's enslaved workers and for convicts at the fort sites.

Altarriba also expressed concern that this group of king's slaves not be abused. He offered to draw up a short set of regulations for their future governance, which would make the captain general or the intendant and the lieutenant vicar general of the troops their protectors. In particular, he wanted to save them from the burden of fees for marrying and having their children baptized, "as another distinction for them," and presumably to encourage both their reproduction and their conformity with good Catholic practice. He was confident that the artillerymen and their families deserved these special privileges "due to their docility, obedience and application to all the work assigned to them, be it in Artillery tasks or in those at the forts in which they have been and are employed."[10]

Though information on these enslaved artillerymen is fragmentary, the early fort works summaries for 1765 listed a group of ninety to ninety-nine king's slaves, the only workers under the artillery brigade, assigned to make *salchichones*, or large fascines, first at La Cabaña and then at the Puerta de Tierra, along the city wall. By July 1765, they were listed at the Atarés fort site, south of the Havana arsenal. This group of men enslaved by the king disappears from the general reviews of the forts' workforce, but the royal commissioner was keeping separate records of the group by the end of 1767, perhaps after most had married and moved into their newly built houses.[11]

Altarriba's recommendations met with royal approval. In response to a royal order, in 1768 he and the new captain general, Antonio Bucareli, published a *reglamento*, or set of ordinances, concerning the enslaved artillery corps and their families. Two sections of the *reglamento* covered the obligations of Spanish officials and the corps' chaplain; the third section covered the obligations of the royal slaves.[12]

The corps fell under the jurisdiction of the captain general for any civil or criminal infractions; lesser officials could only apprehend and return any people enslaved in the royal artillery company who were suspected of crimes. The military officer commanding the corps was to be appointed by the captain general and was charged with keeping scrupulous records of each enslaved person by name, age, ethnic group, and any distinguishing marks. The marital status, partners, and numbers of children of each artilleryman were also to be recorded, along with the number assigned to each family's room.[13]

The intendancy was charged with providing subsistence and clothing for the corpsmen and their families, and the *reglamento* minutely detailed the types of foodstuffs, fabric, and notions required, and their costs. In stark contrast to the rude and utilitarian clothing allotted to fort workers, the artillerymen wore breeches, waistcoats, hose, shoes, and caps with an insignia of the artillery company. Their wives were given fabric for skirts and petticoats, blouses, and a mantilla, along with a bit of scarlet taffeta and ribbon for adornment. The wives also received one pair of stockings and a pair of shoes with buckles.[14]

Rather than the two- to four-peso allowance originally proposed for new parents, the *reglamento* included a fabric allotment for each newborn, to make a set of diapers and swaddling clothes, a shirt, and a little bonnet. In a paragraph on the costs of these clothes for infants, the captain general and the intendant noted that six sets of baby clothes per year would be enough. In a chilling reminder of the specter of infant mortality, they noted that more than six children were typically born in a year, but some died of the local malady called the seven-day disease, making the deceased child's allotted clothes available for other newborns.[15]

The artillerymen's special status was also manifested in their better housing, which allowed them some privacy as a family. Their rooms had beds and two lamps fueled by oil, when available, or by pig's fat. They were not obliged to go to the mess hall and each couple was given provisions to cook in their own quarters "according to their custom." Women and children who had been weaned received a half ration; men and boys over ten years old received a full ration. Women who had recently given birth and the sick were given a supplement that included a bit of chicken, bread, and bacon.[16] Sick or injured artillerymen were sent to the royal hospital for king's slaves, Nuestra Señora del Pilar. When their wives and children were sick, they would be visited by the doctor and surgeon of the Royal Hospital of San Ambrosio and would convalesce in their homes. Any royal slaves too ill or incapacitated to work would continue to live in the artillery quarters and would be cared for by the state until their deaths.[17]

The state expected all who were able-bodied to work. The men were to learn all the parts and workings of the city's artillery. When any male children reached working age, they were to be apprenticed to a master of carpentry, ironworking, or stoneworking, or assigned to artillery work like their fathers. In times of war, the men would serve in the towns to which they were assigned. Their work included moving the carriages and artillery pieces, along with gunpowder and shot. Beyond the heavy work of transporting artillery, these slaves were also trained to position, clean, load, and aim cannons and to attend to any other assigned tasks related to artillery in the fortifications. The most outstanding among the enslaved artillerymen were to be permitted to aim and fire cannons, "in order that they might remedy the lack [*suplir la falta*] of Artillerymen in time of war." An enslaved artilleryman who performed a notable action during wartime could be awarded his liberty if the captain general deemed him worthy of that reward. The elderly among the enslaved would make rope or do other light tasks if they were able. Each night, the corps was subject to a roll call, and they were not allowed to leave their quarters thereafter. If any men were missing, an immediate search was to be carried out.[18]

The employment of the women married to the enslaved artillerymen showed the crown's determination to benefit from both their reproductive and their productive labor. The *reglamento* contended that since the men would be well occupied with their many tasks in the artillery corps, it was "indispensable that the women have some useful occupation." Besides sewing clothes for their husbands and families, these occupations included making rope for the navy and washing clothes for the royal hospitals, "at which they could occupy themselves for part of the year with some utility." The enslaved women could also be hired out part time to "decent homes" with their husband's consent, if they were married. The owners of the homes were expected to provide food and a wage to these women for their work outside the artillery company, a considerable advantage to the state. Between February 1767 and June 1772, the wives of the enslaved artillerymen made rope for use in the arsenal, earning 3,376 pesos 7 reales.[19]

The women likely did not enjoy the full use of their earnings, "since the work of the [artillery] quarters is communal." At least part of their salaries was to be pooled under the control of their supervisors and used to pay six pesos a month to a midwife, for children's clothes beyond the allotment provided by the royal treasury, and for masses to be said for the souls of deceased artillerymen. The *vecinos* who hired the enslaved artillerymen's wives also were responsible for ensuring that the women returned to their quarters accompanied by their husbands or the corporal of the artillery unit.[20]

These descriptions of the working arrangements of those enslaved by the king in Havana's artillery company suggest a substantially different experience from that endured by the state's fort workers. The artillerymen were still subject to a degree of military discipline, with nightly roll call and supervision by white officers, but there is no mention of branding or having to work in irons. In fact, to improve their spirit and enthusiasm, the men were allowed, on holidays, to go out in groups to take a walk and do "what is decently permitted," if accompanied by their white officers. If there were not enough white officers, they could be accompanied by a black member with "good judgment, and whom they will obey," though they had to return to their quarters punctually for meals.[21] The enslaved artillerymen also were allowed some patriarchal authority within their households, through the privacy of their dwellings and preparation of meals and in the chaperoning of their wives when away from home.

The regulations of the artillery company also made provision for the granting of manumission to its slaves. If a couple had twelve live children, they—but presumably not the children—would be emancipated. Extraordinary service in time of war also could bring manumission.[22]

The state made some provision for the fact that, at least initially, all of the adults among the enslaved in the artillery company were born in Africa, though the allowances were designed to ease their adaptation to Spanish norms and customs and to establish something of an esprit de corps. The chaplain assigned to the company was to "keep inviolable" their religious devotions, such as thanking God after eating and saying the rosary each night. He was to hear their confessions yearly and to instruct them "in the Mysteries of Our Holy Faith . . . with all sweetness and gentleness." He had the obligation, however, to be vigilant in maintaining the "purity" of religious practice and reminding them of their place in the Spanish colonial hierarchy by instructing "each one in what he must do in his state." The chaplain had to consult with the supervisor of the company about appropriate punishment in cases of transgressions. The dead were to be buried in the cemetery established for the royal military hospital of San Ambrosio, with the entire company assembled in uniform but "keeping silent." It is not clear whether women and children would have been interred there as well or if their burials would have allowed other kinds of funereal customs.[23]

Most of the ordinances did not explicitly prohibit African cultural practices; rather, they implicitly favored Spanish custom and cultural norms as evidence of good behavior among the artillerymen and their families. The clearest reglamento reference to the African origins of the enslaved expressed a complex blend of paternalistic values and concern for military discipline in dealing with the artillerymen's punishment: "As black bozales they feel every oppression with respect to the liberty with which they have lived in their Country of origin; they will be treated by the governor of the quarters according to their rudeness, correcting their defects and vices with gentleness." Here, colonial officials showed a fatherly regard for the slaves' presumed ignorance of European ways and for their pain at enslavement, advising supervisors to "as much as possible" avoid beatings as punishment. In cases of "disobedience and haughtiness," however, the *reglamento* contended that more severe punishment was deserved and required. Lesser, recurrent misdeeds were to be corrected with imprisonment and half rations, "which is to them the most terrible penalty."[24]

The state used its fort projects as a threat, analogous to the role of sugar plantations in the private sector, for the most difficult to control among the artillerymen, especially those unwilling to see themselves as members of a privileged corps. For instance, thieves would be assigned to the fort works in chains for a time period proportional to what they had taken. If the thief had stolen from the artillery unit or from the homes of his fellow enslaved artillerymen, he also would be flogged in front of the entire company.[25]

The *reglamento* and a series of data on the enslaved artillerymen and their families from December 1767 through November 1768 (table 4.1) gives us a tantalizing but frustratingly incomplete window into the lives of Havana's enslaved artillerymen and their families. The number of king's slaves in the artillery company grew to slightly more than two hundred people over that period as more couples married and the number of children doubled, from ten to twenty by year's end. Commentary by the colonial official filing the monthly summaries indicates that the fort projects served as a site of both punishment and recruitment for the artillery company, though only one enslaved man passed to the forts (no reason is given) and one was recruited from there in 1768. Significantly, there is no mention of desertions or manumissions by any members of the enslaved artillery community over the year.[26]

Table 4.1. King's Slaves and Families in Artillery Companies of Havana, December 1767–November 1768

Date	Single men	Married men	Single women	Married women	Sons	Daughters	Total
December 1767	8	83	7	83	1	9	191
January 1768	9	83	7	83	2	10	194
February 1768	9	83	7	83	3	12	197
March 1768	9	83	7	83	4	11	197
April 1768	7	85	5	85	5	11	198
May 1768	7	85	5	85	5	11	198

Table 4.1 (continued)

Date	Single men	Married men	Single women	Married women	Sons	Daughters	Total
June 1768	7	86	5	86	5	11	200
July 1768	7	86	5	86	5	11	201
September 1768	6	86	4	86	7	12	201
October 1768	6	86	4	86	8	12	202
November 1768	6	86	4	86	7	13	202

Source: "Estado de Revista . . . y de la Artilleria, a los Negros esclavos de Rey destinados al servicio de ella, a las Negras de SM mugeres de aquellos, a sus hijos, y hijas que unos y otras se hallan aquartelados en el Quartel de San Isidro de esta ciudad . . . ," December 13, 1767; January 17, February 21, March 20, April 17, May 12, June 12, July 10, September 11, October 23, and November 27, 1768, Archivo General de Indias, Santo Domingo, 2122.

Note: The summaries did not distinguish possibly widowed enslaved people among those who were single.

The comments also included information on births and deaths to explain changes in the total number of enslaved people living in the artillery quarters month to month. In contrast to the grim mortality rates in the fort works, none of the artillerymen died over the year recorded here. Life was more precarious for the enslaved women and children; twelve children were born in the quarters, while two women and two children died.

Data here also suggests that the reglamento's admonishment to the intendant to "avoid disorders" by finding wives for any of the single or new recruits was taken seriously and may have been successful. The number of single men was reduced from a high of nine in January to six in November. The number of single women fell by the same number, and three married couples were added by the end of 1768. Only one single man was sent to the forts, and no one deserted.

Unfortunately, to date, only a few later glimpses of the enslaved artillerymen and their families have been found. The captain general, the Marqués de la Torre, reported that during his tenure, from 1771 to 1776, "the very useful company of black King's slaves who served in Artillery" had been maintained at full strength by transferring others from the fort works as needed.[27] As renewed war against England approached in early 1777, Charles III reported on the number of crown slaves in Havana in his instructions to the new Captain General Diego José Navarro: "I have in that Plaza [Havana] 350 black slaves with their children: the 100 are well instructed in the use of cannon and are only employed in tasks of this sort; the rest in the fortification works, [there are] those that are worth a lot of money because they are masons, stonecutters, and artisans of other kinds; but there are also others that are nothing more than *peones*."[28]

Some of the skilled royal slaves may have been children of the first generation of artillerymen, trained and sent to work in other sites around Havana. The king may have overstated the numbers of these enslaved men who lived with their children, though some among the workers who remained for many years at the forts may have had families.

By the summer of 1780, the numbers of enslaved artillerymen in Havana had fallen to seventy-six men and continued to shrink, to seventy-two by May 1781, as the Spanish army took thirty royal artillery slaves into battle in the Gulf campaigns.[29] Our next glimpse is a table of the enslaved members of the artillery company from December 1784. By that year, their numbers had fallen substantially compared to the 1760s, to 144 people—seventy males and seventy-four females. The list of males was broken down by age and suggests an aging population, including twelve enslaved males under fifteen years old, thirty-one from fifteen to sixty years of age, and twenty-seven over sixty years old. There were also three free *pardos*, or mulattoes, listed as corporals in the artillery company, raising the question of whether these men had been born of white fathers and enslaved women in the company and then freed. More likely, they were hired from outside as supervisors, as had been common in the 1760s.[30]

The review of 1784 lists a number of free whites still with the company as well: two retired soldiers, the chaplain and his family, plus two sergeants, four corporals, and their families. Unfortunately, no marital status is listed for any of the residents of the company in 1784, but the close correspondence between the numbers of men and of women among the enslaved most likely meant that family groups in a second generation still made up a large portion of the enslaved living in the artillery company almost twenty years after its creation. By 1789, the numbers of enslaved blacks had fallen to fifty-three, thirty of whom were married.[31]

The Spanish state garnered considerable benefit from this community of enslaved artillerymen and their families. Havana now enjoyed a permanent, well-trained group of artillerymen to supplement regular soldiers for defense, and even for offensive campaigns during the American War of Independence. The offspring of the enslaved increased royal assets, while family ties and relative privilege helped to ensure the artillerymen's obedience and loyalty. The considerable investment and care taken to establish this corps of enslaved artillerymen suggests that the state highly valued their skills. In contrast to the basic maintenance and intense vigilance mandated for those enslaved by the king who were assigned to the fort projects, the state took pains to create an esprit de corps among the enslaved artillerymen, with allowances for family life, special housing and clothing, and a system of discipline more like that imposed on free soldiers than on slaves. The lack of evidence of major resistance among the enslaved artillerymen and their families, and the company's longevity, may mean that they also viewed themselves as an elite and that they valued their military training and service.[32]

When war resumed in the late 1770s, some of the enslaved artillerymen were called to action in the Caribbean theater, but the overall participation of the enslaved in combat remained low. Unlike British and French Caribbean colonies, the Spanish Caribbean islands such as Cuba retained white majorities in their populations until the early 1790s, and Spain retained its populous mainland colonies such as Mexico. Therefore, in the 1770s and 1780s, the Spanish Empire still had access to an empire-wide pool of military manpower—white soldiers recruited in Spain, Mexico, and the Caribbean, disciplined militiamen from places such as Havana, and Native American allies from around the circum-Caribbean. At this point, at least, the empire did not require a major resort to enslaved soldiers in combat.

Securing Louisiana

One of the few concessions Spain acquired for its costly support of France in the Seven Years' War was France's cession of Louisiana to its ally. The transfer was unpopular with the colony's French-speaking residents, sparking a rebellion in 1768 that put Spanish governor Antonio de Ulloa to flight.[33] Charles III appointed Alejandro O'Reilly to mount an expedition to reassert Spanish control in his new colony, using Cuba as the staging ground.

The expedition of more than 2,000 men that sailed for New Orleans in 1769 comprised a mix of Spanish soldiers, Havana militiamen (white and of color), and some "distinguished volunteers" from among the Havana elite. To serve the expedition and begin any necessary construction, free artisans were included—seven ironworkers and seven carpenters. No groups of slaves were listed in the expedition reports, though a few likely participated.[34] O'Reilly and his troops arrived in New Orleans in August 1769 and quickly established Spanish authority, arresting the twelve leaders of the rebellion. Six were executed and six were sent to prison in the El Morro fort of Havana.[35]

Since the fort works in Havana still required thousands of workers in 1769, Cuban Captain General Bucareli proposed assigning soldiers from the New Orleans expedition who were guilty of serious crimes ("*delitos feos*") to begin any needed defense works in Louisiana.[36] Once Spanish control was established, however, at least one small group, four enslaved men in total, was assigned to the military hospital in Louisiana to care for sick and wounded soldiers, similar to the enslaved contingent on the staff of the military hospital in Havana.[37] Back in Havana, however, the threat of renewed war with Britain necessitated more extensive use of the enslaved in military occupations.

Enslaved People in the Gulf Campaigns

By the mid-1770s, there had been significant improvement in the defenses of Havana, both in the reorganization of its armed defenders and in its fortifications.[38] The outbreak of armed rebellion against British rule in North America in 1776 emboldened Spain to shift from a predominantly defensive posture to an offensive one. With Britain beleaguered on various fronts, Spain hoped to recoup some of the losses of the 1760s, particularly its colony in Florida. Cuba provided crucial support for the Spanish victories in the northern Caribbean theater, as part of the overall Bourbon strategy of creating scattered diversions around the fringes of the British empire to prevent the concentration of British forces against any one threat.[39]

Unlike the extraordinary resort to state enslavement that refortified Havana after 1763, however, the Gulf campaigns showed Spain's more common strategic, but limited, use of enslaved workers in military service. Spanish commanders brought in veteran white soldiers from around the empire, reassigned disciplined militias (white and of color) from colonies such as Cuba, and recruited Native American fighters from among allies in the Gulf region. The enslaved were part of all these expeditions, but their numbers were small and they were rarely, if ever, officially armed.

In February 1776, the possibility of renewed war with Britain spurred the new minister of the Indies, José de Gálvez, to order a full report on Cuba's military capabilities.[40] Before the formal declaration of war against Britain, in May 1779, Spain also had sent spies into English Florida to reconnoiter defenses and to offer covert aid to the North American rebels.[41] With open war, Spanish New Orleans became the launching site for military attacks against British posts on the Mississippi River and the northern Gulf Coast. Many of the soldiers and supplies were organized through the office of Captain General Diego José Navarro in Havana.

For instance, to mount an expeditionary force against Manchac and Baton Rouge in the fall of 1779, Louisiana governor Bernardo de Gálvez needed troops from Havana to supplement his small garrison of only 370 able-bodied men. Along with the 160 soldiers sent from Havana, Governor Gálvez was able to recruit a similar number of Native American fighters, plus local militia and other volunteers.[42] Since Navarro was unable to send the 4,000 men Gálvez had originally requested, plans to press on to Pensacola were scaled back.

When Gálvez decided to attack Mobile, instead, he again took advantage of a mix of fighters recruited in Cuba, including Spanish regulars and soldiers from the Havana garrison, *pardo* and *moreno* (brown and black) militiamen, and at least one hundred black volunteers as pioneers (*gastadores de acha y machete*), though whether they were enslaved or free was not recorded.[43] Twenty-four slaves did serve in this expedition, but it is not clear whether they were among the pioneers or were employed in other capacities.[44]

When the Spanish finally did launch an attack on Pensacola, beginning in the spring of 1780, they brought together a much larger fighting force, but reliance on enslaved people's labor remained slight. An expedition of more than 7,700 men was sent out from Cadiz in April 1780, but thousands fell ill or died of disease before the attack could be launched. A hurricane scattered many others to shores all around the Caribbean, even as far west as Campeche.[45]

The reconfigured expedition that finally embarked in February 1781 again numbered more than 7,000 men. This force included *pardo* and *moreno* militiamen from Havana, thirty of the enslaved artillerymen of Havana, and some one hundred fort workers of unknown status.[46] Cuba also contributed a combined force of more than 2,000 men—troops, militiamen, and eighty laborers—for the 1782 invasion of New Providence Island in the Bahamas; 425 more men went to Guarico, in Hispaniola, for a subsequently aborted mission to retake Jamaica that same year.[47]

Spanish troops led by Matías de Gálvez, brother of José and father of Bernardo, also had some success during the North American rebellion, retaking contested territory on the Caribbean coast of present-day Honduras and Nicaragua. Maintenance of Spanish control in Honduras after the peace remained elusive, however, as the Cuban captain general twice sent several hundred troops and provisions to reinforce the small Spanish outpost of Trujillo on the Mosquito Coast.[48]

Among the Spanish, white Cubans and free people of color were willing to volunteer for army service in the fight against Great Britain, but naval recruitment proved much more difficult. In 1782, when Spain successfully deployed thousands of men for various expeditions around the Gulf of Mexico, the commander of the naval squadron stationed in Havana, José Solano, pleaded with Captain General Juan Manuel Cagigal to institute various recruitment methods to find the 1,500 men needed to fully man the squadron in port. Solano asked Cagigal to use the matrícula, or sailors' registry, to find men skilled in naval artillery—and any other seamen who had hidden themselves from earlier roundups. He also proposed a sweep of the city for vagrants, criminals, and others to supplement naval crews. Cagigal issued an order that rounded up two hundred men and inducted them into the squadron.[49]

Though it was a help, this number was still insufficient, and Solano urged the captain general to take the extraordinary measure of a general levy. The naval commander also suggested rounding up all Europeans in Havana who could not present a royal license and assigning them to naval service. Cagigal rejected this operation, which he judged "violent . . . and capable of irritating many of the residents who helped with loans to cover emergencies in the treasury." Instead, he chose to target those he deemed socially undesirable, with "the soft measure" of asking trustworthy subjects to draw up a list of "all men who by their relaxed life and customs might have the public reputation of [being] evilly entertained and gamblers by profession," both inside and outside the city walls of Havana and in other towns on the island. This expedient seems to have finally generated enough men to fill all the ships in Havana's naval squadron without resorting to raiding rum shops and bars or a general levy.[50] Even these "soft" recruitment measures raised protests, however, and by late February Cagigal was asking Solano to order the sailors of each ship in the squadron who felt they had been unfairly forced to serve to choose a representative and to bring their cases to the government.[51]

By the summer and fall of 1782, the numbers of sailors in the squadron had fallen again, due to disease and desertion, and Solano resumed pressing his case in letters to various officials. In an August letter to the interim viceroy of New Spain, Martín de Mayorga, Solano claimed that he had done what he could with the "prisoners and faint-hearted Indians Your Excellency has assigned to the Arsenal and wood cutting and the people from the levy that the governor has given me." Saying that the number of seamen for each of the ships in Havana "was half what it should be," Solano again proposed apprehending Europeans without licenses and any other "useful men" who could be dragooned into naval service.[52]

In November, Solano wrote to the minister of Indies, José de Gálvez, that there were fourteen ships in port that needed repairs and crew members and that he had been unable to recruit enough men, even with his appeals to Mayorga and the governor of Yucatan. Solano then decided to disarm two warships, three frigates, and some smaller vessels to fully staff twelve other warships and four smaller vessels for a scheduled rendezvous with the French fleet in Guarico.[53] Even after the official end of Spain's intervention in the American War for Independence, the crown continued to resort to levies to staff royal vessels. One such roundup, in 1787, generated resistance fierce enough that then Captain General Ezpeleta had to rescind the order, to avoid outright rebellion.[54]

A Spanish invasion of Jamaica in the early 1780s never materialized, but the recovery of the Florida colonies and the addition of Louisiana meant that the crown had even more territory in North America to defend from Great Britain and the newly constituted United States. Though Spain's intervention in the American War of Independence had been largely successful in exacting revenge for 1762, it proved costly in both the short and the long terms.[55]

The successes of the Gulf campaign against Great Britain were in large measure due to Spain's ability to marshal the necessary manpower and supplies, an effort in which the participation of Cuban residents, both free and enslaved, proved crucial.[56] Yet the fact that Spanish forces were on the offensive and allied with France reduced the need to rely on the enslaved in military service. On the other hand, the British were stretched to the limit, on the defensive against the rebels in North America and against two imperial rivals in the Caribbean; therefore, they relied more heavily on enslaved soldiers and auxiliaries.

As historians Philip Morgan and Andrew O'Shaughnessy have noted, the British suffered a "fatal isolation" during the American Revolution, with no foreign allies, no friendly ports in mainland North America south of Canada, and the necessity of trying to defend its many Caribbean island colonies from both French and Spanish attack after 1779. In the Caribbean and in southern mainland colonies such as South Carolina, in particular, the British armed slaves and, in some cases, formed them into regiments. By the end of the conflict, in 1783, the British military and their American opponents may have employed as many as 30,000 black men as soldiers, most of them enslaved, setting precedents for Great Britain's later widespread use of enslaved soldiers in the Caribbean, in the 1790s.[57]

The Enslaved as Soldiers During the Haitian Revolution

When waves of slave rebellion and warfare against revolutionary France engulfed the Caribbean, beginning in 1791, France, Britain, and Spain were forced to increase their reliance on black soldiers, both enslaved and free. Spain remained officially neutral during the first years of fighting in Saint-Domingue as whites and free people of color fought in the southern provinces and slaves rebelled in the north. When England and Spain declared war on France in 1793, the Spanish military was again entangled in fighting on the continent and in the Caribbean.

To preserve slavery and colonial rule on Hispaniola, Spain embarked upon what historian David Geggus has called the "daring experiment" of appealing to Saint-Domingue's insurgent black fighters to become Spanish soldiers in return for guarantees of freedom for themselves and their families, privileges, and land somewhere on Hispaniola or elsewhere.[58] By the spring of 1793, British and French officials were also trying to recruit the rebels.[59]

Spain was ultimately the most successful in this effort, recruiting the three main leaders of insurgent black troops: Jean-François, George Biassou, and, for a time, Toussaint Louverture.[60] Their followers, often underfed and ill equipped, were offered freedom, along with uniforms and rations, to fight for Spain as the black auxiliaries of Charles IV. Rather than the groups of perhaps several hundred enslaved men that Spain had employed in earlier conflicts, the black rebel armies in Hispaniola numbered in the thousands by the mid-1790s.[61] Spain had a long history of negotiating with rebellious or fugitive slaves when the situation demanded, yet the experiment in Hispaniola was especially risky in the context of widespread slave rebellion and imperial warfare.[62]

Such an expedient was necessary, in part, due to the decline of the Spanish army in Cuba. In 1786, Madrid administrators ended the expensive policy of reinforcing Spanish American fixed garrisons with a rotation of peninsular battalions, though replacement soldiers still were recruited in Spain and the Canary Islands. By the late 1780s, troops from Havana also had to be sent to garrison the territories in Louisiana and Florida, which they had helped to win during the Spanish intervention in the American War of Independence, reducing troop strength in Havana. Historian Allan Kuethe has noted that the Havana garrison of the 1790s became "a kind of repository for the depraved and the desperate," causing a rise in criminal behavior and desertions among the city's troops.[63] When caught, malefactors often were sentenced to labor at the forts, a boon for administrators trying to maintain Havana's fortifications but a problem for keeping the garrison at full strength.

By the spring of 1793, the regular army in Cuba had fallen in both numbers and quality. Commanders in Cuba were no longer able to recruit sufficient numbers of soldiers on the island or in places such as the Canaries. Spain itself could offer few replacements, as peninsular troops were fighting French revolutionary armies in Europe.[64]

Thus, the daring experiment of recruiting enslaved rebels to the Spanish army in Hispaniola was necessary, and it was initially successful. By early January 1794, the Spanish governor in Santo Domingo, Joaquín García, could report that "many of the parishes of the Northern Part and west [of the French colony of Saint-Domingue] have submitted to the Domination of our Catholic monarch, some by the force of Arms of our Black auxiliaries," others by seeking Spanish protection from English or French republican forces.[65] Yet Spanish colonial officials were uneasy about the necessity of relying so heavily on both the fighting skills and the loyalty of black soldiers. Soon García and others were reporting that most of the men under arms were "undisciplined free mulattos and blacks or black slaves without sense and incapable of subordination." They also feared that these fighters might at some point change sides, if they perceived some advantage in doing so.[66]

Spanish officials had legitimate cause for concern on several counts. On the issue of loyalty, the rebel leaders Jean-François and Biassou remained in Spanish employ, but Toussaint skillfully played all the European participants before he finally left Spanish service and declared for the French Republic in the spring of 1794. The reasons for Toussaint's "about-face" are not entirely clear, but the republican French National Assembly's declaration of general slave emancipation may have been one factor. Another may have been the Spanish and Cuban officers' outright trading in enslaved people and their efforts to protect the property of French royalists, including their enslaved workers.[67]

Spanish officials found their lack of control over their new allies even more alarming. The black military leaders recognized their key role in advancing the Spanish cause and therefore brooked little intervention from Spanish commanders. They chose their own ranks, Jean-François preferring the title of Grand Admiral and George Biassou adopting, among others, the title of "Viceroy of the

Conquered Territories." They also were wined and dined by Spanish officials and demanded flattery and bribes for their services.[68]

Spanish impotence became brutally clear in July 1794, when Jean-François's troops massacred some seven hundred French colonists in the town of Bayajá, at Fort Dauphin in Saint-Domingue. Various accounts in the colonial archives recount the Spanish version of the attack. On July 7, Jean-François entered Bayajá with 450 infantrymen and seventy cavalry. As they advanced on the main square, they came across many white French émigrés from North America, who had come to the garrison seeking protection at Fort Dauphin, now manned by Spanish troops. Quickly, the black soldiers chased down the white colonists on the streets and indoors, putting most to the sword, regardless of gender or age.[69]

This incident generated a lengthy correspondence among French, Spanish, and English diplomats trying to assign blame. Charles IV assured representatives of French landowners in Saint-Domingue that their property rights would be respected and that he would make "the most severe and swift judgment punishing the person or persons that might have been at fault."[70] The Spanish ultimately decided Jean-François was most responsible, though George Biassou was also involved, and that the Spanish troops in Fort Dauphin had made little effort to intervene. However, no official sanction against either of the black military leaders was carried out.[71]

Toussaint's loyalty to Spain was in question for much of 1794 as well, and his ultimate switch to supporting the French republican forces brought a series of Spanish battlefield defeats and Spain's withdrawal from the conflict.[72] The separate peace treaty with France, in 1795, also ceded the Spanish part of Hispaniola to France and gave Spanish families one year to gather their personal effects and move.[73]

The tense peace left Spanish officials with a host of problems. They feared a negative English reaction to Spain's withdrawal from the conflict, and they had to deal with an influx of people of all stations and experience to Cuba. The Cuban captain general, along with his counterpart in Santo Domingo, also were obliged to undertake delicate negotiations to reward the king's black allies, leaving the massacre at Fort Dauphin unpunished though not forgotten. They had to develop a plan to resettle Jean-François and Georges Biassou, their soldiers, and their families somewhere in the Spanish Empire. The crown took its responsibility to these allies seriously, but some officials in the Caribbean complained bitterly about their interactions with the ex-slaves. They found themselves forced to carefully balance the crown's directive to reward the auxiliaries for their service with concerns about potential disruptions in colonies like Cuba, where plantation slavery was growing.

Difficulties began even before Spain withdrew from the conflict. In the spring of 1794, the captain general of Cuba, Luis de Las Casas, returned to Santo Domingo 119 slaves belonging to fleeing refugees, though he allowed the white families to stay in Cuba. When the governor of Santo Domingo complained, Las Casas invoked a royal order of May 21, 1790, prohibiting the importation of slaves or free people of color from French colonies into Spanish territories.[74] After the peace accord, Las Casas still refused to allow slaves traveling with refugees from Santo Domingo to enter Cuba, but he proposed sending the enslaved men to the Isle of Pines and the women to the repository of royal slaves. Until this proposal received royal approval, he suggested assigning the slaves to public works, the perennial choice for all manner of undesirables, though ultimately unsuitable for the empire's black military allies.[75]

When negotiations to resettle the black auxiliaries of Charles IV began, Santo Domingo's Governor García again found himself in a wrangle with Cuban Captain General Las Casas. García's orders were to evacuate the black auxiliaries, because the victorious French refused to allow them to remain and the Spanish crown had promised them resettlement for their loyal service. Las Casas, on the other hand, continued to insist on the royal order of 1790, prohibiting the introduction of any people of color from French colonies into Cuba.[76]

The Spanish governor stationed in Bayajá, the Marqués de Casa Calvo, carried on more direct negotiations with the black rebel leaders in Santo Domingo. His long letter to Las Casas captures well the delicacy of the negotiation and the rancor some officials felt at having to undertake it. Casa Calvo began his letter by attesting to his zeal and patriotic obedience to the king. He offered some observations for Las Casas, after his two years of service at Bayajá in Santo Domingo, and repeated the orders that "charged him with the preservation of the auxiliaries, as the Court [wished], the constitution of the State required, and the necessity of our situation demanded." He noted the expense involved in providing the auxiliaries with clothing and sustenance and complained bitterly that the situation "has seen me forced to treat with a black [man] that although named a general did not leave the realm to which his birth and the principles of slavery consigned him," a position which Casa Calvo found "shameful and perhaps prejudicial" to him personally and to the Spanish cause.[77] Since the war was over, he advocated the immediate abolition of the black fighters' units and titles. Jean-François, his soldiers, and their families, on the other hand, wanted to retain their units, titles, pay, and rations and be given land to resettle as a group in their own town, as they had been promised.[78]

Casa Calvo pointed to the Fort Dauphin massacre and Spanish tolerance of the behavior of the black auxiliaries as having "given them a level of superiority even with us . . . and inspired in their bloody hearts and entrails the unfounded fancy that they had conquered this Plaza and that they had saved the Spanish garrison from the plot" they thought had been planned by the French émigrés from North America. Thus, considering themselves valuable warriors, Jean-François and his men insisted on retaining their arms so they could provide the king with a ready army to defend his realm wherever they finally settled. Casa Calvo claimed to have told them scornfully that the king already had an army and that their only duty was to obey and quit their "projects" immediately. The governor of Bayajá ended his letter by exhorting Las Casas "not to permit in the bosom of the flourishing Island of Cuba . . . these poisonous vipers." He reminded the captain general that "these are the same ones that assassinated their owners, violated their mistresses, and ended [the lives] of many who had properties in this land at the beginning of their insurrection."[79]

In December 1795, when two flotillas of black auxiliaries and their families did arrive in Havana's port, first with George Biassou and then with Jean-François, Las Casas began his own negotiation with Spain's allies with a similar note of fear and lack of grace. Yet the Cuban captain general was able to bargain with more leverage than his counterparts in Santo Domingo. With all the soldiers and their families confined to ships in the harbor, Las Casas refused to allow any of them to disembark, echoing Casa Calvo in commenting that "every colonist imagines his slaves will rebel and the colony will be totally destroyed the moment these individuals arrive. Wretched slaves yesterday, they are today the heroes of a revolution, triumphant, wealthy, and decorated."[80]

Las Casas called two juntas of generals to find a solution that respected the crown's wishes to resettle its allies yet prevented them from supposedly wreaking havoc in Cuba. In the face of Las Casas's insistence on restricting the auxiliaries to their ships, Jean-François at one point sarcastically asked whether he and his entourage were prisoners of the state or vassals of the king, vowing to "obey only the true orders of His Majesty, and no others."[81]

Ultimately, however, the auxiliaries had little choice but to accept resettlement outside of Cuba, in part to avoid being returned to Bayajá and subjected to possible capture by the French. Spanish officials in Havana finally decided that the best plan was to divide up the groups by separating out most of the leaders, or caudillos, as they called them. Spain's allies were to be scattered around the circum-Caribbean in Florida, Trujillo (Guatemala), Campeche (Yucatan), and the island of Trinidad, as well as in Spain.[82]

Thus, despite the opposition of colonial officials in the Caribbean, the freedom of the black troops from Hispaniola was preserved. Jean-François and his entourage of 780 people sailed for Cádiz, Spain, where he remained in the king's service until his death.[83] George Biassou, resettled in Florida and fought again for the king in campaigns against Spain's Native American enemies. When Biassou died, in 1801, he was buried in Saint Augustine with full military honors.[84]

As historian Jane Landers has noted, enslaved fighters were among the most loyal of Spain's auxiliaries in wartime. They could trust the crown's willingness to grant freedom and other rewards for devoted military service and to uphold those rewards despite hostility and discrimination from white officials and soldiers, even in the charged moment of the Haitian Revolution. None of Spain's black allies met the fate of Toussaint, who was betrayed and left to die in prison.[85]

It is also true, however, that Spain never resorted to purchasing numerous slaves directly from Africa for military service, as the British did. In the 1790s, faced with the perennial realities of disease among their European-born troops, warfare on Hispaniola, and rebellions in some of their own Caribbean colonies, the British began forming black slave regiments that were uniformed and armed along European lines. Initially, these black soldiers were purchased or hired out from slave owners in the colonies, but by 1796 British officials favored the outright purchase of enslaved Africans through the transatlantic slave trade. From 1795 to 1808, the British government bought an estimated 13,400 slaves for the West India Regiments, at a cost of approximately 925,000 pounds, making the government the largest individual purchaser of slaves in the empire. By 1807, as abolitionist pressure grew, the British government freed close to 10,000 of its enslaved soldiers and, like the Spanish, ultimately settled them in relatively underpopulated parts of the empire.[86]

Ironically, the Spanish Empire, which had the longest history of employing and rewarding slaves for military service, did not adopt a similar expedient in the 1790s. Several factors may have discouraged the formation of slave regiments in the Spanish military. An important one for colonial officials clearly was the relative newness of large-scale plantation slavery in the Spanish Caribbean. But additionally, unlike in the 1760s, when the state bought thousands of slaves for fort building in Havana, by the 1790s, Spain simply could not muster the resources to do so.

～

Spain's ability to rely on the labor power and military service of people of African descent, enslaved and free, was a crucial element in its ability to retain most of its empire in the face of the bitter and costly warfare of the eighteenth century. Spanish cultural traditions and norms valued military service by all men. These values helped to ensure that the crown and its officials were careful to reward extraordinary valor and loyalty, even of the enslaved, often enough to retain the colonial bond. Given the difficulties of defending its far-flung empire against Britain's growing economic and military power, Spain had few alternatives.[87] With the service of enslaved people and free militiamen of color, Spain's offensive against Great Britain from 1779 to 1783 was deemed a success. During the next decade of relative peace, Spanish policy makers even entertained illusions of returning to the offensive to retake Jamaica, and planned an invasion of the British Isles.[88]

Renewed war against revolutionary France, from 1793 to 1795, and against Britain, from 1796 to 1802 and from 1804 to 1808, on the other hand, brought a chaotic series of reversals. Spain found itself seriously debilitated by the time it withdrew from the fighting on Hispaniola in 1795, and continued war with Britain led to a series of defeats at sea from which the Spanish navy never recovered, especially at the Battle of Trafalgar, in 1805. Cuba remained firmly within the colonial sphere through the nineteenth century, but its role shifted considerably. The island occasionally provided troops and matériel to battles elsewhere (such as in Florida, against the Georgia Patriots, in 1812), but by 1825, Spain's mainland colonies had splintered away.

The foregoing shows that Spain employed enslaved people of African descent more often for the defense of Cuba than for offensive campaigns in the Caribbean. The full range of military occupations and experiences of the enslaved was wide: as uniformed artillerymen or as unskilled fort workers enslaved by the king, as workers hired from private owners, or as allied soldiers who had freed themselves from slavery by force of arms. The crown used the possibility of gaining freedom as a tool to recruit defenders for the empire and as a reward for service. Such tools were more likely to have the desired result if the enslaved had some expectation of actually enjoying those rewards, and the evidence presented here suggests that many enslaved people in Cuba were willing to fight for the king and then actively petitioned for their freedom as recompense for their service and sacrifice. The crown upheld its promise of reward, though only for some, and this promise was always tempered by the embedded prejudices of slavery and colonialism.

Within the slave system, the crown also was willing to create small corps of enslaved people, such as Havana's artillery workers, and to try to win their loyalty with the trappings of military status and privilege—separate quarters, special uniforms, and the encouragement of marriage and family life. In fact, marriage policy for white colonial officials and soldiers was often much more restrictive.[89] However, because Spain's employment of enslaved fighters on the battlefield was generally limited, such employment did not transform the institution of slavery in Cuba or in the empire. Instead, long-standing Spanish norms that valued and rewarded military service by all male subjects extended to some of the enslaved, even in the midst of slave revolution in the 1790s—even until the end of Spanish rule, in 1898. On the other hand, military labor, particularly in the fort works, more closely approximated the experiences of enslaved workers on plantations, characterized by miserable and deadly work regimes with few if any paths to freedom.

Spain's employment of the enslaved in the military did not transform Cuba's economy or the institution of slavery to the extent that state-directed defense construction and development did up to the end of the eighteenth century. Instead, military service had a greater impact on the status of white creoles and the free population of color. The latter gained valuable military experience and prestige through their effective service. Havana's free militiamen of color continued to lobby for privileges, and against discrimination and harassment by government officials, into the early decades of the nineteenth century, pushing against the growing discrimination of an expanding plantation economy based on enslavement of people of African descent.[90] White creoles also gained experience and prestige that they used as leverage to claim more economic, social, and political power.

Defeat for the empire in 1762 had brought benefits for Cuba thereafter. Similarly, Cubans' loyalty and service to Spain during the second half of the eighteenth century allowed the island's white creoles to extract commercial concessions that brought greater access to the Atlantic markets for slaves, sugar, and other commodities and substantially expanded sugar production in Cuba. Ultimately, slavery became more deeply entrenched in the private sector, even as it declined as a major source of labor employed by the state, forcing colonial officials to experiment with other forms of labor coercion to advance defense and public works projects. In particular, the captains general of Cuba extended the reach and centralization of the criminal justice system to control populations considered dangerous and to recruit labor for public works. Several of these experiments ultimately provided models of labor coercion for the private sector as slavery was gradually abolished over the nineteenth century.

5

KEEPING THE PEACE

Civil Construction and Forced Labor in Havana, 1771–1835

In 1777, Felipe de Fondesviela, the Marqués de la Torre, wrote a series of notes to his successor, reflecting on his six years as captain general of Cuba. He claimed as his greatest successes his reforms of policing and the administration of justice in Havana and the advancement of many much-needed public works projects. These two accomplishments were inextricably linked in his thinking and practice. For De la Torre, the extirpation of vice and delinquency through forced labor was a key component of a well-ordered society. Sentencing thousands of criminals to public works was a "gentle method" of correcting the "vice-ridden" (*viciosos*) and advancing "the important works constructed for the common good."[1]

De la Torre was a representative of the enlightened colonial officials who carried out the Bourbons' plans to defend and develop Spain's American empire. He also was the beneficiary of the good work of his two predecessors as captain general; the Count of Ricla and Antonio Bucareli had advanced the fort construction and repair projects considerably by the time De la Torre arrived in Havana in June 1771.[2] The new captain general enjoyed a brief respite from war in the Caribbean theater throughout his term (1771 to 1777) and therefore could devote most of his energies to ensuring internal security and improving the infrastructure in and around the capital city.

De la Torre's successors into the early nineteenth century had to confront more dire circumstances: internal threats to Spanish colonialism and to slavery. Though Cuba remained a Spanish colony until 1898, independence agitation in the early 1800s prompted the crown to impose martial law by 1825. The colonial officials and the Cuban elite also worried about the rapidly increasing population of enslaved Africans as *marronage* and slave rebellion spread. Additionally, the island's slave system was disrupted by British abolitionism, though officials were able to turn this challenge to their advantage, claiming the labor of liberated Africans for the state.

De la Torre arrived at a city in transformation, growing and bustling with new people and enterprise. The infusion of imperial resources for Havana's defenses after 1763 flooded the city and its environs with Mexican silver revenues, enriching property owners and contractors and generating capital for private investment. The increased militarization of Cuba in the 1760s also brought thousands of troops to Havana, and the state appropriated or purchased urban buildings and lands for barracks, parade grounds, warehouses, and fortifications.[3] The presence of more soldiers and sailors may have enhanced security against external threats, but it also led colonial officials to worry about the growing numbers of military deserters and their potential to disturb the social order among the rapidly changing population. Due to their concerns about disruptions, during the 1700s, state authorities added other groups of people to the list of those who required constraints and rehabilitation through forced labor.

Colonial officials ultimately turned potentially disruptive groups in Havana's population into sources of labor for civil construction and urban renewal. Where the Count of Ricla had resorted to purchasing enslaved Africans in the king's name to advance the fort projects of the 1760s, by the 1770s and 1780s, De la Torre and his successors took to experimenting with military levies and patrols to round up deserters to maintain troop numbers and supplement the squads of fort workers. Colonial officials also turned these tactics on the civilian population to recruit nonmilitary workers, expanding patrols to capture vagrants and the unemployed and sentencing petty criminals to forced labor on public projects.

By the last decade of the eighteenth century, another source of forced labor for public works emerged from the expanding enslaved population in Cuba, though the state had ceased buying large numbers of enslaved Africans for its projects in the mid-1760s. In the 1790s, both Cuban elites and colonial officials sought better ways to control the growing numbers of the enslaved who fled captivity. Adopting policies similar to those that centralized the roundup of military deserters, fugitive slaves from around the island were increasingly sent to Havana. When slave owners did not quickly claim those enslaved who had escaped from their work sites, the state sought to benefit from their labor, especially for road building projects. By targeting fugitives from military service and slavery, as well as free people who transgressed the norms of the eighteenth-century social order, the Spanish colonial state was able to remodel the city in ways befitting its growing wealth and status in the empire.

A Growing City and its Hinterland

Havana's increasing importance to imperial defense and development is reflected in the swelling population on the island, especially in and around the capital, over the eighteenth century. At the close of the 1600s Cuba's, population was roughly 50,000 people, with about half living in Havana.[4] In 1762, on the eve of the British siege and occupation of Havana, the island was home to approximately 150,000. Twelve years later, when De la Torre compiled the island's first official census, the island's population was more than 175,000, with almost 97,000 in the Havana region and just over 75,500 in the city. Much of this growth occurred among the island's white population as waves of colonial officials, military engineers, soldiers, sailors, officers, civilian merchants, workers, and others came to Havana. The growing white population suggests that the imperial service economy continued to dominate in Cuba through the 1770s.[5]

Importations of enslaved Africans, on the other hand, did not return to previous annual highs of close to 8,000 people (during the years 1763 to 1765) until the early 1790s, after important changes were made to imperial policy on slave trading to Cuba, in 1789. In the years between 1765 and 1789, yearly imports of enslaved Africans into Cuba ranged from approximately 1,000 to 3,000 people. In 1791, two years after the Spanish crown allowed free trade in the enslaved, annual slave imports had jumped to more than 6,700.[6]

Still, Cuba remained a diversified economy with a steadily growing but not dominant sugar sector until the 1790s. When slave rebellion destroyed the plantation economy of nearby Saint-Domingue, beginning in 1791, a major competitor in the world market for sugar was removed, and Cubans were prepared to take advantage of the opportunity. Commercial concessions over the preceding decades had opened the island's economy to Atlantic markets, and the slave trade was finally released from monopoly contracts in 1789.[7]

Slow but steady growth in the numbers of sugar plantations characterized the period from the mid-1760s to the end of the century. From 1763 to 1768, an average of 1.6 new *ingenios* (sugar mills) were established in the Havana region each year. For the next twenty-five years, the annual average growth in numbers of *ingenios* in the area hovered just under seven per year. By the end of the 1790s, however, an average of twenty *ingenios* per year were established, and the size of individual plantations had increased as well.[8] The growth of *cafetals*, or coffee plantations and coffee production followed a similar trajectory. The first *cafetal* was established to the southwest of Havana in 1748. By 1790, there were fewer than ten *cafetales*, but in 1804 there were eighty-four. By 1841, there were 582 coffee plantations in the region.[9]

To staff these plantations, the enslaved population in and around Havana began to increase rapidly, as did the average numbers of the enslaved per *ingenio* and their productivity.[10] By 1792, a census showed that the human mix of Havana had shifted markedly to a majority of people of color, both enslaved and free, for the first time. This demographic trend continued into first half of the nineteenth century as the enslaved population grew to more than 320,000 by 1846.[11] As the private sector increased its commitment to the use of enslaved people for plantation work, the colonial state began to experiment with coercing the labor of other vulnerable people to carry out civil construction projects and to build the infrastructure of an expanding export economy.

Reforming Vagrants and the "Evilly Entertained"
The rapid demographic and social changes in late eighteenth-century Cuba coincided with an era of growing attention to "unproductive" and "unruly" people in the metropole and the empire, as officials' thinking on imperial political economy evolved.[12] There had been sporadic campaigns against the unemployed poor for centuries, but by the mid-1700s, both official discourse on vagrancy and measures against vagrants increased. The definition of those considered vagrant also expanded over the 1700s, and they, like military deserters, were subjected to capture and forced labor to reform them into more productive subjects.

In a series of royal orders over the eighteenth century, the Spanish crown defined more clearly the category of vagrant and its negative connotations. In a royal order from 1717, the definition of those who could be subject to levies of vagrants was "bad living people" with "no honor." By 1745, the crown had issued another order that expanded its definition of vagrancy and delinquency to cover all who had no trade, home, or income and who lived "not knowing from what licit and honorable means their subsistence might come."[13] The order included both the unemployed and the underemployed who did not find productive activities to occupy their time during dead seasons. The delinquent included gamblers, drunks, the sexually promiscuous or adulterous, pimps, and disobedient children. Crown officials also distinguished between "deserving" beggars, who merited compassion and charity, and "false," able-bodied beggars, who were to be prosecuted as vagrants.[14]

The metropolitan approach also revealed a growing effort to centralize the captured vagrants under royal control and to harness their labor. In the 1730s and 1740s, the Spanish crown ordered that vagrants be rounded up and held in jails, with the able-bodied among them sent to army service or public works. In 1775, Charles III authorized annual levies to round up vagrants, and in the later 1770s, shelters were established in Madrid to hold them. In 1779, when Spain joined France to intervene in the American War of Independence, the king set the term of service for captured vagrants sent to the army at eight years. The crown continued to publish edicts against vagrants, beggars, and foreigners every few years over the next two decades.[15]

In Cuba, official concern about unproductive and potentially harmful behavior grew in response to metropolitan directives but also responded to local disquiet about potential problems in the city's expanding population. For instance, *habaneros'* passion for gambling seems to have grown as the city's population swelled with military men, workers, and those without fixed or permanent employment. In response to a royal order in 1745 reminding officials in the Indies of prohibitions against gambling, Captain General Güemes de Horcasitas had reported few gaming houses in Havana. However, from 1763 onward, each of the captains general sought to outlaw or at least regulate gambling and many types of public merriment to reorient the population toward industriousness and productive pursuits. Though Captain General de la Torre claimed great success in the 1770s in controlling the bad habits of *habaneros*, he admitted that gambling was impossible to eradicate, so the only remedy was to tax the practice. His successor, Diego Navarro, attributed the gambling problem to the growing population of vagrants and people of color, though he noted that all social classes participated in the games. The colonial authorities pointed to the area outside the city walls (*extramuros*) as a site of gambling houses, often run by people of color, where sons of "good families" might be corrupted and led astray. Ultimately, officials chose to issue licenses to operate gaming houses, once it was clear that eradicating them would be impossible.[16]

Another contributing factor to official unease about social order in Cuba was the devastating consequences of natural disasters. The island had faced shortages of provisions for the growing population since the early 1760s. When a new cycle of droughts and punishing storms began, in 1765, it further exacerbated the generalized sense of crisis. For instance, the widely destructive hurricane of October 1768 wreaked sufficient havoc to encourage some forced laborers, slaves, and military men to flee their captivity, especially in areas outside Havana proper. The destruction of more than 5,000 houses outside the city also swelled the number of mendicants looking for relief. Captain General Bucareli sent out groups of soldiers to round up escapees, and the king ordered him to guard against the poor going about the streets or to houses to beg for alms. The king also ordered that vagrants be employed in crown projects or public works, or exiled from Havana altogether.[17] It was Bucareli's successor, De la Torre, who perfected mechanisms of capture and deployment to carry out a major program of urban renewal with the forced labor of people deemed vagrants, criminals, or deserters.

Urban Renewal and Forced Labor Under the Marqués de la Torre, 1771–1777
Human disorder was not the only challenge facing colonial officials in Cuba's capital. Various governors of the second half of the eighteenth century commented on the lamentable state of Havana upon their arrival: rented and inadequate housing for state officers and their staff, streets coursing with mud and garbage, tight quarters within the walled portion of the city for the growing population. Arriving governors' distaste sometimes extended to the city's inhabitants. The Marqués de la Torre initially had a sour view of Cubans, accusing them of being "by nature lazy . . . and given to all manner of vices." He contended that the better class of "decent people," to which he presumably belonged, was constantly assaulted by swarms of working people—"cooks, other tavern workers, ship's boys, and brick layers . . . conmen and riffraff."[18]

The attitudes and policies of the De la Torre as captain general illustrate well various threads of Spanish enlightened absolutism on defense, public order, and forced labor. His predecessors had focused funding and labor on fort repairs and construction; most previous civil construction had been carried out by the Catholic Church and religious orders. De la Torre began one new fort (el Príncipe) while captain general and finished several of the defense projects begun in the 1760s. However, relative peace in the Caribbean (from 1763 to 1779) allowed him to direct much of his attention to civil construction, urban beautification, and improvements in public order. De la Torre did face some adversity during his term. Some of the repair and construction projects were necessary due to damages from the Santa Teresa hurricane of October 1768 and from the effects of an especially destructive hurricane season in 1772, when sixteen storms made landfall in the Caribbean and the Gulf Coast.[19]

Civil projects completed during De la Torre's term in office included street cleaning and some effort at paving, several bridges over rivers around Havana, the addition of wider thoroughfares at the Alameda de Paula, inside the city wall, and at the Paseo Nuevo between the Tierra and Punta doorways, outside the wall. Another major project was the Coliseo Theater, part of a plan to provide a venue for proper public entertainment and to raise revenue to build and maintain the Casa de Recogidas, a home for women of "relaxed" morals.[20] Works begun under De la Torre that were still under construction at the end of his term included the Marimelena dock complex and the rebuilding of the Plaza de Armas, which included a new governor's house, meeting space for the municipal council (*cabildo*), and a new jail.[21]

Unlike the defense projects, the expenses of which were covered largely by imperial subsidies from Mexico's silver production, Havana's rebuilding and infrastructure projects relied mostly on local sources of funding.[22] Road and bridge building and repairs were paid for with contributions from *vecinos* living in areas served by those projects. For instance, street repairs and cleaning in Havana were paid for by city residents, each of whom was assessed based on their ability to pay. As evidence of his evenhandedness, De la Torre reported to the intendant that soldiers and clergy had already paid their share, so he expected no less from other inhabitants.[23]

Thoroughfares leading out of Havana also required the constant attention of officials. In the late 1760s, Captain General Bucareli had begun raising funds from the hacienda owners to the leeward side of Havana for the bridges over the Chorrera River. De la Torre ordered a new collection, several years later, from livestock ranchers in the area, to advance the projects. The Cojímar River bridge to the east of Havana was funded by the sugar mill owners who used it to transport their sugar to Havana's docks. When fundraising for building a bridge at Arroyo Hondo came up short, the captain general reallocated additional funds that had been collected for other public works, such as those for cleaning Havana's streets. Another revenue stream was generated by fines and fees, such as those charged to vendors selling drinks and food on the Alameda de Paula.[24] Additionally, fines charged to people who had transgressed against De la Torre's edict of good government generated slightly more than 7,000 pesos for his public projects.[25]

One source of funding generated conflict between Captain General De la Torre

and two of his intendants, Miguel de Altarriba and Nicolás Rapún, in part because the captain general's charge was to maintain good order, which included
the provisioning of the city, whereas the intendant focused more on imperial
defense. The tax known as the *sisa*, established in the sixteenth century, was
originally designated as funding to build and maintain the *zanja* that supplied
freshwater to Havana from the Chorrera River. After the devastating storms of the
summer and fall of 1772, the aqueduct needed repairs, but according to Intendant
Altarriba, the *sisa* funds had been assigned to other projects. De la Torre wanted
significant repairs to the freshwater canal and to Havana's slaughterhouse, saying he found it "painful" that the intendant seemed to be dragging his feet in
spite of the captain general's exhortations that the provision of freshwater to the
city and its slaughterhouse was an indispensable and urgent concern.[26]

Several months later, the captain general complained to Altarriba's successor,
Nicolás Rapún, that the repairs attempted to date on Havana's aqueduct were
"superficial," insisting that a more formal and long-lasting project would be
the best and most economical plan for a "growing town" (pueblo) like Havana.
Like his predecessor in the intendancy, Rapún replied that *sisa* funds had been
assigned to various projects in the city, including the new building to house the
cabildo and jail. De la Torre insisted that Rapún draw up a thorough accounting of
the assignment of funds so they could agree on a plan that best served the public.
By the summer of 1773, De la Torre had moderated his tone and asked Rapún to
use *sisa* funds for repairs to the slaughterhouse in whatever way the intendant
felt would provide "the greatest savings and economy."[27]

In De la Torre's notes to the next captain general, Diego Navarro, he claimed
success in cleaning up the aqueduct by assigning patrols to prevent people from
washing clothes or bathing themselves or their livestock in the water. He also
noted the repeated repairs made to the channels that served the city's fountains,
but the provision of freshwater to Havana continued to be a problem for subsequent governors.[28] Intendant Rapún did do an accounting of the *sisa de zanja*
funds, in June 1775, showing expenses for the repairs and maintenance of the
canal, along with payouts to the House for Abandoned Children and for land
rentals from several *hacendados*. Rapún also noted that other charges, made under the previous intendant, Altarriba, had left his successor with only a bit over
163,128 pesos in cash in the fund.[29] Later captains general continued to expend
several thousand reales a month on a squad of forced laborers to clear the canal
of mud and to repair fountains in Havana.[30]

One of the largest projects carried out under De la Torre was construction of the Coliseo, a theater for comedies and "decent" entertainments, built at a cost of just over 35,800 pesos. The revenue from the theater was to be used to fund the women's shelter, and both projects were sorely needed in Havana, according to De la Torre.[31] The Casa de Recogidas and theater project reflected Bourbon ideology about reforming social customs and behavior, but it also was a good example of public–private collaboration in public works that responded to local needs and were carried out with local resources.[32] In a speech to the principal *vecinos* of Havana, Captain General De la Torre noted that Havana's bishop had proposed the women's shelter project and that it would be "a work so pleasing to God and so convenient to the republic." The king had agreed to dedicate 1,500 pesos per year to the project from the rents of properties seized from the Jesuits upon their expulsion in 1767.[33]

But De la Torre was most interested in convincing his audience to voluntarily donate money to advance the Coliseo's construction as a charitable gesture, because a portion of the revenue raised from the performances would fund the Casa de Recogidas. He reminded his audience of the peninsular precedents of theaters in Spain funding hospitals and other pious works. He asked each person to "give or loan that which their faculties permit and their charity dictates," adding that "I will be the first." His summary of the benefits of the project encapsulated enlightened officialdom's desire to reform society: "It would lead directly to developing ways to correct vices, avoid scandals, conserve good customs, succor the miserable, honestly entertain the public, beautify the city and increase policing," thus fulfilling all his "wholesome intentions." His case was persuasive enough to generate donations and loans that paid to complete the theater by May 1776.[34]

De la Torre was able to carry out such a wide range of projects in only six years for several reasons. Though war between Great Britain and its North American colonies loomed toward the end of his term, in 1776, peace in the Caribbean theater meant that De la Torre did not have to divert extensive resources to defending the island or mounting expeditions elsewhere. He also enjoyed considerable goodwill from Cubans across social classes, in spite of his initial negative opinion of them.[35] His requests for voluntary contributions and labor for bridge and road repair and construction, in particular, seem to have been fairly successful, since most of these projects were paid for and carried out by the residents who used them.[36] However, his success in public works also rested upon a range of policies that confronted people of the lower classes who resisted their work regimes and the Bourbons' sense of what constituted public order. De la Torre may have developed a good opinion of the "better class" of Cubans during his time on the island, but his enduring distaste for those deemed unproductive and unruly was clear.

When De la Torre turned over the reins of government to his successor, Diego Navarro, in 1777, he highlighted his efforts at improving policing to ensure the "tranquility and good order" of Havana and its benefits in recruiting labor for his ambitious program of public works. His zealous prosecution of "delinquents" had prompted him to designate Saturdays for hearings of criminal cases exclusively, and he exulted over sending 8,263 people to jail in less than six years. The captain general noted, however, that most of the convicts spent little time in jail because the usual punishment was to "send them to public works for more or less time according to the crime."[37]

It is difficult to verify De la Torre's figures, and he may have been including the many hundreds of imperial prisoners who passed through Havana during his term. But if he was able to deploy even half this number of people to the many work sites around Havana, the captain general commanded labor on a scale similar to his predecessors Ricla and Bucareli. The main difference was that De la Torre relied on convicts, not workers enslaved by the state. Thus, colonial officials' shift from employing king's slaves to imperial convicts in defense construction in the late 1760s was mirrored in De la Torre's pursuit of vagrants and delinquents to carry out urban renewal projects in the 1770s, a practice that sought to control the costs of forced labor in public works and to discipline the growing populace of the capital.

Many of the Havana elite seemed to have agreed with De la Torre's assessment of his success in the dual project of improving public order and advancing public works. In a long report near the end of De la Torre's term, well-placed members of Havana's city council and militia units responded to complaints about the captain general's alleged mishandling of criminal justice and the funds raised for public works. His defenders claimed that assigning criminals to public works "reformed the vice-ridden, making them serve society which is the best resolution [satisfacción] for the scandals against the public . . . because the example of punishment advances the utility of work." They also noted that he had exiled 250 delinquents to other presidios in the empire, thereby "exiling idleness; which is the common root of crimes." They cited one specific example of De la Torre's order to the neighborhood justices to constrain celebrations in the social clubs of free blacks (*cabildos de negros*), prohibiting any discharge of rifles, pistols, or fireworks, or indecorous dancing. Any offenders were to be punished severely by closing their club, and individual offenders were to recieve fifty lashes and a year of forced labor in shackles in public works, with a ration but no salary.[38]

In answering other charges, several members of Havana's city council affirmed De la Torre's zeal and scrupulous handling of money for public works, saying that contributions were made spontaneously, partly due to the captain general's laudable example. Several praised the noticeable reduction in crime in Havana during De la Torre's time in office. His defenders made clear their approval of the captain general's exercise of power over criminal justice to generate forced labor for public works.[39]

Imperial Prisoners and State Slaves Under De la Torre

The stacks of memoranda and reports passing among the captain general, the intendants, and other officials, which are now housed in the Archive of the Indies, are full of notices detailing the ebb and flow of forced laborers from other parts of the Spanish Empire through Havana. Some memos contained information on groups of *presidiarios* (state prisoners) sent from Veracruz to Havana. At the end of De la Torre's term, he reported returning a total of 492 to their home regions.[40] Other memos are anonymous reports on people, often deserters from military units or defense works, who were caught around the island and sent to Havana, with requests for payment for their capture. Some memos contain names and considerable detail about individuals caught in the net of enlightened policing.

Unlike the major fort works supervised by royal appointees such as the intendants, the infrastructure projects usually were consigned to Cuban notables, and the practice of keeping detailed summaries of workers on individual projects was not maintained. But it is clear that some of the practices used to generate labor for the imperial defense projects were also applied in internal improvement projects.[41] One example was the case of a black man, Mauricio de Roxas, sent to De la Torre as a prisoner by the captain of the Partido of San Pedro. Roxas claimed he was free and a native of Panama, but officials noted that free status still did not entitle a person of color to carry a knife of any sort, nor did it protect him from forced labor for proscribed behavior. De la Torre sentenced Roxas to work on the Coliseo Theater project, with a ration but no salary, "so that he would be corrected of the vices of drunkenness and evil entertainments that the Captain attributes to him."[42] In another memo from 1774, Intendant Nicolás

Rapún ordered two Englishman caught with contraband by the coast guard to be sentenced to the Coliseo project, in this case for two years.[43] In one unusual case, two English prisoners sentenced to jail in Havana asked to be sent to work on the Alameda de Paula thoroughfare to avoid the unhealthy conditions in the jail. De la Torre agreed, and he paid them a small allowance of half a real per day, after they had signed a deposition saying that they had not been forced to work there.[44]

The larger military population, added to the forced workers in defense projects, meant that the state was constantly trying to stem the tide of desertions. De la Torre established both uniformed and plainclothes patrols to search for fugitives, expanding the practice of designating local residents to apprehend deserters and fugitives begun under his predecessors.[45] Captors notified the captain general of an apprehension and requested reimbursement for maintenance costs, transport, and fees.[46] His office began keeping track of the deserters recaptured in 1775 and claimed to have "applied to Royal works of this Plaza 362 inmates between locals and soldiers of this Garrison" by the end of his term in 1777.[47]

Before 1762, the deputizing of patrols to round up runaways, both enslaved and free, had rested with the local town governments, but this power had been appropriated in moments of crisis, by captains general Ricla, in 1763, and Bucareli, in 1768. These times of emergency had allowed the colonial state to extend its power and, once extended, it rarely returned that power to the localities. Historian Sherry Johnson has argued that the governors of Havana, for several decades after the British occupation of the city, had developed reputations for good government in their attention to the public welfare during disasters, which helped to justify and control resistance to their extension of power.[48] The constant stream of desertions suggests that many of those pressed into military service or defense construction were less appreciative.

Some deserters were able to run far from Havana before recapture. In January 1777, a group of thirteen prisoners was brought to Havana from the town of Trinidad, almost two hundred miles to the southeast. Five captives of the group were returned to the fortifications from which they had escaped. A smaller group, captured even farther afield, in Sancti Spiritus in central Cuba, comprised an army deserter, one from the navy, and a "fugitive guachinango from the Arsenal" named Mariano de la Cruz, though it is not clear whether they had fled Havana together. On occasion, the state could admit a wrongful apprehension, as in the case of Julian de los Reyes, in February of 1777. De la Torre ordered that he be freed and that his captor return the payment for the innocent man's apprehension.[49]

The various types of forced laborers at the state's disposal became a mobile work force for both defense and civil projects. Forced laborers originally assigned to fort works could be diverted to the captain general's urban renewal projects. On De la Torre's order, in 1776, Intendant Juan Ignacio de Urriza delivered four *forzados* from Mexico to the contractor providing hardwood blocks for street paving in Havana, similar to earlier practices of hiring out king's slaves and *presidiarios* to contractors for the fort works.[50] Prisoners working in the defense projects were sometimes hired out to work for private citizens on holidays, though De la Torre felt that too many problems resulted from this particular practice and ordered the intendant to squelch it.[51] Similar patterns of shifting small groups of forced laborers from one project to another as the need arose were practiced in Havana's defense projects as well. The examples here suggest that since the intendants and captains general were so intimately involved with both sets of projects, there were few sharp boundaries between military or defense works and civil projects, at least those promoted by the captain general.

By the time De la Torre arrived in Havana, in 1771, the reliance on workers enslaved by the state for all construction projects, both defense and civil, had been eclipsed by resort to the forced labor of those who had transgressed the norms and laws of the empire. The number of king's slaves working in Havana's fort works had fallen to 423 by 1772, and their numbers declined further, to around 320, over the next several years.[52] Even if De la Torre had wanted to purchase enslaved Africans for civil construction, the flow of the enslaved into Havana through the transatlantic slave trade slowed to trickle at the beginning of his term. The main slave trading company, Compañía Gaditana de Negros, was in the midst of a bankruptcy and reorganization, slowing the numbers of the enslaved imported to Cuba to only 314 in 1771, 220 in 1772, and 283 in 1773. When the terms of a new *asiento* were finally agreed upon, in 1773, importations of the enslaved rebounded to more than 2,000 per year from 1774 through 1777.[53] In his many notes to his successor, Diego Navarro, De la Torre devoted only one to state slaves, "the very useful company of Negro slaves of the King [who are] servants in artillery." He noted that their numbers had been maintained without decline by reassigning enslaved people from the fort works as needed.[54]

The Marqués de la Torre's policies as captain general of Cuba show that, by the 1770s, the state had returned to earlier practices of using small numbers of workers enslaved by the king in strategic tasks, while shifting small mixed groups of workers among various projects, though De la Torre now added a range of civil construction sites to the roster. The growing size and complexity of Havana, in both its spatial and human dimensions, spurred De la Torre and his successors to expand the state's powers of coercion to control the swelling numbers of people trying to escape military service or the more restrictive norms of decent behavior, with the approval of Cuban elites. De la Torre has received much credit in subsequent historiography for his projects to rebuild and beautify Havana, but the darker side of his extension of state power to generate the necessary labor for those projects is less well known.[55] His successors continued to persecute and prosecute the "vice-ridden and evilly entertained," but had to contend with renewed warfare in the Caribbean as well.

Forced Labor and Civil Construction in Wartime, 1779–1783
Colonial officials in Cuba were alert to the possibility of renewed warfare at least as early as 1776, when the British North American colonies rebelled against metropolitan rule. Attention and resources were again focused on Havana's defenses and away from many of the civil projects initiated by the Marqués de la Torre. Two such projects were not completed until more than a decade after his 1777 departure from Cuba.

The extension and rebuilding of the Plaza de Armas—proposed to the crown in 1773—did not break ground until 1776. The first year was dedicated to demolishing existing structures, clearing the square, gathering materials, and laying foundations, at a cost of some 40,000 pesos, mostly from the *sisa de zanja* funds. Little was done for most of the next decade, due to shortages of resources during Spain's intervention in the American War for Independence, beginning in 1779. Even after peace was restored, in 1783, the project languished until the arrival of Captain General Ezpeleta in 1786. He assigned new funds to complete the Plaza de Armas project from a tax to raise money for militia uniforms and organized the importation of bricks and ironwork from Spain for its completion.[56]

Captain General Ezpeleta also succeeded in getting the Havana town council's approval for a tax on carriages to fund street paving, though some residents raised objections. The crown finally approved the carriage tax, and paving began under the next captain general, Las Casas, based on a new plan to use large pebbles as pavers rather than the blocks of wood proposed by De la Torre.[57]

Several of De la Torre's major works fared poorly in the years following his tenure in Havana. At least one of the wooden bridges he had ordered constructed over the San Juan River, to the east of the city, had collapsed by the mid-1780s.

Ezpeleta assigned a royal engineer to design a new stone bridge, which was completed in 1788. Perhaps the most spectacular failure was the ruin of the Coliseo Theater, on which De la Torre had lavished such praise and attention. By 1787, Havana alderman Gabriel de Peñalver y Calvo was proposing to use the theater site to build a new jail for the city, renting out space in the existing jail building to support the women's shelter. Ultimately, Peñalver's proposal failed to gain approval in Madrid.[58]

De la Torre's approach to unruly subjects, on the other hand, had become part of the colonial state's arsenal of policies to maintain social order, staff the army and navy, and carry out public works. The patrols and roundups of deserters of the 1770s became annual levies targeting vagrants and the "evilly entertained" during the war years, from 1779 to 1783, and continued into the later 1780s. During the years of Spain's intervention in the American War for Independence (1779 to 1783), the captains general of Cuba resorted to levies on the free population to recruit troops for the army and navy and laborers for defense works.[59]

The end of hostilities, in 1783, found much of the Cuban population exhausted after the considerable sacrifices demanded by the war effort, which complicated state officials' search for voluntary labor to build and repair roads. The late 1780s and early 1790s also were a boom period in the expansion of plantation production for export and of the importations of enslaved Africans into Cuba, which prompted a reordering of the state's relationship to slave trading and slavery. Cuban elites and colonial officials collaborated to use labor recruitment strategies, developed to harness the labor of the free population defined as deserters and vagrants, on the growing numbers of the enslaved who tried to flee to freedom.

The Sugar Boom and its Transformations

To further stimulate agriculture and to help satisfy the growing private demand for enslaved workers, the Spanish state finally declared free trade in slaves in 1789, which remained in effect until 1817.[60] Recognizing that such free trade would significantly increase the enslaved population of Cuba, the crown also issued new comprehensive instructions on the treatment of the enslaved, in 1789.[61] The general principles of the sections of the thirteenth-century law code, the *Siete Partidas*, that dealt with enslavement, such as humanitarian concern for the well-being of the enslaved and recognition of legitimate avenues to freedom, had been amended over the three centuries of colonial rule in the Americas. Colonists' concerns about bands of fugitive enslaved Africans and growing free populations of color had prompted many municipal ordinances and imperial directives to control the growth of their populations and to regulate their behavior.[62]

The *Siete Partidas* and later regulations of enslavement, up to 1789, had reflected the predominantly urban character of slavery on the peninsula and in Spanish America into the eighteenth century. Since enslaved people were rarely a majority in Spanish colonies, hiring out, living apart from owners, doing skilled work, and purchasing one's freedom had become accepted as legitimate activities for enslaved workers. As Alejandro de la Fuente has noted, although practices such as *coartación*, or self-purchase in installments, had "little support in written law," they were well established in custom, during the late eighteenth and early nineteenth centuries, as rights that enslaved people claimed when in conflict with their enslavers.[63]

The new instructions of 1789 still harked back in many ways to the spirit of earlier Spanish legislation, which stressed the humanity of the enslaved and their right to pursue freedom. The instructions reflected the crown's concerns that previous legislation regulating African enslavement in the Indies was scattered and difficult for officials to make use of effectively. But, most importantly, the 1789 orders reflected a desire by the crown to reiterate humanitarian guidelines and to control abuses, a perspective that was at odds with the interests of Cuban slave owners.

The crown did take some account of the new slave society evolving in Cuba. Faced with the likelihood that a growing proportion of the enslaved Cuban population would be African born, the first chapter of the code ordered that all slave owners be responsible for the Catholic instruction of their enslaved workers. It also reminded owners to relieve the enslaved of working on the requisite festival days. Chapter 2 exhorted owners to adequately feed and clothe the enslaved and their families according to the norms established by municipal authorities and justices.

Chapter 3 reflected the changing role of enslaved labor in the Spanish Empire, particularly the recent shift away from urban to rural agricultural employment. In contrast to the widespread work of enslaved Africans in domestic service and urban employments in Spain and Spanish America up to the eighteenth century, in 1789, the crown declared that "the first and principal occupation of Slaves should be Agriculture and other rural labors, and not the trades of a sedentary life." Other chapters sought to reinforce the obligations of the enslavers to adequately care for their injured or ill enslaved workers and to uphold the crown's encouragement of marriage among the enslaved. While Chapters 8 and 9 dealt with enslaved people's obligations to work and to honor their masters, and the penalties for transgressions, the final five chapters were concerned with detecting "defects, or excesses of owners, or overseers." The new code established a system of official oversight, fines, and penalties against those who abused the enslaved in their care and recognized the *síndico procurador* as the "protector of the slaves."[64]

Cuban slave owners reacted with fear and outrage to the restrictions on their authority to discipline the enslaved as they saw fit. Seventy-one planters petitioned the king in 1790, arguing that "irreparable harm" would come if the law were enforced on the island. The enslaved would rebel and calamity and annihilation would result.[65] In another 1790 petition, Cuban planters cited the rebellion of the enslaved on the Quiebra Hacha plantation in 1727 as a reason to oppose the new regulations on treatment. According to the planters, that rebellion had been so serious that "it was necessary for the government to subdue them with weapons, costing much blood and some lives."[66] By 1794, after the consequences of the slave rebellion in Saint-Domingue were clear, the Council of the Indies accepted the crown's inability to enforce the law and suspended its application, noting that local governments and landowners knew best how to manage the enslaved people in their charge. Thus, the crown also accepted the transformation of Cuba into a plantation economy based on slavery and ruled by slave owners.[67]

Some scholars have argued that the era of free trade in slaves, from 1789 to 1820,[68] was the most brutal of the century of sugar expansion from 1750 to 1850. The sugar mills became "prisons" organized for production, the enslaved were less likely to have access to land to grow some of their own food, and the high ratios of male to female enslaved people discouraged marriages and family life.[69]

The declaration of free trade in the enslaved also dramatically transformed the structure of Cuba's population. From 1783 through 1789, almost 12,000 enslaved people were imported into Cuba. Estimates for the next thirty years show explosive growth in the numbers of the enslaved brought to the island, from 36,426 (1790–1799) to 51,977 (1800–1809) to 110,808 (1810–1819). Even after the first anti–slave trade treaty went into effect, from 1820 through 1839, another 299,541 enslaved Africans were brought to Cuba.[70] People of African descent, both enslaved and free, came to represent a majority of the island's inhabitants as early as 1792, and they maintained that majority into the 1840s. This was a dramatic change for Cuba, which had had a white majority since the conquest had extinguished much of the indigenous population in the sixteenth century.[71]

By 1790, the importance of the defense sector to the Cuban economy had waned as the plantation sector expanded. Havana's forts were mostly completed and the warfare of the 1780s had ceased. *Situado* payments to Cuba from Mexican silver increased somewhat over the 1790s, with renewed fighting in Hispaniola, but never reached the heights of the 1780s.[72] The urban service sector of the economy remained strong with the surge in the exports of sugar through Havana's busy port. The agriculture sector showed a marked shift away from cattle ranching and, to a certain extent, from tobacco, in favor of sugar and coffee production in the hinterland of the city. Some growth in sugar had begun as early as 1740, and Cuban sugar exports had more than tripled, to 378,346 arrobas, by 1760.[73]

Official encouragement and private initiative after the British occupation stimulated further growth that produced nearly 1.5 million arrobas of sugar for export by 1781. Sugar expansion after 1790 increased exports to approximately 2.2 million arrobas in 1800, close to 3.5 million in 1820, and almost 7 million in 1840. Coffee exports also increased, on a somewhat later timeline, from 25,237 arrobas in 1804 to 918,263 arrobas in 1815.[74] Thus, it was no longer mostly defense contracts and state spending that enriched Havana's elite, but they sought access to both old and new institutions of the colonial state to recruit more enslaved labor and to build the transportation network they needed to get their plantation products to port in Havana.

Roadwork and Experiments with Captured Enslaved Fugitives

Before the final decade of the eighteenth century, road building and maintenance had been the province of the island's municipal councils or private landowners. Colonial officials had made some attempts to improve the transport infrastructure around Havana in the eighteenth century, but labor recruitment for such projects was often an obstacle to progress. Captain General de la Torre had been able to build bridges over the various rivers, crossing roads to and from Havana in the mid-1770s, but after the sacrifices made during warfare, from 1779 through 1783, free Cubans were less willing than they had been in the previous twenty years to volunteer for road construction. Of particular concern for colonial officials and planters were the roads and bridges to the south and east of Havana, toward Güines and Matanzas, where some of the greatest sugar and coffee expansion was concentrated.

Captain General Ezpeleta (1785 to 1790) sent numerous requests to his captains of *partido* (district captains, similar to sheriffs) in the region to require local householders to give two days per week to road and bridge building and repair, or to send several enslaved workers or farmhands in their stead. He often received long reports of reasons why local *vecinos* could not or would not comply, particularly from those whose military privileges freed them from labor in public works. To advance the road projects, Ezpeleta gave the contractor in charge of the works access to a number of captured military deserters, fugitive slaves, and escaped convicts. Ultimately, this infusion of forced laborers had some success in improving the road networks between Havana and the growing plantation areas during the second half of the 1780s, though Ezpeleta's successor was not so fortunate.[75]

In the summer of 1790, Luis de Las Casas arrived in Cuba as the new captain general, receiving an effusive welcome from the Havana elite. Most of the fort works had been completed, and the governor's house in the Havana's Plaza de Armas was almost done, with Las Casas being the first to live in it. Las Casas was perceived as a friend to sugar planters, and to cement that relationship, they presented him with a plantation of his own, complete with machinery and enslaved laborers.[76] One way in which Las Casas sought to return the favor and to reap the maximum benefit from his plantations was to advance the road building projects.

His order in late 1790 for all able-bodied men to report for roadwork led to protests and resistance. In January 1791, Las Casas again pressed the captains of *partidos* to force locals to do roadwork, but *vecinos* continued to give excuses for their refusal to participate. Because so many Cubans had served the crown in the military campaigns and island defense during the previous thirty years, they were able to invoke their military *fuero*, or privilege to claim exemption from labor in public works.[77] A severe hurricane in June 1791 caused extensive loss of life and washed out bridges and roads, but further orders from Las Casas to round up the "idle" and "evilly entertained" yielded few laborers for roadwork.

The captain general tried to raise more funds for rebuilding by charging those who used bridges, but the captains of *partidos* protested that such fees would fall too heavily on poor farmers trying to get their produce to market. Las Casas also ordered the captains to report on the numbers of people living in their districts, presumably to know who could be taxed and coerced to work, but again the captains claimed such obstacles as illness and even bad roads as reasons why they could not comply. Ultimately, the captain general admitted defeat on advancing road projects with free laborers.[78]

Las Casas had better luck working with Havana-area planters through quasi-governmental organizations to advance their mutual interests. As a representative of Bourbon enlightened rule and an enthusiastic plantation owner, he supported the Havana elites' efforts to create institutions devoted to improving Cuban agriculture. He had met Cuban planter Francisco Arango y Parreño in Madrid when the latter served as the Havana Municipal Council's representative to the royal court.[79] Arango, Las Casas, and the new intendant, José Pablo Valiente, collaborated in the formation of new organs of influence and power. For instance, with the official blessing of the captain general, the first Patriotic Society of Friends of the Country (Sociedad Patriótica de Amigos del País) was founded in 1792, on the peninsular model, as a forum to research, discuss, and disseminate theories of political economy and more practical reports on agriculture, commerce, and education. The first periodical that was not a government organ, associated with the Sociedad Patriótica, was founded in the same year.[80]

The metropolitan government also authorized the formation, in 1794, of a group known as the Royal Council of Agriculture, Industry and Commerce (Real Consulado de Agricultura, Industria y Comercio). Its membership comprised wealthy landowners, merchants, and high colonial functionaries, including the captain general and the intendant. In contrast to the Sociedad Patriótica, the Consulado was granted revenue from a special tax (avería) as part of its charter to carry out projects.[81] One of its main charges was to improve Cuba's system of roads. Thus, organizations such as the Havana Consulado brought together both Cuban elites and colonial officials to foment plantation development and adjudicate commercial disputes. With its royal charge to improve infrastructure through state and private collaboration, the Consulado became a new vehicle through which to execute public works with forced laborers.[82]

The Spanish crown had tasked the Consulado with "constructing good roads . . . [and] opening canals of navigation and irrigation," among other charges to develop the Cuban countryside. Local governmental bodies, such as the ayuntamientos (municipal councils) and the newly formed Sociedad Patriótica, were to aid the Consulado in its program of public works.[83]

The road system of Cuba at the end of the eighteenth century comprised a modest network of varied provenance and quality. The royal roadway (camino real) linked the major towns from west to east. Smaller roads connected other towns with the camino real or to one another. Road networks from north to south or in the interior of the island were less developed, though planters often cleared roads to connect their own properties and to link up with those of their neighbors. However, the rainy season was particularly devastating to the road system, regularly washing out roads and bridges in rivers of mud and debris.[84] Repair and construction of roads also necessitated substantial inputs of human and animal labor in the period before the incorporation of steam-powered equipment into the enterprise—to dig and haul earth and stone, to level terrain and form a roadbed, and to break large stones into smaller pieces for paving.[85]

Organizing the funds and labor for road projects was no easy task, and the Consulado spent months soliciting reports, proposals, and comments on how to proceed. The members were able to agree to prioritize four projects radiating out from Havana, west to Guanajay, south to Batabanó, southeast to Güines, and east to Matanzas.[86] Within a year of its founding in 1794, prominent members of the Consulado were discussing ways to raise funds in addition to the *avería* for road building projects.

In a 1795 report to the Consulado, wealthy planter Nicolás Calvo y O'Farrill laid out a plan to provide the Havana region with the roadways necessary for its continued development.[87] In keeping with earlier approaches to funding civil infrastructure projects, Calvo proposed several new taxes based on the general principal that those who would benefit most from improved roads should pay the most for their construction. The first recommendation was to charge for the passage of animals over the various bridges surrounding Havana. People on foot would be exempt since they were assumed to be poor. A second source of income would be generated by raising the prices of meat and salt. Calvo did not consider these increases to be a hardship for the city's poor, because the poor did not eat meat, and he noted that "we don't know that anyone has died of hunger in our country [tierra]." He also suggested raising funds with lotteries. An additional 10,000 pesos would be raised from the Consulado's own funds.[88]

Calvo's final proposal highlighted the changes in the Cuban population and economy over the preceding decades. Instead of proposing donations or other consumer taxes to raise the bulk of the necessary funds, he suggested a levy of two pesos per year for each slave owned, of whatever sex, age, or color. Thirty or forty years earlier, such a tax would have generated limited funds from the livestock ranches, vegetable farms, and tobacco fields surrounding Havana that did not rely heavily on enslaved labor. But by 1795, Calvo estimated an enslaved population of 70,000 persons in the jurisdictions in and around Havana, Bejucal, Guanabacoa, Jaruco, Matanzas, Santa María del Rosario, and Santiago, the areas that would benefit most directly from road construction.[89]

Of a total of 231,000 pesos, Calvo expected to raise almost 52 percent (120,000 pesos) through the head tax on enslaved workers. The tax on bridge traffic would bring a modest 30,000 pesos, or 12.9 percent. The higher meat prices and the salt tax combined would raise an estimated 51,000 pesos or 22 percent.[90]

Calvo urged his peers on the Consulado to take advantage of the marked expansion of enslavement on the island by targeting slave-owning export producers, not consumers, as the main and most reliable source of funding for infrastructure building. The Consulado ultimately rejected Calvo's proposal to tie revenue generation to ownership of the enslaved, opting for a land tax instead, a decision that may have hampered the body's fund-raising efforts.[91]

Though it was opposed to taxing planters for the people they enslaved, the Consulado sought other ways to both control and benefit from the growing enslaved population in Cuba. To marshal labor for its projects, its members devised a plan to tap the labor potential of captured fugitive slaves awaiting return to their enslavers.

In 1796, two prominent Consulado members, merchant Joseph Manuel de Torrontégui and planter Francisco Arango y Parreño, presented a report that proposed seeking royal approval for changes in the existing policies on enslaved runaways. Noting that no formal ruling on the handling of enslaved fugitives existed on the island, Torrontégui and Arango decried the state of the countryside "inundated with rancheadores [bounty hunters who captured fugitives on their own or as proxies of individual enslavers or provincial authorities] that abuse their powers with grave prejudice to the Public." The report stated that the only objectives of the policy on fugitives should be to avoid gatherings of runaways, which could be a danger to public safety, and to return the enslaved to the care and supervision of their enslavers as soon as possible. The rancheadores, according to the authors, tended to be unnecessarily cruel, transgressing basic humanity and, perhaps more importantly, injuring the enslavers' property.[92]

Showing parallels to state policies of the previous twenty years that had centralized the disposition of military deserters, the report suggested that the Consulado regulate the expeditions of capture and control the disposition of enslaved fugitives thereafter. This centralization also would have the advantage of bringing together island-wide information on the state of the Cuban enslaved population, as the Consulado's accountant would maintain lists of the captured enslaved fugitives.[93]

Most likely in response to the slave rebellion in nearby Haiti, the report approved of harsher measures to be meted out to enslaved fugitives guilty of forming maroon communities, of rebellion, or of highway robbery. But individual enslaved people "who only flee to escape work" should be treated with gentleness, although their captors were to be paid equal sums in all cases. The report also proposed strict criteria for being considered fugitive: "All the slaves that are found without a paper from their owner, overseer, or driver or with a pass that is one month expired, at three leagues from the haciendas where they grew up, and a league and a half from those where they work, will be taken for fugitives."[94]

Torrontégui and Arango proposed that captured fugitives be brought to the closest justice or provincial captain, within seventy-two hours, and that they should be maintained in public jails, well fed and attended, for up to ten days. If, in that time, the owner appeared and paid all the costs of the enslaved person's capture and maintenance, then the enslaved person would be released to their enslaver. If the enslaver did not appear or could not pay in full, the slave would be transported to Havana, the Consulado's treasury would pay all costs, and the enslaved captive could be assigned to the Consulado's public works projects. Unclaimed enslaved people were categorized as goods without owners or of doubtful ownership. As such, they fell under the jurisdiction of the intendancy and were to be transferred to the state's care and service.[95]

The report ended by asking the king to approve two basic proposals. First, the authors requested that all enslaved fugitives assigned to public works be allowed to remain in that service without time limit, unless the enslaver came forward and could pay the costs of the enslaved person's capture.[96] Second, the authors asked the king to limit or abolish the squads of *rancheadores* under the jurisdiction of provincial justices. Using the language of humanitarianism, the protection of property, and the public good, the Consulado persuaded the king to proclaim a new policy, at the end of 1796, allowing the Consulado to be in charge of the pursuit and capture of enslaved fugitives and to be the major beneficiary of their labor on the island.[97] Over the next nineteen years, the Consulado spent 53,396.6 pesos on the capture of the 15,971 enslaved fugitives who were housed in Havana.[98]

Crown officials and creole planters expended considerable energy on the question of who should control and benefit from the labor of unclaimed enslaved fugitives (*esclavos mostrencos*), even though their numbers were small (twelve from 1797 through 1815).[99] Consulado members were most concerned about recouping from the intendancy the funds expended over years on the unclaimed fugitives' maintenance, especially when those enslaved people had gained some skill and experience in road projects.[100] In 1802, Intendant Luis de Viguri proposed sending captured enslaved people that he might have in custody to the Consulado for roadwork, but he asked that the Consulado guarantee their value. Not surprisingly, the Consulado demurred, arguing that the body did not acquire property and operated entirely in the public's service. Hence, it could not undertake the risks of death or desertion of the workers enslaved by the intendancy.[101]

The Consulado's claim of not owning property ignored the fact that it had purchased enslaved people to undertake two pilot road building projects several years before. The first project, begun in 1796, was improvements to a segment of road in the Havana suburb of Horcón to the southwest. The Consulado invested more than 30,000 pesos and the labor of one hundred men for more than a month on barely one kilometer of road. Part of this cost was the purchase of six enslaved workers at a total of 1,680 pesos, or roughly 280 pesos each. In the fall of 1796, a smaller effort to repave a portion of road from the Puerta de Tierra in Havana's city wall toward the extramural suburb of Guadalupe cost more than 15,000 pesos. The enslaved people and tools purchased by the Consulado could be used in later projects, but most of the laborers were paid a wage and the costs were high.[102]

The Consulado members learned several important lessons from these two early road projects. Though the projects were of a much smaller scale than the fort works of the 1760s, the Consulado discovered that purchasing enslaved people to quickly undertake public works was expensive, and the members soon began looking for other types of forced laborers whose recruitment would cost less.[103] In this case, the Consulado sought enslaved laborers without the outlay of direct purchase by centralizing the capture and disposition of fugitives.

Initially, the Consulado rented a small building to house the enslaved fugitives and grounds on which to keep the animals, equipment, and tools necessary for road construction. These accommodations quickly proved inadequate, and the Consulado gained official approval to begin the construction of a larger and more secure Depósito de Cimarrones (House for Enslaved Fugitives) in 1800, in the extramural zone known as El Cerro.[104] The Consulado reported that almost 16,000 enslaved fugitives entered the Depósito from 1797 through 1815, as shown in table 5.1. Of this total, 13,801 enslaved fugitives were returned to their owners, 738 of the captured were lost to death or desertion, and forty-two were able to prove their status as free persons and were released.[105]

Table 5.1. Fugitives Slaves Entered and Lost to the Havana Depósito, 1797–1815

Year	Slaves from Havana jurisdiction	Slaves from interior areas	Deaths	Desertions	Free	Unclaimed fugitives sent to intendant
1797	140	17	4	1	—	—
1798	337	50	13	6	—	2
1799	424	75	8	4	—	—
1800	441	107	17	25	—	3
1801	675	67	20	12	1	—
1802	857	65	32	31	4	—
1803	1,218	93	22	22	4	—
1804	1,269	86	41	9	8	7
1805	1,303	51	27	27	3	—
1806	1,171	37	24	20	1	—
1807	1,086	35	48	16	—	—
1808	855	82	28	17	1	—
1809	689	53	22	9	1	—
1810	778	34	26	5	3	—
1811	673	65	27	6	6	—
1812	769	26	18	9	7	—
1813	995	16	68	9	1	—
1814	684	30	15	12	2	—
1815	618	989	22	18	—	12
Totals	14,982	15,971	482	256	42	792

Source: "Resumen que presenta a la Junta de Gobierno del Real Consulado su Contaduría, de los Esclavos Cimarrones que han sido depositados en dicha oficina desde 21 de Julio de 1797 que se puso en practica el actual Reglamento de la materia, hasta 31 de Diciembre de 1815," Archivo General de Indias, Ultramar, 320.

The figures offer a number of insights into the dramatic changes wrought in Cuban society by the sugar boom and into some of the boom's effects on the execution of public works. First, the Depósito program was reasonably effective in eventually returning the fugitive enslaved to their enslavers, with 86 percent of the fugitives being returned over the first eighteen years. Second, the figures reflect the early concentration of sugar expansion in the jurisdiction of Havana, with almost 94 percent of the captured fugitives coming from that region. Although this group of laborers was not a static and permanent labor force, in a given year the Consulado had at its disposal the labor of hundreds of enslaved fugitives for whom it only had to pay the Depósito for maintenance and transport. Unlike the crown's defense projects of the 1760s, the Consulado did not have to muster large sums to purchase enslaved laborers for road projects.

Even so, by 1811, the Consulado reported difficulties in covering the costs of maintaining and transporting enslaved fugitives to the Havana Depósito and back to their enslavers. The engineer in charge of the Consulado's public works reported that overall costs for enslaved fugitives came close to what they would have paid for "blacks who were healthy, free, and good workers." Many of the Depósito's captives were "feeble," worn out by the harsh work regimes and punishments meted out by their enslavers or by the lack of food and difficult conditions of their flight. The engineer concluded that the work of two enslaved fugitives did not equal the work of one black worker who was healthy and free.[106]

The Consulado did employ a much smaller contingent of its own enslaved workers in road building, similar to the more permanent squads of king's slaves maintained by the crown for defense works. Their numbers in the Havana Depósito by the early 1830s averaged only seventy-six enslaved workers. Because the Consulado did not have jurisdiction over criminal offenses, convicts were a much smaller part of the road building crews—an average of fifty-three workers in the first two decades of the nineteenth century. By 1833, the average number of convicts had fallen to about fifteen laborers.[107]

A more ambitious project proposed by the Consulado was a canal linking Havana with the fast-growing sugar region of Güines to the southeast. The royal navy had made initial inquiries into building a canal, in the late 1760s, to transport lumber to Havana's shipyard. The Consulado hired the well-regarded team of engineers Felix and Francisco LeMaur to survey the area and report on the work needed to build a canal. By 1801, Alexander von Humboldt traveled the region with the LeMaur brothers and reported that the estimated cost of the canal had ballooned to 1.5 million pesos.[108]

Rather than undertake such a complex and expensive project, the Consulado tried to improve communication between Havana and Güines by contracting out the building of sections of road to the region's landowners and notables, some of who were Consulado members. The contractors' method of recruiting labor for the roadwork closely resembled the attempts by Captain General Las Casas in the early 1790s—requiring area residents to provide a day's labor to the work, either their own labor or that of their enslaved workers. Perhaps because the work was now being organized locally by landowners themselves, instead of by decree from the captain general, the contractors were able to recruit labor more easily and to complete some of the road projects and eleven bridges in the region.[109]

An 1823 report from a member of the Consulado on conditions in the Depósito provides a glimpse of the conditions under which the enslaved fugitives employed in road construction had to live and work. Vicente María Rodrigo reported that the first thing that caught his attention at the Depósito was the barracoon in which the enslaved stayed; its small size and lack of ventilation and flooring offered neither comfort nor safety from the elements. He found the kitchen to have similar defects, being too small to serve the four hundred enslaved people who commonly resided there. Rodrigo also lamented the lack of a chapel and the services of a chaplain for the Consulado's enslaved workers. Another serious problem was the lack of potable water on the Depósito site, which necessitated using some of the enslaved fugitives to transport water rather than to work in the road projects.[110]

Rodrigo presented a plan to improve the structure and the living conditions of the Depósito at a cost of 36,038 pesos, but this plan was deemed too expensive by the rest of the Consulado. He was, however, able to build an infirmary, a chapel, and a larger kitchen and living area for the barracoon. Several barred windows and flooring also were added to the quarters.[111]

The expense of digging a canal to bring water to the site was the costliest improvement in Rodrigo's plan, and had caused his original plan to be turned down. In place of the canal, he was able to construct tanks and a well to provide water for bathing and cleaning, which freed more workers to be assigned to the road projects. Rodrigo also reported that the improvements at the Depósito were responsible for reducing the number of deaths among the inmates, which he listed at seventy in 1820, ninety-three in 1821, and forty-five in 1822. Combining Rodrigo's figures with those of historian Gabino La Rosa Corzo, we see that the average number of inmates in the Depósito in 1820 was 414 enslaved workers and *forzados*, with mortality rates of 16.9 percent for 1820 and 22.4 percent for 1821, falling to 10.8 percent in 1822.[112]

In Rodrigo's report, there is also an indication of another reason why the Consulado's program of road construction and repair proceeded so slowly, beyond the scale and difficulty of the work required. He noted that the Consulado had never drawn up a comprehensive plan for road repair and construction. Work crews and materials were assigned on an ad hoc and provisional basis. The work sites farthest from the Depósito suffered from transport difficulties. The Consulado's materials and labor also were scattered among many other projects in and around the city—for repairs to the city's bridges and wall, for maintenance and cleaning of the Consulado's dock facilities, and for the pontoon crews charged with cleaning the bay.

In spite of having a relatively low-cost group of laborers at its disposal, the Consulado only had modest success in expanding the road system of Cuba. Between 1796 and 1816, even though the Consulado dedicated an average of 31,000 pesos per year to its road projects, only about eight and a half kilometers were completed. A royal order in 1818 approved a plan to almost double the funding, to 60,000 pesos per year, and to include the purchase of four hundred enslaved people at 390 pesos each, although such a large number does not seem to have been purchased. Over the next thirteen years, the Consulado expended some 1.25 million pesos on road construction and repair around Havana in hopes of completing almost eighty kilometers. However, the projects proceeded much more slowly than anticipated, with only 25.4 kilometers completed by 1831.[113] Dramatic improvements in internal transport in Cuba would have to await the construction of railroads in the late 1830s.

In spite of the relative lack of success of some of the projects of the Consulado, their execution was organized in new ways, which had a significant impact on later public works in Cuba. Although the Spanish military remained in charge of most defense works throughout the colonial period,[114] the rise in sugar exports after 1790 provided the funds for the formation of new official bodies with strong creole participation, such as the Consulado, through which organs of the state could carry out internal public works without expending imperial funds. By giving the Consulado the power to pursue, capture, and dispose of the labor of enslaved fugitives, the crown minimized its investment in king's slaves, especially at the higher prices of the 1790s. Imperial funds did not have to be tapped to purchase and maintain enslaved laborers, and the colonial administration still retained some oversight, through the memberships of the captain general and the intendant in the Consulado.

The Consulado also provided an organization through which wealthy Cuban landowners could pursue infrastructure expansion in their own interests, even after the Napoleonic occupation of the peninsula in 1808 disrupted the colonial bond with Spain. The projects' alternative funding and organization continued to provide resources for internal public works after 1810, when imperial monies were diverted to fighting the independence rebellions in Spain's mainland American colonies. The funds and powers granted to the Consulado by the crown allowed the creole elite to pool resources that would have been beyond their reach as individuals. Where internal public works previously had been at the mercy of crown investment or the initiative and resources of individuals and municipalities, the formation of the Consulado began the centralization of resources and planning in a quasi-governmental body responsive to creole interests, especially support for plantation expansion and slavery.

Policing the City and Martial Law

The political economy of state enslavement and other forms of labor coercion to defend and maintain the Spanish American empire was radically transformed after 1820. With the decimation of Spain's navy in the early nineteenth century and the collapse of Spanish rule in the mainland Americas by the 1820s, officials in Cuba no longer employed levies for military service as a way to quell unrest or reduce the numbers of the "evilly entertained." However, the captains general of the first decades of the nineteenth century continued other practices established in the late 1700s, such as increasing and centralizing policing and incarceration, and colonial officials continued to use for public works the labor of those accused of many types of crimes. State enslavement also declined as sugar production expanded, and fears of the "Africanization" of Cuba's population stimulated various schemes to encourage white workers to immigrate, some as free agricultural workers, others under labor contracts. Though the colonial state in Cuba did not return to eighteenth-century levels of ownership of enslaved workers, officials did find ways to exploit the labor of a range of workers for public projects, including some unfortunate souls formerly enslaved and nominally freed by British abolitionism.

Rapid population growth in Havana, which began in the second half of the eighteenth century, accelerated in the early decades of the nineteenth century. When Alexander von Humboldt published his essay on the island of Cuba in Spanish in 1827, he noted that the city's population had more than doubled in the twenty years from 1791 through 1810, from more than 44,000 to just over 96,000. He also reported that the ratio of whites to people of color had shifted from 53 to 47 to 43 to 57 over the same period.[115] A census taken in 1827 showed that the population of Havana and its rural districts had ballooned to 237,828 people, 109,535 of whom were enslaved.[116] Over the 1820s and 1830s, colonial officials continued to target the population of color in an effort to avoid "another Haiti," regulating the mobility of the free and enslaved people of color. They also worried about the mingling of whites with the population of color.

Several of the social ills lamented by Spanish officials of the later 1700s continued to exercise their successors in the early 1800s—especially idleness and gambling. Various edicts and regulations were published to contain gambling by allowing only certain types of games, such as cockfights, billiards, and lotteries, only in cafés and billiard halls, and only until ten o'clock at night. Yet people of all colors and classes wagered at cards, dice, and cockfights, at home and in public. There were rumors that even Captain General Vives had a cock pen on the patio of the Fuerza fortress.[117]

To contain crime over the 1820s, several attempts were made to increase street patrols by day and night and to establish additional corps of men to carry them out. A new regulation of policing, published in 1823, formalized the position of neighborhood watchmen with the title of deputies and established the position of police inspector to oversee three or four neighborhood headquarters. The historian who has most closely studied crime and punishment in 1820s Cuba, Yolanda Díaz Martínez, argues that both the crown and the captains general were most concerned about containing any growth of independence movements on the island during this period and responded vigorously to quash them. With Spain's loss of the mainland empire by the mid-1820s, retaining the now rich colony of Cuba was paramount. Hence, they repressed independence conspiracies like the Rayos y Soles de Bolívar, in 1823, but tolerated social vices such as gambling, and even some street crimes, such as robbery and assault. Captain General Francisco Dionisio Vives and his successor as captain general, Mariano Ricafort, maintained a policy of "apparent restrictions and real tolerance" that reduced threats to the colonial bond but left crime and delinquency largely untouched.[118]

To contain affronts to the restored Bourbon monarchy and colonial rule, Ferdinand VII established military commissions to administer justice in Spain and the remaining colonies, in January 1824.[119] The commissions had the power to try and sentence anyone deemed an enemy of the crown, including any who supported the liberal Spanish constitution of 1812. The commissions also could adjudicate cases of people charged with fomenting upheavals or committing robberies or assaults in the countryside. The commissions endured more or less continuously from 1824 through 1869.[120]

The commission's sentences for members of the Black Eagle conspiracy in 1830 reveal an imperial network of forced labor sites for convicts.[121] Of the eighteen convicted participants in the plot, eight were executed and had their property confiscated, seven were sentenced to ten years in the Spanish presidio of Ceuta in North Africa, and two others were sentenced to shorter terms there. Penalties even for uttering "subversive words" could be severe—six years of forced service in a hospital or public works, or six years confined to La Cabaña fortress— swelling the numbers of convicts in state service. Several other men convicted of running away from their confinement at La Cabaña were sent to finish their sentences in Ceuta. Others were exiled to Spain, though they were not sentenced to a presidio.[122]

In addition to the military commission, the Spanish crown further increased the powers of the captains general of Cuba in 1825. The island's highest military authority now could operate as a governor of a besieged outpost under martial law, which included the ability to exile to Spain any island official, regardless of rank, whose conduct might be prejudicial, and the power to suspend enforcement of any orders or legislation. As one historian has concluded, after 1825, the captain general "could rule Cuba as a military dictatorship."[123]

Creole Planters Ascendant

When the Bourbon monarchy was restored in Spain with the return of Ferdinand VII, in 1823, the crown also rewarded a few loyal Cuban creoles with government posts that previously had been reserved for Spanish-born military officers and bureaucrats.[124] One such creole was Cuban planter Francisco Arango y Parreño. Early in his career, in the 1790s, he had proposed the formation of the Havana Consulado, and he defended slavery and the slave trade to Cuba in the liberal Cortes of Cádiz in 1810. Arango was appointed to the Council of the Indies under Ferdinand VII and became intendant of Cuba in 1824.[125] Due to Arango's ill health, the *habanero* Claudio Martínez de Pinillos, later the Count of Villanueva,[126] was appointed to the Cuban intendancy in 1825.[127]

By the 1820s, the power and resources necessary to carry out public works in Cuba had been divided among peninsular officials and institutions closely allied with creole interests. These new creole institutions exercised power over coerced public laborers and the implementation of public works that was similar to that of the Spanish administration itself. Institutions such as the Havana Consulado, with its funding coming from the most dynamic sector of the imperial economy, ultimately were able to overshadow even the power of the captain general in planning and executing public projects.

Intendant Villanueva understood well both the benefits and the dangers of the expansion of sugar and enslavement in Cuba, noting that "our slaves may rise up, provoking the subsequent ruin of our agriculture, which constitutes all the wealth of this country."[128] Potential internal enemies multiplied as the enslaved population rose into the hundreds of thousands by the 1820s. Paradoxically, imports of enslaved Africans to Cuba expanded most just as the Spanish crown signed treaties with Great Britain to ban the transatlantic slave trade in 1817 and 1835.[129] One grim irony of British efforts to liberate Africans from Spanish slave ships was the creation of a new group of people who were legally free but were forced to labor for the Spanish colonial state in public works.

Abolitionism and the Emancipados

The peninsular upheavals after 1808 produced government penury in Spain. One remedy pursued by the Spanish crown was to give in to British pressure and accept a payment of 400,000 pounds to begin the process of banning the Atlantic slave trade. The brief period of Spain's official encouragement of the slave trade, between 1789 and 1804, had been extended by the Napoleonic invasion of Spain in 1808. However, the liberal Cortes of Cádiz (1810–1814), dependent on British support against the French occupation, undertook the first public Spanish debate on abolishing the slave trade, in April of 1811. When news of the debate reached Cuba, planters felt betrayed by the Cortes and horrified by the possible consequences, should the enslaved population get wind of the discussion. The uncovering, in 1812, of a planned uprising involving slaves, free Afro-Cubans, and whites in several areas on the island, known as the Aponte Rebellion, generated enough fears, both on the island and in the metropole, to end the Cortes's talk of abolishing the slave trade.[130]

However, the issue of the slave trade to Spanish America was not dead in practice. The period from 1811 to 1816 was one of British seizures of Spanish slaving vessels in the Atlantic without any legal basis beyond an internal British law prohibiting the trade. These seizures generated protests and appeals to the British Vice-Admiralty courts. In 1817, diplomatic negotiations between Spain and Britain finally produced a treaty agreement that proclaimed the end of the slave trade from Africa north of the equator to Spanish dominions on May 30,

1820. The mutual right of search was established and seizure was allowed if enslaved people were aboard. The treaty provided detailed conditions for search and seizure and created two courts of mixed commission, one in Sierra Leone and one in Havana, to oversee the operations and the disposition of any enslaved persons aboard the seized vessels. The commissions were allowed to confiscate any of the enslaved on board and to free them.[131]

The British abolitionist campaign against the Spanish slave trade challenged the basic assumptions of Spanish colonial policy, in place since the 1760s, that the prosperity and security of Cuba were tied directly to the maintenance of slavery and the slave trade. Not surprisingly, the Cuban reaction to the treaty was hostile, and planters, with the connivance of Spanish officials, did their best to delay or circumvent the treaty's implementation. When Henry Kilbee arrived in Cuba in 1819 as the first British appointee to the mixed commission in Havana, he commented that "all employés of the Government are directly or indirectly engaged in the traffic."[132] Undoubtedly, these entrenched interests were instrumental in thwarting British efforts at seizing slavers in the Caribbean. No ships were seized in those waters before 1824, although imports of enslaved Africans did decrease from 1820 to 1824.[133]

The treaty did, however, create a group of Africans in Havana who were technically free but not Hispanized, which worried colonial officials. The king issued a royal order in April 1828 resolving that all blacks freed by the treaty of 1817 should be removed from Cuba and transported to another Spanish colony, or even to the peninsula, where they would retain their free status. In spite of this order, several thousand of these freed Africans, *emancipados* or *libertos*, arrived in Cuba in the 1820s.[134] In an exposition to the king, members of Havana's town council expressed their concern that English ships continued capturing numerous "negros," who were then divided up "indistinctly to various persons." Council members proposed that the *emancipados* instead be consigned to the "three corporations" of the city—the town council, the Consulado, and the Patriotic Society (all largely under creole control)—for more consistent training and supervision.[135] Intendant Villanueva was still complaining to the crown of the danger in 1830, noting that this group of freed people would "drag down with their injurious example" that part of the population "that found themselves in servitude." To remedy this problem, the intendant extolled the benefits of assigning these *emancipados* to labor in public works.[136]

Although the state lost legal direct access to the slave trade after the implementation of the treaty of 1817, and imports of enslaved Africans fell briefly in the 1820s, this first step toward abolition gave Cuban officials a new group of forced laborers at their disposal. By 1831, there were more than 3,000 *emancipados* in Cuba, and funds to transport them all off the island were inadequate.[137] The state could no longer openly buy enslaved people from the Atlantic trade in its own name, but it did control the fate of the enslaved who were freed by the mixed commission in Havana. In spite of official protests about the social dangers posed by the *emancipados*, from 1824, when the first ship was seized off the Cuban coast, the captains general began using the freed Africans not only as laborers in public works but also as a source of revenue.[138]

Initially, the treaty of 1817 released the *emancipados* directly to the captains general. Although they were legally free, the *emancipados* were supposed to be kept in Havana and placed with good citizens to learn a trade and be Christianized. This assignment, or consignation, was to last five years for adults and seven years for minors and for women with children who could not work. This "apprenticeship" period was justified by describing the liberated Africans as equivalent to small children, who, by the laws of the land, required a period of tutelage. According to Captain General Ricafort in 1833, these *emancipados* would become accustomed to "a methodical and laborious life" to ensure their "honesty" when their consignations were finished.[139]

The consignations were to be grants, not contracts for sale, but the captains general were known to accept donations. Eventually, the contracts became commodities of speculation and sale, not unlike slave sales. The fate of those who remained *emancipados* was potentially even worse than the fate of those who were enslaved. Slaves at least enjoyed the possibility of freedom through manumission or self-purchase, whereas *emancipados* had little recourse against their fraudulent manipulation by the captains general.[140]

Up to 1831, the vast majority of *emancipados*, some 3,000 people, had been consigned to individuals. Another 374 were placed with institutions. This began to change as the population of *emancipados* in Cuba grew. In June 1832, the captured slaving vessel *Águila* disembarked 601 Africans who had survived the journey, who were then declared free by the mixed commission, bringing the total number of *emancipados* in Cuba to close to 3,800.[141] In April of 1833, Captain General Ricafort was able to send 196 *emancipados* to Trinidad, and another group of 212 the following January, with British approval, but fears of spreading cholera after the 1833 outbreak in Havana halted further transfers, in 1834.[142]

Captain General Ricafort and Intendant Villanueva formed a junta to find a solution to the growing number of liberated Africans on the island, in 1833. The impending declaration of emancipation of slaves in the British Caribbean, and several uprisings among Cuban slaves, increased the urgency felt by officials in Cuba to deal with the problem.[143] In its printed report, the junta praised the disposition of the British governor of Trinidad to receive *emancipados* but lamented the difficult conditions he had imposed. The Cuban government was to cover all the costs of transfer, give Trinidad's governor at least a month's notice for each expedition, and send only groups of *emancipados* that included equal numbers of men and women. The Cuban junta felt that the provision of a month's notice would require the outfitting of a special ship to convey such messages, an expensive enterprise. The sending of equal numbers of men and women also posed a problem, since the slaving vessels generally arrived with an excess of men.[144]

Another solution pursued by the captain general was to increase the numbers of *emancipados* consigned to institutions such as hospitals, convents, and the navy yard, which he felt would ensure greater supervision and training in productive work. One such measure was the consignment by Ricafort of 404 *emancipados* to the building of the Ferdinand VII aqueduct, in 1833. The aqueduct was a project begun by Intendant Villanueva in 1831, to improve the water supply of Havana. In 1834, Ricafort also designated seventy-two *emancipados* for a work detail to build a new jail, though that project was not carried out during his term.[145]

In a report to the king, Captain General Ricafort extolled the many benefits of assigning *emancipados* to such projects, even though this type of assignment was not specifically allowed by the treaty of 1817. These employments would "civilize" the former slaves, train a cohort of masons and bricklayers, and provide freshwater to the city of Havana, all of which, Ricafort said, would benefit the realm. Given Villanueva's support of the use of *emancipados* in public works and his close work with Ricafort on a solution to their growing numbers in the city, the consignment was a logical one.[146]

Villanueva's position and influence as intendant brought *emancipados* to another institution that organized and carried out public works, the Havana Consulado.[147] It is clear that the workforce at the disposal of the Consulado was considerably smaller than that used on the fortification projects in the 1760s. Between 1826 and 1830, the Consulado had an average of 487 workers, both enslaved and nominally free, in the Havana Depósito. Table 5.2 presents figures from 1829, giving a somewhat more detailed breakdown of the statuses of these workers.

Table 5.2. The Workforce of the Havana Depósito, 1829

Month	Fugitive slaves	Others	Total
January	217	269	486
February	185	267	452
March	198	266	464
April	194	262	456
May	226	311	537
June	233	318	551
July	225	319	544
August	202	321	523
September	190	323	513
October	200	325	525
November	195	335	530
December	219	311	530

Source: Gabino La Rosa Corzo, Los cimarrones de Cuba (Havana: Editorial de Ciencias Sociales, 1988), table 7, 54.

Note: The category of "others" included forzados, or free people, often of color, sentenced to public works for crimes such as running illegal businesses, theft, gambling, or carrying arms; enslaved people purchased in the name of the Consulado; emancipados, or Africans, freed by the treaty of 1817, assigned to public works to be acculturated to work.

In contrast to the period of urgent defense works in the 1760s, the Consulado did not purchase large numbers of slaves in its own name for road building. By 1800, prices for enslaved men of prime working age ranged from three hundred to five hundred pesos, two to three times the prices the crown had been able to negotiate in 1764.[148] Even with the growth of sugar revenues, the Consulado did not have access to sufficient funds for the purchase and maintenance of a large group of its own enslaved workers.

However, the emancipados represented a new, supplemental group of coerced workers that the Consulado could add to its squads of purchased and enslaved fugitives without making a major investment. Since one of the charges of the Consulado was the building and maintenance of Cuba's roads, over the next dozen years, the Consulado worked to improve the transportation infrastructure of Cuba. While its workforce of mostly recaptured enslaved fugitives and emancipados was relatively low cost, their numbers proved to be inadequate for the task of significantly increasing the road system around Havana. The Cuban planter elites who served in the Consulado, and the intendant, ultimately resorted to importing indentured or contract laborers from North America, Mexico, and China to build rail lines in Cuba and to work on its plantations.[149]

∼∞

An evolving political crisis in Spain and renewed British efforts to curb the slave trade to Cuba in the 1830s again shifted the context in which laborers for public works projects in and around Havana were recruited and employed. By the early 1830s, political upheaval on the peninsula had made the maintenance of the colonial bond with the rich island of Cuba even more critical. The death of King Ferdinand VII in 1833 touched off a civil war between liberal and absolutist forces in Spain. Queen Isabella II's alliance with the liberal faction raised creole hopes of greater political participation in colonial governance, but there still was the difficult question of the status of slavery and the slave trade.

Both previous liberal constitutional intervals in nineteenth-century Spanish politics (from 1810 to 1814 and from 1820 to 1823) had generated proposals to abolish the trade and to gradually end enslavement. In the 1830s, the Spanish Cortes took two more small steps toward the abolition of slavery, keeping in mind the interests of Cuban enslavers, who feared that any sudden changes in the status of their enslaved workers could spark insurrection. The Cortes abolished slavery on the peninsula by royal decree on March 29, 1836.[150]

The dismal failure of the first treaty to ban slave trading after 1820 produced a new treaty, in 1835, signed by Spain and Great Britain, with stronger provisions. It declared the Spanish slave trade to be "totally and finally abolished in all parts of the world," since the earlier treaty had not banned trade among colonies. It required that condemned vessels be immediately broken up, and it provided for the seizure and condemnation of vessels that carried equipment for trading slaves, even if no enslaved people were found on board. The treaty also provided for the transfer of the *emancipados* to British colonies as a response to stories of abuse by Spanish authorities, but events in Spain and in Cuba militated against any strict observation of the new treaty's provisions.[151] The new treaty was silent on the length of consignments of *emancipados*, and subsequent colonial officials in Cuba continued to deploy the labor of both enslaved and freed Africans in their public construction projects for decades.

The period after 1817 marked the end of state slavery in Cuba as a major form of labor coercion for defense and development. Several hundred king's slaves remained enslaved by various organs of the state over the next fifty-odd years, but purchasing enslaved people in the king's name was no longer legal or affordable as a labor recruitment strategy. Yet Cuba's enslaved population increased dramatically over this same period, in spite of British abolitionism, and the officials and institutions of the state, particularly the captains general and the Havana Consulado, found ways to benefit from the labor of fugitive slaves and the *emancipados.* Though their numbers were lower than the numbers of state slaves employed in the 1760s, these enslaved and freed workers still represented a mobile cohort of workers who could be moved from one project to another as urgency required. By forcing them to work for the state, colonial officials and planters also sought to contain the rapidly expanding population of enslaved and free Africans, whose labor Cuba's elites deemed so necessary to the island's prosperity but whose potential for resistance they feared.

CONCLUSION

State enslavement in Cuba and the Spanish Empire officially ended in July 1870, with the Spanish Cortes's passing of the Moret Law, in the midst of an anticolonial insurrection on the island. Article V of the law freed "all slaves that belong to the State for whatever reason . . . including those who with the title of *emancipado* were under the protection of the State." In keeping with long-standing practice, the law also declared free any enslaved people who fought for the crown against the insurrectionists. Both of these groups of freed people were to enjoy the protection of the state thereafter.[1]

Yet the freedom the Spanish state offered to the enslaved in Cuba in 1870 was incomplete. The Moret Law created the *patronato*, an intermediate status that qualified full liberty with various provisions to ensure some compensation for enslavers and a minimum of disruption in the forced labor system at the core of the island's economy.[2] The period of qualified freedom was extended a decade later, in January 1880, when the Spanish Cortes passed another law that codified an additional eight years of apprenticeship for those supposedly freed in 1870.

Patronos (masters) were still allowed to punish or withhold wages from any people freed under the *patronato* (*patrocinados*) who failed to attend diligently to their work or who disrupted work regimens. Service in public works remained a punishment for any *patrocinado* who failed three times to fulfill their work obligations.[3] *Patrocinados* could end the apprenticeship in various ways, such as by denouncing a *patrono* who punished them abusively or prostituted them. *Patrocinados* who were parents could claim their young children by paying the *patrono* a sum to cover the cost of their care.[4] A royal decree in October 1886 ended the *patronato* and finally completely abolished bonds between former enslavers and enslaved.[5]

This gradual, ambiguous path to abolition regulated and limited the freedom of Cuba's enslaved people in ways that highlight the arguments made in this book. The motives behind the legislation and its implementation demonstrate the uneasy tension between the state's interests, its paternalism, and its exploitation of the enslaved. The state sought to maintain the colonial bond and its sources of revenue and to uphold the authority and property rights of masters for as long as possible. At the same time, the state allowed the enslaved or *patrocinados* some openings to seek redress for abusive treatment, to maintain family ties, and to pursue full freedom, all patterns in place in the Spanish American empire since the sixteenth century. A key difference was the acknowledgment by state officials in 1870 that slavery as an institution would eventually end.

The historical context of the late 1860s and 1870s in which the Moret Law was debated and implemented had been transformed in ways that made the indefinite retention of slavery impossible. The slave trade to Cuba was finally outlawed in 1867, and only Cuba and Puerto Rico maintained legal enslavement, in a much-reduced Spanish American empire, after 1825. A major rebellion by enslaved people in Cuba in 1844 had prompted brutal repression, executions, and exile for thousands Cubans of African descent.[6] An anticolonial insurrection broke out in eastern Cuba in 1868, and its leaders began offering freedom to the enslaved and indentured workers in the region who were willing to fight for their cause, spurring the Spanish state to counter with the offer of gradual emancipation in the Moret Law.[7] The constant search, by both state and private employers in Cuba, for groups of people who could be forced to work, and the continual reconfiguration of the forms of that coercion, well illustrate the deep embedment of forced labor in nineteenth-century Spanish colonialism and in the development of capitalism within and beyond the empire.

This book also has shown how the Spanish state's policies and practices with regard to the ownership and employment of enslaved people in the eighteenth century was a bridge to the explosive expansion of plantation production and enslavement in nineteenth-century Cuba. The cycles of war of the 1700s, especially the British occupation of Havana from 1762 to 1763, compelled Spanish officials to mobilize capital in new ways, to facilitate the private sector's access to enslaved Africans, and to further integrate Cuban exports into Atlantic markets with commercial concessions. These commercial openings were essential to sugar's expansion and also provided Cuba's creole elite with avenues to greater economic and political power, reshaping in turn the colonial state and its labor policies and practices in public works.

The extent, size, and complexity of the projects undertaken by the Spanish state to defend Havana in the 1760s reshaped its own practices of owning and employing enslaved people. Royal slaves (*los esclavos del rey*) had been one group of forced laborers among many for centuries in Spain and the Americas. The crown's purchase of thousands of enslaved Africans to repair and rebuild the city's fortifications immediately following the British occupation of Havana in 1763 was unusual and was accomplished by fomenting the extension of plantations and enslavement on the island. Defense and development were joined in policy and practice to save Havana, develop its hinterland, and retain and maintain the city as a key hub of imperial trade and wealth.

The effects of this unprecedented resort to state enslavement were profound. The state quickly became the largest single enslaver on the island, managing multiple work sites with hundreds of royal slaves, smaller numbers of enslaved people hired out from private owners, and convicts. The fort sites, in particular, anticipated the work regimes that developed on many Cuban plantations by the early nineteenth century—hundreds of enslaved Africans, mostly men, performing difficult, dangerous, and often deadly work, with few opportunities for family life or paths to freedom. Havana's forts also became urban sites of fear and punishment, parallel to Alexander von Humboldt's observation about rural Cuban sugar plantations.[8] Military deserters, rebels, vagrants, pirates, enslaved fugitives, and criminals from around the empire were sentenced to labor in the city's fortifications, marching, often in chains, to their punishment.

There were a few spaces for small numbers of those enslaved by the state—such as the enslaved artillerymen of Havana and their families, or the enslaved defenders of the city during the British siege—to enjoy a somewhat better quality of life or to be rewarded for military service to the crown. When defense considerations were paramount, exemplary military service could lead to freedom, but military labor did not. The evidence presented in this book shows that the site of enslavement, the work required, and the place of that work within imperial priorities—not just whether a person was enslaved in the city or in the countryside—mattered in determining treatment, relative autonomy, and the potential for achieving freedom.

By the late 1760s, the Spanish crown and its officials in Cuba acknowledged the high costs of owning and sustaining its own enslaved labor force and began selling the least skilled among its enslaved workers. Having initially purchased these enslaved Africans at reduced prices, the crown was able to recoup some of the expense of the massive Havana fort projects by selling royal slaves to private enslavers at market prices. However, though the state quickly reversed its shift to extensive ownership and employment of the enslaved for public projects, slave importations to the island and plantation agriculture were not reversed, as hundreds of thousands of enslaved Africans were brought to Cuba by 1840.

After the 1760s, colonial officials continued to carry out extensive public works projects, but their intent, their employment of enslaved workers, and their management often were different from those of the fort projects. The staffing of state projects varied according to the levels of coercion needed to recruit people to do the work and the costs to the state. For example, the Havana naval yard and its shipbuilding capacity were restored after 1763, largely with free workers and several squads of skilled royal slaves working mostly as sawyers or carpenters. Road building and repair were carried out with hired and free labor but did not significantly increase the length of passable roadways in the interior until more labor coercion was applied to recruit road crews from among Cuba's resident population.

From 1770 onward, state officials marshaled arguments about enlightened governance and policing, social control, and imperial defense to justify forcing various groups of people to labor for the state. For example, with a brief period of peace in the mid-1770s the Marqués de la Torre was able to begin a program of urban renewal. He also turned his attention to greater internal social control and generated coerced labor for the construction of new government buildings, street paving, and bridge building by extending the state's definitions of criminal behaviors such as vagrancy and by more vigorously pursuing military deserters. This model of centralized capture of military fugitives was then applied to the roundup of escaped slaves, starting in the 1790s, as the boom in sugar production increased the need to build better roads between plantations and Havana's port.

Once the Spanish state lost control of the slave trade after 1789, and access to Mexican silver in the early 1800s, the costs of purchasing and maintaining thousands of enslaved Africans for its projects was prohibitive. After the Spanish crown signed the first treaty with Great Britain to restrict the transatlantic slave trade to Cuba, in 1817, state purchases of enslaved Africans were further constrained, though officials in Cuba turned those nominally freed by the treaty (emancipados) into wards of the state, forcing many of them to labor in legal limbo for most of their lives.

In the middle decades of the nineteenth century, the Cuban elite experimented with recruiting groups of contract workers—North American contract workers, indigenous people and mestizos from the Yucatan Peninsula, and Chinese indentured workers—to initiate the building of the first railroad lines on the island.[9] However, conditions for both the Yucatecan and Chinese contract laborers were so miserable that their home governments ultimately forbade their indenture in Cuba.[10]

The experience with contracted labor in the middle decades of the nineteenth century made this form of labor coercion attractive after the passage of the Moret Law began the process of emancipation of the enslaved in Cuba. Employers used contracts to qualify the freedom of those liberated by the law. Emancipados under state supervision numbered some 10,000 people in Cuba in 1870. At one public works site, for example, they labored to build a new channel and aqueduct to provide water to the city of Havana. The Cuban governor reported that, rather than release these workers from their labors, they were contracted to continue working for another two to six years, in what he characterized as "mutually advantageous conditions." Thus, the Moret Law both freed and constrained for a second time the freedom of the emancipados.[11]

The law also freed all children born of enslaved mothers and those over sixty years old. Enslavers were required to maintain the younger slaves, but they did not have to pay them wages until they reached eighteen years old. From the ages of eighteen to twenty-two, freed people would earn only half the prevailing wage for whatever work they did. Thus, the law freed the very young and the elderly but few people of working age, revealing the more oppressive side of official paternalism and the state's desire maintain the loyalty of Cuban enslavers with a gradual, compensated abolition. For the enslaved of working age, the Moret Law created some openings to pursue freedom for themselves and their families by appealing to the new Juntas Protectoras that were charged with the implementation of the law, but the process of emancipation for the majority of the enslaved in Cuba was long and slow.[12]

At least one common outcome of state and plantation enslavement grew from the efforts to end both the external trade and slavery itself. Recruiting people to do work that never attracted free workers at low wages in either sector continued to require the search for and experiment with alternative forms of coercion as access to enslaved workers diminished. This process began to hit all branches of the Spanish state's projects of public works in the 1830s. The state had the political advantage of controlling criminal justice, which provided it with a workforce requiring less capital investment than directly purchasing enslaved Africans.

Planters in the second half of the nineteenth century had fewer alternatives, though they, too, resorted to the importation of indentured workers by the mid-1800s and began to experiment with convict and military labor to replace slaves who had died, fled, or purchased their freedom.[13] Additionally, planters had to continually renegotiate the terms of work with their enslaved workers and with the peninsular government, after slave imports began their uneven decline in the 1840s. Thus, expansion of private sugar production and abolitionism certainly cost the Spanish state the power to acquire enslaved workers for public projects, but it retained the advantage in finding alternatives.

We also must take into account the human costs and violence embedded in the physical structures of the Spanish Empire in Havana, the state's role in shaping the institution of slavery, and the experiences of enslaved people both before and after the sugar boom of the early nineteenth century. By attending to these human costs, this study of state slavery has sought to make visible the tremendous labor necessary to construct and reproduce the Spanish Empire in the imperial hub of Havana. The case of Cuba can be usefully compared to other sites of empire building in the Atlantic world, so that this labor—building forts, warehouses, docks, and prisons; soldiering and sailoring; sawing wood; digging and hauling earth and rock; and transporting people and goods—can be included in the accounting of the growth of capitalism and the historical role of imperial states in its development.[14]

NOTES

ABBREVIATIONS

AGI	Archivo General de Indias
AGS	Archivo General de Simancas
AHN	Archivo Histórico Nacional, Madrid
BNE	Biblioteca Nacional de España
doct.	document
exp.	expediente
LCMD	Library of Congress, Manuscript Division
MNM	Museo Naval, Madrid
n.d.	no date
SD	Santo Domingo
SSH	Secretaría y Superintendencia de Hacienda
t.	tomo (volume)

INTRODUCTION

1. Alejandro de Humboldt, Ensayo político sobre la isla de Cuba, ed. Miguel Ángel Puig-Samper, Consuelo Naranjo Orovio, and Armando García González (Madrid: Ediciones Dos Calles, 1998), 101, 107.

2. Humboldt, Ensayo político, 107. The additional fortifications were the westernmost Chorrera Castle, built from 1634 to 1646; El Príncipe, finished in 1789; and Atarés, finished in 1767.

3. There is considerable scholarly consensus on the importance of the imperatives of imperial defense and services to the island's early economic development. See, for instance, Manuel Moreno Fraginals, El ingenio: complejo económico social cubano del azúcar (Barcelona: Crítica, 2001). This edition brings together the three volumes of El ingenio published in Cuba in 1978. See also Moreno Fraginals, "Peculiaridades de la esclavitud en Cuba," Islas 85 (1986): 3–12; Julio Le Riverend Brusone, La Habana, espacio y vida (Madrid: MAPFRE, 1992), 67; Francisco Pérez Guzmán, La Habana clave de un imperio (Havana: Editorial de Ciencias Sociales, 1997), 158–168. This book has the most information to date on state slavery in Havana, particularly those employed in building fortifications. It also treats fort construction in other Cuban cities. Franklin Knight, "Origins of Wealth and the Sugar Revolution in

Cuba, 1750–1850," *Hispanic American Historical Review* 57, no. 2 (1977): 231–253, at 242–243; Allan J. Kuethe, "Havana in the Eighteenth Century," in *Atlantic Port Cities, Economy, Culture and Society in the Atlantic World, 1650–1850*, ed. Franklin W. Knight and Peggy K. Liss (University of Tennessee Press: Knoxville, 1992) 13–39, especially 17–19 and 24–25.

4. Humboldt, *Ensayo político*, 105. For an argument for significant commercial expansion over the whole of the eighteenth century, especially due to slave trading, see Elena A. Schneider, *The Occupation of Havana: War, Trade and Slavery in the Atlantic World* (Williamsburg, VA, and Chapel Hill, Omohundro Institute of Early American History and Culture and University of North Carolina Press, 2018).

5. Elena Schneider, "African Slavery and the Spanish Empire: Imperial Imaginings and Bourbon Reform in Eighteenth-Century Cuba and Beyond," *Journal of Early American History* 5, no. 1 (2015): 3–29.

6. For examples of these attitudes among the Cuban elite, see the essays collected in María Dolores González-Ripoll et al., *El rumor de Haití en Cuba: Temor, raza y rebeldía, 1789–1844* (Madrid: Consejo Superior de Investigaciones Científicas, 2004).

7. Humboldt, *Ensayo político*, 301, 308–309.

8. Humboldt, *Ensayo político*, 302.

9. For works that highlight state support for early sugar development, see Alejandro de la Fuente, "Sugar and Slavery in Early Colonial Cuba," in *Tropical Babylons: Sugar and the Making of the Atlantic World, 1450–1680*, ed. Stuart Schwartz (Chapel Hill: University of North Carolina Press, 2004), 116–126, on establishment of sugar mills with crown support in the sixteenth and seventeenth century; and Kuethe, "Havana in the Eighteenth Century."

10. The present site of the city was neither the colony's original capital nor the original site of the city itself. The first capital was founded on the southeastern coast, at Santiago. In the west, it is likely that two towns were founded toward the end of the conquest period (1511–1514), one on the southern coast and one to the north and west of the Puerto de Carenas, the present site of Havana. The advantages of the northern port for transatlantic shipping became clear to the Spanish (and to pirates) by the middle decades of the 1500s. Alejandro de la Fuente, *Havana and the Atlantic in the Sixteenth Century* (Chapel Hill: University of North Carolina Press, 2008), 4–5; Emilio Roig de Leuchsenring, *La Habana. Apuntes históricos* (Havana: Municipio de la Habana, 1939) 13–22.

11. This was a pattern more common to the Caribbean than to the mainland parts of the Spanish Empire. It will be discussed in greater detail in chapter 1.

12. Most important were subsidies from the viceroyalty of New Spain, generated from the mineral wealth of that colony. Carlos Marichal and Matilde Souto, "La Nueva España y el financiamiento del imperio español en América: Los situados del Caribe en el siglo XVIII," in *El secreto del Imperio Español: Los situados coloniales en el siglo XVIII*, ed. Carlos Marichal and Johanna von Grafenstein (Mexico City: El Colegio de México, 2012), 61–93; and José Manuel Serrano and Allan J. Kuethe, "El situado mexicano y la Cuba borbónica," 95–114, in the same volume. See also Allan J. Kuethe, "Guns, Subsidies, and Commercial Privilege: Some Historical Factors in the Emergence of the Cuban National Character, 1763–1815," *Cuban Studies* 16 (1986): 123–138, especially 129–131.

13. Robin Blackburn, "Why the Second Slavery?," in *Slavery and Historical Capitalism during the Nineteenth Century*, ed. Dale Tomich (Lanham, MD: Lexington, 2017), 3, describes first slavery as "colonial in character, with its legal and socioeconomic underpinnings deriving from the Old World, especially the Mediterranean." For bibliography on second slavery, see note 33.

14. Peter Way's scholarship is fundamental to a perspective that examines the work of warfare. He has focused mostly on the commodification and proletarianization of labor in canal building and military service, though he also shows the expansion of capital, markets, technology, and institutional innovation as parts of those processes. See Way, "Class-Warfare: Primitive Accumulation, Military Revolution and the British War-Worker," in *Beyond Marx: Theorising the Global Labour Relations of the Twenty-first Century*, ed. Marcel van der Linden and Karl Heinz Roth (Leiden: Brill, 2014), 65–87; "'The Scum of Every County, the Refuse of Mankind': Recruiting the British Army in the Eighteenth Century," in *Fighting for a Living: A Comparative History of Military Labour, 1500–2000*, ed. Erik-Jan Zürcher (Amsterdam: Amsterdam University Press, 2013), 291–330; "Black Service . . . White Money: The Peculiar Institution of Military Labor in the British Army During the Seven Years' War," in *Workers Across the Americas: The Transnational Turn in Labor History*, ed. Leon Fink (New York: Oxford University Press, 2011), 57–80; and *Common Labour: Workers and the Digging of North American Canals, 1780–1860* (Cambridge: Cambridge University Press, 1993).

15. Schneider, *Occupation of Havana* (especially chapters 5 and 6) also argues that policy changes after the British occupation of Havana from 1762 to 1763 reduced the openings to freedom and sometimes to privileges and higher status through military service, which previously were possible for enslaved and free people of color.

16. As I have argued elsewhere, "An uneasy balance between force and favor—penal servitude and paternalism, enslavement and manumission, labor tribute and loyalty to a distant lord—all built and maintained the Spanish American empire." Rebellion undermined the colonial bond with Cuba only once repression outweighed paternalism and faith in the mercy and justice of the crown waned, after about 1820. Evelyn P. Jennings, "Sinews of Spain's American Empire: Forced Labor in Cuba from the Sixteenth to the Nineteenth Centuries," in *Building the Atlantic Empires: Unfree Labor and Imperial States in the Political Economy of Capitalism, ca. 1500–1914*, ed. John Donoghue and Evelyn P. Jennings (Leiden: Brill, 2016), 53. For discussion of crown paternalism as a remnant of feudal social relations in the evolution of capitalism in colonial Cuba, see Karen Y. Morrison, "Spanish Imperial Vassalage and the Social Reproduction of Slavery in Colonial Cuba," *Journal of Global Slavery* 3, no. 3 (2018): 261–285.

17. Frank Tannenbaum, *Slave and Citizen: The Negro in the Americas* (New York: Alfred A. Knopf, 1946).

18. Tannenbaum, *Slave and Citizen*, focuses mostly on the differences in the legal status of slaves in Iberian American colonies and their possibilities for achieving freedom (53–56 and 65–88). Tannenbaum also cited Fernando Ortiz, *Hampa-afrocubana: Los negros esclavos, estudio sociológico y de derecho público* (Havana: Revista bimestre cubana, 1916); and Richard Dana, Jr., *To Cuba and Back* (Boston: Tichnor and Fields, 1859). Though Humboldt recognized significant differences between the relative humanity of Spanish versus English laws on slavery, he was less convinced that slaves on plantations in Cuba, in particular, were able to access the purported benefits of Spanish law. Humboldt, *Ensayo político*, 306–311.

19. A good introduction to the scholarship on urban enslavement in the Americas, especially that written in English, is the bibliographic essay at the end of Jorge Cañizares-Esguerra, Matt D. Childs, and James Sidbury eds., *The Black Urban Atlantic in the Age of the Slave Trade* (Philadelphia: University of Pennsylvania Press, 2013), 351–350. On urban slavery in Cuba in particular, see Pedro Deschamps Chapeaux, *El negro en la economía habanera del Siglo XIX* (Havana: Unión de Escritores y Artistas de Cuba,

1971); and *Los cimarrones urbanos* (Havana: Editorial de Ciencias Sociales, 1983). For the nineteenth century, see Fernando Ortiz, "El esclavo urbano," in *Los negros esclavos* (Havana: Editorial de Ciencias Sociales, 1975), 189–196. Also, Robert Paquette, *Sugar Is Made with Blood: The Conspiracy of La Esclaera and the Conflict Between Empires over Slavery in Cuba* (Middletown: Wesleyan University Press, 1988), especially chapter 1, 29–50. More recently, see Philip Howard, *Changing History: Afro-Cuban Cabildos and Societies of Color in the Nineteenth Century* (Baton Rouge: Louisiana State University Press, 1998); María del Carmen Barcia Zequeira, *La otra familia: Parientes, redes, y desendencia de los esclavos en Cuba* (Havana: Casa de la Américas, 2003); and Matt D. Childs, *The 1812 Aponte Rebellion in Cuba and the Struggle against Atlantic Slavery* (Chapel Hill: University of North Carolina Press, 2006).

20. See, for example, Pablo Miguel Sierra Silva, *Urban Slavery in Colonial Mexico: Puebla de los Ángeles 1531–1706* (Cambridge: Cambridge University Press, 2018). Sierra examines the variety of experiences of the enslaved in Puebla, Mexico, at sites such as convents, markets, and textile mills. As he notes, "Understanding specific physical settings within the city allows for a more fruitful engagement with the expectations, limitations and possibilities that the enslaved and their captors confronted on an everyday basis" (22). Christian De Vito, "Connected Singularities: Convict Labour in Late Colonial Spanish America (1760s–1800), in *Micro-Spatial Histories of Global Labour*, ed. Christian G. De Vito and Anne Gerritsen (London: Palgrave, 2018) makes a parallel argument about the study of convict labor through a microspatial analysis that rejects "predetermined categories and units" and "foregrounds specific connections between contexts" (172) both local and global.

21. Francisco Pérez Guzmán, "El modo de vida de esclavos y forzados en las fortificaciones cubanas," *Anuario de estudios americanos* 47 (1990): 241–257; Pérez Guzmán, *La Habana clave*; María Elena Díaz, *The Virgin, the King, and the Royal Slaves of El Cobre* (Stanford, CA: Stanford University Press, 2000). I am very grateful to the late Pérez Guzmán for giving me a copy of his book and discussing my project at an early stage, when I visited Havana in the late 1990s.

The bibliography on state slavery in the Atlantic world is relatively short. Alvin O. Thompson, *Unprofitable Servants: Crown Slaves in Berbice, Guyana, 1803–1831* (Kingston: University of West Indies Press, 2002) looks at the use of crown slaves in Guyana, after its wartime acquisition by Britain in 1803, as an economic failure. Two other full-length treatments discuss state enslavement as a political and military issue rather than an economic one. See Roger N. Buckley, *Slaves in Red Coats: The British West India Regiments, 1795–1815* (New Haven, CT: Yale University Press, 1979); and Peter M. Voelz, *Slave and Soldier: The Military Impact of Blacks in the Colonial Americas* (New York: Garland, 1993). For a broader historical and geographic perspective on military slavery, the essays in Christopher Leslie Brown and Philip D. Morgan, eds., *Arming Slaves from Classical Times to the Modern Age* (New Haven, CT: Yale University Press, 2006) are a good introduction. In addition to the two works by Pérez Guzmán and Díaz that give some attention to the impact of state slavery on economic development in Cuba, see Evelyn Powell Jennings, "'War as the Forcing House of Change': The Case of Cuba in the late Eighteenth Century," *William and Mary Quarterly* 63, no. 3 (July 2005): 411–440; and Vicent Sanz Rozalén, "Los negros del rey. Tabaco y esclavitud en Cuba a comienzos del Siglo XIX," in *Trabajo libre y coactivo en sociedades de plantación*, ed. José Antonio Piqueras Arenas (Madrid: Siglo XXI de España Editores, 2009), 151–176. On state-owned slaves elsewhere in the circum-Caribbean, see Rina Cáceres Gómez, "Slave Wages in Omoa," in *Blacks and Blackness in Central America: Between Race and Place*, ed. Lowell Gudmundson and Justin Wolfe (Durham: Duke University Press, 2010), 130–149; K. J. Kesselring, "'Negroes of the

Crown': The Management of Slaves Forfeited by Grenadian Rebels, 1796–1831," *Journal of the Canadian Historical Association/Revue de la Société historique du Canada* 22, no. 2 (2011): 1–29; and Cécile Vidal, "Public Slavery, Racial Formation, and the Struggle over Honor in French New Orleans, 1718–1769," *Anuario Colombiano de Historia Social y de la Cultura* 43, no. 2 (2016): 155–183.

22. For instance, the majority of royal slaves who built Havana's monumental fortifications after 1763 had a relatively brief, often deadly relationship with the state. Most of them did not create stable communities over generations, as happened in El Cobre, and few had the opportunities to invest their relationship with the state with the layered meanings created by the *cobreros*.

23. The *cobreros'* experience, in some ways, resembled that of maroon communities that were able to wrest concessions from imperial authorities in exchange for providing military labor to defend outposts of the Spanish Empire. See, for instance, Jane Landers, "Gracia Real de Santa Teresa de Mose: A Free Black Town in Spanish Colonial Florida," *American Historical Review*, 95, no. 1 (1990): 9–30.

24. David Eltis, "Free and Coerced Migrations from the Old World to the New," in *Coerced and Free Migration: Global Perspectives*, ed. David Eltis (Stanford, CA: Stanford University Press, 2002), 45.

25. For a perceptive analysis of comparative questions of development in early modern Western Europe, with Spain at the center, see David Ringrose, *Spain, Europe, and the "Spanish Miracle,"* 1700–1900 (Cambridge: Cambridge University Press, 1996).

26. For a thorough discussion of Marx's categories of analysis in the historiography of plantation slave societies, with a discussion of Cuban historians' positions, see Jorge Ibarra Cuesta, *Marx y los historiadores ante la hacienda y la plantación esclavista* (Havana: Editorial de Ciencias Sociales, 2008). Also see José Antonio Piqueras, "Historical Slavery and Capitalism in Cuban Historiography," in *Slavery and Historical Capitalism in the Nineteenth Century*, ed. Dale Tomich (Lanham, MD: Lexington, 2017), 67–122. The foundational work in Cuban scholarship is still Moreno Fraginals, *El ingenio.* See also, Manuel Moreno Fraginals, "Plantations in the Caribbean: Cuba, Puerto Rico, and the Dominican Republic in the Late Nineteenth Century," in *Between Slavery and Free Labor: The Spanish-Speaking Caribbean in the Nineteenth Century*, ed. Manuel Moreno Fraginals, Frank Moya Pons, and Stanley L. Engerman (Baltimore: Johns Hopkins University Press, 1985), 3–21. This essay provides a succinct summary, in English, of Moreno's overall argument. He also discusses the Cuban case in comparison with that of Puerto Rico and Santo Domingo (SD).

27. See, for example, Fe Iglesias Garcia, "The Development of Capitalism in Cuban Sugar Production, 1860–1900," in *Between Slavery and Free Labor: The Spanish-Speaking Caribbean in the Nineteenth Century*, ed. Manuel Moreno Fraginals, Frank Moya Pons, and Stanley L. Engerman (Baltimore: Johns Hopkins University Press, 1985), 55, 72. Iglesias's point is based on her argument that there was no internal labor market in Cuba until the 1890s. See also Francisco López Segrera, "Cuba: Dependence, Plantation Economy, and Social Classes, 1762–1902," in *Between Slavery and Free Labor: The Spanish-Speaking Caribbean in the Nineteenth Century*, ed. Manuel Moreno Fraginals, Frank Moya Pons, and Stanley L. Engerman (Baltimore: Johns Hopkins University Press, 1985), 87, which argues that "the massive introduction of Africans prevented capitalist industrialization" and, following Moreno Fraginals, that Cuba's plantation economy was "really . . . a colonial and dependent capitalist mode of production," suitable for capital accumulation but "incompatible" with industrial mechanization.

28. See especially Rebecca J. Scott, *Slave Emancipation in Cuba: The Transition to Free Labor, 1860–1899* (Princeton: Princeton University Press, 1985). In slavery studies, scholars' emphasis on the agency

of the enslaved was largely a response to interpretations of slavery that focused on slaves as victims. The most extreme example was likely Stanley M. Elkins, *Slavery: A Problem in American Institutional and Intellectual Life* (Chicago: University of Chicago Press, 1959), which claimed that the enslaved were deracinated and infantilized by the horrors and violence of their oppression. Many works since have contested Elkins's notion of the slave as Sambo by emphasizing efforts by the enslaved to exploit any openings in the slave system to lighten their burdens of labor, through culture and family life or through outright rebellion and flight. The bibliography on these topics across the Americas is extensive. Several works serve as introductions to the issues and bibliography, including Walter Johnson, "On Agency," *Journal of Social History* 37, no. 1 (2003): 113–124, which explores connections between discussions of slaves' agency and the New Social History of the 1970s and beyond. In Cuban slavery studies, Gloria García Rodríguez used notarial records and court documents to investigate slaves' own perspectives on their lives and bondage. See García Rodríguez, *La esclavitud desde la esclavitud: La vision de los siervos* (Mexico City: Centro de Investigación Científica Ing. Jorge L. Tamayo, 1996), republished in English as *Voices of the Enslaved in Nineteenth-Century Cuba*, trans. Nancy L. Westrate (Chapel Hill: University of North Carolina Press, 2011), which contains a good introduction to the history and historiography of Cuban slavery, and a brief bibliography.

29. Moreno, "Plantations in the Caribbean," 15; Scott, "Explaining Abolition: Contradiction, Adaptation, and Challenge in Cuban Slave Society, 1860–1886," in *Between Slavery and Free Labor: The Spanish-Speaking Caribbean in the Nineteenth Century*, ed. Manuel Moreno Fraginals, Frank Moya Pons, and Stanley L. Engerman (Baltimore: Johns Hopkins University Press, 1985), 25–53.

30. The dependency perspective has both Marxian and nationalist roots among Cuban scholars. See, for example, Moreno Fraginals, *El ingenio*, which calls commercial institutions set up by the Cuban bourgeoisie in the late 1700s "transitional organisms toward a capitalism castrated by a slave workforce" (89), and Ibarraa Cuesta, *Marx y los historiadores*, 198–205, 279.

31. De la Fuente, *Havana*; Ada Ferrer, *Freedom's Mirror: Cuba and Haiti in the Age of Revolution* (Cambridge: Cambridge University Press, 2014); Josep M. Fradera and Christopher Schmidt-Nowara, eds., *Slavery and Antislavery in Spain's Atlantic Empire* (New York: Berghahn, 2013); Schneider, *Occupation of Havana*.

32. Dale W. Tomich, "Capitalism, Slavery, and World Economy: Historical Theory and Theoretical History," in *Through the Prism of Slavery: Labor, Capital, and World Economy* (Lanham, MD: Rowman and Littlefield, 2004), 4. Tomich discusses the conceptual problems of world-systems theory in relation to slavery and the world economy at 13–17.

33. The bibliography on second slavery has grown extensive, especially since 2000. Tomich himself has published numerous essays and has coedited collections examining different aspects of the development of second slavery in the postrevolutionary Atlantic context. See, for instance, Tomich, *Through the Prism of Slavery*; and Dale Tomich and Michael Zeuske, "Introduction, the Second Slavery: Mass Slavery, World-Economy, and Comparative Microhistories," *Review (Fernand Braudel Center)* 31, no. 2 (2008): 91–100; as well as the essays and their references in Dale Tomich, ed., *The Politics of Second Slavery* (Albany: State University of New York Press, 2016); and Tomich, *Slavery and Historical Capitalism during the Nineteenth Century* (Lanham, MD: Lexington Books, 2017). Also see Javier Laviña and Michael Zeuske, eds., *The Second Slavery: Mass Slaveries in the Americas and in the Atlantic Basin* (Zurich: LIT, 2014); and Ada Ferrer, "Cuban Slavery and Atlantic Antislavery," in *Slavery and Antislavery in*

Spain's Atlantic Empire, ed. Josep M. Fradera and Christopher Schmidt-Nowara (New York: Berghahn, 2013), 134–157. For a critique of the second slavery methodology, see Karen Y. Morrison, "Sustaining Freedom and Second Slavery in Nineteenth-Century Brazil and Cuba," *Latin American Research Review* 53, no. 2 (2018): 411–417.

34. Most influential in this regard are, for instance, Marcel van der Linden, *Workers of the World: Essays Toward a Global Labor History* (Leiden: Brill, 2008); and Tom Brass and Marcel van der Linden, *Free and Unfree Labour: The Debate Continues* (Bern: Peter Lang, 1997). See also the essays in Leon Fink, ed., *Workers Across the Americas: The Transnational Turn in Labor History* (New York: Oxford University Press, 2011), especially part 2 on labor and empire.

35. For an early call to attend to the many entanglements in the Atlantic world, see Eliga H. Gould, "Entangled Histories, Entangled Worlds: The English-Speaking Atlantic as a Spanish Periphery," *American Historical Review* 112, no. 3 (June 2007): 764–786; Gould, "Entangled Atlantic Histories: A Response from the Anglo-American Periphery, *American Historical Review* 112, no. 5 (December 2007): 1414–1422.; and, more recently, Jorge Cañizares Esguerra, *Entangled Empires: The Anglo-Iberian Atlantic, 1500–1830* (Philadelphia: University of Pennsylvania Press, 2018).

36. Peter Linebaugh and Marcus Rediker, *The Many-Headed Hydra: Sailors, Slaves, Commoners, and the Hidden History of the Revolutionary Atlantic* (Boston: Beacon, 2000), 332.

37. Linebaugh and Rediker, *The Many-Headed Hydra*, 42, and all of chapter 2.

38. On disrupting Anglo-Atlantic normativity, see the work of Jorge Cañizares Esguerra, such as *Puritan Conquistadors: Iberianizing the Atlantic 1550–1700* (Stanford, CA: Stanford University Press, 2006), and his edited collection *Entangled Empires*. For a critique of institutional economic interpretations of the Spanish Empire as "absolutist, interventionist, and centralized," thereby stifling innovation and local political and economic development in favor of understanding Spanish America as a "negotiated" empire, see Alejandra Irigoin and Regina Grafe, "Absolutismo negociado: La trayectoria hispana en la formación del estado y el imperio," in *El secreto del Imperio Español: Los situados colonials en el siglo XVIII*, ed. Carlos Marichal and Johanna von Grafenstein (Mexico City: El Colegio de México, 2012), 295–335, quote on 296. The work of John H. Elliott is indispensable for a comparison of the American empires of Spain and Britain, especially Elliott, *Empires of the Atlantic World: Britain and Spain the America 1492–1830* (New Haven, CT: Yale University Press, 2006). Raising questions about the suitability of Atlantic frameworks for understanding the Spanish Empire, see Evelyn P. Jennings, "All in the Family? Colonial Cuba in an Iberian Atlantic Frame," *Bulletin of Hispanic Studies* 91, no. 1 (2014): 83–104.

39. Most considerations of the relationship between enslavement, capitalism, and the industrial revolution in Britain recognize the foundational work of Eric Williams, *Capitalism and Slavery* (1944; Chapel Hill: University of North Carolina Press, 1994). For later evaluations of Williams's thesis, see Barbara L. Solow and Stanley L. Engerman, eds., *British Capitalism and Caribbean Slavery* (Cambridge: Cambridge University Press, 2004); and Joseph E. Inikori, *Africans and the Industrial Revolution in England: A Study in International Trade and Economic Development* (Cambridge: Cambridge University Press, 2002). For more recent examples, see Barbara L. Solow, *The Economic Consequence of the Atlantic Slave Trade* (Lanham, MD: Lexington, 2014); and Dale Tomich, "*Capitalism and Slavery* Revisited: Remaking the Slave Commodity Frontier," in *The Legacy of Eric Williams: Into the Post-Colonial Moment*, ed. Tanya L. Shields (Jackson: University Press of Mississippi, 2015), 172–185. Tomich seeks to revive Williams's thesis about the importance of West Indian slavery to British industrialization by looking beyond the

individual units of the West Indian plantation islands and Britain to show the interrelated processes that produced "the *expansion and differentiation* of slavery" in the nineteenth-century Americas (Cuba, the United States, and Brazil) and the "growth and reorganization of world markets and the international division of labor" (184, emphasis in the original). C. L. R. James, *Black Jacobins: Toussaint L'Ouverture and the San Domingo Revolution*, 2nd ed., revised (New York: Vintage, 1963) is one major exception to the Anglo-Atlantic bias.

40. Sven Beckert, *Empire of Cotton* (New York: Alfred A. Knopf, 2015), 37, 440. Beckert only devotes a few paragraphs to the first three centuries of European colonization, largely dominated by Spanish American gold and silver extraction (1500–1800), which provided the foundation for global trade, though he does note that Spanish American silver bought East Indian textiles "in the first place" (35). He is more interested in connecting the need for plantation labor outside the Spanish Empire to Atlantic slavery and cotton production in English colonies (440–441). For a microanalysis that comes to parallel conclusions about the connections between slavery and capitalism, see Seth Rockman, *Scraping By: Wage Labor, Slavery and Survival in Early Baltimore* (Baltimore: Johns Hopkins University Press, 2009), who notes that "the persistence of coercion," among other features of the labor market in Baltimore, "were not imperfections or temporary contradictions in capitalist development; they were the very foundation of capitalism in the early republic" (9). For a history of the early stages of capitalism, focused on the central role of Spanish America in the globalization of commercial capitalism through silver production and the deeply capitalist social relations in Northern New Spain, see John Tutino, *Making a New World: Founding Capitalism in the Bajío and Spanish North America* (Durham, NC: Duke University Press, 2011).

41. Beckert, *Empire of Cotton*, 29–82.

42. José Antonio Piqueras, *La esclavitud en las Españas. Un lazo transatlántico* (Madrid: La Catarata, 2011), 94–118.

43. Daniel B. Rood, *The Reinvention of Atlantic Slavery: Technology, Labor, Race, and Capitalism in the Greater Caribbean* (New York: Oxford University Press, 2017). Earlier historiography on Cuban development in the nineteenth century points to the 1860s as the definitive reorientation of sugar production. Moreno Fraginals, *El ingenio*, 467–477.

44. Sven Beckert and Christine Desan, in the introduction to their collection of essays on new histories of American capitalism, argue for the need to "reinstall political economy as a category of analysis," "contest the line between public and private," "interrogate connections between slavery and the unfolding of capitalism," and "restore the centrality of violence and coercion to the history of capitalism"—all points that frame the analysis in this book. Sven Beckert and Christine Desan, eds., *American Capitalism: New Histories* (New York: Columbia University Press, 2018), 10–12.

45. For much of the twentieth century, the role of the Spanish state in the dismantling the institution of slavery in Cuba has been more thoroughly documented than its role in slavery's development. See, for instance, Arthur F. Corwin, *Spain and the Abolition of Slavery in Cuba, 1817–1886* (Austin: University of Texas Press, 1967); David Murray, *Odious Commerce: Britain, Spain, and the Abolition of the Cuban Slave Trade* (Cambridge: Cambridge University Press, 1980); Scott, *Slave Emancipation in Cuba*; Christopher Schmidt-Nowara, *Empire and Antislavery: Spain, Cuba, and Puerto Rico, 1833–1874* (Pittsburgh: University of Pittsburgh Press, 1999). More recent scholarship has reset the balance, especially the work of Elena Schneider in "African Slavery" and *The Occupation of Havana*.

46. For an introduction to the vast literature on political economy and its intersections with scholarship on empire, see James D. Tracy, ed., *The Political Economy of Merchant Empires: State Power and World Trade, 1350–1750* (Cambridge: Cambridge University Press, 1991); Sophus A. Reinert and Pernille Røge, eds., *The Political Economy of Empire in the Early Modern World* (Basingstoke: Palgrave Macmillan, 2013); and Robert Fredona and Sophus A. Reinert, eds., *New Perspectives on the History of Political Economy* (Cham: Palgrave Macmillan/Springer, 2018). For a focus on labor in the nexus of political economy and empire, see John Donoghue and Evelyn P. Jennings, eds., *Building the Atlantic Empires: Unfree Labor and Imperial States in the Political Economy of Capitalism, ca. 1500–1914* (Leiden: Brill, 2016).

47. As Sven Beckert has argued, war capitalism was the "engine of capital formation." Beckert, *Empire of Cotton*, 52–53, 60.

48. The website of the state archives of Spain (http://pares.culturaydeporte.gob.es/inicio.html) offers a good introduction to these collections (in Spanish), and there are more detailed introductions to the collections of each archive.

49. On the eighteenth-century reforms of the military in Cuba, see the work of Allan J. Kuethe, particularly Kuethe, *Cuba, 1753–1815: Crown, Military, and Society* (Knoxville: University of Tennessee Press, 1986); Celia María Parcero Torre, *La pérdida de La Habana y las reformas borbónicas en Cuba (1760–1773)* (Ávila: Junta de Castilla y León, 1998); and Sherry Johnson, *Social Transformation of Eighteenth-Century Cuba* (Gainesville: University Press of Florida, 2001). For the Bourbon Reforms more broadly, a good starting point is Allan J. Kuethe and Kenneth J. Andrien, *The Spanish Atlantic World in the Eighteenth Century: War and the Bourbon Reforms, 1713–1796* (New York: Cambridge University Press, 2014). Scholars who have used these documents to discuss royal or state slaves include Pérez Guzmán, *La Habana clave* and "Modo de vida de esclavos y forzados"; Ruth Pike, "Penal Servitude in the Spanish Empire: Presidio Labor in the Eighteenth Century," *Hispanic American Historical Review* 58, no. 1 (1978): 21–40; and De Vito, "Connected Singularities," 171–202. Although Pike and De Vito focus on convict labor, they present data on state slaves as well.

50. Prices of working-age slaves were relatively stable from 1800 to 1850, but British abolitionism raised the political costs of extensive resort to enslaved laborers for public works after 1820. On slave prices from 1790 to 1880, see Laird Bergad, Fe Iglesias García, and María del Carmen Barcia, *The Cuban Slave Market, 1790–1880* (Cambridge: Cambridge University Press, 1995), 11; note 35 addresses the point about the stability of slave prices in the first half of the nineteenth century.

51. The phrase is borrowed from John Brewer, *The Sinews of Power* (New York: Alfred A. Knopf, 1989), who quotes Cicero, *Orationes Philippicae* ("The sinews of War are infinite money") among the book's epigraphs.

CHAPTER 1

1. There is a considerable bibliography on the history of slavery in Spain, though studies of specific towns or regions tend to predominate. The work of William D. Phillips is a notable exception. See Phillips, *Slavery in Medieval and Early Modern Iberia* (Philadelphia: University of Pennsylvania Press, 2014); "Slavery in Spain, Ancient to Early Modern: A Survey of the Historiography since 1990," *Bulletin of the Society for Spanish and Portuguese Historical Studies* 27, no. 2–3 (Winter–Spring 2001–2002): 10–18; *Historia de la esclavitud en España* (Madrid: Editorial Playor, 1990); and "The Old World Background of

Slavery in the Americas," in *Slavery and the Rise of the Atlantic System*, ed. Barbara L. Solow (Cambridge: Cambridge University Press, 1991), 43–61. Also see Alessandro Stella, *Histoires d'esclaves dans la péninsule ibérique* (Paris: École des Hautes Études en Sciences Sociales, 2000); Charles Verlinden, *L'esclavage dans l'Europe médiévale, tome 1, Péninsule ibérique-France* (Brugge: De Tempel, 1955); and Antonio Domínguez Ortiz, "La esclavitud en Castilla durante la Edad Moderna," *Estudios de historia social de España* (Madrid: Consejo Superior de Investigaciones Científicas, 1952), 369–373. On Portugal in this period, see A. C. de C. M. Saunders, *A Social History of Black Slaves and Freedmen in Portugal 1441–1555* (Cambridge: Cambridge University Press, 1982).

2. Phillips, *Historia de la esclavitud en España*, 163–178; *Slavery in Medieval and Early Modern Iberia*, 103–106.

3. Phillips, *Slavery in Medieval and Early Modern Iberia*, 115–116.

4. For a summary of this period, with bibliography, see Phillips, *Historia de la esclavitud en España*, 25–56, 262–264 (on public slaves specifically, 38–39); and *Slavery in Medieval and Early Modern Iberia*, 115–116.

5. Phillips, *Historia de la esclavitud en España*, 94–99.

6. On Seville's slave population, see Alfonso Franco Silva, *La esclavitud en Sevilla y su tierra a fines de la Edad Media* (Seville: Diputación Provincial de Sevilla, 1979), 132–146; and Phillips, *Slavery in Medieval and Early Modern Iberia*, 24, 68–70. A well-known free black member of early Spanish expeditions in the Americas was Juan Garrido, who fought in Hispaniola and Florida and with Cortés in Mexico and California. See Peter Gerhard, "A Black Conquistador in Mexico," *Hispanic American Historical Review* 58, no. 3 (1978): 451–459; Ricardo E. Alegría, *Juan Garrido, el conquistador en las Antillas, Florida, México, y California, c. 1503–1540* (San Juan: Centro de Estudios Avanzados de Puerto Rico y El Caribe, 1990); and Jane Landers, *Black Society in Spanish Florida* (Urbana: University of Illinois Press, 1999), 10–12.

7. Jane Landers, "Transforming Bondsmen into Vassals: Arming Slaves in Colonial Spanish America," in *Arming Slaves from Classical Times to the Modern Age*, ed. Christopher Leslie Brown and Philip D. Morgan (New Haven, CT: Yale University Press, 2006), 120–145; Phillips, *Slavery in Medieval and Early Modern Iberia*, 119–121.

8. Phillips, *Historia de la esclavitud en España*, 105; *Slavery in Medieval and Early Modern Iberia*, 116–121.

9. Virtually all authors who write on slavery in Spain or its colonies treat the *Siete Partidas* as the general legal framework for slavery under Castilian rule in both areas. See, for instance, Verlinden, *L'esclavage*, 290, 593–594; Phillips, *Historia de la esclavitud en España*, 255; and Phillips, *Slavery in Medieval and Early Modern Iberia*, 22. Verlinden (290) also discusses other slave codes on the peninsula, such as the *Code de Tortosa*, which applied in the Kingdom of Aragón in the thirteenth century. The *Siete Partidas* became important for slavery in the Americas because the Crown of Castile was the sole ruler of the new realms in the Indies. The importance some scholars placed on the Castilian legal code's humanity toward slaves in defining the nature of slavery in Hispanic societies sparked scholarly debate for decades. See Tannenbaum, *Slave and Citizen*, 45–53; Herbert S. Klein, *Slavery in the Americas: A Comparative Study of Virginia and Cuba* (Chicago: University of Chicago Press, 1967), 59–66; Alejandro de la Fuente, "Slave Law and Claims-Making in Cuba: The Tannenbaum Debate Revisited," *Law and History Review* 22, no. 2 (Summer 2004): 339–369.

10. Francisco López Estrada and María Teresa López García-Berdoy, eds., *Las Siete Partidas Antología* (Madrid: Editorial Castalia, 1992), 13–38.

11. Partida IV, Título V, and Título XXI, Ley I, in *Las Siete Partidas*, ed. Robert I. Burns, trans. Samuel Scott Parsons (Philadelphia: University of Pennsylvania Press, 2001), 4:901, 977.

12. See the discussion on this question throughout David Brion Davis, *The Problem of Slavery in Western Culture* (1966; New York: Oxford University Press, 1988), especially 58–61, 98–106, 251; on ancient precedents, mostly in Greek, Jewish, and early Christian thought, see 62–90; on the dualism within Christianity that both rationalized slavery and contained ideals of freedom and equality that were "potentially abolitionist," see 89–90. See also Alfonso Franco Silva, *La esclavitud en Andalucía, 1450–1550* (Granada: Universidad de Granada, 1990), 36.

13. Partida VII, Título VIII, Ley II, and Ley XIII, in *Siete Partidas*, 5:1342, 1349. Also see Phillips, *Slavery in Medieval and Early Modern Iberia*, 120–121, 130–131.

14. Partida IV, Título V, Leyes I and II, in *Siete Partidas*, 4:901–902. For a study of these provisions in practice in another Spanish colony, see Herman L. Bennett, *Africans in Colonial Mexico: Absolutism, Christianity, and Afro-Creole Consciousness, 1570–1640* (Bloomington: Indiana University Press, 2003).

15. Partida IV, Título XXI, Ley II, in *Siete Partidas*, 4:977.

16. Tannenbaum, *Slave and Citizen* (65–93) initiates much of the debate and highlights the importance of manumission. Also see Klein, *Slavery in the Americas*, 62. For a later affirmation of Tannenbaum's thesis, see Jane Landers, *Black Society in Spanish Florida* (Champaign: University of Illinois Press, 1999), 1–2. For a more recent discussion of law and slavery in the context of the "Tannenbaum thesis," see Alejandro de la Fuente, María Elena Díaz, and Christopher Schmidt-Nowara, "Forum: What Can Frank Tannenbaum Still Teach Us about the Law of Slavery?" *Law and History Review* 22, no. 2 (Summer 2004): 339–387. For a more recent summary about slaves in Iberia attaining freedom, see Phillips, *Slavery in Medieval and Early Modern Iberia*, 122–145.

17. Partida III, Título V, Ley IV, in *Siete Partidas*, 3:586.

18. Partida IV, Título XXII, Ley I, in *Siete Partidas*, 4:981.

19. Jane Landers's work on Spanish Florida has shown particularly well the skill and perseverance of slaves "working the system" in their own interests and the opportunities provided by Spanish law.

20. Partida IV, Título XXII, Ley III, in *Siete Partidas*, 4:982. For Roman legal parallels, see Phillips, *Historia de la esclavitud en España*, 44.

21. See Evelyn P. Jennings, "Paths to Freedom," in *Paths to Freedom: Manumission in the Atlantic World*, ed. Rosemary Brana-Shute and Randy Sparks (Columbia: University of South Carolina Press, 2009), 121–141; chapter 4 for eighteenth-century Havana. Voelz, *Slave and Soldiers*, chapter 23 (431–450) contains examples from sixteenth-century Cuba, along with many from other Spanish and European American colonies into the nineteenth century.

22. Phillips, *Historia de la esclavitud en España*, says the *peculium* grew out of the Roman practice of employing some slaves as administrators and business agents, who had to be allowed some kind of expense account and control over money (40). Also see Phillips, *Slavery in Medieval and Early Modern Iberia*, 127.

23. Partida III, Títutlo II, Ley VIII, in *Siete Partidas*, 3:539–540.

24. Partida IV, Título XXI, Ley VIII and IX, in *Siete Partidas*, 4:983–984.

25. Maximilliano Barrio Gozalo, *Esclavos y cautivos. Conflicto entre la Cristianidad y el Islam en el Siglo XVIII* (Valladolid: Junta de Castilla y León, 2006), 84, note 194. In 1549, Pope Paul III authorized the employment of male and female Muslim slaves in publicly useful tasks and for domestic service,

though the practice clearly predated the pronouncement. Franco Silva, *La esclavitud en Andalucia*, 36. For estimates of the number of convicts sentenced to the Spanish galleys, see Christian G. De Vito, "The Spanish Empire, 1500–1898," in *A Global History of Convicts and Penal Colonies*, ed. Clare Anderson (London: Bloomsbury Academic, 2018), 71–72.

26. Stella, *Histoires d'esclaves*, 67–70; Maximiliano Barrio Gozalo, "La esclavitud en el mediterráneo occidental en el siglo XVIII. Los esclavos del Rey en España," *Crítica storica* 2 (1980): 207–208.

27. Stella, *Histoires d'esclaves*, 70.

28. Ruth Pike, *Penal Servitude in Early Modern Spain* (Madison: University of Wisconsin Press, 1983), 4–6.

29. After the suppression of the galleys, in 1748, the *arraeces* were no longer assigned to hard labor. Instead, they were incarcerated in castles like the Alcázar of Segovia and were included in exchanges for Christian captives held in North Africa. Barrio Gozalo, "La esclavitud en el mediterráneo occidental," 211–212; and *Esclavos y cautivos*, 141–144.

30. Pike, *Penal Servitude*, 6–10; Barrio Gozalo, "La esclavitud en el mediterráneo occidental," 208–213; Barrio Gozalo, *Esclavos y cautivos*, 145–149.

31. Pike, *Penal Servitude*, attributes the shortage of slaves to the independence of Portugal in 1640 (10). The subsequent reduction in Spain of enslaved blacks from Portuguese slave traders caused slave prices to rise and made private enslavers less willing to volunteer their slaves for state service.

32. For statistics on percentages of enslaved rowers, see Stella, *Histoires d'esclaves*, 88; and Pike, *Penal Servitude*, 8–10. These two authors disagree on the trend in the use of slaves in the Spanish galleys over the seventeenth century. Stella notes a fall in the percentages of slaves at the oars, from 30 percent in 1661 to 20 percent at the end of the century. Pike cites 26 percent of the rowers as slaves in 1612, rising to 41 percent by 1668. Stella does not include Pike's work in his bibliography.

33. Barrio Gozalo, *Esclavos y cautivos*, 162–171.

34. Pike, *Penal Servitude*, 16–26; Barrio Gozalo, *Esclavos y cautivos*, 176–182. On the forced laborers in the galleys during the eighteenth century, see Manuel Martínez Martínez, *Los forzados de marina en España del siglo XVIII (1700–1775)* (Almería: Editorial Universidad de Almería, 2011), 21–55.

35. Franco Silva, *La esclavitud en Andalucía*, contends that Muslim slaves had to convert to be manumitted, since no documentary evidence shows Muslims freed except through exchanges for Christians held in Muslim lands (30).

36. However, beyond funeral rites, Muslim slaves were not allowed to attend religious services at their *mezquita*. Barrio Gozalo, "La esclavitud en el mediterráneo occidental," 215–222; and *Esclavos y cautivos*, 154–158.

37. Pike, *Penal Servitude*, 38; María Elena Díaz, *The Virgin*, 9, 54–73.

38. Pike, *Penal Servitude*, 38; Barrio Gozalo, *Esclavos y cautivos*, 173–174.

39. In his 1493 letter to Ferdinand and Isabella, Columbus offered "as many slaves as they wish to have brought, from among these idolaters." Christopher Columbus, "Letter on the New World (1493)," in *Early Modern Spain: A Documentary History*, ed. Jon Cowans (Philadelphia: University of Pennsylvania Press, 2003), 33.

40. John H. Elliott, *Imperial Spain, 1469–1716* (New York: St. Martin's, 1963), 68, 72. Rebellious Indians continued to be enslaved in the empire into the eighteenth century, especially in frontier areas such as northern New Spain. Some of these captives were transported to Havana's public works proj-

ects. For examples, see David J. Weber, *Bárbaros: Spaniards and Their Savages in the Age of Enlightenment* (New Haven, CT: Yale University Press, 2005), 83–84, 234–241. On the small numbers of Apaches sent to various sites, including Havana, as prisoners of war in the eighteenth century, see Max L. Moorhead, "Spanish Deportations of Hostile Apaches: The Policy and the Practice," *Arizona and the West* 17 (1975): 205–220.

41. Domínguez Ortiz, "La esclavitud en Castilla durante la Edad Moderna," 369–373; Phillips, *Historia de la esclavitud en España*, 167. On the meaning of *encomienda* in Spain and the Americas and its legal precedents, see Francisco J. Andrés Santos, "Encomienda y usufructo en Indias," *Legal History* 69, no. 3–4 (2001): 245–248.

42. Bill M. Donovan, introduction to *The Devastation of the Indies, A Brief Account*, by Bartolomé de Las Casas (Baltimore: Johns Hopkins University Press, 1992), 20.

43. Colin A. Palmer, *Slaves of the White God: Blacks in Mexico, 1570–1650* (Cambridge: Harvard University Press, 1976), 7.

44. Documento XI, "Relación de los esclavos y forçados que quedaron de la galera San Agustín de la Havana," February 28, 1595, in *Documentos para la historia colonial de Cuba: siglos XVI, XVII, XVIII, XIX*, ed. César García del Pino and Alicia Melis Cappa (Havana: Editorial de Ciencias Sociales, 1988), lists forty-five Moorish slaves in a patrol galley's crew of 149 men, which also included ninety-seven convicts with sentences of various lengths and seven others who voluntarily signed on for another tour after completing their sentences (63–67). Frederick P. Bowser, *The African Slave in Colonial Peru, 1524–1650* (Stanford, CA: Stanford University Press, 1974) notes the importation of a few "white slaves" in the conquest and civil war period in Peru (354–355, note 10). The majority of them were Moorish, or Morisco, slaves. James Lockhart, *Spanish Peru 1532–1560: A Social History* (Madison: University of Wisconsin Press, 1968), describes Morisco slaves in Peru in the early conquest period as mostly females, purchased as housekeepers and concubines for Spaniards (196–198). Never numbering more than several hundred over the first decades of conquest, their numbers diminished by the 1550s as more white, free Spanish women began to migrate to the colony.

45. On the slave trade to Spanish America in the sixteenth and early seventeenth centuries, see Enriqueta Vila Vilar, *Hispanoamérica y el comercio de esclavos* (Seville: Escuela de Estudios Hispanoamericanos de Sevilla, 1977); and David Wheat, *Atlantic Africa and the Spanish Caribbean, 1570–1640* (Chapel Hill: University of North Carolina Press, 2016).

46. For a useful bibliography on the use of blacks, enslaved and free, in the conquest of the expanding Spanish Empire, see Voelz, *Slave and Soldier*, 11–14, and 19–20, notes 4–7.

47. Clarence Haring, *The Spanish Empire in America* (New York: Oxford University Press, 1947), 219.

48. Ortiz, *Los negros esclavos*, 47.

49. Vila Vilar, *Hispanoamérica y el comercio de esclavos*, 2.

50. Ortiz, *Los negros esclavos*, 47. Franco Silva, *La esclavitud en Andalucía*, shows few licenses granted from 1513 to 1518, and each license allowed only a handful of enslaved people for each traveler (74).

51. Haring, *Spanish Empire in America*, 219.

52. De la Fuente, *Havana*, 37.

53. Alejandro de la Fuente, "Havana and the Fleet System: Trade and Growth in the Periphery of the Spanish Empire," *Colonial Latin American Review* 5, no. 1 (June 1996). The native population of Cuba on the eve of conquest has been estimated at around 112,000. By 1519, it had been reduced to some

19,000; by 1531, to 7,000. By the mid-1550s, the native population had shrunk to fewer than 3,000. See Louis A. Pérez Jr., *Cuba: Between Reform and Revolution* (New York: Oxford University Press, 1988), 30.

54. Pérez Guzmán, *La Habana clave*, 6; Paul E. Hoffman, *The Spanish Crown and the Defense of the Caribbean, 1535–1585: Precedent, Patrimonialism, and Royal Parsimony* (Baton Rouge: Louisiana State University Press, 1980), 20–21.

55. Pérez Guzmán, *La Habana clave*, 6. The first governor of Cuba established his capital at Santiago de Cuba in 1515. In 1553, the Council of the Indies ordered the governor to move his residence to Havana. In 1594, Havana's municipal status was raised from a town to a city, and in 1607, Havana's de facto status as the Cuban capital was formally established. See Pérez, *Cuba*, 27, 38.

56. De la Fuente, *Havana*, says Havana's population probably reached its nadir in the 1550s, with fewer than forty householders (*vecinos*) and their families (83). Hoffman, *Spanish Crown*, describes Havana's fortifications at this point as little more than a keep and a bailey (97).

57. De la Fuente, *Havana*, 12, 51–80; Levi Marrero, *Cuba, economía y sociedad* (Madrid: Editorial Playor, 1974), 2:138, 141.

58. De la Fuente, *Havana*, 108–110; Marrero, *Cuba*, 2:164, 269–270; Miguel A. Puig-Samper and Consuelo Naranjo Orovio, "El abastemiento de aguas a la ciudad de la Habana: de la Zanja Real al Canal de Vento," in *Obras hidrálulicas en América colonial*, ed. Centro de Estudios Históricos de Obras Públicas y Urbanismo (Madrid: Ministerio de Obras Públicas, Transportes y Medio Ambiente, 1993), 81–83.

59. Marrero, *Cuba*, 2:251–252.

60. Gordon Douglas Inglis, "Historical Demography of Colonial Cuba, 1492–1780" (PhD diss., Texas Christian University, 1979), 60–61; De la Fuente, "Havana and the Fleet System."

61. Lyle N. McAlister, *Spain and Portugal in the New World, 1492–1700* (Minneapolis: University of Minnesota Press, 1984), 220.

62. Hoffman, *Spanish Crown*, 98; Tamara Blanes Martín, "Fortificaciones habaneras. La defensa de La Habana del siglo XVI a la primera mitad del XIX," in *La Habana, Puerto colonial (Siglos XVIII–XIX)*, ed. Agustín Guimerá and Fernando Monge (Madrid: Fundación Portuaria, 2000), 155–157.

63. Hoffman, *Spanish Crown*, 98.

64. On the African captives of the *San Pedro* and their origins in precolonial Upper Guinea, see Wheat, *Atlantic Africa*, 53–67. On numbers of slaves in La Fuerza by 1575, see De la Fuente, *Havana*, 102.

65. Renée Méndez Capote, *Fortalezas de la Habana colonial* (Havana: Editorial Gente Nueva, 1974), 15–16.

66. Hoffman, *Spanish Crown*, 100, 158, and 280, note 66.

67. Frustrating but not unusual. Geoffrey Parker notes that, into the seventeenth century, the building of new fortresses in Europe took at least twenty years. As was the case in the Spanish Empire, throughout early modern Europe the cost of fortifications was usually shared among the state, regional governments, and the community in which the fortifications were being built. Parker, *Military Revolution* (Cambridge: Cambridge University Press, 1988), 39, 172.

68. De la Fuente, "Havana and the Fleet System," argues that Havana's development from the 1560s onward was a product of intracolonial as well as transatlantic shipping and trade. On sixteenth-century defense and fortification around the port, see De la Fuente, *Havana*, 70–77.

69. Hoffman, *Spanish Crown*, table 18, 144.

70. Hoffman, *Spanish Crown*, 141; Marrero, *Cuba*, 2:341–343.

71. De la Fuente and Del Pino, "Havana and the Fleet System"; De la Fuente, *Havana*, 77–79; Marrero, *Cuba*, 2:344.

72. For a different perspective on Drake's attack in Panama and later incursions in the Caribbean, see David Wheat, "Prologue," in *Atlantic Africa*, which focuses on Africans and African-descended slaves and maroons who fought to defend the Spanish Empire. Wheat's argument that "African forced migrants increasingly performed the basic functions of colonization" in the Spanish Caribbean (3) is closely aligned with the thrust of the present book's argument on the centrality of the state's use of enslaved laborers to the defense and development of Cuba.

73. Marrero, *Cuba*, 2:194, 344–345; Hoffman, *Spanish Crown*, 222; De la Fuente, *Havana*, 79; David Wheat, "Mediterranean Slavery, New World Transformations: Galley Slaves in the Spanish Caribbean, 1578–1635," *Slavery & Abolition* 31, no. 3 (2010): 327–344.

74. Marrero, *Cuba*, 2:207–216.

75. Isabelo Macías, *Cuba en la primera mitad del Siglo XVII* (Seville: Consejo Superior de Investigaciones Científicas, 1978), 2. Macías argues that Spain's confrontation with England was in large part responsible for Cuba's economic development in the first part of the seventeenth century.

76. Carla Rahn Phillips, "The Labour Market for Sailors in Spain," in *"Those Emblems of Hell"? European Sailors and the Maritime Labour Market, 1570–1870*, Research in Maritime History, no. 13, ed. Paul van Royen, Jaap Bruijn, and Jan Lucassen (Saint John's: International Maritime Economic History Association, 1997), 333; Phillips, *Six Galleons for the King of Spain* (Baltimore: Johns Hopkins University Press, 1986).

77. Phillips, *Six Galleons*, 119–151; see appendix C, tables 9–13, on mariners' occupations and wages and those of Spanish infantrymen from the late 1500s to 1635.

78. David C. Goodman, *Spanish Naval Power 1589–1665: Reconstruction and Defeat* (Cambridge: Cambridge University Press, 1997), 258–259. Goodman emphasizes currency manipulations that caused drastic fluctuations of inflation and deflation as the main reason for Spain's difficulties in maintaining a navy, along with the extent of Spain's defense commitments relative to its European rivals and the royal treasury's repeated bankruptcies as factors in restricting resources available for naval expansion. Phillips, "Labour Market," argues that physical coercion for recruitment to Spanish naval service was rare, though economic coercion in the form of a lack of viable alternatives likely played an important role in individuals' decisions to go to sea (342). Phillips, *Six Galleons*, gives two examples of forced service but says this coercion likely was rare (116, 141–142).

79. Goodman, *Spanish Naval Power*, 124–131. For a detailed treatment of Spanish shipbuilding and imperial defense in the early seventeenth century, see Phillips, *Six Galleons*.

80. Phillips, *Six Galleons*, especially chapter 9, 203–222; Goodman, *Spanish Naval Power*, 14–24, 36, and 109–137 on shipbuilding.

81. Marrero, *Cuba*, 2:202–203.

82. Blanes Martín, "Fortificaciones habaneras," 155–157. The three forts discussed in this chapter, La Fuerza, La Punta, and El Morro, still stand guard over the entrance to Havana's harbor.

83. José Martín Félix de Arrate, *Llave del Nuevo Mundo antemural de las Indias occidentales* (1761; Havana: Comisión Nacional Cubana de la UNESCO, 1964), 55; Méndez Capote, *Fortalezas de la Habana colonial*, 10, 23–24; Pérez Guzmán, *La Habana clave*, 15; Marrero, *Cuba*, 2:345. Wheat, *Atlantic Africa*, discusses a case of ten Angolans, initially enslaved by Portuguese traders, captured by a French vessel,

and ultimately put ashore for lack of food and water in western Cuba (68–69). Black ranch hands found the group wandering, lost and hungry, and Spanish officials sent them to Havana to determine their owners. Ultimately, they were claimed by the crown and baptized in May and June 1590.

84. Marrero, *Cuba*, 2:42.

85. De la Fuente, *Havana*, 134–135.

86. Macías, *Cuba en la primera mitad del S. XVII*, 65–98; Marrero, *Cuba*, 2:25–44.

87. Marrero, *Cuba*, 2:200–206, quote on 205; De la Fuente and Del Pino, "Havana and the Fleet System."

88. Marrero, *Cuba*, 2:205. A chart on salaries and prices in ship construction from 1589 to 1592 lists the *jornales* of carpenters at 295 maravedis, those of caulkers at 282 maravedis, and those of slaves at 282 maravedis.

89. On local slaves hired out to the shipyards, see De la Fuente, *Havana*, 133.

90. Marrero, *Cuba*, 2:412; Puig-Samper and Naranjo Orovio, "El abastecimiento de aguas," 82–83.

91. Marrero, *Cuba*, 2:414–415.

92. Inglis, "Historical Demography," 85; De la Fuente, *Havana*, 106–107.

93. De la Fuente, "Sugar and Slavery in Early Colonial Cuba," 118; Inglis, "Historical Demography," 85.

94. De la Fuente and Del Pino, "Havana and the Fleet System." Also see Julio Le Riverend, *La Habana, espacio y vida* (Madrid: MAPFRE, 1992), 67.

95. Alejandro de la Fuente García, "El mercado esclavista habanero, 1580–1699: las armazones de esclavos," *Revista de Indias* 50, no. 189 (1990): 377; De la Fuente, *Havana*, 103, 107.

96. Marrero, *Cuba*, notes that Spain enjoyed only twenty-eight days of peace over the seventeenth century (2:87).

97. Goodman, *Spanish Naval Power*, 46; Phillips, *Six Galleons*, chapters 8 and 9, 181–222.

98. Pérez Guzmán, *La Habana*, 16.

99. Pérez Guzmán, *La Habana*, 19–23; Marrero, *Cuba*, 2:145–147.

100. Arrate, *Llave del Nuevo Mundo*, 60; Marrero, *Cuba*, 2:149–154.

101. Marrero, *Cuba*, 2:154; Parcero Torre, *La pérdida*, 22.

102. Díaz, *The Virgin*, especially chapters 8 and 9, 199–260.

103. Díaz, *The Virgin*, 74–75.

104. Palmer, *Slaves of the White God*, 118.

105. De la Fuente, *Havana*, 151–153.

106. The connection between Veracruz and Havana will be discussed in greater detail in subsequent chapters. For an example of royal slaves sent from Havana to Puerto Rico for fort construction in 1574, see Hoffman, *Spanish Crown*, 154.

107. Voelz, *Slave and Soldier*, 24, 34, 46. Landers, "Transforming Bondsmen into Vassals," contains numerous examples from Spanish America (120–145). For the West India Regiments, see Buckley, *Slaves in Red Coats*.

108. On the growing free population of color in Havana and other parts of the Spanish Caribbean from the 1570s to 1640, see Wheat, *Atlantic Africa*.

109. On the evolution of *coartación*, see Manuel Lucena Salmoral, "El derecho de coartación del esclavo en la América española," *Revista de Indias* 59, no. 216 (1999), 357–374. The author argues that in Spanish America, generally, the term *coartación* initially meant all manumissions by self-purchase

or outright grant by owners. He contends that Bourbon commercial reforms, which raised duties paid on slave purchases, led to a shift in the meaning of *coartación*. After 1768, the term was most often restricted to meaning payments in installments by slaves toward their full freedom. On *coartación* in Cuba in the sixteenth century, see María Teresa de Rojas, "Algunos datos sobre los negros esclavos y horros en la Habana del siglo XVI," in *Miscelánea de estudios dedicados a Fernando Ortiz por sus discípulos, colegas y amigos* . . . (Havana: Sociedad Económica de Amigos del País, 1956), 1275–1287. For the early seventeenth century, see Alejandro de la Fuente, "A alforría de escravos em Havana, 1601–1610: primeiras conclusões," *Estudos Econômicos* 20, no. 1 (1990): 139–59; and De la Fuente, *Havana*, 170–179. For the colonial state's use of *coartación* as part of its reward for defending Havana from the British in 1762, see Jennings, "Paths to Freedom," 121–141. For the eighteenth and nineteenth centuries, see Manuel Moreno Fraginals, "Peculiaridades de la esclavitud en Cuba," *Islas* 85 (1986), which cites 43.1 percent of Havana's population in the 1770s as free people of color and discusses *coartación* and other legal avenues to freedom (5, 6–8); Bergad, Iglesias García, and Carmen Barcia, *Cuban Slave Market*, 122–42; and De la Fuente, "Slaves and the Creation of Legal Rights in Cuba: Coartación and Papel," *Hispanic American Historical Review* 87, no. 4 (2007): 659–692. For numerous examples among the royal slaves in Eastern Cuba in the seventeenth and eighteenth century, see Díaz, *The Virgin*.

110. De la Fuente, "Slave Law and Claims-Making," paragraphs 45–46.

111. For early statements on the uniqueness of *coartación* to Cuba, see the comments by John Thrasher in Alexander Humboldt, *The Island of Cuba*, trans. John Thrasher (New York: Derby and Jackson, 1856), 212–213; and the now dated Hubert H. S. Aimes, "Coartación: A Spanish Institution for the Advancement of Slaves into Freedom," *Yale Review* 17 (1909): 412–429. Aimes's evidence is drawn mostly from the eighteenth and nineteenth centuries, after the practice had been well established in custom; it was later codified into law in 1842. Klein, *Slavery in the Americas*, also has evidence mostly from the eighteenth and nineteenth centuries, adding sources such as newspaper advertisements giving a slave's price reduced by the portion she or he had already paid (196–200). Bergad, Iglesias García, and Carmen Barcia take up the topic in *Cuban Slave Market*, but again the actual evidence is mostly from the nineteenth century, especially 133–141. For evidence of *coartación* in other American slave societies, see Lucena Salmoral, "El derecho de coartación"; Douglas Cole Libby and Clothilde Andrade Paiva, "Manumission Practices in Late Eighteenth-Century Brazilian Slave Parish: São José d'El Rey in 1795," *Slavery & Abolition* 21, no. 1 (2000): 96–127.

CHAPTER 2

1. In the Treaty of Madrid of 1670, Spain recognized England's possessions in the Caribbean, most importantly Jamaica, seized in 1655. The Treaty of Ryswyck of 1697 effectively ceded the western half of Hispaniola to France.

2. Stanley J. Stein and Barbara H. Stein, *Silver, Trade, and War: Spain and America in the Making of Early Modern Europe* (Baltimore: Johns Hopkins University Press, 2000), contends that Spain was "stagnant yet imperial" in 1700, just as it faced the combined calamity of civil and international war (4). For a summary of their argument on how Spain's colonialism led to metropolitan dependence and underdevelopment, see their concluding chapter (260–267).

3. Kuethe, *Cuba*, 4.

4. John J. TePaske, "La política española en el Caribe durante los Siglos XVII and XVIII," in *La influencia de España en el Caribe, la Florida y la Luisiana, 1500–1800*, ed. Antonio Acosta and Juan Marchena Fernández (Madrid: Instituto de Cooperación Iberoamericana, 1983), 66–70; McNeill, *Atlantic Empires*, 87–89. On the importance of smuggling and privateering to the development of Havana, see Schneider, *Occupation of Havana*, 82–89.

5. Improvements in the technology of sailing ships made the galleys largely obsolete for warfare by the early 1700s, and the Bourbons' focus on shipbuilding meant that more forced labor was needed on land, in the naval arsenals, rather than as rowers in galleys. However, the crown revived the galleys from 1784 to 1803 and ordered all serious criminal offenders to be assigned there. See Pike, *Penal Servitude*, 51–53, 66–71, 129.

6. De la Fuente, *Havana and the Atlantic*, 127–134; Leví Marrero, *Cuba, economía y sociedad* (Madrid: Editorial Playor, 1978), 8:1.

7. Marrero, *Cuba*, 8:1. Marrero lists the total labor costs from Ruiz de Campos's proposal at 39,391 pesos, of which 15,300 pesos (38.7 percent) was for day wages for the skilled workers, 9,461 pesos (23.9 percent) was for those cutting and hauling wood, and 4,600 pesos (11.6 percent) was for the seamen's salaries.

8. Marrero, *Cuba*, 8:1.

9. Vicente Rodríguez Casado, "La política del reformismo de los primeros Borbones en la Marina de Guerra española," *Anuario de estudios americanos* 25 (1968): 603.

10. José Merino, *La armada española en el Siglo XVIII* (Madrid: Fundación Universitaria Española, 1981), 18–19.

11. G. Douglas Inglis, "The Spanish Naval Shipyard at Havana in the Eighteenth Century," in *New Aspects of Naval History: Selected Papers from the 5th Naval History Symposium* (Baltimore: Nautical and Aviation Publishers, 1985), 48–49, 52.

12. C. R. Phillips, "'Life Blood of the Navy': Recruiting Sailors in Eighteenth-Century Spain," *Mariner's Mirror* 87, no. 4 (2001): 424–425.

13. C. R. Phillips, "Life Blood of the Navy," 426–427.

14. C. R. Phillips, "Life Blood of the Navy," 431.

15. John TePaske notes that Castilian taxpayers never paid anything for imperial defense in the Caribbean. All the funds came from silver remittances or taxes and donations from the colonies. TePaske, "La política española," 68–70, 74. See also Marichal and Souto, "La Nueva España y el financiamiento del imperio español en América," 69–74.

16. Carlos Marichal and Matilde Souto Mantecón, "Silver and Situados: New Spain and the Financing of the Spanish Empire in the Caribbean in the Eighteenth Century," *Hispanic American Historical Review* 74, no. 4 (1994): 599.

17. Calculated from figures of the annual mean of taxes and situado funds assigned to Havana from 1710 to 1759, in Marrero, *Cuba*, 8:57.

18. Mark A. Burkholder and Lyman L. Johnson, *Colonial Latin America*, 4th ed. (Oxford: Oxford University Press, 2010), 139–140.

19. Petition from Don Diego de Salazar to build ships, n.d., Museo Naval, Madrid [hereafter MNM], Colección Guillen, 6.4, folio 53. Other materials are from April 1731. On the characterizations of tobacco and sugar as contradictory development paths, see Fernando Ortiz, *Contrapunteo cubano*

del tabaco y el azúcar (1947; Caracas: Bibilioteca Ayacucho, 1978). For an argument against the view of tobacco and sugar as contradictory, and offering other examples, see the more recent Mercedes García Rodríguez, *La aventura de fundar ingenios: la refacción azucarera en La Habana del siglo XVIII* (Havana: Editorial de Ciencias Sociales, 2004), 25–53.

20. For more detail on the career of Juan de Acosta as a shipwright and *asentista*, see Allan J. Kuethe and José Manuel Serrano Álvarez, "El astillero de la Habana y Trafalgar," *Revista de Indias* 67, no. 241 (2007): 768–769.

21. Salazar petition, MNM, Colección Guillen, 6.4, folios 60, 68, 72.

22. Order dealing with problems with wood cutting in His Majesty's lands, May 12, 1731, MNM, Colección Guillen, 6.4, folio 68.

23. Inglis, "Spanish Naval Shipyard," 50–51.

24. Though financiers such as Salazar did not always profit from their investments with the crown in shipbuilding, the shipyard did generate significant wealth for those who supplied the projects with materials and labor. See Schneider, *Occupation of Havana*, 70–74.

25. José María Gómez Colón, *Memoria sobre la conservación del puerto de La Habana* (Santiago de Cuba: Imprenta de M. A. Martínez, 1851), 113; Le Riverend, *Espacio*, 133; Carlo Venegas Fornias, *La urbanización de las murallas: dependencia y modernidad* (Havana: Ed. Letras Cubanas, 1990), 10; Inglis, "Spanish Naval Shipyard," 49–51.

26. This agreement ended an earlier *asiento* to the Portuguese Cacheu Company, in place from 1696 to 1701.

27. Bibiano Torres Ramírez, *La compañía gaditana de negros* (Seville: Escuela de Estudios Hispano-Americanos de Sevilla, 1973), 2–4. In the mid-eighteenth century, a *pieza de Indias* was understood by slave traders as the virtual equivalent of the strongest enslaved worker, fifteen to thirty years old and in good health. The values of other slaves were determined relative to such a prime slave—*mulecones* (youths nine to fifteen years old) traded at three to two *piezas; muleques* (children four to nine years old) traded at two to one *pieza*. Slaves over thirty years old usually were considered past their prime (28).

28. For a detailed discussion of the treaty negotiations and outcomes, see Stein and Stein, *Silver, Trade, and War*, 136–141. On the organization of the trade in Africa and the Americas, see Colin A. Palmer, *Human Cargoes: The British Slave Trade to Spanish America, 1700–1739* (Urbana: University of Illinois Press, 1981). Also see Schneider, *Occupation of Havana*, 39–41, 89–94.

29. Mercedes García Rodríguez, "El monto de la trata negrera hacia Cuba en el siglo XVIII," in *Cuba: La perla de las Antillas*, ed. Consuelo Naranjo Orovio and Tomás Mallo Gutíerrez (Madrid: Ediciones Dos Calles, 1994), 298–301; Stein and Stein, *Silver, Trade, and War*, 138. An escudo was a gold coin equivalent to approximately 1.25 silver pesos. See Phillips, *Six Galleons*, 228; and, on currency equivalences, McNeill, *Atlantic Empires*, appendix B, 212.

30. Palmer, *Human Cargoes*, table 15, cites 6,387 enslaved people imported by the South Sea Company through Havana from 1715 through 1738 (106).

31. García Rodríguez, *La aventura*, 27–31.

32. García Rodríguez, "El monto," 302–307, at 307. Palmer, *Human Cargoes*, discusses the South Sea Company's problems in greater detail but concludes that its slave trading was "far from unprofitable" and generated "better than good" profits, though Palmer admits the data available to draw such a conclusion is incomplete and possibly unreliable (155).

33. Laura Náter, "The Spanish Empire and Cuban Tobacco in the Seventeenth and Eighteenth Centuries," in *The Atlantic Economy during the Seventeenth and Eighteenth Centuries*, ed. Peter A. Coclanis (Columbia: University of South Carolina Press, 2005), 256–257, 261.

34. The crown suspended the official monopoly from 1720 to 1727 due to revolts by Cuban tobacco growers, who resisted the state's low scale of prices, and by merchants and speculators, who wanted a freer market in tobacco. McNeill, *Atlantic Empires*, 118. For a detailed chronology of the government regulation of tobacco, see Doria C. González Fernández, "Tabaco y poder. La primera factoría de La Habana," in *Tabaco y economía en el Siglo XVIII*, ed. Agustín González Enciso and Rafael Torres Sánchez (Pamplona: Ediciones Universidad de Navarra, 1999), 107–122.

35. On the tobacco monopoly and manufacturing in Mexico, see Susan Dean-Smith, *Bureaucrats, Planters, and Workers: The Making of the Tobacco Monopoly in Bourbon Mexico* (Austin: University of Texas Press, 1992). For essays on the tobacco monopoly in other sites in the Spanish Empire, see Agustín González Enciso and Rafael Torres Sánchez, eds., *Tabaco y economía en el Siglo XVIII* (Pamplona: Ediciones Universidad de Navarra, 1999).

36. McNeill, *Atlantic Empires*, 117–119.

37. González Fernández, "Tabaco y poder," 113, 119. On the first three asientos, from 1734 to 1740, two with José Antonio Tallapiedra and one with the Marqués de Casa Madrid, see Montserrat Gárate Ojanguren, *Comercio ultramarino e ilustración: la Real Compañía de La Habana* (San Sebastián: Real Sociedad Bascongada de los Amigos del País, 1993), 20–21.

38. Marichal and Souto Mantecón, "Silver and Situados," 601.

39. See García Rodríguez, *La aventura*, for two examples of loans from the 1730s, one given by the *factoría* itself, to be repaid from subsequent tobacco harvests (14–15).

40. González Fernández, "Tabaco y poder," 121.

41. María García Rodríguez, "El crédtio hipotecario a los ingenios habaneros (1700–1792)," in *Diez nuevas miradas de historia de Cuba*, ed. J. A. Piqueras Arenas (Castelló de la Plana: Publicaciones de la Universitat Jaume I, 1998), 44–45.

42. McNeill, *Atlantic Empires*, 128.

43. McNeill, *Atlantic Empires*, 128. Cuban planters most likely were correct about the destruction of *ingenios* (sugar mills) in the early decades of the 1700s. The number of mills around Havana from 1700 into the 1720s may have actually declined, a trend not reversed until the 1740s. See Fe Iglesias García, "La estructura agraria de La Habana, 1700–1775," *Arbor* 547–548 (1991): 100.

44. Manuel Barcia, *The Great African Slave Revolt of 1825: Cuba and the Fight for Freedom in Matanzas* (Baton Rouge: Louisiana State University Press, 2012), describes the Quiebra Hacha revolt and its consequences (44–46). The quote is from a 1733 proposal from the count of Casa Bayona to establish a new town at the former site of his Quiebra Hacha planatation (45).

45. Inglis, "Spanish Naval Shipyard," 49.

46. María Sánchez Agustí, *Edificios públicos de La Habana del siglo XVIII* (Valladolid: Universidad de Valladolid, 1984), 22; Gómez Colón, *Memoria sobre la conservación del puerto de la Habana*, 114.

47. Jacques A. Barbier, "Toward a New Chronology for Bourbon Colonialism: The Depositaria de Indias of Cadiz, 1722–1789," *Ibero-amerikanisches Archiv* 6 (1980), table 1, shows very high levels of revenue from the Indies, especially in the early 1730s, levels not equaled again until the 1750s (342).

48. Gárate Ojanguren, *Comercio ultramarino*, gives a brief introduction to joint-stock, chartered trading companies that appeared in the early eighteenth century in Spain (11–13), though they had been part of the growth of commercial capitalism in England, Holland, and France since the seventeenth century.

49. For numerous examples of privateers issued patents by the governors in Havana and Santiago de Cuba over the 1700s, see César García del Pino, "Cuba y las contiendas navales del siglo XVIII," *Arbor* 144 (1993): 9–28.

50. The war of 1739 between England and Spain is often called the War of Jenkins' Ear, after an English ship captain who claimed a Spanish coast guard had boarded his ship and cut off his ear as punishment for smuggling. This warfare became part of the larger conflict known as the War of the Austrian Succession. Palmer, *Human Cargoes*, 130–144; J. H. Parry, *The Spanish Seaborne Empire* (London: Hutchinson, 1966), 297–298; Richard Pares, *War and Trade in the West Indies, 1739–1763* (Oxford: Clarendon, 1936), 60–61; Schneider, *Occupation of Havana*, 94–109.

51. Kuethe, *Cuba*, 9–10.

52. Díaz, *The Virgin*, 298. By the 1730s, El Cobre had four militia companies of royal slaves, led by their own officers. Díaz argues throughout her book (see, for instance, 312) that the defense of Santiago de Cuba, because of its frontier location and small population, necessitated the crown bestowing special occupations and privileges on the royal slaves who lived there. On the use of privateers in defense in the War of Jenkins' Ear, see García del Pino, "Cuba y las contiendas navales," 14–18.

53. Kuethe, *Cuba*, 8–9; Kuethe, "La batalla de Cartagena de 1741: Nuevas perspectivas," *Historiografía y bibliografía americanista* 18 (1974): 21. As Kuethe, *Cuba*, notes, "The slightest change of fortune at any number of points during the siege could easily have meant defeat" (10).

54. Schneider, *Occupation of Havana*, notes that the War of Jenkins' Ear brought flush times to Havana residents through increased regional trade (94–109).

55. Peggy K. Liss, *Atlantic Empires: The Network of Trade and Revolution, 1713–1826* (Baltimore: Johns Hopkins University Press, 1983), 27–29, 76–79; Kuethe, *Cuba*, 10.

56. Stein and Stein, *Silver, Trade, and War*, 196–199. The decision to resume the flotas to Veracruz was reached in 1754, but the first convoy did not sail until 1757.

57. García Rodríguez, "El monto," cites an agent of the South Sea Company bragging, in 1784, that up to 3,700 enslaved Africans were clandestinely imported into Havana in just the eighteen months after the Spanish king ended the company *asiento*, in August 1739 (310). On the Ulibarri y Gamboa contract, see McNeill, *Atlantic Empires*, 130, and 263, note 139.

58. Kuethe and Serrano Álvarez, "El astillero de la Habana y Trafalgar," 763–776.

59. Gárate Ojanguren, *Comercio ultramarino*, 32–39; table 2.2 shows investors in the Royal Company of Havana in the first five years.

60. Gárate Ojanguren, *Comercio ultramarino*, 44–48.

61. "Representación de la Junta de la Compañía," December 19, 1748, Archivo General de Indias [hereafter AGI], Ultramar, 995, 6, 8–12.

62. "Representación," 7–8.

63. For the final contract of the Royal Company of Havana, approved by the king, June 5, 1741, see AGI, Ultramar, 995; "Representación," 8–12. For a discussion of the *fuero militar* in eighteenth-century Cuba, see Johnson, *Social Transformation*, 64–65.

64. AGI, Ultramar, 995 and 996 contain numerous reports by RCH on costs and materials for building specific ships in the 1740s and into the early 1750s, when the company completed its last ships for the navy. Some of the ironwork seems to have been imported from Spain; other items were manufactured in Havana's arsenal. See, for instance, Copy of "Sumario de los Herrajes que se han labrado en el Arzenal . . . December 5, 1748–August 12, 1751," AGI, Ultramar, 996, December 20, 1754.

65. Pliego by Diego de Aróstegui to build ships, December 20, 1740, AGI, Ultramar, 995, 4.

66. Cuentas del Coste y Costas de . . . la Nueva Reina y la Nueva Invencible, November 2, 1744, and Cuentas del Coste y Costas de . . . los nuevos Conquistador y Dragón, September 20, 1745, AGI, Ultramar, 995.

67. Gárate Ojanguren, *Comercio ultramarino*, 70–72.

68. Inglis, "Spanish Naval Shipyard," 51; García del Pino, "Cuba y las contiendas navales," 18.

69. Inglis, "Spanish Naval Shipyard," 49.

70. Gárate Ojanguren, *Comercio ultramarino*, 73.

71. For a concise discussion of both primary and secondary sources' estimates of slave imports to Cuba from 1740 to 1760, see McNeill, *Atlantic Empires*, 167. He concludes that the RCH's imports of enslaved Africans over this period was probably more than 8,000 but less than 11,000.

72. Gárate Ojanguren, *Comercio ultramarino*, tables 2-16a and 2-16b, 110.

73. On lumber gangs in Havana's hinterland, see Marrero, *Cuba*, 8:19.

74. "Nota de los caudales para cortes de maderas . . . August 16–December 30, 1746," AGI, Ultramar, 995. During this particular period, the cost of wood from private individuals exceeded salaries and expenses for the company's own workers by almost 1,600 pesos.

75. "Representación," December 19, 1748, AGI, Ultramar, 995; Relación summarizing amounts invested in various components for shipbuilding, including 236 enslaved people at the sawmill, AGI, Ultramar, 995.

76. Marrero, *Cuba*, 8:18.

77. Marrero, *Cuba*, 8:81.

78. Marrero, *Cuba*, 8:58, 80.

79. Inglis, "Spanish Naval Shipyard," 51; Marrero, *Cuba*, 8:12.

80. Inglis, "Spanish Naval Shipyard," 48. Marrero cites orders from the governor of Santiago de Cuba, Francisco Cagigal de la Vega, in the 1750s, authorizing various skilled *esclavos del rey* to be sent to Havana to serve in the fort works and in naval construction, so that they could save money to purchase their freedom. Marrero, *Cuba*, 8:48.

81. Representación of a meeting of the Junta of the RCH held December 19, 1748, document dated January 9, 1749, AGI, Ultramar, 995, 1, 12.

82. Enrique López Mesa suggests that this contraband trade was carried on by RCH agents. See López Mesa, "La trata negrera en el Puerto de La Habana a mediados del siglo XVIII," in *La Habana: Ciudad portuaria colonial (S. SVIII–XIX)*, ed. Agustín Guimerá and Fernando Monge (Madrid: Fundación Portuaria, 2000), 246–247. Others show contraband trade taking place mostly outside the privileged trading carried out by the RCH. See Gárate Ojanguren, *Comercio ultramarino e ilustración*, on slaves, 107–111; and McNeill, *Atlantic Empires*, on tobacco and slaves, 156–159, 166–167.

83. Representación, 11, 15.

84. Representación, 52–63.

85. Bernardo Joseph de Urrutia y Matos, *Cuba: Fomento de la Isla* (1749; San Juan, Puerto Rico: Ediciones Capiro, 1993), 21, 24.

86. Urrutia, *Cuba*, 36–38.

87. Urrutia, *Cuba*, 42–43.

88. McNeill, *Atlantic Empires*, 133.

89. Gárate Ojanguren, *Comercio ultramarino*, 101–102.

90. Inglis, "Spanish Naval Shipyard," table 2, shows a total of seventy-four ships of the line built in Havana from 1700 to 1799, including forty-seven from 1700 to 1760, twelve from 1740 to 1749, and five from 1750–1759 (52).

91. Gárate Ojanguren, *Comercio ultramarino*, 123–125.

92. Náter, "Spanish Empire and Cuban Tobacco," 264–265; Garate Ojanguren, *Comercio ultramarino*, 118–125.

93. Figures from ships' manifests in the Archive of the Indies show that the total exports of Cuban sugar to Spain from 1754 through 1760 increased by almost three and a half times, from 108,472 to 378,346 arrobas. McNeill, *Atlantic Empires*, table 6.10, 165.

94. Marrero, *Cuba*, 8:79.

95. Allan J. Kuethe, "Decisiones estratégicas y las finanzas militares del XVIII," in *Por la fuerza de las armas, ejército e independencias en Iberoamérica*, ed. Juan Marchena and Manuel Chust (Castelló de la Plana: Universitat Jaume I, 2007), 84–85.

96. Kuethe, *Cuba*, 13–15.

97. Engineer Carlos Dexnaux to Juan Francisco de Güemes y Horcasitas, May 4, 1744, AGI, SD, 1220.

98. Jaime Delgado, "El Conde de Ricla, Capitán-General de Cuba," *Revista de Historia de América*, 55–56 (1963): 55.

99. Francisco Ricaud de Tirgale, "Relación del estado actual de las fortificaciones de la plaza de San Cristobal de la Habana y demas Fuertes y castillos dependientes," 1761, Archivo Histórico National, Madrid [hereafter AHN], Estado, 3025, exp. 3.

100. "Relación instructiva de la consistencia del Castillo proyectado de San Carlos [La Cabaña]," Havana, July 8, 1761, AHN, Estado, 3025, exp. 3.

101. AHN, Estado, 3025, exp. 3; Delgado, "El Conde de Ricla," 70–74; Kuethe, *Cuba*, 21; Parcero Torre, *La pérdida*, 44.

102. Parcero, *La pérdida*, 48–49, 66.

103. Schneider, *Occupation of Havana*, 126. Kuethe, *Cuba*, discusses varying estimates of the size of the British invasion forces (16, and note 40).

104. MNM, Colección Vargas Ponce, t. 2, doct. 135, folios 549–551. For a detailed description of the British attack and siege of Havana based on archival materials from both Spanish and British sources, see Schneider, *Occupation of Havana*, 113–162.

105. Schneider, *Occupation of Havana*, cites 30,000 as the total number of evacuees from Havana (135).

106. MNM, Colección Vargas Ponce, t. 2, doct. 135, folios 551–554; Parcero, *La pérdida*, 128; Kuethe, *Cuba*, 17–20; Pedro José Guiteras, *Historia de la conquista de la Habana* (1762; Philadelphia: Parry and Macmillan, 1856), 75–86; César García del Pino, *La toma de La Habana por los ingleses y sus antecedentes* (Havana: Editorial de Ciencias Sociales, 2002), 74–77.

107. *An Authentic Journal of the Siege of the Havana. By an Officer* (London: T. Jefferys, 1762), 15–16 (emphasis in original).

108. García del Pino, *La toma*, 79–81.

109. MNM, Colección Vargas Ponce, t. 2, doct. 135, folios 555–556; Kuethe, *Cuba*, 18–19; Schneider, *Occupation of Havana*, 126–134, 151–152.

110. For a general discussion of yellow fever's impact on the Caribbean, see J. R. McNeill, *Mosquito Empires: Ecology and War in the Greater Caribbean, 1620–1914* (Cambridge: Cambridge University Press, 2010), especially chapter 5, 135–194. See McNeill, *Atlantic Empires*, on Cuba's disease environment more specifically (39–42) and on the role of yellow fever in Spanish defense policy and in the British siege of Havana in 1762 (101–104). McNeill argues that the British victory at Havana was something of a fluke. Had yellow fever asserted itself two weeks earlier, Spanish defensive strategy would have retained its reputation for efficacy. García del Pino, *La toma*, disputes the importance of disease in British casualties in a larger argument that stresses the Cubans' intense resistance to the invasion (75). Schneider, *Occupation of Havana*, discusses the precarity of the British position by July 1762, due losses of troops to yellow fever, and also emphasizes the fierce resistance, especially by people of color, both enslaved and free (120–125, 143–151, 160–161).

111. *Authentic Journal*, 22–23 (emphasis in original). Although the British had secured the Chorrera River mouth to ensure a water supply, the water still had to be transported by ship from west to east, past the city, landed, and then transported to troops on the eastern side of the bay.

112. MNM, Colección Vargas Ponce, t. 2, doct. 135, folios 556–557.

113. *Authentic Journal*, 25.

114. Guiteras, *Historia de la conquista de la Habana*, 42–43, 71–73. Guiteras lists 1,400 to 1,500 enslaved people donated by Cuban owners to the defense effort, plus about three hundred *esclavos del rey*. He also notes, on the British side, 1,000 enslaved people purchased in Martinique and six hundred from Jamaica. The first number may be an error, given later estimates, such as those by Daniel E. Walker and by Schnieder. Walker, "Colony versus Crown: Raising Black Troops for the British Siege on Havana, 1762," *Journal of Caribbean History* 33 no. 1–2 (1999), cites almost four hundred slaves purchased by the British in Martinique and Antigua, one hundred more hired out from Saint Christopher (Saint Kitts), along with thirty-six slaves and fifty free colored troops from Jamaica (74–83). Thus, there were two hundred enslaved people who accompanied the initial British landing, for a total of some six hundred enslaved people with the expedition at the time of the original assault. Walker argues that the reluctance of Jamaican planters to arm their slaves stymied British efforts to recruit large numbers of enslaved people for service in the expedition. Schneider, *Occupation of Havana*, cites one hundred enslaved people purchased in Martinique by Albemarle and another five hundred from Antigua and Saint Kitts (128).

115. Matt D. Childs, *The 1812 Aponte Rebellion in Cuba and the Struggle against Atlantic Slavery* (Chapel Hill: University of North Carolina Press, 2006), 24. Schneider, *Occupation of Havana*, discusses the efforts of enslaved people on all sides to benefit from war and chaos, to improve their situations by passing across lines of status, imperial, and cultural identification (151–156).

116. For more on grants of liberty to slaves who fought the British invasion, see Schneider, *Occupation of Havana*, 144–145; and García del Pino, *La toma*, 92. Also see Jennings, "Paths to Freedom," 121–141.

117. Parcero, *La pérdida*, says they were "*miqueletes* negros," the name suggesting that they carried firearms (155). García del Pino, *La toma*, describes the "Compañía de Miqueletes" as composed of sixty white men and 150 black men (111). Also see Schneider, *Occupation of Havana*, 144.

118. *Authentic Journal*, 18.

119. MNM, Colección Vargas Ponce, t. 2, doct. 135, folio 556, Kuethe, *Cuba*, 56; Guiteras, *Historia de la conquista*, 132–133.

120. *Authentic Journal*, 30. The natives would have been white Creoles, not indigenous people. Allan Kuethe argues that the Spanish regulars generally fought well but that the local militia contributed very little to the city's defense. For instance, Kuethe, *Cuba*, discusses a corps of volunteer lancers sent to halt the advance of British troops on El Morro, which failed when, "upon hearing the unfamiliar sound of gunfire, the militia panicked and fled, leaving the veteran dragoons so badly outnumbered that they were forced to withdraw" (19–20).

121. *Authentic Journal*, 32, journal entries for July 23–27.

122. García del Pino, *La toma*, 111–118.

123. MNM, Colección Vargas Ponce, t. 2, doct. 135, folios 557–558; *Authentic Journal*, 32–35; Schneider, *Occupation of Havana*, 113–118.

124. *Authentic Journal*, 35–40.

125. "Relación de los oficiales de la Armada que han sido muertos y heridos y prisioneros en el Sitio de la Habana," August 29, 1762, Archivo General de Simancas [hereafter AGS], Marina, Expediciones a Indias, 426, exp. 2; Kuethe, *Cuba*, 19.

126. *Authentic Journal*, 41.

127. McNeill, *Atlantic Empires*, 104.

128. Articles of Capitulation, Havana, August 12, 1762, AGS, Marina, 426, exp. 10, article 6, 11, 12.

129. Parcero, *La pérdida*, 187–188.

130. Articles of Capitulation, Havana, August 12, 1762, AGS, Marina, 426, exp. 10, article 3, 9, 14.

131. Kuethe, *Cuba*, 21. Parcero, *La pérdida*, estimates the British booty at more than 3 million pesos by including forced donations and confiscations from Havana residents and sales of the king's goods, including sugar, tobacco, and naval stores (176–182). Schneider, *Occupation of Havana*, is the source for 1.8 million pesos in silver and trade goods (177).

132. For a review of the data and debates on sugar expansion and the slave trade to Cuba prior to 1762, see McNeill, *Atlantic Empires*, 162–170; on state tax policy on sugar imports to Spain, see 165–166. For evidence against the argument that the British occupation brought a period of prosperity to Havana, see Leví Marrero, *Cuba, economía y sociedad* (Madrid: Editorial Playor, 1984), 10:144; and Parcero, *La pérdida* (157). A major argument in Schneider, *Occupation of Havana*, is that the interpenetration of interests and commercial activities of British and Spanish subjects in the Caribbean, especially in slave trading, was substantial from the seventeenth century onward.

133. Aimes, *History of Slavery in Cuba*, provided an early, incorrect estimate of 10,700 enslaved Africans imported during the occupation (23, 33, 37), which skewed scholarly discussion of the importance of the British occupation for some time. For the figure of between 3,000 and 4,000, see Schneider, *Occupation of Havana*, which argues that Lord Albemarle's greed constrained the slave trade to *habaneros* by giving Liverpool merchant John Kennion a monopoly on slave trading to Havana (205–207). For estimates closer to 4,000, see Tornero Tinajero, *Crecimiento económico*, 35.

134. For population estimates from the 1755 tour of the island by Havana's bishop, Pedro Agustín Morell de Santa Cruz, see César García del Pino, ed., *La visita eclesiástica* (Havana: Editorial de Ciencias Sociales, 1985), 24–25. For scholarly estimates of the island-wide and city population and a critique of several higher estimates, see McNeill, *Atlantic Empires*, 33–45.

CHAPTER 3

1. Tamara Blanes Martín, "Fortificaciones habaneras, la defensa de La Habana, del siglo XVI a la primera mitad del XIX," in *La Habana, Puerto colonial (Siglos XVIII XIX)*, coor. Agustín Guimerá and Fernando Monge (Madrid: Fundación Portuaria, 2000), 159.

2. In exchange for the return of Havana, other provisions of the peace included ceding to Britain Florida and all Spanish territory in North America east of the Mississippi, tolerating British logwood cutters in Honduras, and renouncing any rights to Newfoundland fishing. Spain also had to return Colônia do Sacramento (in Rio de la Plata) to Portugal. France sought to soften the blow of these losses by ceding Louisiana to its Spanish ally. See John Lynch, *Bourbon Spain, 1700–1808* (Oxford: Blackwell, 1989), 318.

3. Allan J. Kuethe and Lowell Blaisdell, "The Esquilache Government and the Reforms of Charles III in Cuba," *Jarbuch für Geschichte von Staat, Wirtschaft und Gesellschaft Lateinamerikas* 19 (1982): 120–129.

4. Delgado, "El Conde de Ricla," 63; Kuethe, *Cuba*, 18–23; Parcero Torre, *La pérdida*, 42–66.

5. Prado's sentence included perpetual deprivation from further military commissions, exile to a distance of forty leagues from the Madrid court for ten years, and the confiscation of his property to compensate the crown for the loss of its funds to the British. On the trial and sentencing of Prado and the other military high commanders in Cuba during the British siege, see Delgado, "El Conde de Ricla," 70–74; Kuethe, *Cuba*, 20–23.

6. By the eighteenth century, the position of captain general included the supreme military command of Cuba and its subordinate territories—that is, Spanish Florida, Apalache, and/or Louisiana, depending on the time period. The captain general also was the highest political authority on the island and the governor of the city of Havana and its surrounding jurisdiction. There was a second governor appointed in Santiago de Cuba, in eastern Cuba, but he was subordinate to the captain general stationed in Havana. Juan B. Amores Carredano, *Cuba en la época de Ezpeleta (1785–1790)* (Pamplona: Ediciones Universidad de Navarra, 2000), 283–284. For the bundle of instructions for Ricla on taking possession of the Plaza of Havana, March 29, 1763, see AGI, SD, 1211. Interestingly, the urgency of Ricla's charge had prompted the king to originally grant Ricla "absolute authority and jurisdiction." The document was subsequently altered to read "wide [*amplia*] authority and jurisdiction."

7. On the military reforms of the Bourbons in Cuba, see Kuethe, *Cuba*. On Ricla's proposals specifically, see chapter 2, 24–49.

8. Royal instructions to Ricla, March 29, 1763, AGI, SD, 1211.

9. Count of Ricla to Julián Arriaga, July 23 and 27, 1763, AGI, SD, 1212. See also AGI, SD, 2119.

10. Royal instructions to Ricla, March 29, 1763, AGI, SD, 1211.

11. Review extracts for January 17 through December 19, 1763, list the king's eight slaves by name. AGI, Cuba, 337.

12. Gloria García Rodríguez, "El mercado de fuerza de trabajo en Cuba: El comercio esclavista (1760–1789)," in *La esclavitud en Cuba* (Havana: Editorial Academia, 1986), 126–129; "Balance of black slaves of both sexes bought on the King's account by the Count of Ricla from taking possession of the Captaincy-General to May 18, 1765," AGS, Secretaría y Superintendencia de Hacienda [hereafter SSH], 2344; Notice of contract with Miles Barber to deliver 600–700 slaves to Joseph Antonio Uque Osorio, April 28, 1763, AGI, SD, 1212.

13. Count of Ricla to Julián Arriaga, July 27, 1763, AGI, SD, 1212. Ricla said he hoped to obtain four hundred to five hundred slaves donated by private owners, and some "Guachinango Indians" from New Spain. See Kuethe, *Cuba*, for an example of a Havana creole militia officer, Colonel Luis José de Aguiar, who donated eight slaves to this effort (56). Schnieder, *Occupation of Havana*, discusses the case of the Marques de Jústiz de Santa Ana offering enslaved workers and funds to Ricla, though earlier he had refused to provide Prado with workers (235). Delgado, "El Conde de Ricla," gives the figure of seven hundred donated workers from surrounding sugar estates clearing the La Cabaña hill, though this number may have included two hundred soldier volunteers from the Fijo and Córdoba regiments in Havana, who were paid one and a half reales per day (92). See Parcero Torre, *La pérdida*, 222. Pérez Guzmán, *La Habana clave*, cites around 450 donated slaves employed in 1763 to prepare the ground for the forts at La Cabaña and Atarés (72).

14. García Rodríguez, "El mercado de fuerza de trabajo," 129.

15. Torres Ramírez, *La compañía gaditana de negros*, 28.

16. Expedientes sobre contratar, from Nicolas Colonado, August 19, 1763, bundle dated 1763–1765, AGI, SD, 1647.

17. Spain annexed the West African colonies of Fernando Po and Annabon in 1778. A Cuban expedition, with enslaved people brought directly from Senegal, only arrived in Havana twenty years later. Moreno Fraginals, *El ingenio*, 38; Tornero Tinajero, *Crecimiento económico*, 39; Schnieder, *Occupation of Havana*, 275–278.

18. Gárate Ojanguren, *Comercio ultramarino*, 111; Torre Ramírez, *Compañía gaditana*, 115–116.

19. Gárate Ojanguren, *Comericio ultramarino*, 160; Tornero Tinajero, *Crecimiento económico*, 35; Parcero Torre, *La pérdida de La Habana*, 215.

20. Bundle dated October 1765, AGI, SD, 1647.

21. García Rodríguez, "El mercado de fuerza," 130.

22. Tornero Tinajero, *Crecimiento económico*, 37.

23. Schnieder, *Occupation of Havana*, details the many commercial ties that British merchants had with Cuba for many decades before and after the siege of 1762; on Ricla's order of 40,000 bricks from New York through a French merchant, see 250.

24. Scholars have put forth different figures for the RCH's slave imports during Ricla's administration. Working with mostly Cuban records, García Rodríguez, "El mercado de fuerza," cites 5,645 slaves imported by the company from December 1763 to the end of 1764 (135). Using documents in Spanish archives, Tornero, *Crecimiento económico*, cites 5,037 slaves imported by the company from November 1763 through April 1765 (36).

25. Balance sheet of state slaves purchased under Ricla from June 30, 1763, to May 18 1765, AGS, SSH, 2344. Levi Marrero says that Ricla took 350 of the slaves bought from Coppinger and sold them to

tobacco growers in 1763. By the late eighteenth century, the royal tobacco factory also employed king's slaves, 168 of whom were women, as tobacco rollers. Levi Marrero, *Cuba: economía y sociedad* (Madrid: Playor, 1984), 11:33, 58. For the gender breakdown, see Tornero Tinajero, *Crecimiento económico*, 36.

26. Based on the estimate of 3,200 enslaved persons imported over the eleven-month occupation, or an average of 290 slaves imported per month. During Ricla's administration, a rough total of 8,000 enslaved persons, arriving from September 1763 to May 1765, yields an average of 380 slaves imported per month for twenty-one months. On Albemarle's profiteering and restrictions on travel during the occupation, see Schneider, *Occupation of Havana*, 205–209; on the estimate of 3,200 enslaved Africans imported, 206.

27. Estado of the expenses and costs of the fortification works of Havana from July 7, 1763, to December 31, 1772, AGI, SD, 2129.

28. Pérez Guzmán, *La Habana*, 254–255. For examples, see index of letters of the Count of Ricla, Havana, April 22, 1764, AGI, SD, 1211. On the new hospital, see number 24 in the index; and Luis A. de Arce, *El Real Hospital Nuestra Señora del Pilar en el Siglo XVIII (Un hospital para los esclavos del Rey) 1764–1793* (Havana: Ministerio de Salud Pública, 1969), 17, 29–30. For hospital costs in 1764, see Estado of fort expenses of Havana from July 7, 1763, to December 21, 1772, AGI, SD, 2129.

29. "Extracto de revista . . . por don Nicolas Joseph Rapun . . . [sobre] los individuos que se hallan empleados en el Hospital Real de San Ambrosio de la Havana para la asistencia de los enfermos de las Tropas de ella," n.d. But, bundled with papers sent to Madrid in February 1765, AGI, SD, 1647 lists twenty-three free employees, and six Guachinangos and seven royal slaves as nurses. "Relación de empleados y sirvientes . . . del Hospital Real de San Ambrosio," Havana, December 21, 1767, AGI, SD, 2122 lists nine "negros del rey" by name. In addition to those with African ethnonyms, the other enslaved nurses were Pedro Onofre, Sebastian Fernecio, Juan Vicuña, and Joseph Bulcan. There also are monthly registers of employees in the Royal Hospital of San Ambrosio that list the enslaved attendants by name, dated January 31, February 20, March 31, April 30, May 31, June 5, September 30, October 31, and November 3, 1768. See AGI, SD, 2122.

30. The meanings and significance of these African ethnonyms continues to be a subject of debate among scholars, in part because they did not necessarily designate home cultural regions of enslaved Africans. Moreover, Europeans assigned meanings and characteristics to groups of enslaved people with these ethnonyms, often revealing their worries as enslavers about maintaining subordination and discipline rather than an understanding of cultural differences among groups of enslaved Africans. On African ethnicities in the early colonial period in the Spanish Caribbean, see Wheat, *Atlantic Africa*. For African ethnicities in Cuba as a source of knowledge and skills in warfare in the period from the 1790s into the 1820s, see Manuel Barcia, *Great African Slave Revolt*. On Africans' identities in Cuba and their formation of sodalities or *cabildos de nación* in the eighteenth century, see Jane G. Landers, *Atlantic Creoles in the Age of Revolution* (Cambridge, MA: Harvard University Press, 2010), 144–150. For the nineteenth century, see Howard, *Changing History*; and Childs, *1812 Aponte Rebellion*, 95–119. A good introduction to the historiography and debates is also given in Matt D. Childs, "Re-creating African Ethnic Identities in Cuba," in *The Black Urban Atlantic in the Age of the Slave Trade*, ed. Jorge Cañizares-Esguerra, Matt D. Childs, and James Sidbury (Philadelphia: University of Pennsylvania Press, 2013), 85–100.

31. For example, see AGS, SSH, 2342 for papers and memos from 1763 discussing the behavior of some Cubans under the occupation, among them Sebastian Peñalver and Gonzalo Recio Oquendo.

The Marqués del Real Transporte, the Count of Superunda, Diego Tabares, and several other officials were tried in Spain along with Captain General Prado. See Kuethe, *Cuba*, 20–23. On elite women in Havana, see Sherry Johnson, "'Señora en sus clases no ordinarias': Enemy Collaborators or Courageous Defenders of the Family?" *Cuban Studies* 34 (2003), 22.

32. Amores, *Cuba*, contains a chart of all the titles of Castile granted in Cuba up to 1790 (65–69).

33. Arriaga to Ricla, May 13, 1763, AGI, SD, 1212.

34. Field Marshal Alejandro O'Reilly arrived in Cuba with Ricla as the subinspector general of the militias and the regular army, charged with reforming the island's military units after the British occupation. Bibiano Torres Ramírez, "Alejandro O'Reilly en Cuba," *Anuario de estudios americanos* 24 (1967): 1357–1388; Kuethe, *Cuba*, 30–32.

35. Ricla to Arriaga, November 1763, AGI, SD, 1212.

36. Certification of the liberty granted to different slaves who distinguished themselves during the siege of Havana, November 1763, AGI, SD, 1212.

37. Ricla to Arriaga, November 1763, AGI, SD, 1212.

38. For a more detailed discussion of the manumission of Havana's slaves who served the crown during the British siege, see Jennings, "Paths to Freedom," 121–141. The total number of the enslaved who were freed fully or in part by the state, in the records I've consulted, came to more than 140. Schneider, *Occupation of Havana*, cites some additional records from the Cuban national archive's protocols, which mention two enslaved men who were freed and several other men of color who appealed directly to the king and were freed, to arrive at the total of 175 people freed by 1764 (243–249). She also contends that the "manumission process was glaringly incomplete," due to the dozens of enslaved people who presented themselves for rewards but were denied (246).

39. On the evolution of the customary practice of *coartación* and of *pedir papel*, or the enslaved asking their owners to sell them to another, see De la Fuente, "Slaves and the Creation of Legal Rights in Cuba." De la Fuente argues that both were claimed as rights by the enslaved in the nineteenth century and were largely upheld by government officials and courts, but they often were contested by slave owners as the plantation economy expanded in Cuba over the 1800s.

40. Altarriba to Ricla, May 24, 1765, AGI, SD, 1647, on the compensation paid per freed slave, which would have been approximately 20 percent below market prices for a *pieza de Indias* (250 pesos) between 1763 and 1765. See Torres Ramírez, *Compañía gaditana*, 115. For other compensation arrangements, see Ricla to Arriaga, November 1763, AGI, SD, 1212.

41. Ricla to Squilache, December 14, 1763, AGS, SSH, 2342.

42. Ricla to Squilache December 14, 1763, AGS, SSH, 2342. For a fuller discussion of the commercial reform in Cuba under Ricla and the participating members of the Havana elite, see Allan J. Kuethe and G. Douglas Inglis, "Absolutism and Enlightened Reform: Charles III, the Establishment of the *Alcabala*, and Commercial Reorganization in Cuba," *Past and Present* 199 (1985): 118–143.

43. Copy of O'Reilly report for Arriaga, April 1, 1764, AGS, SSH, 2342. In this passage, O'Reilly also mentioned the "lack of justice," because Cuba had no higher court, or *audiencia*, until after 1797, when Santo Domingo was lost to the French and that colony's high court was moved to Cuba. Other Bourbon officials also recognized the need to import more enslaved workers. For similar views from the Marquis of Esquilache and Pedro Rodríguez Campomanes, see Tornero Tinajero, *Crecimiento económico*, 23–28.

44. O'Reilly report, April 1, 1764, AGS, SSH, 2342.

45. Torres Ramírez, *Compañía gaditana*, 38–40, 53–56, 66–68, 85, 121–131.

46. Torres Ramírez, *Compañía gaditana*, 171–179. Torres's figures from the Spanish archives are not continuous for the entire 1765–1779 period, but he suggests a total of some 24,010 enslaved Africans imported through Havana and Santiago de Cuba over this period. Using Cuban archival materials, García Rodríguez, "El mercado de fuerza de trabajo," table 2, cites a total of 23,544 slaves imported to Cuba during these years—21,634 through Havana and 1,910 through Santiago (136).

47. Kuethe and Inglis, "Absolutism," 128–129; Reglamento establishing the *alcabala* in Cuba, 1764, AGS, SSH, 2342.

48. Kuethe and Inglis, "Absolutism," 123–134.

49. Kuethe and Inglis, "Absolutism," 130–141.

50. Copy of royal order of October 16, 1765, AGS, SSH, 2342. There continues to be debate about the importance and degree of innovation represented by the 1765 Reglamento. John Fisher calls it the "first step in the process of revolutionary commercial reform" under the eighteenth-century Bourbons. Fisher, *Commercial Relations between Spain and Spanish America in the Era of Free Trade, 1778–1796* (Liverpool: Center for Latin American Studies, 1985), 10. Kuethe and Inglis, "Absolutism," see reform realized through cooperation between Cuban elites and royal objectives as a common theme in Bourbon policy but call the degree to which the Cádiz Consulado was ignored and injured by the new Reglamento of 1765 "truly revolutionary" (134–140). Stanley J. Stein and Barbara H. Stein, on the other hand, conclude that "the government had limited change essentially to meeting Cuba's needs" and feared to extend freer trade to the wealthiest parts of the empire, such as New Spain. Stein and Stein, *Apogee of Empire* (Baltimore: Johns Hopkins University Press, 2003), 78–79.

51. Torres Ramírez, *Compañía gaditana*, 39, 57–63; Kuethe and Inglis, "Absolutism," 140.

52. Kuethe, "Guns, Subsidies," table 1, covering the period 1763 to 1773, shows that Mexican *situado* income in Cuba was between 1 million and 2 million pesos every year except 1764, when it fell to 483,485 pesos (130). Marichal and Souto, "La Nueva España y el financiamiento del imperio español en América," notes that the *situados* of the middle decades of the 1700s were destined for land (including fortifications), navy, and tobacco purchases but sometimes contained extraordinary funds (80). José Manuel Serrano and Allan J. Kuethe note the importance of the infusions of silver from New Spain to Havana in financing both the fortification and the defense of the city and the early years of sugar plantation expansion. Serrano and Kuethe, "El situado mexicano y la Cuba borbónica," in *El secreto del Imperio Español: Los situados coloniales en el siglo XVIII*, ed. Carlos Marichal and Johanna von Grafenstein (Mexico City: El Colegio de México, 2012), 112–114.

53. Guiteras, *Historia de la conquista*, 75–83.

54. Inglis, "Spanish Naval Shipyard," 53–54.

55. Copies of these records for most of the 1760s are in AGI, SD, 1862. See also Inglis, "Spanish Naval Shipyard," 54.

56. June 1763 to May 1764, AGI, SD, 1862, no. 19.

57. March 1 to December 31, 1765, AGI, SD, 1862, no number.

58. AGI, SD, 1862, no. 19 and 28.

59. AGI, SD, 1862, no. 19.

60. AGI, SD, 1862, contains accounts with numerous entries for payouts for the capture, transport, and maintenance of deserters and their captors.

61. AGI, SD, 1862. This rough estimate is based on the entries for food rations at the customary one real per day for forced workers and one and a half reales per day for free workers.

62. AGI, SD, 1862, no. 18 and 19. See "Cuenta y relación . . ." for the branch of the naval squadron (no. 18) and ship construction (no. 19), dated July 7, 1763 through May 12, 1764. The records indicate that enslaved workers and convicts were given rations valued at one real per day, usually listed at monthly intervals. The rations payouts are an inconsistent measure of the numbers of workers, however, since they are rarely comprehensive and often do not divide out to whole numbers.

63. AGI, SD, 1862, no. 18 and 19. For instance, wages for all the carpenters, caulkers, and masons listed in the shipyard's accounts for March 1764 totaled 85,078 reales, while hired enslaved laborers and a small group of free workers and crown slaves working in carpentry were paid 8,719 reales that month.

64. "Cuenta y relación . . ." for the naval squadron, May 12, 1764, to February 15, 1765, AGI, SD, 1862, no. 29.

65. AGI, SD, 1862, no. 29. A convict who worked in the office also received a pair of shoes and a suit of clothes.

66. AGI, SD, 1862, no. 29.

67. AGI, SD, 1862, no. 28.

68. AGI, SD, 1862, no. 29.

69. Ricla to Esquilache, October 27, 1764, AGS, SSH, 2342, reported on a convoy carrying British merchants sailing out of the city on September 11, 1764. Seven other merchants were allowed to stay, however, among them Cornelius Coppinger, who continued to contract with the state to import enslaved Africans and bricks, ultimately marrying into the Cuban elite and becoming a landowner. See Amores, *Cuba*, 76.

70. Reglamento for the better protection of the royal treasury, Havana, March 28, 1764, AGS, SSH, 2342.

71. Arriaga to Esquilace, June 19, 1764, AGI, SD, 1647.

72. Díaz, *The Virgin*.

73. Esquilache to Ricla, October 12, 1764, AGI, SD, 1647, on the king's appointment of Altarriba; William Whately Pierson Jr., "The Establishment and Early Functioning of the Intendencia of Cuba," *James Sprunt Historical Studies* 19, no. 2 (1927): 74–133; Kuethe, *Cuba*, 70–71.

74. Convict numbers may have increased after 1765, when freer trade within the empire increased the numbers of routes and destinations of convict transport around the empire. De Vito, "Spanish Empire," 77.

75. "Estado[s] de revista . . . ," December 13, 1767; February 17, February 21, March 20, April 17, May 15, May 31, June 19, September 18, and October 30, 1768, AGI, SD, 2122.

76. Index of the letters of the Conde de Ricla, Havana, September 31, 1764, AGI, SD, 1211; AGI, SD, 2122.

77. After October 1765, the carters were no longer listed separately in the summaries of the 1760s. All the figures in this paragraph are taken from monthly summaries of workers at the fort sites, found in AGI, SD, 1647 (for 1765) and 2122 (for December 13, 1767, and ten summaries from 1768).

78. AGI, SD, 2136. Free skilled workers were to be given a salary of eight reales per day and were to be assigned king's slaves, "not convicts," to be trained in their trade. See also Pérez Guzmán, *La Habana*, 84.

79. "Extracto de revista . . . hecho por don Nicolas Joseph Rapun . . . [sobre] los individuos que se hallen empleados en el Hospital Real de San Ambrosio de la Habana para la asistencia de los enfermos de las Tropas de ella," n.d., but in a bundle with papers from February 1765, AGI, SD, 1647. AGI, SD, 2122 contains listings of the hospital's employees for the following dates: December 31, 1767; and January 31, February 20, March 31, April 30, May 31, June 30, September 30, October 31, and November 3, 1768.

80. Pérez Guzmán, *La Habana clave*, suggests that crown reluctance to retain large groups of royal slaves was due to fraud by officials who diverted slaves to their own use (77). This certainly could have added to the already substantial expense of maintaining thousands of royal slaves on the fort projects.

81. Kuethe, "Havana in the Eighteenth Century," 24.

82. Altarriba to Esquilache, May 27, 1765, AGS, SSH, 2343, on the complications of organizing payments to departed merchants through their agents in Havana, and several proposals for the introduction of black slaves, provisions for their sustenance, and bricks for the building projects.

83. "Estados de Revista . . . ," AGI, SD, 1647 and 2122.

84. "Estado que manifiesta los gastos, y costos . . . December 31, 1772," AGI, SD, 2129. Also see Altarriba to Esquilache, November 5, 1765, AGI, SD, 1647; Pérez Guzmán, *La Habana clave*, 99–101.

85. Decree by Ricla, March 3, 1764, AGI, SD, 1212.

86. Pérez Guzmán, *La Habana clave*, 101–106.

87. Estevan Llano de Velasco to Esquilache, February 5, 1765, AGS, SSH, 2343.

88. Pérez Guzmán, *La Habana clave*, 55, reproduces this report dated October 23, 1764. The report listed thirty-three prisoners as having died during the same time period.

89. Pérez Guzmán, "Modo de vida," 245.

90. Altarriba to Esquilache, April 1765, AGI, SD, 1647; Pérez Guzmán, "Modo de vida," 245. Pérez Guzmán, *La Habana*, argues that even during the cruelest years of sugar plantation slavery in Cuba, slaves were not subject to as oppressive a system of vigilance and control as they were at the fort sites (101).

91. AGI, SD, 1647 and 2122.

92. Pérez Guzmán, *La Habana*, 246–252, especially 251–252. Contrary to the corruption cited by La Cabaña supervisor Estevan Llano de Velasco, Pérez Guzmán argues that it was not a serious problem; since the enslaved would be sold after their stint in the fortification works, the state took considerable precautions (regular inspections, penalties for irregularities in the provisions, and so on) to provide adequate food.

93. Altarriba to Esquilache, August 16, 1765, AGI, SD, 1647.

94. Statement of the foodstuffs and quantities under Ricla and Altarriba, April 10, 1766, AGS, SSH, 2344.

95. Arriaga report to the crown, December 22, 1763, on the customary clothing allowance, AGI, SD, 1647. Letter dated April 25, 1764, requesting manufacture of these garments in Spain and their remission to Cuba.

96. Pérez Guzmán, "Modo de vida," 252; and *La Habana*, 91–92.

97. Pérez Guzmán, "Modo de vida," 252–253.

98. Pérez Guzmán, "Modo de vida," 255. The quote is from the regulation of religious instruction.

99. Contract with M. Sanchez, signed by the intendant, Miguel de Altarriba, August 19, 1765, AGI, SD, 1647.

100. Report by Nicolas Joseph Rapun, October 5, 1765, AGI, SD, 1647.

101. Altarriba to Ricla, June 4, 1765, AGI, SD, 1647.

102. "Estado que manifiesta los gastos, y costos . . . ," December 31, 1772, AGI, SD, 2129.

103. See, for instance, "Relacion de cargo y Data de esta Thesoreria general," November 5, 1765, AGI, SD, 1647, which lists receipts for sales of enslaved blacks from March 1 to August 31 at 220,960 reales out of a total of nearly 11.4 million reales.

104. "Estado que manifiesta los gastos, y costos . . . ," December 31, 1772, AGI, SD, 2129.

105. For more on Antonio Bucareli's tenure, see Ramiro Guerra y Sánchez, *Manual de Historia de Cuba* (Havana: Cultural, S. A., 1938), 173–176.

106. Cartas de los intendentes de Cuba, no. 611, AGI, SD, 1647.

107. Bucareli to Arriaga, May 3, 1768, AGI, SD, 2122.

108. Bucareli to Arriaga, May 28, 1768, bundle dated August 13, 1768, AGI, SD, 2122.

109. Jorge L. Lizardi Pollock, "Presidios, presidiarios y desertores: los desterrados de Nueva España, 1777–1797," in *El Caribe en los intereses imperiales, 1750–1815,* ed. Johanna von Grafenstein (San Juan Mixcoac: Instituto de Investigaciones Dr. José María Luis Mora, 2000), 21–23. Lizardi Pollock reports that the Mexican *audiencia* sentenced 19,410 prisoners to some kind of exile and forced labor, but he does not give a specific time period (27). On empire-wide circuits of convict transportation and shifts over the eighteenth century, see De Vito, "Spanish Empire."

110. Bucareli to Arriaga, May 28, 1768, bundle dated August 13, 1768, AGI, SD, 2122.

111. Beaumont to Ricla, June 15, 1765, AGI, SD, 1212. This file also contains other materials on the organization of work in the Santiago forts.

112. Díaz, *The Virgin,* discusses the state's efforts and the *cobreros'* resistance to fort work over the seventeenth and eighteenth centuries (224–245). She cites a "general looseness of the labor system," with high desertion rates and protests (238). In any case, the number of *cobreros* even potentially available for fort work was less than two hundred men for most of the eighteenth century.

113. Bucareli to Arriaga, May 3 and June 8, 1768. In a letter dated June 13, 1768, Bucareli lists eight reports sent in 1766, four in 1767. AGI, SD, 2122.

114. AGI, SD, 2122; Parcero Torre, *La pérdida de La Habana,* 270.

115. Bucareli to Arriaga, bundle dated September 4, 1768, AGI, SD, 2122.

116. Resolutions of the second Junta Extraordinaria, which met on June 11, 1768, bundle dated September 4, 1768, AGI, SD, 2122. On the extent of state debt held by private citizens in the 1770s, see Parcero Torre, *La pérdida de La Habana,* 270.

117. Bucareli to Arriaga, September 14, 1768, AGI, SD, 2122.

118. Bucareli to Arriaga, December 27, 1769, AGI, SD, 1223.

119. Abarca to Altarriba, July 19, 1769, AGI, SD, 1647.

120. Altarriba to Bucareli, May 31, 1769, AGI, SD, 1647.

121. "Estado que manifiesta los gastos, y costos . . . ," December 31, 1772, AGI, SD, 2129.

122. De la Torre, AGI, SD, 1211, bundle dated 1776.

123. De la Torre, AGI, SD, 1211, bundle dated 1776.

124. "Estado que comprende el numero de forzados . . . ," Havana, January 29, 1775, AGI, SD, 1211.

125. Luis Huet to Captain General Juan Manuel de Cagigal, July 29, 1782, AGI, Cuba, 1311. Huet notes the scarcity of laborers and the lack of prisoners, "that for years have not come from the Kingdom of New Spain." The numbers of convict laborers arriving from Mexico may have increased after the peace in 1783. Working from Mexican archival sources, historian Jorge Lizardi Pollock determined that the highest number of prisoners was sent to Havana in the years 1785 and 1786. Lizardi Pollock, "Presidios, presidiarios, y desertores," 23.

126. Huet to Cagigal, September 7 and October 6, 1782, AGI, Cuba, 1311.

127. Huet to Cagigal, Havana, October 28, 1782, AGI, Cuba, 1311.

128. Huet to Cagigal, November 8, 1782; Cagigal to Huet, November 10, 1782; and Huet to Cagigal, December 6, 1782, AGI, Cuba, 1311.

129. Huet to Navarro, September 16, 1779; and Navarro to Huet, with names of mill owners who should contribute slaves for a two-month period, September 3, 1779, AGI, SD, 1247. See also Pérez Guzmán, La Habana, 78–79.

130. AGS, Guerra, 7242, exp. 20, no. 193.

131. For works on the "hardening" of the slave regime in Cuba as the production of sugar on plantations increased after 1790, see Verena Martínez-Alier, Marriage, Class and Colour in Nineteenth-Century Cuba: A Study of Racial Attitudes and Sexual Values in a Slave Society (1974; Ann Arbor: University of Michigan Press, 1989); Gwendolyn Midlo Hall, Social Control in Slave Plantation Societies: A Comparison of St. Domingue and Cuba (Baltimore: Johns Hopkins University Press, 1971); Paquette, Sugar Is Made with Blood; and Pedro Deschamps Chapeaux, El negro en la economía habanera del Siglo XIX.

132. See Sherry Johnson, "'La Guerra Contra los Habitantes de los Arrabales': Changing Patterns of Land Use and Land Tenancy in and Around Havana, 1763–1800," Hispanic American Historical Review 77, no. 2 (1997): 181–209. Johnson suggests several possible reasons for the crown's shift to greater compensation for confiscated property: the mysterious death of Agustín Crame, the chief engineer charged with most of the confiscations after 1763; official concern about maintaining the loyalty of the Havana elite as Spain entered the American War of Independence; or the tardy realization of longer-term intentions to provide compensation. She concludes that military spending "brought economic benefits that began almost from the moment royal administrators disembarked in 1763. Equally important, royal policies benefited many levels of Havana's society" (208).

133. Kuethe, "Havana in the Eighteenth Century," 24.

134. See, for instance, Franklin W. Knight, "Origins of Wealth and Sugar Revolution in Cuba," 231–253, especially 242. For a summary of scholarship on revenues from defense spending in Cuba, see Kuethe, "Havana in the Eighteenth Century," 14–25.

CHAPTER 4

1. As J. H. Elliott has noted, the increase in British power after the Seven Years' War was so great that it was only a matter of time before Spain and France would reunite to challenge it. Elliott, Empires of the Atlantic World, 295.

2. Tornero Tinajero, *Crecimiento económico*, cites 255,377 slaves legally imported to Cuba from 1790 to 1819, with more likely entering illegally (50). Childs, *The 1812 Aponte Rebellion*, table 2.1, summarizes slave import estimates from nineteenth- and twentieth-century sources (50). The lowest is by Humboldt (225,474); the highest is by Juan Pérez de la Riva (369,300). The Slave Voyages Transatlantic Slave Trade database estimates that 213,795 enslaved Africans were imported into Cuba from 1790 to 1820, including 91,741 in the five years from 1816 through 1820 alone. See Slave Voyages, "Trans-Atlantic Slave Trade—Estimates," http://slavevoyages.org/assessment/estimates (accessed January 30, 2020).

3. Sources on the Cuban militia men of color include Pedro Deschamp Chapeaux, *Los batallones de pardos y morenos libres* (Havana: Editorial Arte y Literatura, 1976); Herbert S. Klein, "The Colored Militia of Cuba, 1568–1868," *Caribbean Studies* 6, no. 2 (1966): 17–27; María del Carmen Barcia, *Los ilustres apellidos: Negros en la Habana colonial* (Havana: Ediciones Boloña, 2009); and Schneider, *Occupation of Havana*, 294–303.

4. Estado of Havana's two artillery companies, July 1, 1765, AGI, SD, 1220; Arriaga to Ricla, January 12, 1765, AGI, SD, 1212.

5. The colonial state's establishment of a community of enslaved artillerymen and their families is briefly discussed in the context of the policies of slave owners (private owners of haciendas and plantations, religious orders such as the Jesuits, and the colonial state) toward family formation among the enslaved in eighteenth-century Cuba. See Mercedes García Rodríguez, "Los matrimonios entre esclavos: sexo y reproducción en la Cuba del Siglo XVIII," in *Nuevas voces, viejos asuntos: Panorama de la reciente historiografía cubana*, ed. Ivette García González and Ricardo Quiza Moreno (Havana: Editorial de Ciencias Sociales, 2005), 83–87. This is also mentioned in Sherry Johnson, "'Señoras en sus clases no ordinarias': Enemy Collaborators or Courageous Defender of the Family?," *Cuban Studies/Estudios cubanos*, 34 (2003): 27–28; and Schneider, *Occupation of Havana*, 253–255.

6. Fortification expenses for February to March 1764, AGS, SSH, 2343. On construction of beds, Altarriba to Esquilache, February 26, 1766, AGS, SSH, 2344.

7. Estado of the Real Cuerpo de Artillería, July 1, 1765, AGI, SD, 1220.

8. Arriaga to Ricla, January 12, 1765, AGI, SD, 1212; Altarriba to Esquilache, February 26, 1766, AGS, SSH, 2344.

9. Altarriba to Esquilache, February 25, 1766, AGS, SSH, 2344. A portion of this letter is also quoted in García Rodríguez, "Los matrimonios," 85.

10. Altarriba to Esquilache, February 26, 1766, AGS, SSH, 2344.

11. Fortification workforce summaries for March 9, April 24, May 28, June 30, July 31, August 24, and October 26, 1765, AGI, SD, 1647.

12. *Reglamento para el govierno militar, politico, y economico de la Compañía de Artillería compuesta de negros de S.M. y sus familias* (Havana: D. Blas de los Olivos, 1768), at Houghton Library, Harvard University, 2004-3. When I first consulted this document at the Houghton Library, it was part of the José Escoto Cuban History and Literature Collection. The *Reglamento* has since been removed from the Escoto Collection. The number 2004-3 is an accession number and may change when the library catalogs this document in the future. Other scholars who have discussed the enslaved artillerymen of Havana and used the *Reglamento* as a source include Johnson, "Señoras en sus clases no ordinarias," 27–28; and Schneider, *Occupation of Havana*, 253–255.

13. *Reglamento*, 2. Unfortunately, I have not yet located these detailed records of individual artillerymen and their family members.

14. *Reglamento*, 2, 11–19.

15. *Reglamento*, 14–15.

16. *Reglamento*, 18.

17. *Reglamento*, 5–6.

18. *Reglamento*, 3, 5, 8–10; quote on 10.

19. *Reglamento*, 3–4; Arriaga to Altarriba, May 18, 1773, AGI, Cuba, 1153. Arriaga noted the king's approval of allowing the enslaved women more use of this money. On work outside the barracks, see Johnson, "Señoras en sus clases," 27.

20. *Reglamento*, 3–4.

21. *Reglamento*, 6.

22. *Reglamento*, 10, 14.

23. *Reglamento*, 6 and 8.

24. *Reglamento*, 4.

25. *Reglamento*, 4.

26. *Estados* of Havana's artillery slaves for the dates December 13, 1767; and January 17, February 21, March 20, April 17, May 12, June 12, July 10, September 11, October 23, and November 27, 1768, AGI, SD, 2122. Sherry Johnson discusses one African-born man, Antonio Abad del Rey, whose surname suggests that he was enslaved by the king. Del Rey was emancipated, along with his African-born wife, sometime between the 1760s and 1788. As a free man, he joined Havana's *moreno* militia company, enjoyed the military *fuero*, and amassed considerable wealth by the time of his death in 1796. Johnson speculates that he may have been a member of the enslaved artillery corps before his emancipation, but there is as yet no direct evidence to confirm that. Johnson, "Señoras no ordinarias," 28–29.

27. "Cargos y esculpaciones," AHN, Consejos, 20892, 2nd packet, folios 197–198.

28. Orders from the King to Diego Josef Navarro, January 6, 1777, AGI, SD, 1217, 39.

29. Reports of the artillery force dated the first days of June to December 1780, and January, February, April, and May 1781, AGI, Cuba, 1247. Also Garcini to Navarro, notice no. 239, March 13, 1781, on the embarkation of thirty royal artillery slaves with the army of operation.

30. *Estado* of the artillery company slaves, December 31, 1784, AGI, Cuba, 1371.

31. Amores, *Cuba*, also notes that thirty-eight of the artillery company slaves in 1789 were *bozales* (born in Africa); fifteen were born in the Americas (423, note 29).

32. Landers, *Blacks in Spanish Florida*, also mentions the existence of a group of enslaved artillerymen attached to the artillery corps in Saint Augustine, Florida, in the 1790s (207).

33. On environmental crises as a factor in the New Orleans rebellion against the Spanish takeover, see Sherry Johnson, *Climate and Catastrophe in Cuba and the Atlantic World in the Age of Revolution* (Chapel Hill: University of North Carolina Press, 2011), 81–82, 90–91.

34. Various reports on troops, munitions, and supplies for Alejandro O'Reilly's Louisiana expedition of 1769, AGI, PC, 1070.

35. AGI, SD, 1648, no. 678, 773; Kuethe, *Cuba*, 90–91.

36. Bucareli to Altarriba, December 11, 1769, AGI, SD, 1648, no. 799.

37. Reglamento of Havana treasury obligations to province of Louisiana, February 23, 1770, AGI, SD, 1223.

38. Kuethe, *Cuba*, 24–49.

39. Thomas E. Chávez, *Spain and the Independence of the United States: An Intrinsic Gift* (Albuquerque: University of New Mexico Press, 2002), 10, 15–16.

40. Kuethe, *Cuba*, 96.

41. Packet of correspondence on the declaration of war against Great Britain, AGI, SD, 1229, no. 550.

42. Kuethe, *Cuba*, 100.

43. AGI, Cuba, 1247, no. 63.

44. Kuethe, *Cuba*, 104.

45. See Johnson, *Climate and Catastrophe*, chapter 5, on the effects of storms on the Gulf campaigns.

46. Garcini to Navarro, March 13, 1781, AGI, Cuba, 1247, no. 239.

47. Kuethe, *Cuba*, 117.

48. Captain General Ezpeleta sent reinforcements in 1786 and 1787. Amores, *Cuba*, 463–470.

49. Josef Solano to Juan Manuel Cagigal, January 8, 1782, AGI, SD, 1234, no. 180.

50. Juan Manuel Cagigal to José de Gálvez, February 20, 1782, AGI, SD, 1234, no. 180.

51. Juan Manuel Cagigal to Josef Solano, February 20, 1782, AGI, SD, 1234.

52. Josef Solano to Martín Mayorga, August 28, 1782, AGI, SD, 1234.

53. Josef Solano to José de Gálvez, November 10, 1782, AGI, SD, 1234, no. 8. Captain General Cagigal ordered Solano to remain in port, however. Josef Solano to José Gálvez, November 18, 1782, AGI, SD, 1234, no. 11; Kuethe, *Cuba*, 117.

54. Amores, *Cuba*, 418, note 12.

55. It addition to the costs of the Caribbean campaigns, the Peace of Paris in 1783 returned east Florida to Spain in exchange for the Bahamas. Amores, *Cuba*, 415. Historian John Lynch has gone so far as to say that the cost of the "victory" of 1783 became an impediment to further reform in Spain or its empire. Lynch, *Bourbon Spain*, 327.

56. Correspondence on the formation of a militia artillery company of color for the Pensacola campaign, AGI, Cuba, 1247, no. 203; John Walton Caughey, *Bernardo de Gálvez in Louisiana, 1776–1783* (Gretna, LA: Pelican, 1972), 208; Kuethe, *Cuba*, 106–112.

57. Philip D. Morgan and Andrew Jackson O'Shaughnessy, "Arming Slaves in the American Revolution," in *Arming Slaves from Classical Times to the Modern Age*, ed. Christopher Leslie Brown and Philip D. Morgan (New Haven, CT: Yale University Press, 2006), 187, 198–199.

58. David Geggus, "The Great Powers and the Haitian Revolution," in *Haitian Revolutionary Studies* (Bloomington: Indiana University Press, 2002), 175.

59. Various letters from Pedro de Acuña to Luis de las Casas in early 1793, AGS, Guerra, 7161, exp. 1.

60. Jean-François appears in some Spanish documents as Juan Francisco, and George Biassou is sometimes given as Jorge Biasou.

61. David Geggus, "The Slave Leaders in Exile: Spain's Resettlement of Its Black Auxiliary Troops," in *Haitian Revolutionary Studies* (Bloomington: Indiana University Press, 2002), 179–180. Geggus cites

figures from around 5,000 troops to a high of 14,000, which he says is most likely an exaggeration. Jane Landers says Biassou's army alone reached 40,000 men at its peak. Landers, *Black Society in Spanish Florida*, 209.

62. David Geggus, "The Arming of Slaves in the Haitian Revolution," in *Arming Slaves from Classical Times to the Modern Age*, ed. Christopher Leslie Brown and Philip D. Morgan (New Haven, CT: Yale University Press, 2006), 220–221; and Landers, "Transforming Bondsmen into Vassals," 129–131. On the recruitment of the black auxiliaries of Charles IV, see Ferrer, *Freedom's Mirror*, 83–145.

63. Kuethe, *Cuba*, 128–129, at 142.

64. Kuethe, *Cuba*, 140–145.

65. Joaquín García to Gabriel de Aristizabal, January 8, 1794, AGS, Guerra, 7159, exp. 5, no. 20.

66. AGS, Guerra, 7159, exp. 5, no. 19, 24, 25.

67. David Geggus, "The 'Volte-Face' of Toussaint Louverture," in *Haitian Revolutionary Studies* (Bloomington: Indiana University Press, 2002), 119–136; Ferrer, *Freedom's Mirror*, 97–100, 107–125.

68. Geggus, "Arming of Slaves," 222; Landers, *Black Society*, 209; Ferrer, *Freedom's Mirror*, 100–103.

69. Reports by José Antonio de Urizar, July 9, 15, and 25, 1793, AGS, Guerra, 7159, exp. 1, no. 3, 4, 5. Also many reports in AGI, Estado, 5A; and AGS, Estado, 8150.

70. Duque de Alcudia to Carlos de Irujo, October 22, 1794, AGS, Estado, 8150.

71. AGS, Estado, 8150 contains numerous examples of the diplomatic correspondence on the Fort Dauphin massacre. See also Landers, "Transforming Bondsmen into Vassals," which discusses several versions of the events, one blaming Jean-François's confessor, Father Vázquez, for giving the order to begin the slaughter (131–132). Jean-François himself claimed he had controlled his own forces and blamed Biassou and his men for the atrocities (143, note 62). Madrid officials did note that the extent of the massacre may have been partly due to the cowardice of the Spanish troops, who retired to the fort and did not intervene; see AGS, Guerra, 7161, exp. 1, no. 84. Ferrer, *Freedom's Mirror*, argues that Cuban military officials who were in Hispaniola when the massacre was carried out understood clearly the dangers of even the talk of emancipation for the slave society developing in Cuba (120–124). Hence, for them, the Haitian Revolution was not a specter but rather a bloody reality.

72. Geggus, "Volte Face," 119–136; Ferrer, *Freedom's Mirror*, 115–125.

73. Notice of the treaty in Manuel Godoy to Marqués del Campo, September 8, 1795, AGS, Estado, 8150. On the cession of Santo Domingo to France and the disposition of Spanish residents, see AGI, Estado, 5A, no. 15, 17.

74. Joaquín García to Las Casas, April 3, 1794, AGI, Estado, 5A, no. 22.

75. "Parafo de una Junta de Generales celebrada en Havana en 22 de Diciembre de 1795," AGI, Estado, 5A, no. 22, 3.

76. Las Casas to García, December 17, 1795, AGI, Estado, 5A, no. 24; Ferrer, *Freedom's Mirror*, 131–138.

77. Marqués de Casa Calvo to Las Casas, December 31, 1795, AGI, Estado, 5A, no. 23.

78. Casa Calvo to Las Casas, December 31, 1795; García to Godoy, February 2, 1796, AGI, Estado, no. 36, 1; Landers, "Transforming Bondsmen into Vassals," 132.

79. Casa Calvo to Las Casas, December 31, 1795. On Casa Calvo's slave trading while in Hispaniola, see Ferrer, *Freedom's Mirror*, 140–141.

80. Geggus, "Slave Leaders in Exile," 182–183.

81. Quoted in Las Casas to Godoy, January 25, 1796, AGI, Estado, 5A, no. 28.

82. Las Casas to Godoy, January 25, 1796.

83. Estado of the auxiliary army of Santo Domingo, December 31, 1795, AGI, Estado, 5A, no. 23, lists 707 total migrants—91 officers, 240 troops, 284 women, and 92 children. Las Casas to Godoy, January 25, 1796, updated the total to 780.

84. Geggus, "Slave Leaders in Exile," 182–203. On George Biassou's life in Florida, see Landers, "Transforming Bondsmen into Rebels," 134–137; and Black Society, 211–220.

85. Landers, "Transforming Bondsmen into Vassals," 131.

86. Buckley, Slaves in Red Coats, 55–56, 79.

87. Landers, "Transforming Bondsmen into Vassals," 136–137.

88. Kuethe, Cuba, 128.

89. Johnson, Social Transformation, 101–102, shows that Spanish-born men stationed in the American colonies were prohibited from marrying locally without official permission. Charles III later promulgated even more restrictive measures to constrain marriages across racial and class lines.

90. Landers, Atlantic Creoles in the Age of Revolution, 138–174; Schneider, Occupation of Havana, 294–303.

CHAPTER 5

1. Marqués de la Torre, "Apuntes sobre las principales providencias y operaciones durante mi mando en la Isla de Cuba desde el dia 18 de Noviembre de 1771 hasta el de la fecha en que lo he entregado a mi successor el Sor. Dn. Diego Jph. Navarro," Havana, June 11, 1777, Library of Congress, Manuscript Division [hereafter LCMD], Domingo del Monte Collection, box 3, no. 9, folio 5.

2. Letters announcing De la Torres's appointment (August 9, 1771) and arrival in Havana on June 7, 1771 (November 18, 1771), Archivo Nacional de Cuba, Correspondencia de los Capitanes-Generales, legajo 30-A, exp. 37.

3. Johnson, "Arrabales"; Kuethe, "Eighteenth-Century Havana."

4. Inglis, Historical Demography, appendix 1, 159–160.

5. Inglis, Historical Demography, 156. For data from the 1774 census, see Kenneth F. Kiple, Blacks in Colonial Cuba, 1774–1899 (Gainesville: University Press of Florida, 1976), 84; and Inglis, Historical Demography, 110, 159. Inglis notes that the census of 1774 did include sailors assigned to the warships in Havana, while the census of 1778 did not. Inglis's dissertation undertakes a careful evaluation of both the 1774 and the 1778 censuses.

6. For numbers of slaves imported from 1763 to 1790, see García Rodríguez, "El mercado de fuerza," table 2 (136). For five nineteenth- and twentieth-century scholars' estimates of slave imports to Cuba from 1790 to 1820, see Childs, Aponte, table 2.1 (50). For disembarkations of slaves in Cuba from 1783 to 1840, see Slave Voyages, "Transatlantic Slave Trade—Estimates." Slave imports into Cuba fluctuated between 2,100 to close to 6,700 people per year over the 1790s.

7. Major works that detail Cuba's eighteenth-century economic transformation include Moreno Fraginals, El ingenio. A number of Moreno Fraginals's conclusions have been modified by subsequent research and interpretation. For instance, García Rodríguez, La Aventura, documents Cuban landowners' investments in the factors of sugar production (land, enslaved workers, draft animals,

buildings, and mills) before 1762, when slave prices were higher than they were in the second half of the eighteenth century (25–27). Tornero Tinajero, *Crecimiento económico*, argues that the sugar boom in Cuba was the result of a "pact" between the Cuban oligarchy and metropolitan interests, not in spite of imperial interests (148).

8. For a useful summary of the growth of the numbers and sizes of sugar *ingenios* in western Cuba in the eighteenth century, see Mercedes García Rodríguez, "De productores empíricos a hacendados ilustrados," in *Francisco Arango y la invención de la Cuba azucarera*, ed. María Dolores González-Ripoll and Izaskun Álvarez Cuartero (Salamanca: Universidad de Salamanca, 2010), 85–104; for figures on numbers of new *ingenios* from 1692 to 1800, see table 1 (88). García Rodríguez notes that in the 1700s the Havana region extended from the western tip of the island to the province of Matanzas, not including the Zapata Swamp (86). Also see Tornero, *Crecimiento económico*, 141–193.

9. William Van Norman Jr., *Shade-Grown Slavery: The Lives of Slaves on Coffee Plantations in Cuba* (Nashville: Vanderbilt University Press, 2013), 11.

10. The average yearly yield of sugar per *ingenio* in western Cuba grew from forty-nine tons in 1761 to fifty-eight tons in 1792; by 1804, it was 127 tons. Moreno Fraginals, *El ingenio*, table 1 (147). For more general discussion of the transformations of sugar production in Cuba from 1760 into the early 1800s, see *El ingenio*, 27–86; and Tornero Tinajero, *Crecimiento económico*, 141–193.

11. Kiple, *Blacks in Colonial Cuba*, 30, 47; *Cuadro estadístico de la siempre fiel isla de Cuba correspondiente al año de 1846* (Havana: Imprenta del Gobierno y Capitanía General, 1847). Kiple's book usefully compares the censuses of the eighteenth and nineteenth centuries and the population estimates that appeared in many secondary sources to sort through discrepancies and errors.

12. The bibliography on political economy in the eighteenth-century Spanish Empire is extensive. Several works that focus fully or in part on Cuba include Gabriel Paquette, *Enlightenment, Governance, and Reform in Spain and its Empire, 1759–1808* (New York: Palgrave, 2008); and Elena A. Schneider, "African Slavery and the Spanish Empire: Imperial Imaginings and Bourbon Reform in Eighteenth-Century Cuba and Beyond," *Journal of Early American History* 5, no. 1 (2015): 3–29.

13. Real Órden, April 30, 1745, in Rosa María Pérez Estévez, *El problema de los vagos en la España del Siglo XVIII* (Madrid: Confederación Española de Cajas de Ahorros, 1976), 61.

14. Pérez Estévez, *El problema de los vagos*, 56–81. Similar characterizations were articulated and drove policy in late eighteenth-century Mexico. See Silvia M. Arrom, *Containing the Poor: The Mexico City Poor House, 1774–1871* (Durham, NC: Duke University Press, 2000), 23.

15. Luis Miguel Enciso Recio, "Prólogo," in Pérez Estévez, *El problema de los vagos*, lists bands published in Madrid on vagrants, the idle poor, and foreigners in 1783, 1786, 1789, 1790, 1791, and 1798 (16–17).

16. Amores, *Cuba en la época de Ezpeleta*, 115–116, including note 151.

17. Johnson, *Crisis and Catastrophe*, 69–91. Johnson also discusses the rebellion against the Spanish occupation of Louisiana in the context of the devastating weather patterns of the late 1760s.

18. Amores, *Cuba en la época de Ezpeleta*, 117, note 153; 105, note 125.

19. King to Bucareli, November 19, 1769, José Augusto Escoto Cuban History and Literature Collection, ca. 1574–1922 (MS Span 52), Houghton Library, Harvard University; Johnson, *Climate and Catastrophe*, 92–94.

20. "Cargos y Esculpaciones del Sr. Mqs de la Torre," October 25, 1777, AHN, Consejos, 6a, 20892, folios 162–163. Such a shelter for "those unhappy women who sought their living in the foolish commerce with men" had been proposed several times in the 1700s, but was not carried out until De la Torre's tenure as captain general.

21. Miguel Josef de Azanza, "Noticia formada de orden del Señor Marqués de la Torre, Gobernador y Capitan General de la Isla de Cuba, de los caudales que se han invertido en la Havana y sus cercanías, y de los repartimientos y arbitrios que los han producido," Havana, April 12, 1777, AHN, Consejos, 20892, 6a, folios 30–36. For a discussion of the evolution of the buildings in the Plaza de Armas from the sixteenth through the twentieth centuries, with illustrations, see Roberto Segre, *La Plaza de Armas de la Habana: sinfonía urbana inconclusa* (Havana: Editorial Arte y Literatura, 1995).

22. For figures on the size of the subsidies for land defenses (troops and fortifications), the navy, and tobacco from the 1750s through the 1780s, see Marichal and Souto, "La Nueva España y el financiamiento del imperio español en América," 80.

23. De la Torre to Altarriba, Havana, July 23, 1772, AGI, Cuba, 1154, no.185.

24. For a summary of sources of funds and total expenditures in each project under De la Torre, see Azanza, "Noticia formada," AHN, Consejos, 20892, folios 33–35.

25. "Cargos y Esculpaciones del Sr. Mqs. De la Torre," Havana, October 25, 1777, AHN, Consejos, 6a, 20892, folio 4.

26. De la Torre to Altarriba, February 25, 1773, AGI, Cuba, 1154, no. 314.

27. De la Torre to Rapún, April 14, 1773, AGI, Cuba, 1154, no. 342; April 26, 1773, no. 352; and July 28, 1773, no. 403.

28. De la Torre, "Apuntes sobre las principales providencias . . . ," June 11, 1777.

29. "Liquidación, que en Conformidad de decreto del Sor. Nicolas Josef Rapun Yntendente de Exercito, su fecha 11 del mes de la fecha forma la contaduria principal de Exercito de la Ysla de Cuba, por las cantidades que han tenido entrada en la Thesoreria Gral. Procedentes del Arbitrio de Sisa de Zanja . . . ," June 30, 1775, AGI, Cuba, 115, 3.

30. Antonio Ramon del Valle, "Instruccion para la Secretaria del Governador y Captain-General," n.d., but included in packet for Diego Navarro from the crown, dated January 6, 1777, AGI, SD, 1217. On water canal repairs in the late 1780s, see Amores, *Cuba en la época de Ezpeleta*, 410.

31. Azanza, "Noticia formada," AHN, Consejos, 20892, folio 31b; De la Torre, "Apuntes sobre las principales," LCMD, Del Monte Collection, box 3, folios 7–8.

32. Sylvia Arrom makes a similar point about the poorhouse of Mexico City, which was built in 1774, saying that such initiatives were not simply responses to supposedly enlightened metropolitan directives. She claims that "in some ways Mexico City was on the cutting edge of Spanish social policy," particularly in banning begging three years earlier than in Madrid. See Arrom, *Containing the Poor*, 17. Interestingly, the viceroy in New Spain in the early 1770s was Antonio María de Bucareli, De la Torre's predecessor as captain general of Cuba.

33. On the Jesuits in Cuba, see Mercedes García Rodríguez, *Misticismo y capitales: la Compañía de Jesús en la economía habanera del siglo XVIII* (Havana: Editorial de Ciencias Sociales, 2000).

34. Jacobo de Pezuela, *Ensayo histórico de la isla de Cuba* (New York: Imp. Española de R. Rafael, 1842), 256–259, 261.

35. Amores, *Cuba en la época de Ezpeleta*, notes that De la Torre enjoyed a good reputation in Cuban historiography over the nineteenth and twentieth centuries due to his efforts to beautify Havana, his encouragement of slave trading and commercial agriculture, and likely for the "good number" of titles of Castile that were bestowed upon members of the Havana elite during his tenure as captain general (11). Johnson, *Crisis and Catastrophe*, especially chapter 7, summarizes her argument about the enlightened rule of Charles III and his appointed governors in Havana from 1763 to 1789 and its benefits for Cubans (193–202). She contrasts the contentious period of rule by Captain General Las Casas (1790 to 1796) with the earlier period of good government that De la Torre represented.

36. De la Torre, "Apuntes sobre las principales providencias," LCMD, Del Monte Collection, box 3, no. 6–8.

37. De la Torre, "Apuntes sobre las principales providencias," LCMD, Del Monte Collection, box 3, no. 4.

38. "Cargos y esculpaciones," AHN, Consejos, 6a, 20892, folios 42–43 and 141.

39. Quotes from "Cargos y esculpaciones," October 3, 1777, signed by Domingo Joseph de la Barrera, el Mqs. De Villa Alta, AHN, Consejos, 6a, 20892, folio 98. Other examples, from Havana Cabildo meetings, in folios 100–103.

40. De la Torre, "Apuntes sobre las principales providencias," LCMD, Del Monte Collection, box 3, no. 90.

41. For examples of the many memos and notices during De la Torre's tenure, see AGI, Cuba, 1153 and 1154.

42. De la Torre to Rapun, August 24, 1774, AGI, Cuba, 1154.

43. Rapún to De la Torre, December 26, 1774, AGI, Cuba, 1154, no. 707. In the 1760s, smugglers were likely to be sentenced to the fort works, as we saw in chapter 3.

44. Altarriba to De la Torre, August 13, 1772, AGI, Cuba, 1154, no. 195; and August 16, 1772, no. 200.

45. De la Torre, "Apuntes sobre las principales providencias," June 11, 1777, box 3, no. 3–4, folios 2–3.

46. For numerous examples, see AGI, Cuba, 1153.

47. De la Torre, "Apuntes sobre las principales providencias," LCMD, Del Monte Collection, box 3, no. 92.

48. Johnson, *Crisis and Catastrophe*, chapter 4, 92–122.

49. Urriza to De la Torre, January 9, 1777, AGI, Cuba, 1153, no. 1168; Urriza to De la Torre, April 8, 1777, no. 1237; and Urriza to De la Torre, February 19, 1777, no. 1193. For more on the Guachinangos, or Indian or mestizo prisoners, sent to Havana from Veracruz, see chapter 3.

50. Urriza to De la Torre, March 20, 1776, AGI, Cuba, 1153, no. 921. Intendant Nicolás Rapún died while in office. See memo, March 5, 1776, AGI, Cuba, 1153, no. 1023.

51. Urriza to De la Torre, January 14, 1777, AGI, Cuba, 1153, no. 1174.

52. The number of king's slaves working at Havana's fort appears in De Vito, "Connected Singularities," table 7.1, 175; and "Estado que comprehende el numero de forzados existentes . . . en la Cavaña, y Loma de Arostegui . . . ," October 30 and November 27, 1774, and January 29, February 27, and March 26, 1775, AGI, SD, 1211.

53. For details on the collapse of the first *asiento* of the Compañía Gaditana, see Torres Ramírez, *La compañía gadtiana*, 65–104. Figures on slave imports to Cuba from 1771 to 1777 are from García, "Comercio esclavista," table 2, 136.

54. De la Torre, "Apuntes sobre las principales providencias," LCMD, Del Monte Collection, box 3, no. 116.

55. A good example of nineteenth-century historians' effusive praise for De la Torre's improvements in the social order and infrastructure of Havana is Jacobo de Pezuela, *Ensayo histórico de Cuba*, chapter 16, which claims that, in the Marquis, "talent, enlightenment and such superior understanding shone" as to eclipse all of his predecessors in the reformist administration of Charles III (251).

56. Antonio Ramon del Valle, "Instruccion para la Secretaria del Govierno y Capitanía General," n.d., but filed with the king's instruction to the incoming captain general, Diego Navarro, dated January 6, 1777, AGI, SD, 1217. Del Valle noted that the governor's house project had been suspended for insufficient funds. For further detail on the difficulties and final completion of the governor's house, see Amores, *Cuba en la época de Ezpeleta*, 392–399.

57. Amores, *Cuba en la época de Ezpeleta*, 400–402.

58. Amores, *Cuba en la época de Ezpeleta*, 399–400. Amores notes that Peñalver offered to fund part of the jail project in hopes of pursuing a title of Castile from the crown.

59. For example, in 1781, Captain-General Juan Manuel de Cagigal rounded up men to serve in his expedition the following year against Providence Island in the Bahamas. Antonio J. Valdés, *Historia de la Isla de Cuba y en especial de la Habana* (Havana: Oficina de la Cena, 1813), 1:192. On sweeps of Havana that netted men for Spanish ships stationed there during this same period, see Josef Solano to Juan Manuel Cagigal, January 8, 1782, and Juan Manuel Cagigal to José de Gálvez, February 20, 1782, AGI, SD, 1234, no. 180.

60. "R. C. [Real Cédula] Concediendo la libertad para el comercio de esclavos en las Antillas Mayores y Caracas, Madrid 29 de febrero de 1789," in Manuel Lucena Salmoral, *Regulación de la esclavitud negra en las colonias de América Española (1503–1886): Documentos para su estudio* (Alcalá de Henares: Universidad de Alcalá, 2005), 246–248.

61. The text of the May 31, 1789, "Real Cédula e Instrucción Circular a Indias, sobre la educación, trato y ocupación de los esclavos" is reproduced in Ortiz, *Los negros esclavos*, apéndice, 274–280; and in Manuel Lucena Salmoral, *Los códigos negros de la América española* (Alcalá: Edciones UNESCO, Universidad de Alcalá, 1996), appendix 4, 279–284.

62. Examples of this legislation are compiled in several sources: Lucena Salmoral, *Regulación de la esclavitud*; Richard Konetzke, *Colección de documentos para la historia de la formación social de Hispanoamérica: 1493–1810*, vol. 1 (Madrid: Consejo Superior de Investigaciones Científicas, 1962); and Ortiz, *Los negros esclavos*, 267–274. For an extended discussion of *cimarronaje* (flight by the enslaved) and ordinances to control free populations of color, see Klein, *Slavery in the Americas*, 68–76. The thrust of Klein's argument is that the moral attitude of the *Siete Partidas* continued to manifest itself in the slave legislation of later centuries. For a different interpretation, see Knight, *Slave Society in Cuba*, 124–126.

63. De la Fuente, "Slaves and the Creation of Legal Rights in Cuba," 663.

64. Luceno Salmoral, *Los códigos negros*, 280–284; Ortiz, *Los negros esclavos*, 275–280. The office of the *síndico procurador* was established in the Spanish colonies in 1766 "to provide legal representation

for slaves and mediate in their conflicts with masters." Though some of the *síndicos* were slave owners themselves, over time their intervention in disputes between the enslaved and their enslavers inserted the state more directly into these relationships, to the dismay of owners, as the enslaved claimed precedent and customary rights to *coartación* (gradual self-purchase at a fixed price) and to *pedir papel* (request for sale to another owner). The Cuban Slave Code of 1842 codified these rights. See De la Fuente, "Slaves and the Creation of Legal Rights in Cuba," 659–692, at 665. Scott, *Slave Emancipation in Cuba*, discusses the role of *síndicos* after gradual emancipation began, in 1870 (75–80).

65. Ferrer, *Freedom's Mirror*, 26–29, at 27.

66. Barcia, *Great African Slave Revolt*, 46.

67. "Resolucion del Consejo de Indias suspendiendo 'los efectos' de la Real Cédula de 1789 sobre la educación, trato, y ocupación de los esclavos," Madrid, March 17, 1794, in Lucena Salmoral, *Regulación de la esclavitud negra*, 260–264. For a comparison of the Reglamento of 1789 with the subsequent Cuban slave codes of 1842 and 1844, see Manuel Barcia Paz, *Con el látigo de la ira: Legislación, represión y control en las plantaciones cubanas, 1790–1870* (Havana: Editorial de Ciencias Sociales, 2000), especially chapter 2, 19–36.

68. The slave trade from Africa was officially ended by the Treaty of 1817, but enforcement began in 1820. See Real Cédula from the Spanish king with orders on complying with the treaty between Spain and England to abolish the slave trade, 1818, Archivo General Militar de Segovia, section 2, division 3, legajo 77. This file also contains a copy of the treaty.

69. Moreno, *El ingenio*, 36–37.

70. For yearly estimates of slaves disembarked in Cuba from 1783 through 1840, see Slave Voyages, "Trans-Atlantic Slave Trade—Estimates."

71. Ramón de la Sagra, *Historia económica-política y estadística de la isla de Cuba . . .* (Havana: Viudas de Aroza y Soler, 1831), 4; Kiple, *Blacks in Colonial Cuba*, 30; *Cuadro estadístico de la siempre fiel isla de Cuba correspondiente al año de 1846* (Havana: Imprenta del Gobierno y Capitanía General, 1847).

72. The Mexican *situado* payments that supported Cuban defense reached an early peak in 1769, at just over 2.2 million pesos, with the fortification projects after the British occupation. In 1782, payments reached their highest total, nearly 7.9 million pesos, at the height of Spanish involvement in the American War of Independence. By the end of the decade (1789), the payments had fallen to 549,032 pesos. Kuethe, "Guns, Subsidies, and Commercial Privilege," 130.

73. McNeill, *Atlantic Empires*, table 6.10, 165. McNeill estimates an annual total of 108,472 arrobas of sugar exported from Cuba to Spain in 1754. The total for 1760 is 378,346 arrobas. The Cuban arroba equaled 25 pounds, or 11.36 kilograms. McNeill, *Atlantic Empires*, appendix B, 212.

74. For sugar and coffee exports through the port of Havana from 1773 through 1840, see Tornero Tinajero, *Crecimiento económico*, appendix 3, 285.

75. Amores, *Cuba en la época de Ezpeleta*, 405–408. For reports on some of the projects in the 1790s, see Nicolas Calvo y O'Farrill, "'Memoria sobre los medios que convendrá adoptar para que tuviese La Habana los caminos necesarios.' Presentada al Consulado por la diputación que con este objeto nombró," Havana, 1795, AGI, Ultramar, 170; and Biblioteca Nacional de España [hereafter BNE], VE 1233-14.

76. It was illegal for Las Casas to own plantations in his own name, so they were registered to others, but he shortly purchased a second plantation, which grew to be one of the largest in Cuba. Ferrer, *Freedom's Mirror*, 29–31.

77. Johnson, *Social Transformation*, 128–130.

78. Juan B. Amores Carredano, "Ordenanzas de gobierno local en la isla de Cuba (1765–1786)," *Revista Complutense de Historia de América* 30 (2004): 104; Johnson, *Social Transformation*, 132–137.

79. María Dolores González-Ripoll Navarro, *Cuba. La isla de los ensayos. Cultura y sociedad (1790–1815)* (Madrid: Consejo Superior de Investigaciones Científicas, Centro de Humanidades, Instituto de Historia Departamento de Historia de América, 1999), 83.

80. On the peninsular antecedents and the founding of the Havana Society, see R. J. Shafer, *The Economic Societies in the Spanish World (1763–1821)* (Syracuse, NY: Syracuse University Press, 1958), especially 178–333. Also see González-Ripoll Navarro, *Cuba*, 165.

81. De la Sagra, *Historia económico-política y estadística*, 232. The *avería* consisted of a 0.5 percent tax on all agricultural goods imported and exported through Cuban ports and began to be charged in October 1794. A tax called the additional *avería* was instituted in December 1817 to restore to the Consulado the sum of 25,000 pesos that it had donated to the anti-independence expeditions in Spanish America. Even after that sum had been recovered, the Consulado was allowed to continue collecting a total tax of 0.75 percent. On the founding of the Consulado, see Shafer, *Economic Societies*, 183; and H. E. Friedlaender, *Historia económica de Cuba* (Havana: Biblioteca de Historia, Filosofía y Sociología, 1944), 131–133.

82. Peter. J. Lampros, "Merchant–Planter Cooperation and Conflict: The Havana Consulado, 1794–1832" (PhD diss., Tulane University, 1980). For a report on the state of Cuba's roads and possible sources of funding for their repair, see Calvo y O'Farrill, "Memoria sobre los medios," AGI, Ultramar, 170, BNE, VE 1233-14. For the Torrentégui and Arango report, see "Informe que presentó en 9 de Junio de 1796 a la Junta de Gobierno del Real Consulado de Agricultura y Comercio de esta ciudad e isla cuando examinó la mencionada Real Junta el Reglamento y Arancel de capturas de esclavos cimarrones y propuso al Rey su reforma," Havana, 1796, BNE, VE 1238-12, 5. Though Calvo y O'Farrill is listed as the author, the report was signed by Joseph Ricardo O'Farrill and Francisco Arango as well.

83. The Consulado charter is quoted and discussed in Lampros, "Merchant–Planter Cooperation and Conflict," 490.

84. Lampros, "Merchant–Planter Cooperation and Conflict," 491–492.

85. José Antonio Saco, *Memoria sobre caminos en la isla de Cuba* (New York: G. F. Bunce, 1830), discusses in detail road building techniques in Cuba in comparison with England, before and after the era of the macadam method of road construction (12–53).

86. Lampros, "Merchant–Planter Cooperation and Conflict," 493–497.

87. Calvo y O'Farrill owned the *ingenio* Nueva Holanda, among the largest and most technologically advanced plantations in Cuba at the time. Ferrer, *Freedom's Mirror*, 146.

88. BNE, VE 1233-14, 1–7, at 3.

89. BNE, VE 1233-14, 10.

90. BNE, VE 1233-14, 11.

91. Lampros, *Merchant–Planter Cooperation and Conflict*, 494–495.

92. BNE, VE 1233-14, 5, 9–11.

93. BNE, VE 1233-14, 11–14.

94. BNE, VE 1233-14, 22–23, 27.

95. BNE, VE 1233-14, 27–29.

96. The report's authors did not think the enslaver should have to pay for maintenance of the enslaved when they were under the charge of the Consulado, only for their maintenance and transport to Havana, but the authors also thought that the Consulado should not have to pay wages to the enslavers for the public labor of their enslaved workers. BNE, VE 1233–14, 28.

97. Gabino La Rosa Corzo, Los cimarrones de Cuba (Havana: Editorial de Ciencias Sociales, 1988), 34.

98. "Resumen de los costos sin reintegro que ha erogado el Consulado en los quince mil nuevecientos setenta y unos Esclavos cimarrones manifestados en el anterior Estado," AGI, Ultramar, 320, 8,

99. "Resumen que presenta a la Junta de Gobierno del Real Consulado su Contaduría, de los Esclavos Cimarrones que han sido depositados en dicha oficina desde 21 de Julio de 1797 que se puso en practica el actual Reglamento de la materia, hasta 31 de Diciembre de 1815," AGI, Ultramar, 320, 7.

100. Copy of a memo from the junta consular to Intendant Luis de Viguri, August 27, 1800, AGI, SD, 2195.

101. Copy of reply of the Consulado to Intendant Luis de Viguri, October 18, 1802, AGI, SD, 2195.

102. Lampros, "Merchant–Planter Cooperation and Conflict," 499; Marrero, Cuba: economía y sociedad (Madrid: Playor, 1984), 11:149.

103. Lampros, "Merchant–Planter Cooperation and Conflict," 500–501.

104. La Rosa Corzo, Los cimarrones de Cuba, 39.

105. La Rosa Corzo, Los cimarrones de Cuba, table 2, 242.

106. "Dictamen del Ingeniero Director Diputado de obras Consulares," August 31, 1811, in Resumen que presenta a la Junta de Gobierno del Real Consulado, AGI, Ultramar, 320, 3.

107. La Rosa Corzo, Los cimarrones de Cuba, 58–59.

108. Lampros, "Merchant–Planter Cooperation and Conflict," 504–508; Humboldt, Ensayo político, 273–275.

109. Lampros, "Merchant–Planter Cooperation and Conflict," 521.

110. Vicente María Rodrigo, report to the Havana Consulado on abuses in the Depósito de cimarrones, 1823, AHN, Ultramar, 9, 2, doct. 9, 2.

111. AHN, Ultramar, 9, 2, doct. 9, 2–3.

112. AHN, Ultramar, 9, 2, doct. 11, 2; La Rosa Corzo, Los cimarrones de Cuba, table 5, 48.

113. Marrero, Cuba, 11:149.

114. The Consulado did carry out some projects, more focused on the defense of commerce than of the island itself, by building some towers along the northern coast and outfitting coastal patrols to intercept pirate vessels. Lampros, "Merchant–Planter Cooperation and Conflict," 440.

115. Humboldt, Ensayo político sobre la isla de Cuba, 111–115, 118.

116. De la Sagra, Historia económico-política y estadística, 6. De la Sagra's figures differ somewhat from Humboldt's, but the trends of growth are similar.

117. Yolanda Díaz Martínez, Visión de la otra Habana: Vigilancia, delito, y control social en los inicios del siglo XIX (Santiago de Cuba: Editorial Oriente, 2011), 55–60.

118. Díaz Martínez, Visión de la otra Habana, 83–84, 166–167.

119. On the early years of disruptions in the Spanish colonial bond with Cuba during the Napoleonic era, see Sigfrido Vázquez Cienfuegos, La Junta de la Habana: Adaptación del pacto colonial en Cuba en vísperas de la independencies hispanoamericanas, 1808–1810 (Seville: Consejo Superior de Investigaciones

Científicas, Universidad de Sevilla, Diputación de Sevilla, 2013). On the first republican period, see Juan B. Amores Carredano and Alain Santos Fuentes, "El conflict entre las élites locales y las autoridades cubanas en torno a la aplicación de la Constitución de Cádiz (1812–1814)," *Espacio, tiempo, y forma* 30 (2018): 17–31.

120. Joaquín Llaverías, *La Comisión Militar Ejecutiva y Permanente de la Isla de Cuba* (Havana: El Siglo XX, 1929), 8, 52–55. Military commissions were suppressed in Spain in October 1824 and finally abolished in 1834, but the captain general of Cuba at that time, Miguel Tacón, retained the commissions, due to what he saw as continued threats from criminals and subversives.

121. For a discussion of the imperial network of penal transportation from the 1830s to 1886, see Christian De Vito, "Punishment and Labour Relations: Cuba between Abolition and Empire (1835–1886)," *Crime, Histoire & Sociétés/Crime, History & Societies* 22, no. 1 (2018): 53–79. De Vito emphasizes the role of plural regimes of punishment ("punitive pluralism") that functioned simultaneously as the labor force in all sectors became more diverse through the long process of ending the slave trade, slavery, and Spanish colonialism in Cuba.

122. Llaverías, *La Comisión Militar*, appendix Q, reproduces a report from December 25, 1837, listing all the cases heard by the Military Commission in Cuba and their outcomes, from its inception to the end of 1837—a total of 205 cases from 1824 through 1837 (181–186). On various internal threats and conspiracies in the early 1820s, see Barcia, *Great African Slave Revolt*, 39–41.

123. "Royal Decree Granting Absolute Powers to the Captain-General of Cuba (1825)," trans. Luis Martínez-Fernández, in *Encyclopedia of Cuba: People, History, Culture*, vol. 2, ed. Luis Martínez-Fernández, D. H. Figueredo, Louis A. Pérez, Jr., and Luis González (Westport, CT: Greenwood, 2003), appendix 5, 624. Quote is from Paquette, *Sugar Is Made with Blood*, 48–49.

124. Paquette, *Sugar Is Made with Blood*, 85.

125. For an in-depth examination of Francisco Arango y Parreño's life, work, and legacies, see the essays in María Dolores González-Ripoll and Izaskun Álvarez Cuartero, eds., *Francisco Arango y la invención de la Cuba azucarera* (Salamanca: Ediciones Universidad de Salamanca, 2009).

126. Martínez de Pinillos assumed his father's title of Count of Villanueva in 1829.

127. Claudio Martínez de Pinillos to Secretary of State, 1822, AGI, Ultramar, 180; Juan Pérez de la Riva, ed., *Correspondencia del Capitán General Don Miguel de Tacón* (Havana: Consejo Nacional de Cultura, 1963), appendix, 339–341; Manuel Barcia, "El Conde de Villanueva y la alternativa de la Cuba Grande: una aproximación a la labor de Claudio Martínez de Pinillos al frente de la Intendencia de Hacienda de la Isla de Cuba, 1825–1851," in *Francisco Arango y la invención de la Cuba azucarera*, ed. María Dolores González-Ripoll and Izaskun Álvarez Cuartero (Salamanca: Ediciones Universidad Salamanca, 2009), 291–292.

128. Barcia, *Great African Slave Revolt*, 2. On slave revolts in the early 1800s, see Ferrer, *Freedom's Mirror*, 213–223; and Barcia, *Great African Slave Revolt*, 51–67.

129. The number of enslaved people imported into Cuba from 1810 through 1815 averaged 5,027 per year. From 1816, the year before the first anti–slave trade treaty was signed, through 1820, when the interdiction of slave ships was first allowed, imports of the enslaved averaged 18,548 per year. Imports fell off somewhat for the next four years, but in 1825, 24,192 enslaved Africans entered Cuba. For the four years after the signing of the second anti–slave trade treaty, in 1835, imports of the enslaved never fell below 20,000 people. Slave Voyages, "Trans-Atlantic Slave Trade—Estimates."

130. For the most extensive investigation of the Aponte Rebellion, see Childs, 1812 *Aponte Rebellion;* on the Cortes's debates, 32. See also Ferrer, *Freedom's Mirror,* 264–27; on the Cortes's debates and their publication, connections to events in Haiti, and the Aponte Rebellion, 271–328.

131. For a copy of the treaty, inserted into a royal decree with other copied documents about the enforcement of the ban, see "Real Cédula . . . por la cual se manda guardar y cumplir el tratado que va inserto," copy of the treaty, articles I, II, V, IX, February 9, 1818, Archivo Militar de Segovia, 77, división 3, sección 2.

132. Murray, *Odious Commerce,* 77. For a detailed discussion of the treaty and the Cuban reaction, see 68–88.

133. Slave Voyages, "Trans-Atlantic Slave Trade—Estimates."

134. "Buques mercantes Españoles," Havana, June 30, 1841, AHN, Estado, 8035, 11, no. 18, contains a table showing Spanish ships captured, with 2,697 enslaved Africans abroad brought to Cuba and freed from 1824 through 1829.

135. Ayuntamiento of Havana to Secretary of State, November 4, 1829, AHN, Estado, 8033, 18, no. 1.

136. Villanueva to Secretary of State, July 28, 1830, AHN, Estado, 8033, 22, no. 2. Contemporary documents use both the words *liberto* and *emancipado* to refer to the people freed by the treaty of 1817. In the scholarly literature, *emancipado* is more commonly used.

137. Inés Roldán de Montaud, "En los borrosos confines de la libertad: el caso de los negros emancipados en Cuba, 1817–1870," *Revista de Indias* 71, no. 251 (2011): 162, table 1. Murray, *Odious Commerce,* cites approximately 2,300 (276).

138. Most of the works on the ending of the slave trade, especially Murray, *Odious Commerce,* discuss the *emancipados* in Cuba. See also Roldán de Montaud, "Origen," 559–641; and "En los borrosos confines de la libertad." In the latter essay, Roldán de Montaud also uses the phrase "receptive Africans" to identify this group. See also Luis Martínez Fernández, "The Havana Anglo-Spanish Commission for the Suppression of the Slave Trade and Cuba's Emancipados," *Slavery & Abolition* 16, no. 2 (1995): 205–225.

139. Mariano Ricafort to Secretary of State, January 30, 1833, AHN, Estado, 6374-1, no. 15. Ricafort began this letter by reviewing the policies that had been followed with regard to the *emancipados* since the 1817 treaty. Also see Roldán de Montaud, "Origen," 563.

140. For an example of an *emancipado* who lost his freedom, see Oscar Grandio Moraguez, "Dobo: A Liberated African in Nineteenth-Century Havana," *Slave Voyages,* https://www.slavevoyages.org/voyage/essays. Gabino was "consigned" for fifteen years, appealed to the British consul, and received his freedom paper, but was then arrested and deported to Ceuta for allegedly fomenting an uprising. Also discussed in Roldán de Montaud, "Los borrosos confines de la libertad," 169.

141. Roldán de Montaud, "Los borrosos confine de la libertad," Table 1, 162. Murray, *Odious Commerce,* 277–278 has somewhat different figures.

142. Ricafort to Secretary of State, August 27, 1833, AHN, Estado, 6374, 36, no.1 on the deaths of thousands of people of color from cholera. Roldán de Montaud, "Los borrosos confines de la libertad," 165; Murray, *Odious Commerce,* 279–280.

143. Villanueva to Secretary of State, August 30, 1833, AHN, Estado, 8034, 21, no. 1.

144. AHN, Estado, 8034, 16 nos. 2 and 4 contain a copy of the conditions for transport of Cuban *emancipados* to Trinidad and Villanueva's letter to the Secretary of State outlining the problems with these conditions.

145. Ricafort to Secretary of State, January 30, 1833, AHN, Estado, 6374, 1, no. 15; Mariano Ricafort, "Al Público," El Noticioso y Lucero, May 30, 1834, 3, quoted in Juan Pérez de la Riva, ed. *Correspondencia reservada del Capitán General Don Miguel Tacón, 1834–1836* (Havana: Biblioteca Nacional de José Martí, 1963), 118, ft. 19.

146. Ricafort to Secretary of State, January30, 1833, AHN, Estado, 6374, 1, no. 15.

147. LaRosa Corzo, *Los cimarrones de Cuba*, 50.

148. Bergad, Iglesias, and Barcia, *The Cuban Slave Market*, Figure 5.7, 90 and Table B.2 174–185.

149. For more detail on the importation of contract laborers to Cuba to build railroads, see Evelyn P. Jennings, "The Path to Sweet Success: Free and Unfree Laobr in the Building of Roads and Rails in Havana, Cuba, 1790–1835," *International Review of Social History* 64, Special Issue 27 (2019): 149–171.

150. Arthur F. Corwin, *Spain and the Abolition of Slavery in Cuba 1817–1886* (New York: Octagon Books, 1967) 63–64.

151. Murray, *Odious Commerce*, 92–113. Roldán de Montaud, "Los borrosos confines de la libertad," 165–166.

CONCLUSION

1. "Decreto de abolición de la esclavitud en la forma y bajo las reglas que se expresan [Ley Moret o de libertad de vientres], San Idelfonso 4 de julio de 1870," in *Regulación de la esclavitud negra en las colonias de América Española (1503–1886): Documentos para su estudio*, ed. Manuel Lucena Salmoral (Alcalá: Universidad de Alcalá and Universidad de Murcia, 2005), 349–351.

2. "Decreto de abolición de la esclavitud . . . 4 de julio de 1870," 349–351.

3. "Ley de supresión de la esclavitud y del patronato, Madrid, 13 de febrero de 1880," in Lucena Salmoral, *Regulación de la esclavitud negra*, 376. On the 1880 law and its consequences, see Scott, *Slave Emancipation in Cuba*, 123–171.

4. "Decreto de abolición de la esclavitud . . . ," 350. On the *patronato* and *patrocinados'* active pursuit of freedom through the apprenticeship period, see Scott, *Slave Emancipation in Cuba*, 127–197.

5. "Real Decreto de abolición del patronato, Madrid, 7 de octubre de 1886," in Lucena Salmoral, *Regulación de la esclavitud negra*, 381–383.

6. On the slave rebellions of the mid-1840s collectively known La Escalera, and an introduction to the bibliography, see Aisha K. Finch, *Rethinking Slave Rebellion in Cuba: La Escalera and the Insurgencies of 1841–1844* (Chapel Hill: University of North Carolina Press, 2015); Michelle Reid-Vázquez, *The Year of the Lash: Free People of Color in Cuba and the Nineteenth-Century Atlantic World* (Athens: University of Georgia Press, 2011); and Paquette, *Sugar Is Made with Blood*.

7. Scott, *Slave Emancipation in Cuba*, 45–62. On the ambiguous and shifting policies toward emancipation of the enslaved in insurgent territory, see Ada Ferrer, *Insurgent Cuba: Race, Nation, and Revolution, 1868–1898* (Chapel Hill: University of North Carolina Press, 1999), 15–42.

8. Humboldt, *Ensayo político*, 273–276.

9. To date, we do not have a clear idea of how many people ultimately came to Cuba from Yucatan in the mid-nineteenth century; estimates range from 730 to 10,000. The higher number is from Paul Estrade, "Los colonos como sustitutos de los esclavos negros," in *Cuba la perla de las Antillas: Actas de las I Jornadas sobre 'Cuba y su historia,'* ed. Consuelo Naranjo Orovio and Tomás Mallo Gutiérrez (Madrid:

Dos Calles, 1994), 97. See also Jason M. Yaremko, *Indigenous Passages to Cuba, 1515–1900* (Gainesville: University Press of Florida, 2016), 112. Lisa Yun, *The Coolie Speaks: Chinese Indentured Laborers and African Slaves in Cuba* (Philadelphia: Temple University Press, 2008), table 1.3, cites 138,156 Chinese as having embarked from China to Cuba from 1847 to 1873, and 121,810 who actually landed (19). For a comparison of Yucatecan and Chinese indentures in Cuba and the differing imperial ideologies about their places in Cuba's slave society, see Evelyn P. Jennings, "'Some Unhappy Indians Trafficked by Force': Race, Status, and Work Discipline in Mid-Nineteenth Century Cuba," in *Human Bondage in the Cultural Contact Zone*, ed. Raphael Hörmann and Gesa Mackenthun (Münster: Waxmann, 2010), 209–225.

10. Yaremko, *Indigenous Passages*, 115; David Northrup, *Indentured Labor in the Age of Imperialism, 1834–1922* (Cambridge: Cambridge University Press, 1995), 143.

10. French doctor Henri Dumont spent time in Cuba, beginning in 1864, treating enslaved people of African descent on eleven plantations and at a public works site at the Springs of Vento (Manatiales de Vento) in Havana. He was interested in pathologies among the enslaved and in their cultural traditions. At the Vento site in Havana, he photographed several enslaved and *emancipado/a* men and women working at the site. See Henry Dumont, *Los orígenes de la antropología en el Caribe*, ed. Lourdes S. Dominguez and Gabino La Rosa (San Juan: Ediciones Puerto, 2013); on Dumont's life and work, see the editors' introduction, "Los orígenes de la antropología en el Caribe," 15–77; for the photographs of the *emancipados* in Vento, see figure 1 (104), figure 6 (123), and figures 13 and 14 (148–149). For the captain general's quote, see Scott, *Slave Emancipation in Cuba*, 71.

12. Scott, *Slave Emancipation in Cuba*, 63–83.

13. Scott, *Slave Emancipation in Cuba*, 100–105; De Vito, "Punishment and Labour Relations," 66.

14. The essays in Donoghue and Jennings, *Building the Atlantic Empires*, offer a comparative perspective on these issues.

BIBLIOGRAPHY

PRIMARY SOURCES

Archivo General de Indias (Seville)
    Santo Domingo
    Papeles de Cuba
    Ultramar

Archivo General de Simancas
    Estado
    Guerra
    Marina
    Secretaría y Superintendencia de Hacienda

Archivo General Militar de Segovia

Archivo Histórico Nacional (Madrid)
    Consejos
    Estado

Archivo Nacional de Cuba (Havana)
    Correspondencia de los Capitanes-Generales

Biblioteca Nacional de España (Madrid)

Houghton Library, Harvard University, Cambridge, Massachusetts
    José Escoto Cuban History and Literature Collection

Library of Congress, Washington, DC
    Manuscript Division, Domingo del Monte Collection

Museo Naval, Madrid
Colección Guillen
Colección Vargas Ponce

PUBLISHED PRIMARY SOURCES

Arrate, José Félix Martin de. *Llave del Nuevo Mundo antemural de las Indias occidentales*. La Habana: Comisión Nacional Cubana de la UNESCO, 1964 [1761].

An Authentic Journal of the Siege of the Havana. By an Officer. London: T. Jefferys, 1762.

Columbus, Christopher. "Letter on the New World (1493)." In *Early Modern Spain: A Documentary History*, edited by Jon Cowans, 28–33. Philadelphia: University of Pennsylvania Press, 2003.

Dana, Richard Jr. *To Cuba and Back*. Boston: Tichnor and Fields, 1859.

Dumont, Henry. *Los orígenes de la antropología en el Caribe*. Edited by Lourdes S. Dominguez and Gabino La Rosa. San Juan: Ediciones Puerto, 2013.

García del Pino, César, and Alicia Melis Cappa, eds. *Documentos para la historia colonial de Cuba: siglos XVI, XVII, XVIII, XIX*. Havana: Editorial de Ciencias Sociales, 1988.

Gómez Colón, José María. *Memoria sobre la conservación del puerto de La Habana*. Santiago de Cuba: Imprenta de M. A. Martínez, 1851.

Guiteras, Pedro José. *Historia de la conquista de la Habana*. 1762. Philadelphia: Parry and Macmillan, 1856.

Humboldt, Alejandro de. *Ensayo político sobre la isla de Cuba*. Edited by Miguel Ángel Puig-Samper, Consuelo Naranjo Orovio, and Armando García González. Madrid: Ediciones Dos Calles, 1998.

Humboldt, Alexander. *The Island of Cuba*. Translated by John Thrasher. New York: Derby and Jackson, 1856.

Konetzke, Richard. *Colección de documentos para la historia de la formación social de Hispanoamérica: 1493–1810*. Vol. 1. Madrid: Consejo Superior de Investigaciones Científicas, 1962.

Las Siete Partidas. Edited by Robert I. Burns. Translated by Samuel Scott Parsons. Philadelphia: University of Pennsylvania Press, 2001.

Morell de Santa Cruz, Pedro Agustín. *La visita eclesiástica*. Edited by César García del Pino. Havana: Editorial de Ciencias Sociales, 1985.

Pezuela, Jacobo de. *Ensayo histórico de la isla de Cuba*. New York: Imp. Española de R. Rafael. 1842.

Saco, José Antonio. *Memoria sobre caminos en la isla de Cuba*. New York: G. F. Bunce, 1830.

Sagra, Ramón de la. *Historia económica-política y estadística de la isla de Cuba*. Havana: Viudas de Aroza y Soler, 1831.

Urrutia y Matos, Bernardo Joseph de. *Cuba: Fomento de la Isla*. 1749. San Juan, Puerto Rico: Ediciones Capiro, 1993.

Valdés, Antonio J. *Historia de la Isla de Cuba y en especial de la Habana*. Vol. 1. Havana: Oficina de la Cena, 1813.

Zamora y Coronado, José María. *Biblioteca de legislación ultramarina*. Tomo 5, *Letras P–S*. Madrid: Alegría y Charlain, 1844.

SECONDARY SOURCES

Aimes, Hubert. *History of Slavery in Cuba, 1511–1868*. New York: Knickerbocker, 1907.

Alegría, Ricardo E. *Juan Garrido, el conquistador en las Antillas, Florida, México, y California, c. 1503–1540*. San Juan: Centro de Estudios Avanzados de Puerto Rico y El Caribe, 1990.

Amores Carredano, Juan B. *Cuba en la época de Ezpeleta (1785–1790)*. Pamplona: Ediciones Universidad de Navarra, 2000.

———. "Ordenanzas de gobierno local en la isla de Cuba (1765–1786)." *Revista Complutense de Historia de América*, 30 (2004): 95–109.

Amores Carredano, Juan B., and Alain Santos Fuentes. "El conflict entre las élites locales y las autoridades cubanas en torno a la aplicación de la Constitución de Cádiz (1812–1814)." *Espacio, tiempo, y forma*, 30 (2018): 17–31.

Arce, Luis A. De. *El Real Hospital Nuestra Señora del Pilar en el Siglo XVIII (Un hospital para los esclavos del Rey) 1764–1793*. Havana: Ministerio de Salud Pública, 1969.

Arrom, Silvia M. *Containing the Poor: The Mexico City Poor House, 1774–1871*. Durham, NC: Duke University Press, 2000.

Barbier, Jacques A. "Toward a New Chronology for Bourbon Colonialism: The Depositaria de Indias of Cadiz, 1722–1789." *Ibero-amerikanisches Archiv* 6 (1980): 335–353.

Barcia, Manuel. "El Conde de Villanueva y la alternativa de la Cuba Grande: una aproximación a la labor de Claudio Martínez de Pinillos al frente de la Intendencia de Hacienda de la Isla de Cuba, 1825–1851." In *Francisco Arango y la invención de la Cuba azucarera*, edited by María Dolores González-Ripoll and Izaskun Álvarez Cuartero, 289–299. Salamanca: Ediciones Universidad Salamanca, 2009.

———. *The Great African Slave Revolt of 1825: Cuba and the Fight for Freedom in Matanzas*. Baton Rouge: Louisiana State University Press, 2012.

Barcia, María del Carmen *Los ilustres apellidos: Negros en la Habana colonial*. Havana: Ediciones Boloña, 2009.

Barcia Paz, Manuel. *Con el látigo de la ira: legislación, represión y control en las plantaciones cubanas, 1790–1870*. Havana: Editorial de Ciencias Sociales, 2000.

Barcia Zequeira, María del Carmen. *La otra familia: Parientes, redes, y desendencia de los esclavos en Cuba*. Havana: Casa de las Américas, 2003.

Barrio Gozalo, Maximilliano. "La esclavitud en el mediterráneo occidental en el siglo XVIII. Los esclavos del Rey en España." *Critica storica* 2 (1980): 199–256.

———. *Esclavos y cautivos. Conflicto entre la Cristianidad y el Islam en el Siglo XVIII*. Valladolid: Junta de Castilla y León, 2006.

Beckert, Sven, and Christine Desan, eds. *American Capitalism: New Histories*. New York: Columbia University Press, 2018.

———. *Empire of Cotton*. New York: Alfred A. Knopf, 2015.

Bergad, Laird, Fe Iglesias García, and María del Carmen Barcia. *The Cuban Slave Market, 1790–1880*. New York: Cambridge University Press, 1995.

Bennett, Herman L. *Africans in Colonial Mexico: Absolutism, Christianity, and Afro-Creole Consciousness, 1570–1640*. Bloomington: Indiana University Press, 2003.

Blackburn, Robin. *The Making of New World Slavery*. London: Verso, 1997.

———. "Why the Second Slavery?" In *Slavery and Historical Capitalism During the Nineteenth Century*, edited by Dale Tomich, 1–36. Lanham, MD: Lexington, 2017.

Blanes Martín, Tamara. "Fortificaciones habanera, la defensa de La Habana, del siglo XVI a la primera mitad del XIX." In *La Habana, Puerto colonial (Siglos XVIII–XIX)*, edited by Agustín Guimerá and Fernando Monge, 154–175. Madrid: Fundación Portuaria, 2000.

Bowser, Frederick. *The African Slave in Colonial Peru*. Stanford: Stanford University Press, 1974.

Brass, Tom, and Marcel van der Linden. *Free and Unfree Labour: The Debate Continues*. Bern: Peter Lang, 1997.

Brehony, Margaret. "Irish Migration to Cuba, 1835–1845: Empire, Ethnicity, Slavery and 'Free' Labour." PhD diss., National University of Ireland, Galway, 2012.

Brewer, John. *The Sinews of Power*. New York: Alfred A. Knopf, 1989.

Brown, Christopher Leslie, and Philip D. Morgan, eds. *Arming Slaves from Classical Times to the Modern Age*. New Haven, CT: Yale University Press, 2006.

Buckley, Roger N. *Slaves in Red Coats. The British West India Regiments, 1795–1815*. New Haven, CT: Yale University Press, 1979.

Burkholder, Mark A., and Lyman L. Johnson. *Colonial Latin America*. 4th ed. Oxford: Oxford University Press, 2010.

Cáceres Gómez, Rina. "Slave Wages in Omoa." In *Blacks and Blackness in Central America: Between Race and Place*, edited by Lowell Gudmundson and Justin Wolfe, 130–149. Durham, NC: Duke University Press, 2010.

Camacho-Cárdenas, Enrique. "Early 19th Century Ports, Fortifications and New Foundations along Cuba's North-West Coast." In *From Colonies to Countries in the North Caribbean: Military Engineers in the Development of Cities and Territories*, edited by Pedro Luengo-Gutiérrez and Gene Allen Smith, 73–90. Newcastle upon Tyne: Cambridge Scholars, 2016.

Cañizares-Esguerra, Jorge. *Entangled Empires: The Anglo-Iberian Atlantic, 1500–1830*. Philadelphia: University of Pennsylvania Press, 2018.

———. *Puritan Conquistadors: Iberianizing the Atlantic 1550–1700*. Stanford: Stanford University Press, 2006.

Cañizares-Esguerra, Jorge, Matt D. Childs, and James Sidbury, eds. *The Black Urban Atlantic in the Age of the Slave Trade*. Philadelphia: University of Pennsylvania Press, 2013.

Carroll, Patrick. *Blacks in Colonial Veracruz*. Austin: University of Texas Press, 1991.

Caughey, John Walton. *Bernardo de Gálvez in Louisiana, 1776–1783*. Gretna, LA: Pelican, 1972.

Chávez, Thomas E. *Spain and the Independence of the United States: An Intrinsic Gift*. Albuquerque: University of New Mexico Press, 2002.

Childs, Matt D. *The 1812 Aponte Rebellion in Cuba and the Struggle Against Atlantic Slavery*. Chapel Hill: University of North Carolina Press, 2006.

———. "Re-creating African Ethnic Identities in Cuba." In *The Black Urban Atlantic in the Age of the Slave Trade*, edited by Jorge Cañizares Esguerra, Matt D. Childs, and James Sidbury, 85–100. Philadelphia: University of Pennsylvania Press, 2013.

Corwin, Arthur F. *Spain and the Abolition of Slavery in Cuba, 1817–1886*. Austin: University of Texas Press, 1967.

Davis, David Brion. *The Problem of Slavery in Western Culture*. 1966. New York: Oxford University Press, 1988.

Dean-Smith, Susan. *Bureaucrats, Planters, and Workers: The Making of the Tobacco Monopoly in Bourbon Mexico*. Austin: University of Texas Press, 1992.

Delgado, Jaime. "El Conde de Ricla, Capitán-General de Cuba." *Revista de Historia de América* 55–56 (1963): 41–138.

Deschamps Chapeaux, Pedro. *Los batallones de pardos y morenos libres*. Havana: Editorial Arte y Literatura, 1976.

———. *Los cimarrones urbanos*. Havana: Editorial de Ciencias Sociales, 1983.

———. *El negro en la economía habanera del Siglo XIX*. Havana: Union de Escritores y Artistas de Cuba, 1971.

De Vito, Christian. "Connected Singularities: Convict Labour in Late Colonial Spanish America (1760s–1800)." In *Micro-Spatial Histories of Global Labour*, edited by Christian G. De Vito and Anne Gerritsen, 171–202. London: Palgrave, 2018.

———. "Punishment and Labour Relations: Cuba between Abolition and Empire (1835–1886)." *Crime, Histoire & Sociétés/Crime, History & Societies* 22, no. 1 (2018): 53–79.

———. "The Spanish Empire, 1500–1898." In *A Global History of Convicts and Penal Colonies*, edited by Clare Anderson, 65–96. London: Bloomsbury Academic, 2018.

Díaz, María Elena. *The Virgin, the King, and the Royal Slaves of El Cobre*. Stanford, CA: Stanford University Press, 2000.

Díaz Martínez, Yolanda. *Visión de la otra Habana: vigilancia, delito, y control social en los incios del siglo XIX*. Santiago de Cuba: Editorial Oriente, 2011.

Domínguez Ortiz, Antonio. "La esclavitud en Castilla durante la Edad Moderna." In *Estudios de Historia social en España*, 369–428. Madrid: Consejo Superior de Investigaciones Científicas, 1952.

Donoghue, John, and Evelyn P. Jennings, eds. Building the Atlantic Empires: Unfree Labor and Imperial States in the Political Economy of Capitalism, ca. 1500–1914. Leiden: Brill, 2016.

Donovan, Bill M. Introduction to The Devastation of the Indies, A Brief Account, by Bartolomé de Las Casas. Baltimore: Johns Hopkins University Press, 1992.

Elkins, Stanley M. Slavery: A Problem in American Institutional and Intellectual Life. Chicago: University of Chicago Press, 1959.

Elliott, John H. Empires of the Atlantic World: Britain and Spain in America 1492–1830. New Haven, CT: Yale University Press, 2006.

———. Imperial Spain, 1469–1716. New York: St. Martin's, 1963.

Eltis, David. "Free and Coerced Migrations from the Old World to the New." In Coerced and Free Migration: Global Perspectives, edited by David Eltis, 34–74. Stanford, CA: Stanford University Press, 2002.

———. The Rise of African Slavery in the Americas. Cambridge: Cambridge University Press, 2000.

Eltis, David, Frank D. Lewis, and Kenneth L. Sokoloff, eds. Slavery in the Development of the Americas. Cambridge University Press, 2004.

Estrade, Paul. "Los colonos como sustitutos de los esclavos negros." In Cuba la perla de las Antillas: Actas de las I Jornadas sobre 'Cuba y su historia,' edited by Consuelo Naranjo Orovio and Tomás Mallo Gutiérrez, 93–107. Madrid: Dos Calles, 1994.

Ferrer, Ada. "Cuban Slavery and Atlantic Antislavery." In Slavery and Antislavery in Spain's Atlantic Empire, edited by Josep M. Fradera and Christopher Schmidt-Nowara, 134–157. New York: Berghahn, 2013.

———. Freedom's Mirror: Cuba and Haiti in the Age of Revolution. Cambridge: Cambridge University Press, 2014.

———. Insurgent Cuba: Race, Nation, and Revolution, 1868–1898. Chapel Hill: University of North Carolina Press, 1999.

Finch, Aisha K. Rethinking Slave Rebellion in Cuba: La Escalera and the Insurgencies of 1841–1844. Chapel Hill: University of North Carolina Press, 2015.

Fink, Leon, ed. Workers Across the Americas: The Transnational Turn in Labor History. New York: Oxford University Press, 2011.

Fisher, John. Commercial Relations Between Spain and Spanish America in the Era of Free Trade, 1778–1796. Liverpool: Center for Latin American Studies, 1985.

Fradera, Josep M. The Imperial Nation: Citizens and Subjects in the British, French, Spanish, and American Empires. Translated by Ruth McKay. Princeton, NJ: Princeton University Press, 2018.

Fradera, Josep M., and Christopher Schmidt-Nowara, eds. Slavery and Antislavery in Spain's Atlantic Empire. New York: Berghahn, 2013.

Franco Silva, Alfonso. La esclavitud en Andalucía, 1450–1550. Granada: Universidad de Granada, 1990.

———. *La esclavitud en Sevilla y su tierra a fines de la Edad Media*. Seville: Diputación Provincial de Sevilla, 1979.

Fredona, Robert, and Sophus A. Reinert, eds. *New Perspectives on the History of Political Economy*. Cham: Palgrave Macmillan/Springer, 2018.

Friedlaender, H. E. *Historia económica de Cuba*. Havana: Biblioteca de Historia, Filosofía y Sociología, 1944.

Fuente, Alejandro de la. "A alforría de escravos em Havana, 1601–1610: primeiras conclusões." *Estudos Econômicos* 20, no. 1 (January–April 1990): 139–159.

———. *Havana and the Atlantic in the Sixteenth Century*. Chapel Hill: University of North Carolina Press, 2008.

———. "Havana and the Fleet System: Trade and Growth in the Periphery of the Spanish Empire." *Colonial Latin American Review* 5, no. 1 (June 1996).

———. "El mercado esclavista habanero, 1580–1699: las armazones de esclavos." *Revista de Indias* 50, no. 189 (1990): 371–395.

———. "Slave Law and Claims-Making in Cuba: The Tannenbaum Debate Revisited." *Law and History Review* 22, no. 2 (Summer 2004): 339–369. http://www.historycooperative .org/journals/lhr/22.2/forum_fuente.html.

———. "Slaves and the Creation of Legal Rights in Cuba: Coartación and Papel." *Hispanic American Historical Review* 87, no. 4 (November 2007): 659–692.

———. "Sugar and Slavery in Early Colonial Cuba." In *Tropical Babylons: Sugar and the Making of the Atlantic World, 1450–1680*, ed. Stuart Schwartz, 115–157. Chapel Hill: University of North Carolina Press, 2004.

Fuente, Alejandro de la, María Elena Díaz, and Christopher Schmidt-Nowara. "Forum: What Can Frank Tannenbaum Still Teach Us about the Law of Slavery?" *Law and History Review* 22, no. 2 (Summer 2004): 339–387.

Gárate Ojanguren, Montserrat. *Comercio ultramarino e ilustración: la Real Compañía de La Habana*. San Sebastián: Real Sociedad Bascongada de los Amigos del País, 1993.

García del Pino, César. "Cuba y las contiendas navales del siglo XVIII." *Arbor* 144 (1993): 9–29.

———. *La toma de La Habana por los ingleses y sus antecedentes*. Havana: Editorial de Ciencias Sociales, 2002.

García Rodríguez, Gloria. *La esclavitud desde la esclavitud: La visión de los siervos*. Mexico City: Centro de Investigación Científica Ing. Jorge L. Tamayo, 1996.

———. "El mercado de fuerza de trabajo en Cuba: El comercio esclavista (1760–1789)." In *La esclavitud en Cuba*, 124–148. Havana: Instituto de Ciencias Históricas, Academia de Ciencias de Cuba, 1986.

———. *Voices of the Enslaved in Nineteenth-Century Cuba*. Translated by Nancy L. Westrate. Chapel Hill: University of North Carolina Press, 2011.

García Rodríguez, Mercedes. *La aventura de fundar ingenios: la refacción azucarera en La Habana del siglo XVIII*. Havana: Editorial de Ciencias Sociales, 2004.

———. "El crédtio hipotecario a los ingenios habaneros (1700–1792)." In *Diez nuevas miradas de historia de Cuba*, edited by J. A. Piqueras Arenas, 41–56. Castelló de la Plana: Publicaciones de la Universitat Jaume I, 1998.

———. "Los matrimonios entre esclavos: sexo y reproducción en la Cuba del Siglo XVIII." In *Nuevas voces, viejos asuntos: Panorama de la reciente historiografía cubana*, edited by Ivette Gárcia González and Ricardo Quiza Moreno, 65–96. Havana: Editorial de Ciencias Sociales, 2005.

———. *Misticismo y capitales: la Compañía de Jesús en la economía habanera del siglo XVIII*. Havana: Editorial de Ciencias Sociales, 2000.

———. "El monto de la trata negrera hacia Cuba en el siglo XVIII." In *Cuba: La perla de las Antillas*, edited by Consuelo Naranjo Orovio and Tomás Mallo Gutíerrez, 297–311. Madrid: Ediciones Dos Calles, 1994.

———. "De productores empíricos a hacendados ilustrados." In *Francisco Arango y la invención de la Cuba azucarera*, edited by María Dolores González-Ripoll and Izaskun Álvarez Cuartero, 85–104. Salamanca: Universidad de Salamanca, 2010.

Geggus, David. "The Arming of Slaves in the Haitian Revolution." In *Arming Slaves from Classical Times to the Modern Age*, edited by Christopher Leslie Brown and Philip D. Morgan, 209–232. New Haven, CT: Yale University Press, 2006.

———. *Haitian Revolutionary Studies*. Bloomington: Indiana University Press, 2002.

Gerhard, Peter. "A Black Conquistador in Mexico." *Hispanic American Historical Review* 58, no. 3 (August 1978): 451–459.

González Enciso, Agustín, and Rafael Torres Sánchez, eds. *Tabaco y economía en el Siglo XVIII*. Pamplona: Ediciones Universidad de Navarra, 1999.

González Fernández, Doria C. "Tabaco y poder. La primera factoría de La Habana." In *Tabaco y economía en el Siglo XVIII*, edited by Agustín González Enciso and Rafael Torres Sánchez, 107–122. Pamplona: Ediciones Universidad de Navarra, 1999.

González-Ripoll Navarro, María Dolores. *Cuba. La isla de los ensayos. Cultura y sociedad (1790–1815)*. Madrid: Consejo Superior de Investigaciones Científicas, Centro de Humanidades, Instituto de Historia Departamento de Historia de América, 1999.

González-Ripoll Navarro, María Dolores, and Izaskun Álvarez Cuartero, eds. *Francisco Arango y la invención de la Cuba azucarera*. Salamanca: Ediciones Universidad de Salamanca, 2009.

González-Ripoll Navarro, María Dolores, Consuelo Naranjo, Ada Ferrer, Gloria García, and Josef Opatrn´ y, eds. *El rumor de Haití en Cuba: Temor, raza y rebeldía, 1789–1844*. Madrid: Consejo Superior de Investigaciones Científicas, 2004.

Goodman, David C. *Spanish Naval Power 1589–1665: Reconstruction and Defeat*. Cambridge: Cambridge University Press, 1997.

Gould, Eliga H. "Entangled Atlantic Histories: A Response from the Anglo-American Periphery." *American Historical Review* 112, no. 5 (December 2007): 1414–1422.

———. "Entangled Histories, Entangled Worlds: The English-Speaking Atlantic as a Spanish Periphery." *American Historical Review* 112, no. 3 (June 2007): 764–786.

Grandio Moraguez, Oscar. "Dobo: A Liberated African in Nineteenth-Century Havana." *Slave Voyages.* https://www.slavevoyages.org/voyage/essays.

Guerra y Sánchez, Ramiro. *Manual de Historia de Cuba.* Havana: Cultural, S. A, 1938.

Hall, Gwendolyn Midlo. *Social Control in Slave Plantation Societies: A Comparison of St. Domingue and Cuba.* Baltimore: Johns Hopkins University Press, 1971.

Haring, Clarence. *The Spanish Empire in America.* New York: Oxford University Press, 1947.

Hoffman, Paul E. *The Spanish Crown and the Defense of the Caribbean, 1535–1585: Precedent, Patrimonialism, and Royal Parsimony.* Baton Rouge: Louisiana State University Press, 1980.

Howard, Philip. *Changing History: Afro-Cuban Cabildos and Societies of Color in the Nineteenth Century.* Baton Rouge: Louisiana State University Press, 1998.

Ibarra Cuesta, Jorge. *Marx y los historiadores ante la hacienda y la plantación esclavista.* Havana: Editorial de Ciencias Sociales, 2008.

Iglesias García, Fe. "The Development of Capitalism in Cuban Sugar Production, 1860–1900." In *Between Slavery and Free Labor: The Spanish-Speaking Caribbean in the Nineteenth Century,* edited by Manuel Moreno Fraginals, Frank Moya Pons, and Stanley L. Engerman, 54–75. Baltimore: Johns Hopkins University Press, 1985.

———. "La estructura agraria de La Habana, 1700–1775." *Arbor* 547–548 (1991): 91–113.

Inglis, G. Douglas. "Historical Demography of Colonial Cuba, 1492–1780." PhD diss., Texas Christian University, 1979.

———. "The Spanish Naval Shipyard at Havana in the Eighteenth Century." In *New Aspects of Naval History: Selected Papers from the 5th Naval History Symposium,* 47–58. Baltimore: Nautical and Aviation Publishers, 1985.

Inikori, Joseph E. *Africans and the Industrial Revolution in England: A Study in International Trade and Economic Development.* Cambridge: Cambridge University Press, 2002.

Irigoin, Alejandra, and Regina Grafe. "Absolutismo negociado: La trayectoria hispana en la formación del estado y el imperio." In *El secreto del imperio español y los situados coloniales en el siglo XVIII,* edited by Carlos Marichal and Johanna von Grafestein, 295–335. Mexico City: El Colegio de México, Instituto Mora, 2012.

James, C. L. R. *Black Jacobins: Toussaint L'Ouverture and the San Domingo Revolution.* 2nd ed., revised. New York: Vintage, 1963.

Jennings, Evelyn P. "All in the Family? Colonial Cuba in an Iberian Atlantic Frame." *Bulletin of Hispanic Studies* 91, no. 1 (2014): 83–104.

———. "In 'the Language of the Criminal': Slavery and Colonialism in Ibero-America." *Latin American Research Review* 49, no. 2 (Summer 2014): 282–294.

———. "Paths to Freedom: Imperial Defense and Manumission in Havana, 1762–1800." In *Paths to Freedom: Manumission in the Atlantic World,* edited by Rosemary Brana-Shute and Randy J. Sparks. Columbia: University of South Carolina Press, 2009, 121–141.

———. "Paths to Sweet Success: Free and Unfree Labor in the Building of Roads and Rails in Havana, Cuba, 1790–1835." *International Review of Social History* 64, no. S27 (2019): 149–171.

———. "The Sinews of Spain's American Empire: Forced Labor in Cuba from the Sixteenth to the Nineteenth Centuries." In *Building the Atlantic Empires: Unfree Labor and Imperial States in the Political Economy of Capitalism, ca. 1500–1914*, edited by John Donoghue and Evelyn P. Jennings, 25–23. Leiden: Brill, 2016.

———. "'Some Unhappy Indians Trafficked by Force': Race, Status, and Work Discipline in Mid-Nineteenth-Century Cuba." In *Human Bondage in the Cultural Contact Zone*, edited by Raphael Hörmann and Gesa Mackenthun, 209–225. Münster: Waxmann, 2010.

———. "'War as the Forcing House of Change': The Case of Cuba in the Late Eighteenth Century." *William and Mary Quarterly* 63, no. 3 (July 2005): 411–440.

Johnson, Sherry. *Climate and Catastrophe in Cuba and the Atlantic World in the Age of Revolution.* Chapel Hill: University of North Carolina Press, 2011.

———. "'La Guerra Contra los Habitantes de los Arrabales': Changing Patterns of Land Use and Land Tenancy in and Around Havana, 1763–1800." *Hispanic American Historical Review* 77, no. 2 (1997): 181–209.

———. "'Señoras en sus clases no ordinarias': Enemy Collaborators or Courageous Defenders of the Family?" *Cuban Studies* 34 (2003): 11–37.

———. *Social Transformation of Eighteenth-Century Cuba.* Gainesville: University Press of Florida, 2001.

Johnson, Walter. "On Agency," *Journal of Social History* 37, no. 1 (2003): 113–124.

Kesselring, K. J. "'Negroes of the Crown': The Management of Slaves Forfeited by Grenadian Rebels, 1796–1831." *Journal of the Canadian Historical Association/Revue de la Société historique du Canada* 22, no. 2 (2011): 1–29.

Kiple, Kenneth F. *Blacks in Colonial Cuba, 1774–1899.* Gainesville: University Press of Florida, 1976.

Klein, Herbert S. "The Colored Militia of Cuba, 1568–1868." *Caribbean Studies* 6, no. 2 (1966): 17–27.

———. *Slavery in the Americas: A Comparative Study of Virginia and Cuba.* Chicago: University of Chicago Press, 1967.

Knight, Franklin W. "Origins of Wealth and the Sugar Revolution in Cuba, 1750–1850." *Hispanic American Historical Review* 57, no. 2 (1977): 231–253.

———. *Slave Society in Cuba during the Nineteenth Century.* Madison: University of Wisconsin Press, 1970.

Kuethe, Allan J. "La batalla de Cartagena de 1741: Nuevas perspectivas." *Historiografía y bibliografía americanista* 18 (1974): 19–38.

———. *Cuba, 1753–1815: Crown, Military, and Society.* Knoxville: University of Tennessee Press, 1986.

———. "Decisiones estratégicas y las finanzas militares del XVIII." In *Por la fuerza de las armas, ejército e independencias en Iberoamérica*, edited by Juan Marchena and Manuel Chust, 81–100. Castelló de la Plana: Universitat Jaume I, 2007.

———. "Guns, Subsidies, and Commercial Privilege: Some Historical Factors in the Emergence of the Cuban National Character, 1763–1815." *Cuban Studies* 16 (1986): 123–138.

———. "Havana in the Eighteenth Century." In *Atlantic Port Cities, Economy, Culture and Society in the Atlantic World, 1650–1850*, edited by Franklin W. Knight and Peggy K. Liss, 13–39. Knoxville: University of Tennessee Press, 1992.

———. "El situado mexicano, los azucareros y la fidelidad cubana: comparaciones con Puerto Rico Y Nueva Granada." In *Las Antillas en la era de las luces y la revolución*, edited by José A. Piqueras, 301–318. Madrid: Siglo XXI, 2005.

Kuethe, Allan J., and Kenneth Andrien. *The Spanish Atlantic World in the Eighteenth Century: War and the Bourbon Reforms, 1713–1796*. New York: Cambridge University Press, 2014.

Kuethe, Allan J., and Lowell Blaisdell. "The Esquilache Government and the Reforms of Charles III in Cuba." *Jarbuch für Geschichte von Staat, Wirtschaft und Gesellschaft Lateinamerikas* 19 (1982): 117–136.

Kuethe, Allan J., and G. Douglas Inglis. "Absolutism and Enlightened Reform: Charles III, the Establishment of the *Alcabala*, and Commercial Reorganization in Cuba." *Past and Present* 199 (November 1985): 118–143.

Kuethe, Allan J., and José Manuel Serrano Álvarez. "El astillero de la Habana y Trafalgar." *Revista de Indias* 67, no. 241 (2007): 763–776.

Lampros, Peter. J. "Merchant-Planter Cooperation and Conflict: The Havana Consulado, 1794–1832." PhD diss., Tulane University, 1980.

Landers, Jane G. *Atlantic Creoles in the Age of Revolution*. Cambridge, MA: Harvard University Press, 2010.

———. *Black Society in Spanish Florida*. Urbana: University of Illinois Press, 1999.

———. "Gracia Real de Santa Teresa de Mose: A Free Black Town in Spanish Colonial Florida." *American Historical Review* 95, no. 1 (1990): 9–30.

———. "Transforming Bondsmen into Vassals." In *Arming Slaves from Classical Times to the Modern Age*, edited by Christopher Leslie Brown and Philip D. Morgan, 120–147. New Haven, CT: Yale University Press, 2006.

La Rosa Corzo, Gabino. *Los cimarrones de Cuba*. Havana: Editorial de Ciencias Sociales, 1988.

Laviña, Javier, and Michael Zeuske, eds. *The Second Slavery: Mass Slaveries in the Americas and in the Atlantic Basin*. Zurich: LIT, 2014.

Lawrence, Mark. *Spain's First Carlist War, 1833–1840*. New York: Palgrave Macmillan, 2014.

Le Riverend Brusone, Julio. *La Habana, espacio y vida*. Madrid: MAPFRE, 1992.

Libby, Douglas Cole, and Clothilde Andrade Paiva. "Manumission Practices in Late Eighteenth-Century Brazilian Slave Parish: São José d'El Rey in 1795." *Slavery & Abolition* 21, no. 1 (April 2000): 96–127.

Linebaugh, Peter, and Marcus Rediker. *The Many-Headed Hydra: Sailors, Slaves, Commoners, and the Hidden History of the Revolutionary Atlantic*. Boston: Beacon, 2000.

Liss, Peggy K. *Atlantic Empires: The Networks of Trade and Revolution, 1713–1826*. Baltimore: Johns Hopkins University Press, 1983.

Lizardi Pollock, Jorge L. "Presidios, presidiarios y desertores: los desterrados de Nueva España, 1777–1797." In *El Caribe en los intereses imperiales, 1750–1815*, edited by Johanna von Grafenstein, 20–45. San Juan Mixcoac: Instituto de Investigaciones Dr. José María Luis Mora, 2000.

Llaverías, Joaquín. *La Comisión Militar Ejecutiva y Permanente de la Isla de Cuba*. Havana: El Siglo XX, 1929.

Lockhart, James. *Spanish Peru 1532–1560: A Social History*. Madison: University of Wisconsin Press, 1968.

López Estrada, Francisco, and María Teresa López García-Berdoy, eds. *Las Siete Partidas Antología*. Madrid: Editorial Castalia, 1992.

López Mesa, Enrique. "La trata negrera en el Puerto de La Habana a mediados del siglo XVIII." In *La Habana: Ciudad portuaria colonial (S. SVIII–XIX)*, edited by Agustín Guimerá and Fernando Monge, 246–253. Madrid: Fundación Portuaria, 2000.

López Segrera, Francisco. "Cuba: Dependence, Plantation Economy, and Social Classes, 1762–1902." In *Between Slavery and Free Labor: The Spanish-Speaking Caribbean in the Nineteenth Century*, edited by Manuel Moreno Fraginals, Frank Moya Pons, and Stanley L. Engerman, 77–93. Baltimore: Johns Hopkins University Press, 1985.

Lucena Salmoral, Manuel. *Los códigos negros de la América española*. Alcalá: Edciones UNESCO, Universidad de Alcalá, 1996.

———. "El derecho de coartación del esclavo en la América española." *Revista de Indias* 59, no. 216 (1999): 357–374.

———. *Regulación de la esclavitud negra en las colonias de América Española (1503–1886): Documentos para su estudio*. Alcalá de Henares: Universidad de Alcalá, 2005.

Lynch, John. *Bourbon Spain, 1700–1808*. Oxford: Blackwell, 1989.

Macías, Isabelo. *Cuba en la primera mitad del Siglo XVII*. Seville: Consejo Superior de Investigaciones Científicas, 1978.

Marichal, Carlos, and Matilde Souto Mantecón. "La Nueva España y el financiamiento del imperio español en América: Los situados para el Caribe en el Siglo XVIII." In *El secreto del imperio español: Los situados coloniales en el Siglo XVIII*, edited by Carlos Marichal and Johanna von Grafenstein, 61–93. San Juan Mixcoac: Instituto de Investigaciones de Dr. José María Luis Mora, 2012.

———. "Silver and Situados." *Hispanic American Historical Review* 74, no. 4 (1994): 587–613.

Marrero, Leví. *Cuba: economía y sociedad*. 15 vols. Madrid: Playor, S. A., 1972–1988.

Martínez-Alier, Verena. *Marriage, Class and Colour in Nineteenth-Century Cuba: A Study of Racial Attitudes and Sexual Values in a Slave Society.* 1974. Ann Arbor: University of Michigan Press, 1989.

Martínez-Fernández, Luis, D. H. Figueredo, Louis A. Pérez Jr., and Luis González. *Encyclopedia of Cuba: People, History, Culture.* Vol. 2. Westport, CT: Greenwood, 2003.

———. "The Havana Anglo-Spanish Commission for the Suppression of the Slave Trade and Cuba's Emancipados." *Slavery & Abolition* 16, no. 2 (August 1995): 205–225.

Martínez Martínez, Manuel. *Los forzados de marina en España del siglo XVIII (1700–1775).* Almería: Editorial Universidad de Almería, 2011.

McAlister, Lyle N. *Spain and Portugal in the New World, 1492–1700.* Minneapolis: University of Minnesota Press, 1984.

McNeill, John Robert. *Atlantic Empires of France and Spain: Louisbourg and Havana, 1700–1763.* Chapel Hill: University of North Carolina Press, 1985.

———. *Mosquito Empires: Ecology and War in the Greater Caribbean, 1620–1914.* Cambridge: Cambridge University Press, 2010.

Méndez Capote, Renée. *Fortalezas de la Habana colonial.* La Habana: Editorial Gente Nueva, 1974.

Merino, José. *La armada española en el Siglo XVIII.* Madrid: Fundación Universitaria Española, 1981.

Moorhead, Max L. "Spanish Deportations of Hostile Apaches: The Policy and the Practice." *Arizona and the West* 17 (1975): 205–220.

Moreno Fraginals, Manuel. *El ingenio: complejo económico social cubano del azúcar.* 1978. Barcelona: Crítica, 2001.

———. "Peculiaridades de la esclavitud en Cuba." *Islas* 85 (1986): 3–12.

———. "Plantations in the Caribbean: Cuba, Puerto Rico, and the Dominican Republic in the Late Nineteenth Century." In *Between Slavery and Free Labor: The Spanish-Speaking Caribbean in the Nineteenth Century,* edited by Manuel Moreno Fraginals, Frank Moya Pons, and Stanley L. Engerman, 3–21. Baltimore: Johns Hopkins University Press, 1985.

Morgan, Philip D., and Andrew Jackson O'Shaughnessy. "Arming Slaves in the American Revolution." In *Arming Slaves from Classical Times to the Modern Age,* edited by Christopher Leslie Brown and Philip D. Morgan, 180–208. New Haven: Yale University Press, 2006.

Morrison, Karen Y. "Spanish Imperial Vassalage and the Social Reproduction of Slavery in Colonial Cuba." *Journal of Global Slavery* 3, no. 3 (2018): 261–285.

———. "Sustaining Freedom and Second Slavery in Nineteenth-Century Brazil and Cuba." *Latin American Research Review* 53, no. 2 (2018): 411–417.

Moyano Bazzani, Eduardo L. "El ferrocarril cubano, una expresión del crecimiento económico." In *Cuba la perla de la Antillas: Actas de las I Jornadas sobre "Cuba y su historia,"* edited by Consuelo Naranjo Orovio and Tomás Mallo Gutiérrez, 325–334. Madrid: Consejo Superior de Investigaciones Científicas, 1994.

———. *La nueva frontera del azúcar: el ferrocarril y la economía cubana del Siglo XIX*. Madrid: Consejo Superior de Investigación, 1991.

Murray, David. *Odious Commerce: Britain, Spain and the Abolition of the Cuban Slave Trade*. Cambridge: Cambridge University Press, 1980.

Náter, Laura. "The Spanish Empire and Cuban Tobacco in the Seventeenth and Eighteenth Centuries." In *The Atlantic Economy during the Seventeenth and Eighteenth Centuries*, edited by Peter A. Coclanis, 252–276. Columbia: University of South Carolina Press, 2005.

Ortiz, Fernando. *Contrapunteo cubano del tabaco y el azúcar*. 1947. Caracas: Bibilioteca Ayacucho, 1978.

———. *Hampa-afrocubana: Los negros esclavos, estudio sociológico y de derecho público*. Havana: Revista bimestre cubana, 1916.

———. *Los negros esclavos*. Havana: Editorial de Ciencias Sociales, 1975.

Palmer, Colin. *Human Cargoes: The British Slave Trade to Spanish America, 1700–1739*. Champaign: University of Illinois Press, 1981.

———. *Slaves of the White God*. Cambridge, MA: Harvard University Press, 1976.

Paquette, Gabriel. *Enlightenment, Governance, and Reform in Spain and its Empire, 1759–1808*. New York: Palgrave, 2008.

Paquette, Robert. *Sugar Is Made with Blood: The Conspiracy of La Esclaera and the Conflict Between Empires over Slavery in Cuba*. Middletown, CT: Wesleyan University Press, 1988.

Parcero Torre, Celia María. *La pérdida de La Habana y las reformas borbónicas en Cuba (1760–1773)*. Ávila: Junta de Castilla y León, 1998.

Pares, Richard. *War and Trade in the West Indies, 1739–1763*. Oxford: Clarendon, 1936.

Parker, Geoffrey. *The Military Revolution*. Cambridge: Cambridge University Press, 1988.

Parry, J. H. *The Spanish Seaborne Empire*. London: Hutchinson, 1966.

Pérez, Louis A. Jr. *Cuba: Between Reform and Revolution*. 3rd ed. New York: Oxford University Press, 2006.

Pérez Estévez, Rosa María. *El problema de los vagos en la España del Siglo XVIII*. Madrid: Confederación Española de Cajas de Ahorros, 1976.

Pérez Guzmán, Francisco. *La Habana clave de un imperio*. Havana: Editorial de Ciencias Sociales, 1997.

———. "Modo de vida de esclavos y forzados en las fortificaciones de Cuba: Siglo XVIII." *Anuario de estudios americanos* 47 (1990): 241–257.

Phillips, Carla Rahn. "The Labour Market for Sailors in Spain." In *"Those Emblems of Hell"? European Sailors and the Maritime Labour Market, 1570–1870*. Research in Maritime History, no. 13, edited by Paul C. van Royen, Jaap R. Bruijn and Jan Lucassen, 329–348. St. John's, Newfoundland: International Maritime Economic History Association, 1997.

———. "Life Blood of the Navy: Recruiting Sailors in Eighteenth-Century Spain." *The Mariner's Mirror* 87, no. 4 (2001): 420–445.

———. *Six Galleons for the King of Spain*. Baltimore: Johns Hopkins University Press, 1986.

Phillips, William D. *Historia de la esclavitud en España*. Madrid: Editorial Playor, 1990.

———. "The Old World Background of Slavery in the Americas." In *Slavery and the Rise of the Atlantic System*, edited by Barbara L. Solow, 43–61. Cambridge: Cambridge University Press, 1991.

———. *Slavery in Medieval and Early Modern Iberia*. Philadelphia: University of Pennsylvania Press, 2014.

———. "Slavery in Spain, Ancient to Early Modern: A Survey of the Historiography since 1990." *Bulletin of the Society for Spanish and Portuguese Historical Studies* 27, no. 2–3 (Winter–Spring 2001–2002): 10–18.

Pierson, William Whately Jr. "The Establishment and Early Functioning of the Intendencia of Cuba." *James Sprunt Historical Studies* 19, no. 2 (1927): 74–133.

Pike, Ruth. *Penal Servitude in Early Modern Spain*. Madison: University of Wisconsin Press, 1983.

———. "Penal Servitude in the Spanish Empire: Presidio Labor in the Eighteenth Century." *Hispanic American Historical Review* 58, no. 1 (1978): 21–40.

Piqueras, José Antonio. *La esclavitud en las Españas. Un lazo transatlántico*. Madrid: La Catarata, 2011.

———. "Historical Slavery and Capitalism in Cuban Historiography." In *Slavery and Historical Capitalism in the Nineteenth Century*, edited by Dale Tomich, 67–122. Lanham, MD: Lexington, 2017.

Puig-Samper, Miguel A., and Consuelo Naranjo Orovio. "El abastemiento de aguas a la ciudad de la Habana: de la Zanja Real al Canal de Vento." In *Obras hidrálulicas en América colonia*, ed. Centro de Estudios Históricos de Obras Públicas y Urbanismo, 81–93. Madrid: Ministerio de Obras Públicas, Transportes y Medio Ambiente, 1993.

Reid-Vázquez, Michelle. *The Year of the Lash: Free People of Color in Cuba and the Nineteenth-Century Atlantic World*. Athens: University of Georgia Press, 2011.

Reinert, Sophus A., and Pernille Røge, eds. *The Political Economy of Empire in the Early Modern World*. Basingstoke: Palgrave Macmillan, 2013.

Restall, Matthew. "Black Conquistadors: Armed Africans in Early Spanish America," *The Americas* 57, no. 2 (2000):171–205.

Ringrose, David. *Spain, Europe, and the "Spanish Miracle," 1700–1900*. Cambridge: Cambridge University Press, 1996.

Rockman, Seth. *Scraping By: Wage Labor, Slavery and Survival in Early Baltimore*. Baltimore: Johns Hopkins University Press, 2009.

Rodríguez Casado, Vicente. "La política del reformismo de los primeros Borbones en la Marina de Guerra española." *Anuario de estudios americanos* 25 (1968): 601–618.

Roig de Leuchsenring, Emilio. *La Habana. Apuntes históricos*. Havana: Municipio de la Habana, 1939.

Rojas, María Teresa de. "Algunos datos sobre los negros esclavos y horros en la Habana del siglo XVI." In Miscelánea de estudios dedicados a Fernando Ortiz por sus discípulos, colegas y amigos, 1275–1287. Havana: Sociedad Económica de Amigos del País, 1956.

Roldán de Montaud, Inés. "En los borrosos confines de la libertad: el caso de los negros emancipados en Cuba, 1817–1870." Revista de Indias 71, no. 251 (2011): 159–192.

———. "Origen, evolución y supresión del grupo de negros 'emancipados' en Cuba (1817–1870)." Revista de Indias 42 (July December 1982): 559–641.

Rood, Daniel B. The Reinvention of Atlantic Slavery: Technology, Labor, Race, and Capitalism in the Greater Caribbean. New York: Oxford University Press, 2017.

Sánchez Agustí, María. Edifícios públicos de La Habana del siglo XVIII. Valladolid: Universidad de Valladolid, 1984.

Santos, Francisco J. Andrés. "Encomienda y usufructo en Indias." Legal History 69, no. 3–4 (2001): 245–270.

Sanz Rozalén, Vicent. "Los negros del rey. Tabaco y esclavitud en Cuba a comienzos del Siglo XIX." In Trabajo libre y coactivo en sociedades de plantación, edited by José Antonio Piqueras Arenas, 151–176. Madrid: Siglo XXI de España Editores, 2009.

Saunders, A. C. de C. M. A Social History of Black Slaves and Freedmen in Portugal 1441–1555. Cambridge: Cambridge University Press, 1982.

Schmidt-Nowara, Christopher. Empire and Antislavery: Spain, Cuba, and Puerto Rico, 1833–1874. Pittsburgh: University of Pittsburgh Press, 1999.

Schneider, Elena A. "African Slavery and the Spanish Empire: Imperial Imaginings and Bourbon Reform in Eighteenth-Century Cuba and Beyond." Journal of Early American History 5, no. 1 (2015): 3–29.

———. The Occupation of Havana: War, Trade, and Slavery in the Atlantic World. Williamsburg, VA, and Chapel Hill: Omohundro Institute of Early American History and Culture and University of North Carolina Press, 2018.

Scott, Rebecca J. "Explaining Abolition: Contradiction, Adaptation, and Challenge in Cuban Slave Society, 1860–1886." In Between Slavery and Free Labor: The Spanish-Speaking Caribbean in the Nineteenth Century, edited by Manuel Moreno Fraginals, Frank Moya Pons, and Stanley L. Engerman, 25–53. Baltimore: Johns Hopkins University Press, 1985.

———. Slave Emancipation in Cuba: The Transition to Free Labor, 1860–1899. Princeton, NJ: Princeton University Press, 1985.

Segre, Roberto. La Plaza de Armas de la Habana: sinfonía urbana inconclusa. Havana: Editorial Arte y Literatura, 1995.

Serrano, José Manuel, and Allan J. Kuethe. "El situado mexicano y la Cuba borbónica." In El secreto del Imperio Español: Los situados coloniales en el siglo XVIII, edited by Carlos Marichal and Johanna von Grafenstein, 95–114. Mexico City: El Colegio de México, 2012.

Serrano, Violeta. Crónicas del primer ferrocarril de Cuba. Havana: Departamento de Orientación Revolucionario del Comité Central del Partido Comunista de Cuba, 1973.

Shafer, R. J. *The Economic Societies in the Spanish World (1763–1821)*. Syracuse, NY: Syracuse University Press, 1958.

Sierra Silva, Pablo Miguel. *Urban Slavery in Colonial Mexico: Puebla de los Ángeles 1531–1706*. Cambridge: Cambridge University Press, 2018.

Solow, Barbara L. *The Economic Consequence of the Atlantic Slave Trade*. Lanham, MD: Lexington, 2014.

Solow, Barbara L., and Stanley L. Engerman, eds. *British Capitalism and Caribbean Slavery*. Cambridge: Cambridge University Press, 2004.

Stein, Stanley J., and Barbara H. Stein. *Apogee of Empire*. Baltimore: Johns Hopkins University Press, 2003.

———. *Silver, Trade, and War: Spain and America in the Making of Early Modern Europe*. Baltimore: Johns Hopkins University Press, 2000.

Stella, Alessandro. *Histoires d'esclaves dans la péninsule ibérique*. Paris: École des Hautes Études en Sciences Sociales, 2000.

Tannenbaum, Frank. *Slave and Citizen: The Negro in the Americas*. New York: Alfred A. Knopf, 1946.

TePaske, John J. "La política española en el Caribe durante los Siglos XVII and XVIII." In *La influencia de España en el Caribe, la Florida y la Luisiana, 1500–1800*, ed. Antonio Acosta and Juan Marchena Fernández, 61–87. Madrid: Instituto de Cooperación Iberoamericana, 1983.

Thompson, Alvin O. *Unprofitable Servants. Crown Slaves in Berbice, Guyana, 1803–1831*. Kingston: University of West Indies Press, 2002.

Tomich, Dale W. "*Capitalism and Slavery* Revisited: Remaking the Slave Commodity Frontier." In *The Legacy of Eric Williams: Into the Post-Colonial Moment*, edited by Tanya L. Shields, 172–185. Jackson: University Press of Mississippi, 2015.

———. *Slavery and Historical Capitalism during the Nineteenth Century*. Lanham, MD: Lexington, 2017.

———. *Through the Prism of Slavery: Labor, Capital, and World Economy*. Lanham, MD: Rowman and Littlefield, 2004.

———, ed. *The Politics of Second Slavery*. Albany: State University of New York Press, 2016.

Tomich, Dale, and Michael Zeuske. "Introduction, the Second Slavery: Mass Slavery, World-Economy, and Comparative Microhistories." *Review (Fernand Braudel Center)* 31, no. 2 (2008): 91–98.

Tornero Tinajero, Pablo. *Crecimiento económico y transformaciones sociales: Esclavos, hacendados y comerciantes en la Cuba colonial (1760–1840)*. Madrid: Ministerio de Trabajo y Seguridad Social, 1996.

Torres Ramírez, Bibiano. "Alejandro O'Reilly en Cuba." *Anuario de estudios americanos* 24 (1967): 1357–1388.

———. *La compañía gaditana de negros*. Seville: Escuela de Estudios Hispano-Americanos de Sevilla, 1973.

Tracy, James D., ed. *The Political Economy of Merchant Empires: State Power and World Trade, 1350–1750*. Cambridge: Cambridge University Press, 1991.

Tutino, John. *Making a New World: Founding Capitalism in the Bajío and Spanish North America*. Durham, NC: Duke University Press, 2011.

Valdés, Antonio J. *Historia de la Isla de Cuba y en especial de la Habana*. Vol. 1. Havana: Oficina de la Cena, 1813.

Van der Linden, Marcel. *Workers of the World: Essays Toward a Global Labor History*. Leiden: Brill, 2008.

Van Norman, William Jr. *Shade-Grown Slavery: The Lives of Slaves on Coffee Plantations in Cuba*. Nashville: Vanderbilt University Press, 2013.

Vázquez Cienfuegos, Sigfrido. *La Junta de la Habana: Adaptación del pacto colonial en Cuba en vísperas de la independencies hispanoamericanas, 1808–1810*. Seville: Consejo Superior de Investigaciones Científicas, Universidad de Sevilla, Diputación de Sevilla, 2013.

Venegas Fornias, Carlos. *La urbanización de las murallas: dependencia y modernidad*. Havana: Editorial Letras Cubanas, 1990.

Verlinden, Charles. *L'esclavage dans l'Europe médiévale, tome 1, Péninsule ibérique-France*. Brugge: De Tempel, 1955.

Vidal, Cécile. "Public Slavery, Racial Formation, and the Struggle over Honor in French New Orleans, 1718–1769." *Anuario Colombiano de Historia Social y de la Cultura* 43, no. 2 (2016): 155–183.

Vila Vilar, Enriqueta. *Hispanoamérica y el comercio de esclavos*. Seville: Escuela de Estudios Hispanoamericanos de Sevilla, 1977.

Voelz, Peter M. *Slave and Soldier, the Military Impact of Blacks in the Colonial Americas*. New York: Garland, 1993.

Walker, Daniel E. "Colony versus Crown: Raising Black Troops for the British Siege on Havana, 1762." *The Journal of Caribbean History* 33, no. 1–2 (1999): 74–83.

Way, Peter. "Black Service . . . White Money: The Peculiar Institution of Military Labor in the British Army During the Seven Years' War." In *Workers Across the Americas: The Transnational Turn in Labor History*, edited by Leon Fink, 57–80. New York: Oxford University Press, 2011.

———. "Class-Warfare: Primitive Accumulation, Military Revolution and the British War-Worker." In *Beyond Marx: Theorising the Global Labour Relations of the Twenty-First Century*, ed. Marcel van der Linden and Karl Heinz Roth. Leiden and Boston: Brill, 2014.

———. *Common Labour: Workers and the Digging of North American Canals, 1780–1860*. Cambridge: Cambridge University Press, 1993.

———. "'The Scum of Every County, the Refuse of Mankind': Recruiting the British Army in the Eighteenth Century." In *Fighting for a Living: A Comparative History of Military Labour, 1500–2000*, edited by Erik-Jan Zürcher, 291–330. Amsterdam: Amsterdam University Press, 2013.

Weber, David J. *Bárbaros: Spaniards and Their Savages in the Age of Enlightenment*. New Haven, CT: Yale University Press, 2005.

Wheat, David. *Atlantic Africa and the Spanish Caribbean, 1570–1640*. Chapel Hill: University of North Carolina Press, 2016.

———. "Mediterranean Slavery, New World Transformations: Galley Slaves in the Spanish Caribbean, 1578–1635." *Slavery & Abolition* 31, no. 3 (September 2010): 327–344.

Williams, Eric. *Capitalism and Slavery*. 1944. Chapel Hill: University of North Carolina Press, 1994.

Yaremko, Jason M. *Indigenous Passages to Cuba, 1515–1900*. Gainesville: University Press of Florida, 2016.

Yun, Lisa. *The Coolie Speaks: Chinese Indentured Laborers and African Slaves in Cuba*. Philadelphia: Temple University Press, 2008.

Zanetti, Oscar, and Alejandro García. *Sugar and Railroads: A Cuban History, 1837–1959*. Translated by Franklin W. Knight and Mary Todd. Chapel Hill: University of North Carolina Press, 1987.

INDEX